ROMNEY MARSH

Coastal and Landscape Change
through the Ages

Dengemarsh Road, Dungeness.

Oxford University School of Archaeology
Monograph No. 56

ROMNEY MARSH

Coastal and Landscape Change through the Ages

Edited by
Antony Long, Stephen Hipkin and Helen Clarke

Oxford University School of Archaeology
2002

Published by the Oxford University School of Archaeology
Institute of Archaeology
Beaumont Street
Oxford

Distributed by
Oxbow Books, Park End Place, Oxford OX1 1HN

Distributed in North America by
The David Brown Book Company
PO Box 511, Oakville, CT 06779

ISBN 0 947816 57 7

Printed in Great Britain at
The Short Run Press, Exeter

Contents

Acknowledgements

Publication of this volume has been made possible by the generous support
of the following:

The Romney Marsh Research Trust

The Marc Fitch Fund

Kent RDA

and

Märit and Hans Rausing Charitable Foundation

Cover photograph kindly provided by Mr Christopher Shore, FRPS

Frontispiece photograph kindly provided by Mr Terry Hulf

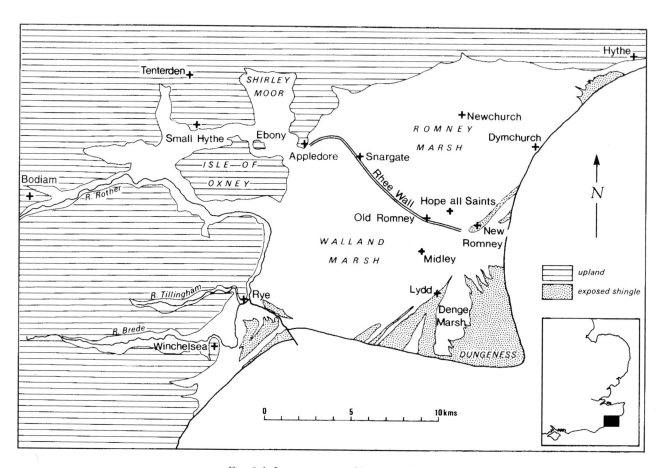

Fig. 0.1. Location map of Romney Marsh.

Foreword

Romney Marsh: The Changing Landscape

Antony Long, Stephen Hipkin and Helen Clarke

Introduction

This monograph is about Romney Marsh, a triangular-shaped landmass which projects into Rye Bay and the eastern English Channel (Fig. 0.1). Though wide, these marshlands also possess hidden depths; indeed sink a borehole in almost any place on the marsh and one will find not *terra firma* but instead a wet, unconsolidated sequence of sands, silts, clays and peat. These sediments, which extend to depths of 10 or 20 m or more, have formed over the last 10,000 years or so as the sea has vacilated across the region. It is, then, perhaps no surprise that this special place has long attracted study into its geomorphology, archaeology and history. Up until the 1980s this work was completed largely in an *ad hoc* manner, by interested individuals with their own research agenda. This changed in 1984 with the establishment of the Romney Marsh-Dungeness Research Group, whose aim was 'to approach jointly the problem of the evolution, human occupation and reclamation of the whole marshland from Fairlight to Hythe, and up the valleys of the Rother, Tillingham and Brede' (*The Romney Marsh Irregular* 1, 1985).

Reincarnated in 1987 as the Romney Marsh Research Trust, the Trust has encouraged a proliferation of research on the marsh which has been supported in various ways by its membership (which now exceed 350), donations from local organisations and companies, charities and government organisations. The Trust is committed to the dissemination of this research at lectures and field days, and through informal publication in the remarkably regular *Romney Marsh Irregular*, and, in academic papers and research monographs.

This Monograph

This is the fourth Romney Marsh research monograph to be published by the Trust since 1988. As previously we present a set of related papers which address geomorphological, archaeological and historical aspects of the Trust's research. In scope, the papers vary. Some deal with localised aspects of the marsh and its history, but most seek to address wider scale issues of geographic and academic interest. Wherever possible, we have encouraged the contributors to synthesise existing knowledge and to look beyond the five metre contour which too frequently restricts our research. The papers respect the stylistic conventions of each respective discipline; those concerned with the geomorphology of the marsh tend to cite ages in calibrated years before present (cal. yr BP – that is before AD 1950), whilst those dealing with the last 2000 years or so adopt the AD timescale. Referencing styles also vary subtly between contributions. We present the papers in a broadly chronological sequence, starting with those with a prehistoric focus and moving gradually towards the present.

The monograph opens with a comprehensive review of the vegetation history of the Romney Marsh region by Martyn Waller. There are now 28 pollen diagrams from the marsh, which makes it one of the most intensively studied coastal wetlands in the UK. The distribution of sites, from the valleys in the west, where the peats are oldest and thickest, to the thinner and more expansive main marsh peat which accumulated during the mid Holocene (*c.* 7000 to 2000 cal. yr BP), enables Waller to explore early tree migration to the area, the impact of prehistoric (mesolithic and neolithic) peoples on the region, as well as the influence of sea-level change, climate and freshwater run-off from the Weald on vegetation patterns. This is the second major coastal lowland on which Martyn Waller has worked, the other being the much larger Fenland of East Anglia (Waller 1994). It is interesting to compare the two, as much from a vegetation perspective as from the way in which the research itself has been conducted. As Waller notes, a key difference has been the more deliberate site selection criteria used on Romney Marsh. This has led to the development a comprehensive spatial network of sites that has enabled the identification of trends in vegetation that are clearly the product of identifiable processes (natural and human). This contrasts with Fenland, where a more haphazard approach to sampling has complicated efforts to identify driving forces behind the changes in vegetation observed.

This review is followed by an important study on the deepest sediment yet recorded from Romney Marsh, at Tilling Green, Rye. By retrieving samples from depths in excess of 20 m below ground surface with a percussion drilling rig, Waller and Kirby are able to tackle the long-standing and important issue of early Holocene sea-level change, coastal evolution and vegetation history. They demonstrate conclusively that interpretations based on poorly constrained borehole sediments collected in the 1960s are incorrect, and develop a revised history which is more in keeping with what limited comparable sea level data exist from Sussex and East Kent.

The mid Holocene saw profound changes to the shorelines of Romney Marsh. As the rate of ice-sheet melt fell, so global and local rates of sea-level rise declined sharply. At this time the shingle and sand barrier of the Dungeness Foreland probably began to extend across Rye Bay, providing protection for the accumulation of thick deposits of sand, silt, clay and then peat across Walland and Romney Marshes. The peat forming vegetation communities were inundated once more between *c.* 3200 and 1000 cal. yr BP. Previously published data suggest that this inundation was a gradual affair, probably associated with the expansion of a tidal inlet from the Hythe area (Long *et al.* 1988). Spencer and Woodland present new evidence for the changes in shoreline during the mid Holocene, based on sediments retrieved from close to the town of Lydd. This is an important part of the marsh, lying at the interface between the shingle complex of Dungeness and the lower energy marsh deposits behind. Using a comparatively untested technique of testate amoebae analysis, Spencer and Woodland reconstruct watertable and salinity changes associated with a relatively short-lived period of peat formation at Scotney Marsh. This work builds on Spencer's Ph.D thesis (funded entirely by the Trust in conjunction with Brett Gravel), and shows the potential of testate amoebae for tracking subtle scale changes in watertable height and salinity, which are themselves driven by wider scale changes in sea level. Their study confirms previous suggestions of a gradual

submergence of the peat-forming communities in the late Holocene.

As the tidal waters flooded across the marsh, so networks of tidal creeks and larger tidal channels developed. These were important conduits for water, sediment and energy, and their reconstruction is central to efforts to understand the present marshland landscape. The Soil Survey (Green 1968) used variations in soil texture and chemistry, as well as subtle changes in ground level (themselves a product of differential compaction of the creek/channel sediments compared with the generally finer-grained adjoining marsh sediments) to map the former extent of creeks. Determining changing depositional conditions in these creeks forms a focus in a review of the use of foraminfera in palaeoenvironmental studies on the marsh. Thus, Evans and Kirby show how one major channel – the Wainway on Walland Marsh – infilled with sediment prior to reclamation. As with the testate amoebae, foraminifera are a relatively infrequently used environmental indicator on the marsh, but one which offers significant potential for resolving differences in intertidal environment, which the more commonly used diatoms appear unable to detect.

The post-peat sediments bridge the prehistoric and historic periods on the marsh and, as such, they provide perhaps the most fertile ground for the interdisciplinary research which the Trust seeks to promote. In a holistic paper, Plater and colleagues develop a broad scale model of coastal change during the late Holocene, which links human activity in the catchment (such as vegetation disturbance) with the deposition of thick suites of post-peat sediments across the Romney Marsh region. This study provides important insights into the often very rapid landscape changes that occurred in the past on Romney Marsh. For example, Stupple's Ph.D research on the infilling of the Wainway channel demonstrates the significance of short-lived episodes of very rapid channel infilling which have hitherto lain unidentified. Plater and colleagues go on to explore the possible links between the deposition of the post-peat sediments (the sands, silts and clays so often seen in roadside ditches across the marsh) and the evolution of Dungeness Foreland itself.

The theme of large-scale landscape reconstruction is developed further by Rippon, who reviews a model of coastal and landscape change in Romney Marsh during the last 2000 years, first proposed by Green (1988). Rippon highlights the enormous potential of landscape studies for reconstructing reclamation and land-use history, as well as coastal and sea-level change. Comparisons with other studies completed in Essex, the Thames estuary, and the Severn Estuary demonstrate how similar, at a macro-level at least, the marshlands of these very different settings can be.

The issue of reclamation landscapes is also pursued by Gardiner, who describes the 'antediluvian' landscape of Walland Marsh. Adopting concepts developed by coastal geomorphologists working on contemporary saltmarshes, Gardiner identifies a range of landscape and creek types, from which he proposes different stages of reclamation and landscape change. The most striking aspect of this paper is the persistence of landscape topography through time, a persistence which once again highlights the potential of the present landscape as an insight into the more distant past.

The two papers that follow, by Allen and Eddison, address more detailed aspects of the Romney Marsh landscape and raise questions of wider significance. Both papers are concerned with a narrow ribbon of marshland which extends from Appledore to New Romney. Allen suggests that the Rumenesea is a watercourse and later sea wall which, he proposes, formed a bridging seabank between the Wealden scarp and New Romney. His interpretation of consistent variations in ground elevations across the axis of the Rumenesea supports a hypothesis that the Rumenesea marks the initial (Saxon) coastal defence which allowed Romney Marsh proper to be colonised and reclaimed. Eddison focuses her attention on the neighbouring (and in places superimposed) Rhee Wall, a more upstanding marshland monument which was constructed in the 13th century in an effort to divert water from the upland to flush out the silting harbour at Romney. There are clear differences of opinion between these papers regarding the age, origin and wider importance of these two watercourses, differences that may only resolved with excavation and further field study.

The incentive for reclamation was clearly strong on Romney Marsh. As Rippon explains, the benefits of reclamation far outweighed the significant costs involved in both the initial reclamation and also in subsequent water management and coastal defence construction and maintenance. The papers of Allen and Eddison bring us to the Medieval period, by the end of which the marsh had become dominated by a pastoral economy which was heavily dependent on sheep. However, one of the biggest challenges still facing historians of the region is to chart the origins and development of the pastoral economy that dominated Romney Marsh by the mid-16th century.

The last decade has seen a number of contributions by historians and archaeologists that have shed light on the process of agrarian change and depopulation in particular parts of the marsh during the late-medieval period, but, as the editors of the third Romney Marsh monograph pointed out, it is difficult to distinguish trends general to the whole marsh from changes which were purely local. Nor are the available manuscript sources always easy to interpret, a point emphasised by Sheila Sweetinburgh in her examination of peasant land holding and the land market in Appledore, 1400–1470. Sweetinburgh tentatively concludes that although few individuals were able to build up large holdings, pragmatic peasants viewed land, not least, as a valuable and flexible capital asset, 'useful in the raising of liquidity through mortgaging, leasing or selling where the cash raised might be employed for other purposes'.

For large-scale accumulations of land in the hands of livestock farmers, Sweetinburgh suggests, it is necessary to look elsewhere – to the butcher/graziers of east Kent towns especially – and to the generation farming in the late-15th and early-16th centuries. Gillian Draper (1998) and Andrew Butcher (unpublished) have both offered tangible evidence for the significance of town-dwelling farmers as sponsors of agrarian transformation at the turn of the 15th century, though by the 1520s, Draper suggests, the lessees of demesne lands belonging to All Souls College were more often gentry who lived away from the marsh, and who were prepared to pay higher rents for the privilege.

It is difficult to detect the precise chronology and direction of region-wide trends in the pattern of farming on Romney marsh before the 16th century. However, developments between the Elizabethan period and the mid-19th century are now much clearer, thanks to Stephen Hipkin's (1998; 2000; forthcoming) exploitation of the remarkable scot book material that survives within the archives of the Commissioners for Sewers for the Level of Romney Marsh, Walland Marsh and Denge Marsh. These data identify the 17th century as the crucial period in the emergence of the larger tenant farmer. Between the early Jacobean period and 1699, tenant farmers occupying more than 200 acres doubled their share of the land on the Level of Romney Marsh, and, by the turn of the 17th century, larger occupiers held 57% of the 43,000 acres assessed for taxes levied to maintain sewers and sea defences across the region. During the early-18th century large tenant farmers further increased their share of the land, and by 1746 they occupied 60% of the region. Finally, by 1768 two-thirds of the privately owned land across the region was in the hands of the 89 owners, each possessing more than 100 acres.

These long-term trends were the product of the difficult economic climate for wool growers that persisted throughout the period, and of weak consumer demand for foodstuffs after the mid-17th century, when England's population ceased expanding. In such conditions, profitability for livestock farmers came to depend more heavily on increasing productivity and output to compensate for lower margins, which favoured farmers with capital to invest - not least - in the leasing of additional pasture, thus creating larger farms. Capital-rich farmers were also able to transfer some of the costs of expansion by driving hard bargains with rentiers, who were in a weak position to defend their rent income as competition for tenancies abated. Marsh rents fell sharply in some parts of the region between the 1650s and 1670s, and although there was something of a recovery during the 1690s, the indications thus far are that rents remained fairly flat during the first half of the 18th century.

After 1750, however, pressure exerted on supply by renewed national population growth was pushing up food prices, and improved conditions for meat producers made tenancies on the marsh once again an attractive proposition for upland farmers, the very people who had tended to withdraw from the marsh in disproportionate numbers during the early-18th century. Consequently, specialist marsh graziers found they could no longer assemble large farms at relatively low rents, and they also had to compete in a contracting leasehold sector as more proprietors were seduced by the rewards of direct farming. The proportion of owner-occupied land across the region rose from 8% in 1768 to 20% by 1834. During the later-18th and early-19th centuries competition for tenancies on the marsh became sufficiently robust and widespread to prevent any further drift towards the consolidation of more land in the hands of fewer tenants.

The clear implication of the scot book data is that trends in the evolution of the agrarian economy of Romney Marsh throughout the early modern period were heavily influenced by decisions reached in farmhouses well away from the marsh. Anne Davison's examination of aspects of the symbiotic relationship between marsh and upland holdings represents the first fruits of ongoing research which promises to increase greatly our knowledge of farming regimes in the marsh and its hinterland during the 18th century. It is already clear not only that many farmers ran upland and marsh holdings in conjunction, but also that a significant body of farmers who were formal tenants (or owners) only in the marsh relied on the willingness of tenants (or owners) with upland holdings to agist (pasture for a rent per head) livestock on their land, and vice versa. Thus, upland farmers sought to buy summer pasturage for cattle from tenants on the marsh, and marsh graziers bought space on upland pasture for vulnerable lambs in winter. But the 'particularly convenient and useful arrangement' did not stop here. Upland farmers agisted livestock on each other's lands, and marsh graziers did the same. The widespread practice of agistment brought an invaluable degree of flexibility to the business of farming, but it also involved risks, both that animals consigned to other farmers might not be well-kept, and that in times of high demand agistment costs might spiral. For the historian too, agistment is a risky business, for, even when detectable, the contribution of agistment to effective farm size is notoriously difficult to quantify. But it is quite clear that research into farming on Romney Marsh cannot advance any further without fully taking into account the multi-regional context within which it was so often practised.

As his working financial notebooks show, Daniel Langdon, one of the larger tenant farmers on the marshes during the early-18th century, relied on his father-in-law at Ulcombe for the safe-keeping of his lambs during winter. But Langdon's 'almanacs' and surviving correspondence also offer many other valuable insights into farming practice on the marsh during the mid 1720s, and into the pattern of Langdon's dealings with the metropolitan market. Between 1705 and 1751 Langdon was also a pivotal figure in the political and bureaucratic apparatuses of the Level and Liberty of Romney Marsh, and Hipkin offers an account of the private commercial and public

worlds of this most conspicuous of men. Utilising the hitherto neglected fiscal and administrative records of the Level and Liberty of Romney Marsh, Hipkin draws attention to the often-strained relations between marsh farmers and the oligarchic clique controlling the drainage authority during the early-Hanoverian period. Much else remains to be extracted from this rich archival seam.

By the late-16th century many county gentry owned land on Romney Marsh, and prominent amongst them were the Hales and Scott families. In the last paper of the monograph, Mark Merry and Catherine Richardson offer an interpretation of the part played by Romney Marsh holdings in the construction and perpetuation of family identity during the early modern period through an examination of their testamentary strategies and of the self-conscious rhetoric of identity employed in their wills. Whereas the Scott family lost its place among leading proprietors on the marsh during the 17th century, the Hales family became more prominent. But for both families, Merry and Richardson suggest, the importance of marsh holdings was not merely economic, for they also served 'to anchor the families firmly within the regional society in which they operated as land owners, social and cultural leaders and officers'. Once again, however, since it is clear that marsh holdings need to be viewed within the overall context of gentry proprietorship, Merry and Richardson also direct our attention to the application of family codes of practice with respect to land held far from the marsh.

Progress and Prospects

Geomorphology

Fifteen years ago our knowledge of the prehistory of Romney Marsh was heavily reliant on the results of the Soil Survey (Green 1968). Though a superb backdrop for much recent work, the survey provided relatively little information regarding the age and origin of the deeper marsh sediments, including the main marsh peat. So, a major area of progress in the last 15 years has been our improved understanding of this significant element of the stratigraphic architecture of the Romney Marsh region. We now have a reasonably robust chronology for vegetation and shoreline change, a record which compares well with that observed in other coastal lowlands in southern England (e.g. in the Solent, the Thames and the Severn Estuary; Long *et al.* 2000; Long 2000) and implies that the changes in shoreline observed are not simply the product of local processes. Our understanding of trends in relative sea level are entirely a product of research completed since 1988. Now we need to develop a history unaffected by pervasive compaction, something eminently achievable given our knowledge of the stratigraphy of the study area. Much progress has also been made in our understanding of the depositional origin and age of the sediments which abut and intermingle with the shingle beach ridges of Dungeness Foreland. Although some radiocarbon dates exist from deep boreholes beneath the Dungeness power station, our chronology for shingle beach deposition remains incomplete, as highlighted in the paper by Plater and colleagues in this volume. Lastly, the links between the uplands and the lowlands of the Romney Marsh region continue to pose more questions than we have answers. For example, the dramatic differences in valley stratigraphy as one moves from the coastal deposits downstream of Bodiam to the valley deposits upstream raise major questions regarding the nature of sediment transferral from upland to lowland regions.

Archaeology

From an archaeological perspective, a useful starting point for assessing progress is to review the gazetteer of archaeological discoveries in Romney Marsh and its surroundings presented in the first monograph produced by the Trust (Woodcock 1988, fig. 16.1). This gazetteer is limited to prehistoric, Roman and Saxon sites, with post-Norman Conquest features disregarded, so the distribution is not a true reflection of occupation and activity on the Marsh; the past thousand years, the time of the most active human intervention in the Marsh, are a blank. Figure 0.2 is an adaptation of Woodcock's 1988 map, with the addition of letters A to Q, denoting sites which have been investigated with the support of the Romney Marsh Research Trust since its inception. There has been a radical change in approach to the archaeology of Romney Marsh during the lifetime of the Trust, with a pronounced swing in favour of the medieval period. A truer picture of activity and occupation over the past 2000 years would emerge if all medieval and post-medieval sites were mapped (for example, medieval churches or late medieval/post-medieval vernacular buildings), but the published additions are confined to the Trust's work. In 1988, 250 sites were noted, with no more than a dozen having been subjected to archaeological excavations. The rest represent accidental discoveries of pottery, coins or other artefacts, or sites observed through aerial photography. Today's version presents a slightly different picture. Only 16 new sites are shown, but almost half of these have been the subject of more or less extensive archaeological excavation (Table 0.1).

The interdisciplinary nature of the Trust's work can be seen in the collaboration between archaeologists, historians and environmental scientists in the investigation of some sites, notably Broomhill. Excavation formed part of that collaboration and there have also been other excavations since 1988. They have largely been funded by commercial firms in advance of development such as gravel digging. Some, such as the Lydd Quarry sites, have recovered large areas and revealed hitherto unsuspected settlement patterns. The exciting results from Anglo-Saxon *Sandtun* are likewise the result of developer-funded excavations,

but the Broomhill site was mainly supported by grants from East Sussex County Council and the Romney Marsh Research Trust. All excavations are costly exercises, however valuable their results, and future investigations may have to rely on cheaper alternatives. 'Non-intervention archaeology' or 'landscape archaeology' are the phrases most often on the lips of archaeologists in 2002. This is probably the way forward, and we are fortunate that aspects of this have already been put into practice by the Trust over the past 15 years notably the surveys of the fabric of standing buildings, and non-intrusive fieldwalking.

Bennell's and Harris's surveys of the 12th-century fabric of the churches of Hope All Saints, All Saints Burmarsh and St Nicholas New Romney produced exciting results, including the hypothesis that there was a school of masons working on the marsh churches during the 12th century. There are at least seven other churches on the marsh with late 11th- or early 12th-century masonry; surveys of these could test the hypothesis at a small cost and could be supplemented by the geological analysis of the church fabric begun by Pearson and Potter. Although some domestic buildings have been surveyed, there is scope for much more work, notably in Lydd and New Romney. Reeves' fieldwalking on Romney Marsh proper (Reeves 1995b) has revealed a multitude of features of all dates and yet, as she states, has covered only a fragment of the marsh. Such a strategy pursued elsewhere on the marsh would have a similar potential, and would be a cost-effective way of discovering evidence for the history of Romney Marsh as a whole. Similar landscape studies have begun in a small way in the river valleys, concentrating on the changing river lines and settlements, and these have already produced interesting results. The history of the marsh has been illuminated through archaeology and other disciplines, and the potential of non-intrusive archaeological techniques has been realised. If, as one suspects, financial resources diminish over the next few years, the members of the Trust should be able to carry out this type of research, which can yield valuable results, with the smaller resources at their disposal.

History

The agenda for future historical research on the marsh is crowded. The transition from the late-medieval agrarian economy is still far from well understood and, notwithstanding contributions to the present monograph, there is a pressing need for more multi-regional conceptualisation of developments on Romney Marsh. Above all, perhaps, it is time to put an end to the neglect of towns in the marsh region and its hinterland. As mentioned above, there is evidence to suggest that town-dwelling farmers were sponsors of late-medieval agrarian change, and, as Hipkin (this volume) shows, much of the wealth of the leading citizens of late-Stuart New Romney derived from livestock farming on the marsh. Is such evidence indicative of an enduring pattern, and if so, for how long did it endure?

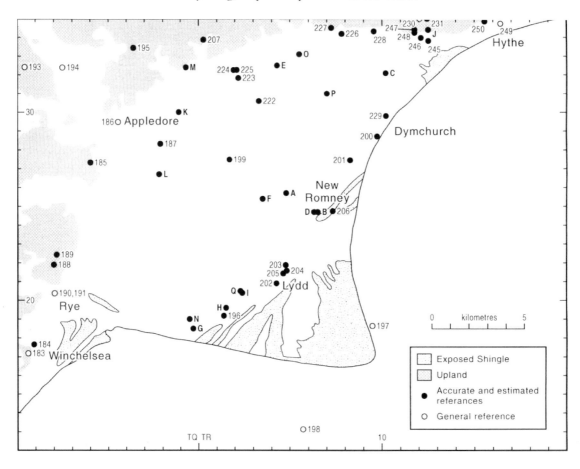

Fig. 0.2. Location map showing archaeological investigations funded by the Romney Marsh Research Trust since 1988.

More generally, and despite the wealth of evidence in corporate archives, little attention has been paid to members of the Cinque Ports confederation over recent years (with the exception of early modern Rye). It must be a priority for the Romney Marsh Research Trust to assist in filling these gaps in our knowledge.

Conclusion

This monograph shows, beyond doubt, the dynamism of the Romney Marsh landscape over many thousands of years. There is a growing debate across the disciplines, especially focussed on the time window which encompasses the end of peat formation and the cessation of major land reclamation (*c*. AD 200 to AD 1700). The Romney Marsh ports, and the people who lived in them, are important to our understanding of the Romney Marsh landscape through the ages, yet in prehistory and during the historic period, we know too little about the patterns of coastal change and changing economic fortunes at the three great inlets at Hythe, Romney and Rye. These places, where people and land meet the sea, are the foci of the past and they remain the foci for much of the present

population of the marsh. It is perhaps to these areas above all else where we should direct our attention in the years to come, and these areas where the fruits of interdisciplinary research will be found in greatest abundance.

Acknowledgments
A large number of people have helped in the preparation of this monograph. Particular thanks are expressed to the authors of all papers who put so much effort into this publication and kept so well to a tight timetable. We are also very grateful to the many reviewers of the papers, especially Martyn Waller, whose critical evaluations are so important to the quality of this and previous monographs. This is the fourth monograph produced with the support of the Professor Barry Cunliffe, a founder Trust member and Chair of the Oxford University School for Archaeology. We thank him and OUSA for their continued interest. Particular thanks are given to Liz King and Val Lamb for their care and advice during the production of this monograph. Fellow members of the Research Committee helped in the development of the original project outline, whilst Margaret Bird helped greatly in the search for financial support.

Table 0.1. Archaeological investigations funded by the Romney Marsh Research Trust since 1988.

HOPE ALL SAINTS Kent: TR 048257
A   *Medieval.* Survey of fabric of ruined 12th-century church and fieldwalking in surroundings.
(Bennell 1990; 1995; Bennell and Harris 1989)

NEW ROMNEY Kent. TR 065247
B   *Medieval.* Survey of fabric of 12th-century tower of St Nicholas church.
(Harris 1990)

BURMARSH Kent. TR 102321
C   *Medieval.* Survey of fabric of north wall of 12th-century chancel of church.
(Harris 1991)

NEW ROMNEY Kent. TR 063247
D   *Medieval.* Survey of 14th-century house, West Street.
(Harris 1992)

LYDD Kent. TR 04320
E   *Medieval and later.* Survey of buildings, 1500–1750.
(Dickinson 1994)

OLD ROMNEY Kent. TR 035254
F   *Medieval.* Fieldwalking east and north of St Clement's church.
(Gardiner 1992; 1994)

BROOMHILL East Sussex. TQ 978185
G   *Medieval.* Excavation, fieldwalking and environmental survey of the lost church and its surroundings.
(Gardiner 1986; 1988a; 1988b; 1989; 1990)

SCOTNEY COURT Kent. TR 015196
H   *Late Iron Age/Roman.* Excavation of salt-working site.
(Barber 1991)

LYDD NEW QUARRY Kent. TR 024204
I   *Roman and medieval.* Excavation of settlements and salt workings.
(Barber 1998; Grieg 1992; Priestly-Bell 2001)

WEST HYTHE Kent. TR 125344
J   *Saxon and medieval.* Excavation of settlement of *Sandtun.*
(Cross 1997; Cross *et al.* 2001)

SMALLHYTHE Kent. TQ 894300
K   *Medieval.* Excavation and field survey of shipbuilding site.
(Clarke 2000; Clarke and Milne 2002)

BODIAM East Sussex. TQ 785267
L   *Roman and medieval.* Excavation and survey of Roman road and approaches to bridge across the Rother.
(Aldridge and Clarke 2001)

SHIRLEY MOOR Kent. TQ 932324
M   *Multi-period* and interdisciplinary investigation of vegetation and human activity.
(Long 1996; Long D. *et al.* 1998; Priestly-Bell and Beck 1999)

CAMBER East Sussex. TQ 958190
N   *Medieval or later.* Accidental discovery of ships' timbers.
(Bloomfield 1988)

ROMNEY MARSH PROPER 1 Kent. Centred on TR 055313
O   *Multi-period* fieldwalking
(Reeves 1991; 1993; 1995a)

ROMNEY MARSH PROPER 2 Kent. Centred on TR 070310
P   *Multi-period* earthwork survey
(Reeves 1995b)

WAINWAY, Kent. Centred on TR 023205
Q   *Multi-period* and interdisciplinary landscape study.
(Eddison 2001)

References

Aldridge, N. and Clarke, H. 2001. In search of Bodiam bridge, *The Romney Marsh Irregular* **18**, 16–22.

Barber, L. 1991. A salt-working site at Scotney Court Gravel Pit, Lydd, *The Romney Marsh Irregular* **6**, 5.

Barber, L. 1998. Medieval rural settlement and economy at Lydd, in J. Eddison, M. Gardiner and A. Long (eds) *Romney Marsh: Environmental Change and Human Occupation in a Coastal Lowland* (Oxford University Committee for Archaeology **46**), 89–108.

Bennell, M. 1990. Survey at Hope All Saints, *The Romney Marsh Irregular* **5**, 6.

Bennell, M. 1995. Hope All Saints: a survey and discussion of the ruins and earthworks, in J. Eddison (ed.) *Romney Marsh: The Debatable Ground* (Oxford University Committee for Archaeology **41**), 99–106.

Bennell, M. and Harris, R. 1989. Surveys at Hope All Saints, *The Romney Marsh Irregular* **4**, 2.

Bloomfield 1988. The evolution of the east side of Rye Bay, *The Romney Marsh Irregular* **3**, 2–5.

Clarke, H. 2000. Early harbours along the River Rother, *The Romney Marsh Irregular* **16**, 11–13.

Clarke, H. and Milne, G. 2002. A medieval shipyard at Smallhythe, *The Romney Marsh Irregular* **19**, 12–22.

Cross, R. 1997. Archaeology at West Hythe. *The Romney Marsh Irregular* **12**, 6–7.

Dickinson 1994. Survey of buildings in Lydd 1500–1750, *The Romney Marsh Irregular* **9**, 5.

Draper, G. 1998. The farmers of Canterbury Cathedral Priory and All Soles College Oxford on Romney Marsh *c.* 1443–1545, in J. Eddison, M. Gardiner and A. Long (eds) *Romney Marsh: Environmental Change and Human Occupation in a Coastal Lowland* (Oxford University Committee for Archaeology Monograph **46**), 109–28. Oxford.

Eddison, J. 2001. The Wainway project, *The Romney Marsh Irregular* **18**, 12–16.

Gardiner, M. 1986. Excavations at Broomhill church, Camber, East Sussex, 1985, *The Romney Marsh Irregular* **2**, 6–8.

Gardiner, M. 1988a. Excavation at Broomhill, *The Romney Marsh Irregular* **3**, 7–8.

Gardiner, M. 1988b. Medieval settlement and society in the Broomhill area, and excavations at Broomhill church, in J. Eddison and C. Green (eds) *Romney Marsh: Evolution, Occupation, Reclamation* (Oxford University Committee for Archaeology **24**), 112–27.

Gardiner, M. 1989. Broomhill 1988, *The Romney Marsh Irregular* **4**, 3–5.

Gardiner, M. 1990. Broomhill 1989, *The Romney Marsh Irregular* **5**, 2–3.

Gardiner, M. 1992. Old Romney: the search for the early medieval port, *The Romney Marsh Irregular* **7**, 2–3.

Gardiner, M. 1994. Old Romney: an examination of the evidence for a lost port, *Archaeologia Cantiana* **116**, 329–45.

Gardiner, M., Cross, R., Macpherson-Grant, N. and Riddler, I. 2001. Continental trade and non-urban ports in Mid-Anglo-Saxon England: the excavations at Sandtun, West Hythe, Kent, *Archaeological Journal* **158**, 161–290.

Green, C. 1988. Palaeogeography of marine inlets of the Romney Marsh area, in J. Eddison and C. Green (eds), *Romney Marsh: Evolution, Occupation, Reclamation* (Oxford University Committee for Archaeology Monograph **46**), 167–74. Oxford.

Green, R.D. 1968. *Soils of Romney Marsh,* Soil Survey of Great Britain, Bulletin No. 4.

Grieg, J. 1988. Plant Resources, in G. Astill and A. Grant (eds) *The Countryside of Medieval England,* Blackwells, 149–87. Oxford.

Grieg, I.M., 1992. Archaeology at Lydd New Quarry, *The Romney Marsh Irregular* **7**, 6–7.

Harris, R. 1990. The rubble stonework of St Nicholas, New Romney, *The Romney Marsh Irregular* **5**, 6–7.

Harris, R. 1991. Twelfth century stonework at All Saints, Burmarsh, *The Romney Marsh Irregular* **6**, 3.

Harris, R. 1992. 3–4 West Street, New Romney, *The Romney Marsh Irregular* **7**, 5.

Hipkin, S. 1998. Land occupation in the Level of Romney Marsh during the late 16th and early 17th centuries, in J. Eddison, M. Gardiner and A. Long (eds) *Romney Marsh: Environmental Change and Human Occupation in a Coastal Lowland* (Oxford University Committee for Archaeology Monograph **46**), 147–63. Oxford.

Hipkin, S. 2000. Tenant farming and short-term leasing on Romney Marsh, 1587–1705, *Economic History Review* **LIII**, 4, 646–76.

Hipkin, S. forthcoming. The structure of land ownership and land occupation in the Romney Marsh region, 1646–1834.

Long, A.J. 2000. The mid and late Holocene evolution of Romney Marsh and the Thames Estuary, in S. Rippon (ed.) *Archaeology in the Severn Estuary* **11**, 55–68.

Long, A., Waller, M., Hughes, P. and Spencer, C. 1998. The Holocene depositional history of Romney Marsh proper, in J. Eddison, M. Gardiner and A. Long (eds) *Romney Marsh: Environmental Change and Human Occupation in a Coastal Lowland* (Oxford University Committee for Archaeology Monograph **46**), 45–63. Oxford.

Long, A.J., Scaife, R.G. and Edwards, R.J. 2000. Stratigraphic architecture, relative sea level, and models of estuary development in southern England: New data from Southampton Water, in K. Pye and J.R.L. Allen (eds) *Coastal and Estuarine Environments: Sedimentology, Geomorphology and Geoarchaeology* (Geological Society, London, Special Publications **175**), 253–79.

Long, D. 1996. Investigations of the archaeology and past vegetation of the Shirley Moor area of Romney Marsh, *The Romney Marsh Irregular* **11**, 4–5.

Long, D., Waller, M. And McCarthy, P. 1998. The vegetation history, stratigraphy and pollen data for the Shirley Moor region, in J. Eddison, M. Gardiner and A. Long (eds) *Romney Marsh: Environmental Change and Human Occupation in a Coastal Lowland* (Oxford University Committee for Archaeology **46**), 31–44.

Pearson, A. and Potter, J. 2001. Church-building on Romney Marsh, *The Romney Marsh Irregular* **17**, 15–16.

Priestly-Bell, G. and Beck, R. 1999. Shirley Moor wooden structure (an interim report), *The Romney Marsh Irregular* **14**, 3–4.

Reeves, A. 1991. Field survey of Romney Marsh Proper; interim report, *The Romney Marsh Irregular* **6**, 6–7.

Reeves, A. 1993. Romney Marsh: the field walking evidence, *The Romney Marsh Irregular* **8**, 6.

Reeves, A. 1995a. Romney Marsh earthworks, *The Romney Marsh Irregular* **10**, 2–3.

Reeves, A. 1995b. Romney Marsh: the fieldwalking evidence, in J. Eddison (ed.) *Romney Marsh: The Debatable Ground* (Oxford University Committee for Archaeology **41**), 78–91.

Waller, M. 1994. *The Fenland Project, Number 9: Flandrian Environmental Change in Fenland.* East Anglian Archaeology **70**, Cambridge.

Woodcock, A. 1988. Gazetteer of Prehistoric, Roman and Saxon sites in Romney Marsh and the surrounding area, in J. Eddison and C. Green (eds) *Romney Marsh: Evolution, Occupation and Reclamation* (Oxford University Committee for Archaeology **24**), 177–85. Oxford.

Romney Marsh: Coastal and Landscape Change through the Ages
(ed. A. Long, S. Hipkin and H. Clarke), OUSA Monograph 56, 2002, 01–21

1. The Holocene Vegetation History of the Romney Marsh Region

Martyn Waller

Twenty-eight radiocarbon dated pollen profiles constructed from organic sediments within the depositional complex of Romney Marsh are used to evaluate the Holocene vegetation history of the region. Data obtained from the valleys and edges of the marshland provide information on the former vegetation of adjacent areas of the Weald. Dates derived for the Holocene arrival of Pinus sylvestris, Ulmus, Tilia *and* Fraxinus excelsior *from Pannel Bridge are some of the earliest recorded in Britain and unusually* Alnus glutinosa *appears to have been present during the early Holocene. This site also contains evidence for the creation of temporary openings within the woodland canopy during the Mesolithic. The data available for the mid Holocene (c. 7800–4000 cal. yr BP) are particularly extensive and suggest the Wealden woodlands were dominated by* Tilia cordata. *Human impact on the vegetation during the late Holocene appears not to have been uniform. Notably, woodland clearance occurred earlier (c. 4000 cal. yr BP, during the early Bronze Age) in the Brede and Pannel valleys than along the northern edge of the marshland and in the Rother Valley. Clear spatial and temporal trends have been identified in the vegetation of the valleys and marshland during the formation of the "main marsh peat". Fen carr dominated by* Alnus glutinosa *persisted in the valleys for c. 3000 cal. yr maintained by base-rich run-off and rising relative sea level. This community grades into a base-poor variant (with more* Betula *and* Salix*) on the marshland. At sites distant from the upland, acidophilic vegetation developed. Wetter conditions c. 2750 cal. yr BP promoted the establishment of an ombrotrophic bog over parts of Walland Marsh. Sites situated close to and within the shingle complex are dominated by herb taxa with little evidence for the successional development of scrub. The paper concludes by summarising the major outstanding issues.*

Introduction

Incorporated within the Holocene (post-glacial) sequences of the Romney Marsh depositional complex are organic sediments. Using standard palaeoecological techniques, in particular pollen analysis (see Faegri and Iversen 1989; Moore *et al.* 1991), these sediments can be used to reconstruct vegetation history. Up until the 1980s the organic deposits of the Romney Marsh region were poorly understood and their potential to provide information on past vegetation remained unexploited. This situation has now been transformed. Not only has the nature, extent and age of these deposits been clarified, but 28 radiocarbon-dated pollen profiles have been published (Table 1.1). These contain a wealth of information on the vegetation history of not only the former wetland areas

(the valleys and marshland) but also the adjacent upland/dryland and the shingle beaches (Fig. 1.1).

In the context of south-eastern England, the spatially and temporally extensive organic deposits of the Romney Marsh area, represent an exceptional resource. It is the absence of such deposits that has regularly been cited (e.g. Scaife 1982; 1988) as the explanation for the relative scarcity of pollen-based vegetation reconstructions from this region. Studies of the Romney Marsh deposits are beginning to redress this imbalance and provide answers to a number of key questions. The importance of this region arises from the proximity of the Continent and the juxtaposition of sharply contrasting geologies. Little information has been available on the timing of the arrival of tree taxa during the Holocene. However, the spread of

Table 1.1. Radiocarbon dated pollen diagrams from the Romney Marsh Region.

No.	Site	Date Range (cal. yr BP) or approximate age	Pollen sum	Primary publication
1	Pannel Bridge	11300 – post 2000	TLP-*Alnus*	Waller 1993
2	Brede Bridge	6800 – 3600	TLP-*Alnus*	Waller 1994a
3	Old Place 80	6400 – 1700	TLP-*Alnus*	Waller 1998
4	Rye bypass 11	*c.* 6300	TLP	Long *et al.* 1996
5	Tillingham Valley TGC	9700 – 9200	TLP	Waller and Kirby 2002
6	Tillingham Valley TG11	*c.* 7800	TLP	Waller and Kirby 2002
7	Rye bypass 27	*c.* 1700	TLP	Long *et al.* 1996
8	Rye bypass 31	*c.* 5200	TLP	Long *et al.* 1996
9	Rye bypass 33	*c.* 3200	TLP	Long *et al.* 1996
10	Chapel Bank	6300 – 3600	TLP-*Alnus*	Long, D. *et al.* 1998
11	Horsemarsh Sewer	6300 – 3300	TLP	Waller *et al.* 1999
12	The Dowels	5700 – 2300	TLP	Waller *et al.* 1999
13	Hope Farm	5100 – 1800	TLP	Waller *et al.* 1999
14	Brookland	4900 – 1800	TLP	Long and Innes 1995
15	Little Cheyne Court	5000 – 950	TLP	Waller *et al.* 1999
16	Broomhill A	3800 – 3300	AP+Group	Tooley and Switsur 1988
17	Broomhill 1	3700 – 3300	AP+Group	Tooley and Switsur 1988
18	Midley 10B	4050 – 2200	TLP	Long and Innes 1993
19	Midley 2B	*c.* 2900	TLP	Long and Innes 1993
20	Midley 6B	*c.* 3200	TLP	Long and Innes 1993
21	Scotney Marsh AY17	*c.* 3300 – 2350	TLP	Spencer *et al.* 1998
22	Scotney Marsh AW63	*c.* 3700 and *c.* 3100	TLP	Spencer *et al.* 1998
23	Scotney Marsh AW-AX 67	*c.* 3900 and 3000 – 2800	TLP	Spencer *et al.* 1998
24	Scotney Marsh A-B 27	*c.* 2700	TLP	Spencer *et al.* 1998
25	Scotney Marsh G60	*c.* 3300	TLP	Spencer *et al.* 1998
26	Wickmaryholm Pit	post 1950	TLP	Long and Hughes 1995
27	Romney Marsh 7	4600 – 2300	TLP	Long, A. *et al.* 1998
28	Romney Marsh 18	3500 – 3000	TLP	Long, A. *et al.* 1998

a number of taxa, from glacial refugia, is likely to have occurred via the south-east of England. The importance of geology, as an influence on the composition of the woodlands of the region prior to extensive human modification, and to the pattern of this interference, has also been the subject of debate. The Holocene deposits of Romney Marsh abut the acidic geologies of the Weald. Traditionally these have been seen as supporting a natural woodland cover dominated by *Quercus* (oak). The sandier lithologies have been regarded as being susceptible to early human interference. In contrast, the heavier more intractable soils (e.g. those developed on the Weald Clay)

are often presumed to have remained well wooded into the historic period. In addition to studies of dryland vegetation history, as a result of their extent, the organic deposits of Romney Marsh also present a significant opportunity to examine spatial and temporal trends in the development of coastal wetland vegetation.

After detailing the organic deposits of the Romney Marsh region and considering the interpretation of the pollen diagrams, this paper reviews the evidence currently available to reconstruct the vegetation of dryland, wetland and shingle areas during the Holocene. The discussion focuses on the issues of wider significance, both in terms

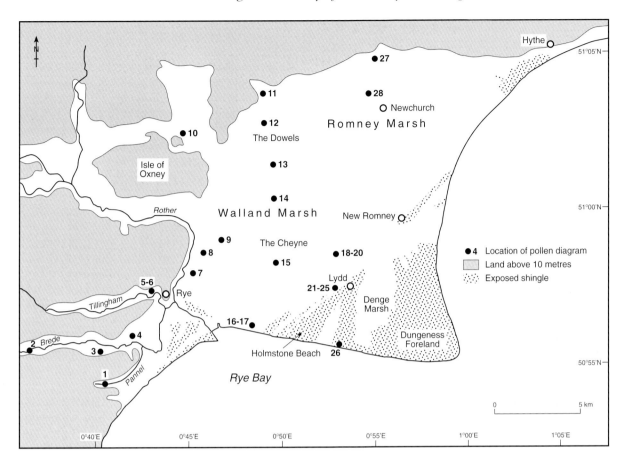

Fig. 1.1. The Romney Marsh region showing the location of the radiocarbon dated pollen diagrams (see Table 1.1 for a key to the numbers).

of the vegetation history of south-eastern England and the development of wetland vegetation in coastal lowland areas.

In spite of being constructed in the relatively recent past, there are a number of inconsistencies between the published pollen diagrams from the Romney Marsh region. Differences in nomenclature have influenced the way in which taxa are referred to on the pollen diagrams. Here the scheme of Bennett (1994) has been followed throughout. There are also important differences in the pollen sums used. In most of the pollen diagrams, pollen taxa are expressed proportionally as a percentage of the pollen and spores counted from a particular sample. The most widely used procedure in recent years has been to express land plants as a percentage of the total land pollen (%TLP) counted (Moore *et al*. 1991). The pollen of aquatics, and pteridophytes spores, are expressed as percentages of a sum in which they are included (%TLP+Aq. and %TLP+Pter. respectively). In many of the sequences from the Romney Marsh area, very high frequencies of *Alnus glutinosa* (alder) are recorded (indicating the local occurrence of fen carr/woodland). As a consequence of pollen counts being expressed in proportions, changes in the other taxa tend to mirror those of *Alnus glutinosa*.

Where wetland vegetation changes have not been the primary focus of the investigation, namely the studies of dryland vegetation history made in the valleys (e.g. Waller 1993; 1994a; 1998; Long, D. *et al*. 1998), the practice has therefore been to exclude *Alnus glutinosa* from the pollen sum (%TLP-*Alnus*). Diagrams from the marshland, where wetland vegetation changes are of principal interest, have generally used a TLP pollen sum. However, Tooley and Switsur (1988) adopted an alternative sum consisting of tree (arboreal) pollen, both to express tree pollen frequencies (%AP) and other groups (%AP+Group).

All the radiocarbon dates mentioned in the text are expressed in calendar years before the present (cal. yr BP) using the mean calibrated age derived from the updated (4.3) version of the program CALIB (Stuiver and Reimer 1993).

The Organic Deposits of the Romney Marsh Region

While thin organic layers occur at depth (Waller 1987; Waller and Kirby 2002), the bulk of the organic sediments of the region are part of a single extensive deposit, the "main marsh peat", found between *c*. -6 m and 4 m

Ordnance Datum (OD). In the upper parts of the valleys, this deposit grades into fluvial clays and silts (Waller *et al.* 1988). It is thickest (*c.* 6.5 m) in the middle parts of the valleys (e.g. Brede Bridge, Bodiam) where it occurs within 1 m of the present surface. Over most of the lower valley areas and Walland Marsh the "main marsh peat" is more deeply buried, though surface outcrops occur, particularly in the vicinity of The Dowels (Green 1968). While a thin layer extends out from the upland edge towards New-church, this deposit is largely absent from Romney Marsh proper (Long, A.J. *et al.* 1998). Organic sediments also occur within the degraded barrier system. At some locations to the north of the gravel outcrop these deposits may represent extensions of the "main marsh peat". However, organic sediments have also formed in open waterbodies between the shingle ridges (Long and Hughes 1995).

The "main marsh peat" is markedly diachronous (Long, A.J. *et al.* 1998; Waller *et al.* 1999) and in general terms provides palaeoecological information for the mid Holocene in the valleys (e.g. *c.* 6800–3500 cal. yr BP at Brede Bridge) and the mid/later Holocene (e.g. *c.* 5000–950 BP at Little Cheyne Court) on Walland Marsh. This layer accumulated rapidly and it has been possible to obtain pollen records with a good temporal resolution (< 150 cal. yr between samples at the sites on Walland Marsh). This is particularly the case for the mid Holocene, when ground water-levels were driven upwards by rising relative sea level (Waller *et al.* 1999), at sites where there is little overburden and hence subsequent compaction. At Pannel Bridge and Brede Bridge interpolation between radiocarbon dates give accumulation rates of 5 to 6 cal. yr cm^{-1} during the mid Holocene (Waller 1993; 1994a). Advantage has been taken of these rates at Brede Bridge to obtain high temporal resolution of critical events by sampling contiguous levels (Waller 1994a).

A number of wetland terrestrial vegetation communities are represented within the "main marsh peat". They can be divided into two basic types: eutrophic (base-rich) and oligotrophic (base-poor). The former included reedswamp, fen (here used to refer to open herb-dominated vegetation) and fen carr/woodland. The latter community was particularly extensive during the formation of this deposit, with *Alnus glutinosa* frequently the dominant species. These communities remain in contact with groundwater and are comparatively well supplied with nutrients. The oligotrophic communities included those that remain in contact with groundwater but receive few nutrients (here termed poor fen), and 'ombrotrophic' vegetation (also termed raised bog) where peat has accumulated above the groundwater level. Ombrotrophic communities are dependent upon precipitation and dust for supplies of water and nutrients and are characterised by the presence of Sphagna (bog mosses), Ericaceae (heathers) and/or Cyperaceae (sedges) particularly the genus *Eriophorum* (cotton grasses).

The Interpretation of the Romney Marsh Pollen Diagrams

Pollen diagrams constructed from peats situated in coastal lowland areas such as Romney Marsh pose particular problems of interpretation (Waller 1993; Waller 1998). A key consideration is the source area from which pollen was derived. This will be influenced both by the nature of the *in-situ* peat-forming community and the position of the pollen site within the wetland area. In pollen diagrams constructed from peats much of the pollen (here termed local pollen) is likely to have been derived from the wetland vegetation growing *in-situ* or immediately adjacent to a site. The quantity of pollen produced is much greater in some communities (particularly fen woodland) than others (such as ombrotrophic bog). The proportion derived from distance (here termed extra-local if originating from within a few hundred metres of a site, and regional if originating from greater distances), varies accordingly. Even the structure of the vegetation needs to be considered. Woodland, for example, acts as a filter (Tauber 1965) so that the pollen source area for fen carr/woodland is likely to be considerably smaller than for the open wetland communities.

Position in the wetland area is important as the representation of pollen taxa is strongly influenced by dispersal bias, with wind-pollinated and tall plants likely to be increasingly over-represented in the extra-local and regional components. Studies at Old Place in the Brede Valley (Waller 1998) demonstrate that the representation of dryland taxa varies in relation to distance from the dryland edge. Locations close to this edge have higher proportions of poorly dispersed dryland types such as *Tilia* (lime) and Cereal-type pollen as extra-local pollen is maximised. Pollen sites positioned adjacent to dryland (in the valleys and along the fringes of the marshland) therefore offer the best opportunity of accurately re-constructing the vegetation of upland areas, though it cannot be assumed that the vegetation reconstructed at any one site will be typical for the region (Waller 1998). The pollen record at more distant sites (on Walland and Romney Marshes and adjacent to the gravel outcrop) is likely be dominated by wetland types. Dryland pollen may derive from a large (though rather uncertain) source area, but will be heavily distorted by dispersal bias.

These factors will influence pollen stratigraphy. Changes in the *in-situ* vegetation (e.g. from fen woodland to fen) and in the distance between a site and a source area affect the pollen deposited at any given site through time (Waller 1994b; 1998). It should be noted that due to rising sea level, expansion in the wetland area is a feature of British coastal lowland areas, including Romney Marsh, during much of the Holocene.

An additional difficulty lies in identifying the community from which certain pollen taxa derive. Taxa originating from ombrotrophic bog and waterbodies are usually distinctive (comprising acidophilous species and aquatics and marginal aquatics respectively). However, many taxa including *Betula* (birch), Poaceae (grasses), Cyperaceae, *Urtica* (nettles), Apiaceae (carrot family) and Brassicaceae (cabbage family) associated with eutrophic wetland vegetation (e.g. fen carr, fen, reedswamp) also occur in dryland communities. In coastal lowlands this problem is compounded by the proximity of other open habitats including saltmarsh. This brings into question the origin of additional taxa, including a number often regarded as indicators of human activity e.g. Cheno-podiaceae (goosefoot family) and *Artemisia*-type (worm-woods).

Dryland Vegetation History

Deposits of early Holocene age (*c.* 11,400–7800 cal. yr BP) are scarce in the Romney Marsh region. Only the comparatively shallow and highly localised sequence at Pannel Bridge (Waller 1993) spans this period. Sediments dated to the interval *c.* 9700–9200 cal. yr BP and to *c.* 7800 cal. yr BP have additionally been recovered at depth in the Tillingham Valley (Waller and Kirby 2002).

The basal pollen assemblage at Pannel Bridge (PB-1) is largely derived from organic silts and contains a mixture of tree and herb pollen (Fig. 1.2). The former suggest that woodland, with both *Betula* and *Pinus sylvestris* (pine) present, developed rapidly (by *c.* 11,400 cal. yr BP) in the Pannel Valley in response to climatic warming at the opening of the Holocene. The herb pollen (comprising Cyperaceae and Poaceae) was probably largely derived from plants growing on the wet valley floor. The persistent occurrence of *Alnus glutinosa* pollen (and macrofossils from 1075–1100 cm) suggests this taxon was also present to take advantage of these conditions. However, some caution is required in the interpretation of PB-1 as pre-Quaternary spores are common and this assemblage may contain material reworked from the preceding late-glacial period (including the *Betula* and herb pollen).

Hazel (*Corylus avellana*) was abundant in the early Holocene woodlands of Britain (Godwin 1975) and high *Corylus avellana*-type frequencies are accordingly recorded both at Pannel Bridge (PB-2) and in the Tillingham Valley (TGC) sequence (Waller and Kirby, 2002). Both diagrams also indicate that *Quercus* and *Ulmus* (elm) became established in the Romney Marsh region during this period. For *Corylus avellana*-type frequencies to remain high from 10,200 to 8200 cal. yr BP, suggests hazel was able to out-compete these species from certain habitats. It may have been favoured by the particular climatic conditions (relatively cold winters and cool summers) prevailing in the early Holocene (Huntley 1993). *Quercus* and *Ulmus* are likely to have been confined to the more sandy and acidic areas.

The rapid rise in *Tilia* pollen at Pannel Bridge (the PB-2/3 boundary) marks the establishment of the woodland communities that characterised the dryland of the region

during the mid Holocene (*c.* 7800–4000 cal. yr BP). With peat formation becoming widespread in the valleys (*c.* 6800 cal. yr BP) before spreading out across the marshland, the number of sites available to reconstruct vegetation history increases considerably during this period.

The mid Holocene pollen assemblages of the valleys are dominated by tree pollen. *Tilia* frequencies of 5–20% TLP-*Alnus* are recorded at Pannel Bridge, Brede Bridge, Old Place and Chapel Bank. *Tilia* is insect pollinated and flowers in the summer when wind velocities through the canopy are lowest (Huntley and Birks 1983). Frequencies of 5% TLP-*Alnus* are sufficient to infer that lime occurred in some abundance, while higher percentages probably indicate the occurrence of lime-dominated woodland within the pollen source areas. Only a few grains of *Tilia platyphyllos* (large-leaved lime) pollen have been recorded and it is likely that the main species involved was *Tilia cordata* (small-leaved lime). Macrofossils (fruits) recorded at Pannel Bridge, Brede Bridge and Old Place are certainly attributable to the latter taxon. Other major constituents of the mid Holocene woodlands included *Quercus* and *Corylus avellana*. The lower pollen frequencies of the latter species recorded at Pannel Bridge after *c.* 8200 cal. yr BP suggest hazel became restricted to the under-storey. *Ulmus* (prior to 5800 cal. yr BP) and *Fraxinus excelsior* (ash) (after *c.* 6700 cal. yr BP) were clearly also present and the latter species is again heavily under-represented in the pollen record (Huntley and Birks 1983). *Betula* pollen is scarce (generally <5% TLP-*Alnus*) at the valley sites, though fruits are consistently recorded leading Waller (1993) to suggest its occurrence as a gap-phase species. Subsequent work on Walland Marsh (Waller *et al.* 1999) indicates the presence here of *Betula* within fen woodland and this now seems a more likely source for these very widely dispersed fruits.

The pre-5800 cal. yr BP (Mesolithic) assemblages from Romney Marsh consistently contain small quantities of herb pollen and fluctuations in the representation of tree taxa, including *Tilia*, are common. Most of the herb taxa can be attributed to either fen, e.g. Cyperaceae, Apiaceae and *Lotus* (birds-foot trefoil), or brackish, e.g. Cheno-podiaceae and *Artemisia*-type, environments. However, the irregular presence of, and peaks in, *Plantago lanceo-lata* (ribwort plantain), *Rumex acetosa/acetosella* (sorrel) and possibly Poaceae pollen, and *Pteridium aquilinum* (bracken) spores at Pannel Bridge (during PB-2b, 3a, 3b and 3c) are suggestive of the creation of temporary openings within the woodland canopy during the Meso-lithic (Waller 1993). These may be the product of human activity or natural processes such as senescence, wind-throw or the presence of herbivores (including wild cattle, boar and beaver).

A mid Holocene decline in *Ulmus* pollen is a consistent feature of the Romney Marsh pollen record. It can be distinguished at all the sites which pre-date *c.* 5800 cal. yr BP (Pannel Bridge, Brede Bridge, Old Place, Chapel Bank and Horsemarsh Sewer). At Pannel Bridge the elm decline

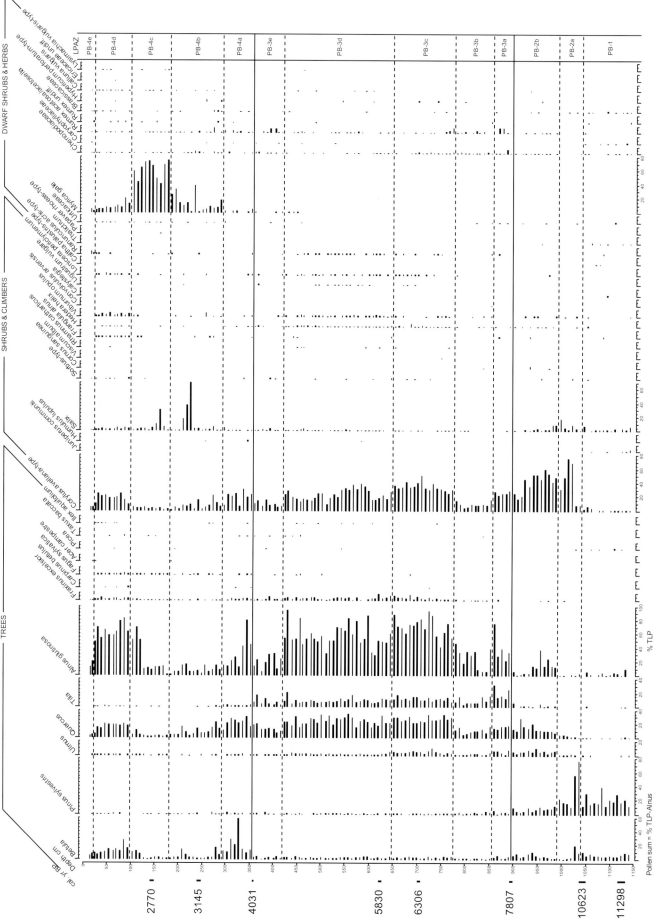

Fig. 1.2. Percentage pollen diagram from Pannel Bridge (after Waller 1993). The radiocarbon dates are expressed as the mean calibrated age.

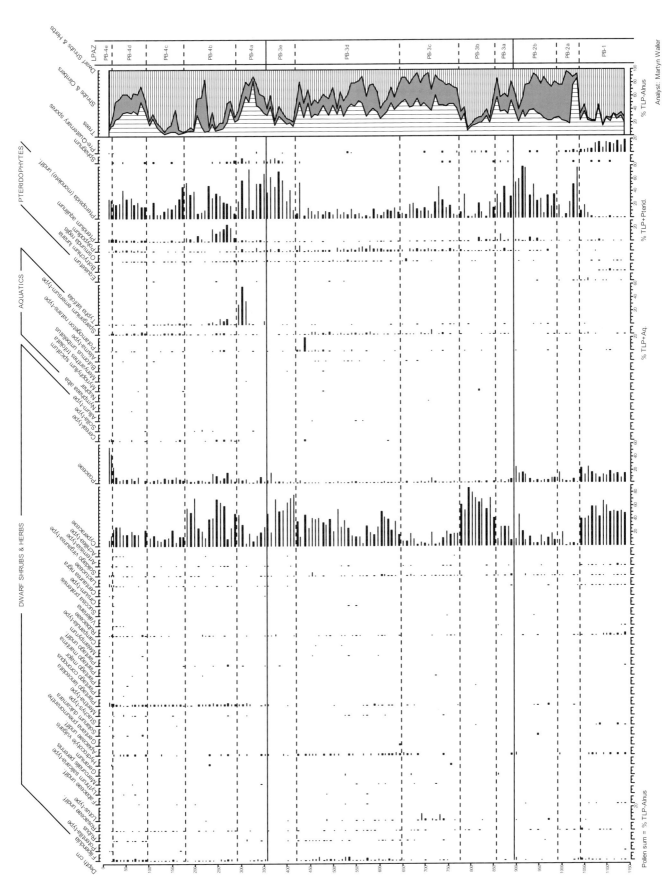

Fig. 1.2. continued.

(the PB-3c/3d boundary) has been dated to 5830 cal. yr BP (5040 ± 80 radiocarbon years BP) clearly associating this event with changes seen in pollen diagrams throughout north-west Europe *c.* 5000 radiocarbon years BP (Godwin 1975). Although only directly dated at one site, the available evidence suggests that the *Ulmus* decline is for all practical purposes a synchronous horizon in the Romney Marsh region and it is probably the only biostratigraphic change which can confidently be used for correlation. *Ulmus* percentages vary considerably between sites prior to the decline (*c.* 10% to 3% TLP-*Alnus*) and it is most easily distinguished by the very low percentages (always <1% TLP-*Alnus*) which occur immediately afterwards.

The *Ulmus* decline has been the subject of much speculation in recent years with human activity and disease, or a combination of the two, being the most favoured explanations (Birks 1986; Hirons and Edwards 1986; Girling 1988; Peglar 1993). At both Pannel Bridge and Brede Bridge, there is evidence for woodland disturbance accompanying the *Ulmus* decline. Fluctuations occur in the abundance of other tree taxa (most notably temporary declines in *Tilia*), *Plantago lanceolata* occurs consistently and the first Cereal-type pollen grains appear. To examine these changes in more detail a high resolution record of the *Ulmus* decline was obtained at Brede Bridge (Waller 1994a). Contiguous 1 cm samples revealed three stages in the behaviour of *Ulmus*; a stage with consistently high values, a stage where they steadily decline (which lasted *c.* 60 cal. yr) and finally a stage of fluctuating but generally low values. Signs of human activity (temporary clearances lasting *c.* 30 to 35 cal. yr) occur during the first two stages, though the lack of conformity between the changes in *Ulmus* values and phases of woodland disturbance suggest an additional selective process was operating upon *Ulmus* (Waller 1994a). Given that the *Ulmus* decline is such a widespread phenomenon it appears most likely that this factor was disease. As has been suggested by other authors, that this event coincides with evidence for human activity is probably a consequence of humans either exploiting the open areas created by the dead elms or facilitating the spread of the pathogen. Subsequently *Ulmus* percentages never regain their pre *c.* 5800 cal. yr BP values, suggesting that the elm decline marks the first virulent occurrence of a pathogen. Gradual recoveries are punctuated by further sudden declines (one of which occurred *c.* 4500 cal. yr BP at both Pannel Bridge and Brede Bridge) indicating further outbreaks.

Aside from the scarcity of elm, the post-*Ulmus* decline dryland woodlands of the region appear little changed in the period *c.* 5800 to 4000 cal. yr BP. However, at both Pannel Bridge and Brede Bridge, a general up-core decline in *Tilia* percentages can be discerned. This phenomenon is likely to be a product of the expansion in wetland area during the mid Holocene resulting in an increase in the distance between sites and dryland source areas and consequently a gradual decline in, poorly dispersed, *Tilia* pollen (Waller 1994b). In addition, at Brede Bridge, two abrupt falls in *Tilia* values occur after *c.* 4600 cal. yr BP (Waller 1994a). They are accompanied by changes in the representation of other tree taxa (*Quercus* also declines, while *Corylus avellana*-type, *Fraxinus excelsior* and *Betula* increase) and increases in Poaceae and *Plantago lanceolata*. Human activity is strongly indicated and these events are probably early or distant manifestations of the *c.* 4000 cal. yr BP decline in *Tilia*.

At Pannel Bridge the sudden drop in *Tilia* values dated to *c.* 4000 cal. yr BP (the PB-3e/4a boundary) marks the opening of the late Holocene (Waller 1993). Both the abrupt nature and the timing of this decline are paralleled at Brede Bridge, where a high-resolution record has again been obtained (Waller 1994a). Declines in *Tilia* pollen have long been associated with human activity (e.g. Turner 1962), with woodland dominated by *Tilia* likely to have been preferentially destroyed as a result of growing on the soils best suited for cultivation and/or because of the value of the tree, which can be used for leaf fodder, timber or bast fibre (Godwin 1975).

The detailed investigations at Brede Bridge highlight the abruptness of the *Tilia* decline. The major drop in *Tilia* values (from >10% to <1% TLP-*Alnus*) occurs across three contiguous 1 cm samples (Waller 1994a), along with falls in *Quercus* and *Corylus avellana*-type and corresponding increases in herb pollen (notably Poaceae, Cyperaceae and *Plantago lanceolata*). The sudden changes in the representation of taxa with poorly dispersed pollen suggest that woodland on the slopes adjacent to the site was being destroyed. The rise in *Plantago lanceolata* implies the subsequent development of grassland and pastoralism, though cultivation is also indicated by the regular occurrence of Cereal-type pollen. Cultivation was certainly occurring at Old Place (Waller 1998), where, at sites close to the valley side, values for Cereal-type pollen (which is very heavily under-represented) are unusually high (>1% TLP-*Alnus*). At Pannel Bridge, although Poaceae values increase, the major beneficiary of the decline in *Tilia* was *Betula*, suggesting rapid woodland regeneration. The subsequent persistence of *Tilia* at Pannel Bridge (in contrast to the sites in the Brede Valley) may be the result of vegetative regrowth.

In contrast to the Brede and Pannel valleys, *Tilia*-dominated woodlands persisted into the late Holocene in the Rother Valley and along the northern edge of the marshland. Although *Tilia* pollen virtually disappears from Romney Marsh borehole 7 *c.* 3900 cal. yr BP, other indicators of human activity remain scarce. At sites close to the upland, Chapel Bank (Long, D. *et al.* 1998) and Horsemarsh Sewer (Waller *et al.* 1999), high *Tilia* values (5 to 10% TLP-*Alnus*) are recorded through to the end of peat formation (*c.* 3600 cal. yr BP and *c.* 3300 cal. yr BP respectively). Values for Poaceae and *Plantago lanceolata* remain low.

The only site investigated to date, close to the upland where peat formation continued well into the late Holocene, is Pannel Bridge. Here a further phase of woodland disturbance occurs at the opening of PB-4b, *c.* 3400 cal. yr BP. Again human activity is implicated. *Quercus, Betula, Corylus avellana*-type values are reduced, *Tilia* virtually disappears, while *Pteridium aquilinum* and *Plantago lanceolata* frequencies increase and Cereal-type grains appear. Unfortunately, from *c.* 3400 cal. yr BP onwards the vegetation history of dryland in the Pannel Valley is obscured by major fluctuations in local taxa, notably Cyperaceae and *Myrica gale* (bog myrtle). In addition, the chronology above 142 cm is insecure with radiocarbon dating prevented by modern rootlet contamination. Although there are indications of limited woodland regeneration towards the end of PB-4b (*c.* 3000 cal. yr BP), the relatively open conditions instigated around Pannel Bridge at the start of PB-4b probably persisted until the beginning of PB-4d. The major increases in *Betula, Quercus* and *Corylus avellana*-type at the PB-4c/4d boundary are clear evidence of woodland regeneration. When this occurred is uncertain. The assumption of a constant rate of sedimentation above 142 cm would place this phase as commencing *c.* 2000 cal. yr BP. In apparent contrast support for increased human activity in the region in the period *c.* 2600 to *c.* 950 cal. yr BP is provided by the Little Cheyne Court sequence on Walland Marsh (Waller *et al.* 1999) through higher *Plantago lanceolata* values and the irregular occurrence of Cereal-type pollen (Fig. 1.3).

Wetland Vegetation History

Although the "main marsh peat" formed diachronously, the pollen diagrams suggest the vegetation changes that accompanied the initial stages of peat development were very similar. Saltmarsh was replaced by a transitional reedswamp community, with the macrofossil remains of *Phragmites* (common reed) particularly abundant at the lithological boundary. Subsequently, emergent aquatic communities/fen, with high frequencies of Poaceae, Cyperaceae and *Sparganium emersum*-type (bur-reed/reedmace) pollen, developed and persisted for several hundred cal. yr. At all sites, except those within or on the edge of the barrier system (Broomhill, Wickmaryholm and Scotney Marsh), tree taxa then invaded, though at this stage important differences emerge between the valley, edge of the marshland and the mid-marshland sites.

At the valley sites (e.g. Chapel Bank, Brede Bridge, Old Place and Pannel Bridge), peat accumulation largely occurred within fen carr/woodland environments. *Alnus glutinosa,* with pollen percentages exceeding 40% TLP and macrofossil remains abundant, was the dominant taxon from *c.* 6800 to 3900 cal. yr BP. A large number of associated shrub and herb taxa have also been recorded. The shrubs include *Rhamnus catharticus* (buckthorn) *Frangula alnus* (alder buckthorn), *Ligustrum vulgare* (privet), *Viburnum opulus* (guelder rose) and *Salix* (willow) all of which are insect pollinated and therefore

likely to be heavily under-represented in the pollen record, compared with the wind pollinated *Alnus glutinosa.* Herb taxa unambiguously associated with such conditions, or for which macrofossil evidence confirms a local origin, include *Ranunculus acris*-type (buttercups), *Filipendula ulmaria* (meadowsweet) *Lythrum salicaria* (purple loosestrife), Apiaceae undiff., *Lysimachia vulgaris*-type (yellow loosestrife), Rubiaceae (bedstraw family), *Lycopus europaeus* (gipsywort), *Rubus* (bramble), *Valeriana* (valerian), *Solidago virgaurea*-type (members of the daisy family) and Cyperaceae. Several aquatic taxa occur persistently, notably *Alisma*–type (water plantain) and *Sparganium emersum*-type. The spores of *Polypodium* (polypody), an epiphyte on alder, *Osmunda regalis* (royal fern) and other ferns are also abundant at some sites. Such vegetation appears closely analogous to modern fen woodlands, specifically the *Alnus glutinosa-Carex paniculata* communities of Rodwell (1991), which are associated with floodplains and are under the influence of eutrophic groundwater.

Spatial and temporal variations are evident within the *Alnus glutinosa*-dominated pollen assemblages of the valleys. The production of multiple profiles from the Brede Valley at Old Place indicates that wetter and more open conditions (and higher Cyperaceae values) prevailed towards the centre of the valley, while drier conditions (fen woodland possibly with *Quercus*) occurred at the valley margins (Waller 1998). Environmental variations may also be reflected in other spatial differences, for example, the unusually high percentages of Apiaceae at Chapel Bank (Long, D. *et al.* 1998) and *Viburnum opulus* at Brede Bridge (Waller 1994). Many of the temporal changes appear short-lived. Fluctuations in *Alnus glutinosa* values (of up to *c.* 20% TLP) frequently occur between adjacent samples. They are attributable to the vagaries of pollen dispersal beneath an alder dominated canopy, with very high *Alnus glutinosa* percentages (over 90% TLP) likely to be the product of the macrofossil deposition of inflorescences (Waller, 1993). With respect to herb and aquatic taxa such variations probably reflect changes in the distribution of wetland plants in relation to the sampled sites, resulting from, for example, temporary openings in the canopy and the migration of water channels. Long-term changes in abundance also occur. For example, pollen values for *Filipendula* consistently increase in the post-*Ulmus* decline assemblages of both the Brede and Pannel valleys, indicating more open conditions (Waller 1998).

Alnus glutinosa-dominated vegetation was also widespread on the marshland during the formation of the "main marsh peat". In particular, the early stages of peat growth appear to have favoured establishment, with alder invading from *c.* 5600 cal. yr BP at Horsemarsh Sewer (Waller *et al.* 1999) to *c.* 3500 cal. yr BP at Romney Marsh borehole 18 (Long, A.J. *et al.* 1998). Only at the sites likely to be most distant from the input of base-rich waters (Little Cheyne Court and possibly Midley) was alder apparently absent, being replaced by *Betula* (Waller *et al.* 1999).

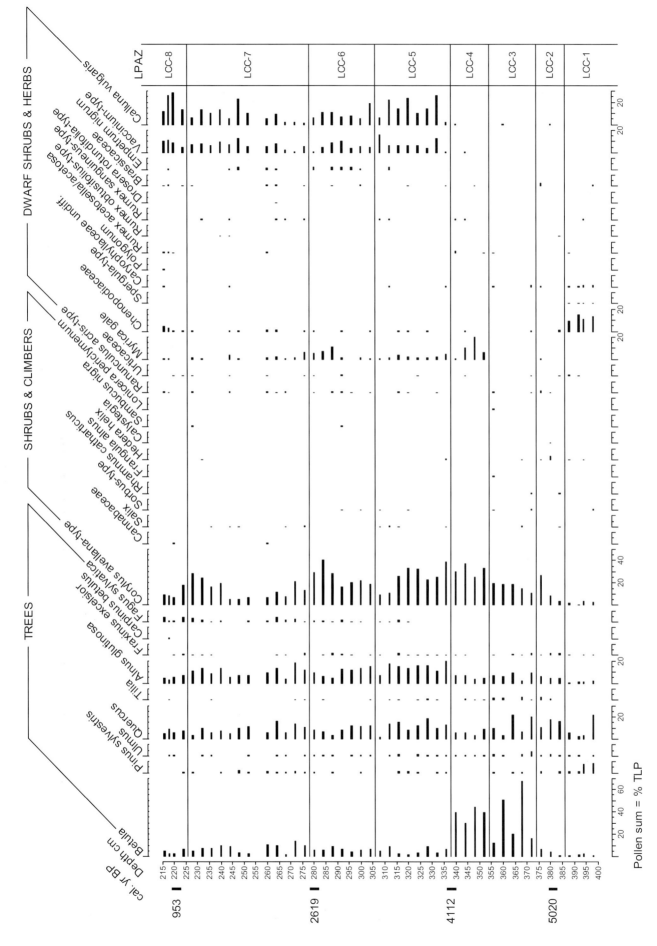

Fig. 1.3. Percentage pollen diagram from Little Cheyne Court: Walland Marsh (after Waller et al. 1999). The radiocarbon dates are expressed as the mean calibrated age.

Fig. 1.3. continued.

The *Alnus glutinosa* communities of the marshland appear to represent a base poor facies when compared to the valleys sites, with fewer taxa recorded and notably more *Betula* and *Salix* pollen. Conditions along the northern edge of the marshland (Horsemarsh Sewer and The Dowels) were sufficient to maintain alder throughout the period of peat formation (*c.* 5600 to 2300 cal. yr BP). However, sites further out into the marshland record a shift away from alder.

Oligotrophic conditions prevailed at Little Cheyne Court from *c.* 5000 to *c.* 950 cal. yr BP. The pollen evidence here (Fig. 1.3) is supplemented by plant macrofossil investigations (Waller *et al.* 1999). High values for *Betula*, *Myrica gale*, ferns and *Sphagnum* (during LCC-3/4) indicate the early development of a poor fen environment. This community was replaced by more open oligotrophic vegetation and ultimately ombrotrophic bog. The Ericaceae, both *Calluna vulgaris* (heather) and *Vaccinium*-type (bilberry/cranberry) and *Sphagnum* (including *Sphagnum* section *Cuspidata* indicative of wet conditions) were initially (LCC-5) prominent in the former community. During LCC-6 *Sphagnum* values drop and there are increases in Cyperaceae and Poaceae pollen. The abundance of *Eriophorum* rhizomes and regular occurrence of *Empetrum nigrum* (crowberry) pollen suggest that this assemblage represents a phase of relatively dry conditions. The LCC-6/7 boundary is accompanied by a stratigraphic change to a peat rich in the remains of *Sphagnum imbricatum* spp. *austinii*. This taxon is strongly associated with ombrotrophic conditions, and indicates that from *c.* 2600 cal. yr BP onwards (for *c.* 1500 cal. yr) peat growth at Little Cheyne Court occurred independently of the ground water-table. In addition to the high *Sphagnum* values, other indicators of the wet acidic conditions at this time include the only record of *Drosera rotundifolia*-type (sundew) pollen (an insectivorous species) from the Romney Marsh region.

During the late Holocene, oligotrophic communities must have extended over large parts of Walland Marsh. In the west, humified peats from the Rye bypass boreholes (Long *et al.* 1996) contain high *Calluna vulgaris*, *Myrica gale* and *Sphagnum* values which predate *c.* 3150 cal. yr BP (borehole 33) and *c.* 1650 cal. yr BP (borehole 27). At Pannel Bridge, *Myrica gale* (pollen and macrofossils) and Cyperaceae are abundant in the post-3300 cal. yr BP assemblages (Waller 1993). The situation is less clear to the north of Little Cheyne Court where high *Alnus glutinosa* values are replaced by Cyperaceae and *Myrica gale* at Brookland *c.* 3950 cal. yr BP and Cyperaceae, followed by *Salix* then *Myrica gale*, at Hope Farm *c.* 3550 cal. yr BP (Waller *et al.* 1999). Assemblages dominated by Cyperaceae, *Salix* and *Myrica gale* are difficult to characterise in terms of modern communities. In the absence of macrofossil evidence, the Cyperaceae and *Salix* pollen could have been derived from either eutrophic or oligotrophic vegetation. However, the presence of *Myrica gale* confirms a decline in the groundwater influence since, in modern fen systems, *Myrica gale* occurs on elevated surfaces or where the lateral movement of water is inhibited (Wheeler 1980). In the east at Midley, where peat formation began *c.* 3900 cal. yr BP, it is difficult to separate the local from the regional components of the pollen rain. High *Betula* and Cyperaceae values suggest oligotrophic conditions, though pollen of *Myrica gale* was not separated from *Corylus avellana* (Long and Innes 1993, 1995). There are no unambiguous signs of acidification in the post *Alnus glutinosa* dominated assemblages of Romney Marsh proper, though the eroded upper contact of the peat at Romney Marsh borehole 18 contains some evidence for such a phase (Long, A.J. *et al.* 1998).

The cessation of peat growth and renewed marine inundation appear to have followed complex patterns (Long, A.J. *et al.* 1998; Waller *et al.* 1999). Marine/brackish conditions may have returned to Romney Marsh proper as early as *c.* 3000 cal. yr BP, however, clear indications of rising water-levels (the establishment of emergent aquatic and reedswamp communities) are absent until immediately prior to the inundation of The Dowels and Midley *c.* 2300 cal. yr BP (Long, A.J. *et al.* 1998). Peat formation at Hope Farm, Brookland, Rye bypass borehole 27 and Old Place ceased *c.* 1800–1700 cal. yr BP. However, independent of the ground water-table, the bog vegetation at Little Cheyne Court was able to keep growing and survived for a further *c.* 900 cal. yr after the flooding of these surrounding sites. The extent of this peat island is unknown. In the valleys peat formation only continued into the late Holocene at Pannel Bridge (Waller 1993).

Shingle Vegetation History

The shingle beaches of Dungeness are today floristically rich and support a variety of habitat types. These range, in what is regarded as being both a spatial (landward) and temporal development, from a pioneering *Rumex-Glaucium* community, through *Arrhenatherum-Silene* grassland, to scrub communities with dwarf *Cytisus scoparius* (broom) and species such as *Sambucus nigra* (elder), *Prunus spinosa* (blackthorn), *Ulex europaeus* (gorse) and *Taxus baccata* (yew) (Scott 1965; Hubbard 1970). In addition, largely confined to Holmstone beach, there are thickets dominated by *Ilex aquifolium* (holly). The status and history of this 'wood' is unclear. Peterken and Hubbard (1972) favour a natural origin before AD 800, though it has only existed with certainty for the last 460 years.

Pollen investigations from sites adjacent to, and within, the gravel complex have the potential to offer a new perspective on the status of these communities. Diagrams have been constructed from two locations on the edge of Broomhill Level (Tooley and Switsur 1988), five sites from the Lydd area (Spencer *et al.* 1998) and, most importantly, from Wickmaryholm Pit, which is contained within the shingle ridges of Lydd Beach (Long and Hughes 1995). The pollen records probably extend from *c.* 3700 cal. yr BP (at Broomhill) to beyond *c.* 700 cal. yr BP (at Wickmaryholm Pit). Unfortunately, the upper two dates from Wickmaryholm Pit (Fig. 1.4) are inverted indicating the contamination of one or both samples (Long and Hughes 1995).

The pollen assemblages from these sites generally have high values for submerged and floating-leaved aquatic plants, confirming their origin within waterbodies. At Wickmaryholm Pit, both *Myriophyllum alterniflorum* (alternate water-milfoil) and *Potamogeton natans*-type (pondweeds) are continuously recorded. High values for Poaceae and Cyperaceae are also a consistent feature. At Wickmaryholm Pit these taxa form *c.* 25–55% TLP. The open shingle communities of the region clearly therefore have a long and persistent history. Other herb taxa likely to have been derived from such vegetation, recorded in the Wickmaryholm Pit diagram, include the Caryophyllaceae (pink family), Brassicaceae, *Rumex* (dock), Apiaceae and *Campanula*-type (members of the bellflower family) pollen. Elements of both the pioneer and grassland communities appear to be represented, though due to the problems associated with achieving taxonomic precision in pollen identifications, it is not possible to be certain.

Unfortunately many of the characteristic elements of the modern scrub communities of the shingle are likely to be heavily under-represented in the pollen record. This is certainly the case with the Fabaceae (pea family) and makes it difficult to draw inferences from the absence of *Ulex*-type (which includes both *Cytisus scoparius* and *Ulex europaeus*) from the pollen records. However, the general scarcity of shrub pollen from these sequences, particularly from Wickmaryholm Pit (the *Corylus avellana*-type is likely to have been regionally derived), is of note. It suggests scrub is unlikely to have been the dominant vegetation cover on nearby areas of shingle. Some of these sequences are short-lived and probably only coincide with the early stages of shingle vegetation development. However, others persist for over 700 years and thus might be expected to have continued into the scrub stages. Human activity has been recorded on the shingle in the Lydd area back to the Bronze Age (Eddison 2000) and scrub development may have been retarded through heavy grazing and/or the collection of woody material for fuel. *Ilex aquifolium* has only been recorded, at very low frequency, in one sample (*c.* 3300 cal. yr BP) at Broomhill (Tooley and Switsur 1988). Although general regarded as a sparse pollen producer, *Ilex aquifolium* pollen is occasionally recorded in some abundance (e.g. Scaife 1982). Therefore, while not conclusive, from the pollen records it seems likely that *Ilex aquifolium* was not extensively distributed on the shingle in the past and Holmstone 'wood' may not have as long a history as has previously been supposed.

Discussion

The Holocene Arrival of Tree Taxa

Information contained in the Romney Marsh pollen diagrams as to the first Holocene appearance of tree taxa is significant because of the scarcity of data from south-eastern England and the likelihood that many species including *Pinus sylvestris*, *Ulmus*, *Alnus glutinosa*, *Tilia*, *Fraxinus excelsior* and *Fagus sylvatica* (beech) spread into Britain via this region (Birks 1989; Bennett 1995). Comparable information is only available from the recently published site of Holywell Coombe, Folkestone (Bennett and Preece 1998). Both the timing of their arrival and subsequent expansion is of interest, though in practice these processes are both difficult to detect and distinguish using pollen data (Bennett 1986; Birks 1989). To detect first presence, Birks (1989) advocates the use of the rational-limit (the point at which pollen values begin a sustained rise) for well represented taxa and the empirical-limit (when taxa first become consistently present) for under-represented taxa.

Despite uncertainties over the presence of reworked pollen and the sediment accumulation rate, the Pannel Bridge sequence remains the most useful when considering the post-glacial immigration of tree taxa into the Romney Marsh region. Application of the Birks (1989) criteria suggest *Betula* and *Pinus* were present before *c.* 11,400 cal. yr BP, *Corylus avellana c.* 10,500 cal. yr BP, *Quercus c.* 10,300 cal. yr BP, *Alnus glutinosa c.* 9500 cal. yr BP, *Tilia c.* 9300 cal. yr BP, *Fraxinus excelsior c.* 7400 cal. yr BP and *Fagus sylvatica c.* 4000 cal. yr BP. Values for *Ulmus*, a well represented taxon, rise *c.* 9500 cal. yr BP, though this taxa never attains high frequencies in this region and its earlier appearance is probably indicated by the consistent presence of *Ulmus* pollen from *c.* 10, 300 cal. yr BP at Pannel Bridge and *c.* 9700 cal. yr BP in the Tillingham Valley (TGC) sequence (Waller and Kirby 2002). Unfortunately, TGC and the other newly published diagrams from the Tillingham and Brede valleys (Waller and Kirby 2002) add little extra information. *Tilia* is absent and *Alnus glutinosa* scarce in the TGC sequence, though organic sedimentation ceased *c.* 9300 cal. yr BP. The short diagrams from the Tillingham (TG11) and Brede (OP16) valleys serve only to confirm the presence of these taxa about the time they appear to have been rapidly expanding at Pannel Bridge. They do, however, suggest *Fraxinus excelsior* was present from *c.* 7800 cal. yr BP. In addition, the Brede Bridge data (Waller 1994a) indicate *Fagus sylvatica* was present in the region from *c.* 4500 cal. yr BP.

In general terms the data derived from the Romney Marsh region conform to the patterns of tree-spreading proposed by Birks (1989). The presence of *Pinus sylvestris* from *c.* 11,400 cal. yr BP at Pannel Bridge is consistent with the findings of Birks (1989) who indicates the arrival of pine into Britain via the south-east (prior to *c.* 10,700

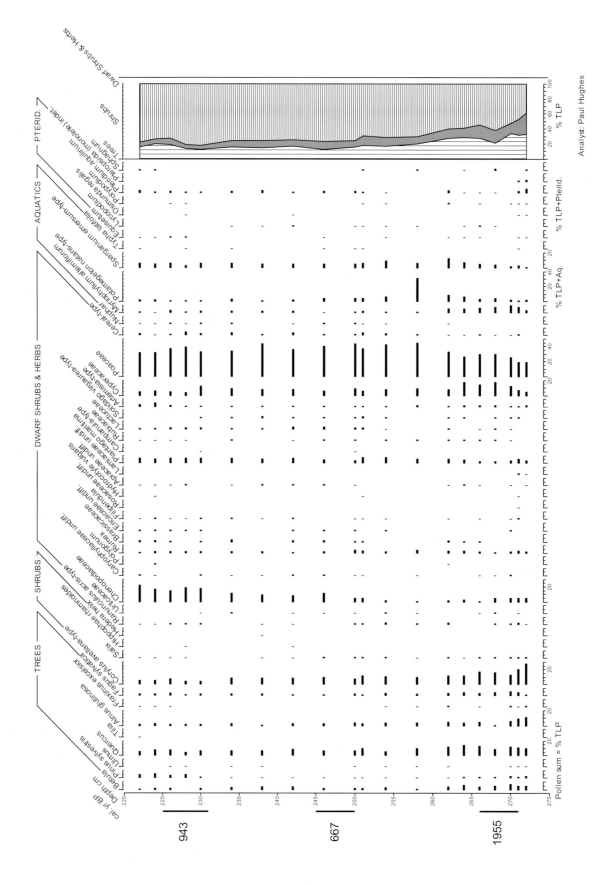

Fig. 1.4. Percentage pollen diagram from Wickmaryholm Pit core W20 (after Long and Hughes 1995). The radiocarbon dates are expressed as the mean calibrated age.

cal. yr BP), although it is earlier than the date (*c.* 11,100 cal. yr BP) Bennett and Preece (1998) derive from Holywell Coombe. The date obtained for *Corylus avellana*–type at Pannel Bridge is, at *c.* 10,500 cal. yr BP, slightly later than that from Holywell Coombe (*c.* 10,700 cal. yr BP) though with the rise protracted, the rational-limit of this type is more difficult to define at Pannel Bridge. Both sites are consistent with *Corylus avellana* becoming established first in Britain at sites around the Irish Sea (Birks 1989). The appearances of *Quercus* and *Ulmus* are not well dated at Holywell Coombe though appear compatible with the dates derived from Pannel Bridge (of *c.* 10,300 cal. yr BP). These data are consistent with the spread of oak from western Britain and an early presence for *Ulmus* in south-eastern England (Birks 1989). Birks (1989) also shows *Tilia* becoming established first in the south-east (prior to 8300 cal. yr BP). The interpolated date derived from Pannel Bridge (*c.* 9300 cal. yr BP) is much earlier than from Holywell Coombe (8400 cal. yr BP), though *Tilia* pollen has been reported from *c.* 9000 cal. yr BP in the Thames estuary (Devoy 1980). The presence of *Fraxinus excelsior,* from *c.* 7800 cal. yr BP, in the Brede and Tillingham valleys, and *Fagus sylvatica,* from *c.* 4500 cal. yr BP, at Brede Bridge, correspond well with the patterns of spread via south-eastern England derived by Birks (1989) from very restricted datasets.

It is the arrival and expansion of *Alnus glutinosa* that has generated the most debate (e.g. Chambers and Price 1985; Bush and Hall 1987; Bennett and Birks 1990; Tallantire 1992). Geographical trends have proved difficult to establish, leading to the suggestion that alder spread across Britain during the early Holocene before expanding when conditions became locally favourable (Bennett and Birks 1990). Recent work suggests the *Alnus* genus may even have been present during the late-glacial (Wilkinson *et al.* 2000). The occurrence of alder pollen and particularly macrofossils in the early Holocene at Pannel Bridge offers support for these suggestions. One of the aims of the attempt to retrieve deposits of a late-glacial/early Holocene age from Tilling Green (Waller and Kirby 2002) was to provide further information on this matter. Unfortunately the Tilling Green pollen diagram coincides with the lowest *Alnus glutinosa* values at Pannel Bridge. From the data currently available it seems likely that alder was present in the Romney Marsh area at the opening of the Holocene, though suitable areas were initially restricted. Although sea level was rising rapidly, the wetland areas generated would have been quickly submerged. Sites such as Pannel Bridge (where a small wetland area developed at a comparatively high altitude) would have been limited. It was the slowing down in the rate of sea-level rise from *c.* 7800 cal. yr BP onwards (Waller and Kirby 2002), and the consequent extension of freshwater habitats, that provided the impetus for the major and sustained regional expansion of this taxon.

Woodland Modification During the Mesolithic

Woodland modification prior to the adoption of agriculture has been the subject of much debate over the last thirty years (e.g. Smith 1970; Smith 1984; Bennett *et al.* 1990; Simmons 1993; 1996). The sand strata of the Weald, as a result of well-drained soils and supposedly relatively open natural vegetation, have long been seen as vulnerable to such interference. The distribution of Mesolithic finds (e.g. Jacobi 1978; Mellars and Reinhardt 1978) and pollen analysis (Dimbleby 1985) has lead to the belief that such areas were subject to early clearance leading to the development of heathland. In addition to changes in the structure of the vegetation, such activity may have influenced the representation of tree taxa, with *Alnus glutinosa* possibly benefiting (Bush and Hall 1987; Chambers and Elliott 1989). The Pannel Bridge pollen diagram appears to offer an excellent opportunity to elucidate this matter as not only are the slopes surrounding the site largely developed on the sandy lithologies of the Hasting Beds Group, but a number of Mesolithic flint scatters occur in the Pannel Valley (Holgate and Woodcock 1988). One, situated only *c.* 70 m north of the Pannel Bridge pollen site, excavated by Holgate and Woodcock (1988; 1989), is thought to represent the remains of short-stay camps visited intermittently during the later Mesolithic.

The Pannel Bridge pollen diagram, in particular the predominance of tree and shrub pollen in PB-2 and PB-3a and the shift to *Tilia* dominated woodland from *c.* 7800 cal. yr BP, suggests that human activity did not have a major influence on dryland vegetation development during the Mesolithic. The mid Holocene abundance of *Tilia* throughout the region also argues against a widespread and lasting impact. Lime is generally associated with undisturbed woodland. This does not preclude an influence in the immediate vicinity of the archaeological sites and, as already noted, there is good evidence for the woodland of the Pannel Valley not being completely closed-canopy in the period *c.* 8900 to 7300 cal. yr BP (during PB-2b, 3a and 3b). Temporary openings, which would be consistent with the archaeological evidence, appear to be indicated. However, that human activity was responsible for all, or even most, of the openings is by no means certain. Correlation between the pollen and archaeological records is hampered by the irregular occupation occurring over a long, but imprecisely known, period. The openings could also have been produced by natural processes, from which, in the absence of unambiguous indicators of anthropogenic activity (prior to the adoption of agriculture), human activity cannot be conclusively separated.

Vegetation disturbance would be expected to increase run-off and it is therefore possible that the Mesolithic activity in the Pannel Valley promoted peat formation and the early establishment and expansion (*c.* 9500 cal. yr BP, the interpolated date for the PB-2a/2b boundary) of *Alnus glutinosa.* Such conditions would, however, have inevitably developed in response to rising sea level. Although the Pannel Bridge site could not have been directly affected until *c*. 8000 cal. yr BP (see Waller and Kirby 2002), the apparent age discrepancy may be explained by the PB-2a assemblage accumulating over a long period and/or including a break in sedimentation. The landward shifting coastline was certainly responsible for the high Cyperaceae values in PB-3b. These coincide with the maximum inland penetration of marine/brackish conditions (which reached to within *c*. 100 m of the Pannel Bridge site) prior to the development of the "main marsh peat" (Waller 1993).

Woodland Composition in the Mid and Late Holocene

The pollen assemblages from the valleys and edge of the marshland suggest the traditional view, that the Weald was covered by oak woodland prior to extensive human interference, needs to be modified. *Tilia cordata* was clearly prominent, though geology and topography would be expected to produce local variations in woodland composition. Unfortunately it is unrealistic to attempt to assess such variations simply by comparing pollen percentages between sites. In particular, variations in *Tilia* frequencies are as likely to reflect differences in the distance between sites and dryland sources areas, as they are differences in vegetation composition (Waller 1998). The dryland areas adjoining the marshland are geologically complex. The catchments of the rivers draining into the western side of the region are largely developed on the Hastings Beds Group (interbedded clay, siltstone and sandstones), while immediately adjacent to the northern edge of the marshland the Weald Clay outcrops. The data currently available suggest *Tilia* was an important woodland component on the latter as well as the former. *Tilia* frequencies at Horsemarsh Sewer during the mid Holocene are consistently >5% TLP-*Alnus* (note the diagram published in Waller *et al*. 1999 uses a TLP sum). *Tilia* is also consistently recorded, though at comparatively low percentages (maximum >2.5% TLP-*Alnus*) in Romney Marsh borehole 7 through to *c*. 3900 cal. yr BP (Long, A.J. *et al*. 1998, where a TLP sum was used). However, this site is distant from the upland edge and dominated by wetland pollen.

Topographically the region can be divided into slopes and plateaux. It is possible that the *Tilia* dominated woodlands were largely confined to the lower slopes, while *Quercus* preferentially occupied the waterlogged plateau areas. The occurrence of distinct fen edge communities, where *Tilia* was favoured by seepage, has been suggested by a number of authors (Kelly and Osborne 1964; Godwin 1975; Thorley 1981; Brown 1988). The occurrence of very high *Tilia* pollen percentages at sites adjacent to dryland (>30% TLP-*Alnus* at Old Place) and the occurrence of macrofossils strongly support the contention that *Tilia* dominated woodland occupied the lower slopes.

Unfortunately, due to *Tilia* pollen being poorly dispersed, it is difficult to make any assessment of its abundance away from the dryland edge.

Evidence for the importance of *Tilia* in the woodlands of the mid Holocene can be found in pollen diagrams constructed at sites across south-eastern England (Greig 1982; Waller 1994a). Direct comparisons of the pollen percentages between sites is, for the same reasons as noted in the Romney Marsh region, probably unwise. However, even at this scale there is no evidence for lime being confined to particular lithologies. For example, high *Tilia* values have been recorded at a site located at the base of the chalk in the Ouse Valley (Waller and Hamilton 2000). One suggestion is that the pre-clearance soils of south-eastern England displayed a much greater degree of uniformity than today as a result of a blanketing cover of loess (Perrin *et al*. 1974; Burrin 1981; 1988).

Fagus sylvatica and *Carpinus betulus* (hornbeam) are common woodland constituents in the region today and it is often assumed that this also reflects the natural vegetation cover. The Holocene history of these taxa in Britain is poorly understood. Both are generally, though not universally, regarded as native to south-eastern England. Godwin (1975) indicated they were present, but scarce, in the mid Holocene, their subsequent expansion being facilitated by woodland disturbance.

The history of *Fagus sylvatica* in the Romney Marsh region appears to follow this pattern. Although present from at least *c*. 4500 cal. yr BP values remain low (<1% TLP-*Alnus*), until the immediate post-*Tilia* decline assemblages at Brede Bridge. *Fagus sylvatica* values also rise after the clearance phase dated to *c*. 3400 cal. yr BP at Pannel Bridge, when an increase in *Fagus sylvatica* in the regional pollen rain is indicated by its persistent occurrence in the Little Cheyne Court diagram (LCC-5 see Fig. 1.3). The highest pollen values recorded (*c*. 3% TLP) are from at latter site after *c*. 2500 cal. yr BP (during LCC-7 and LCC-8). Such increases are consistent with the progressive expansion of beech as secondary woodland developed in the region.

Such woodland would also be expected to support *Carpinus betulus*, a taxon often heavily exploited through woodland management techniques such as coppicing. Grains of *Carpinus betulus* are recorded in the Romney Marsh pollen diagrams from *c*. 6300 cal. yr BP. However, in contrast to *Fagus sylvatica*, values do not rise significantly during the late Holocene. Indeed *Carpinus betulus* has yet to be recorded at values >1% of the pollen sums used. It is difficult to see how this taxon could have occurred in any abundance, in woodlands close to the valleys or marshland, prior to the last 1000 years.

Human Activity During the Mid and Late Holocene

Temporary woodland clearings are indicated during the early Holocene at Pannel Bridge and there is good evidence for the human exploitation of open areas from the *Ulmus* decline onwards. However, woodland with *Tilia* seems to have remained the principal vegetation cover in the Romney Marsh region into the late Neolithic. The first extensive openings, marked by the declines in *Tilia* pollen at Brede Bridge and Pannel Bridge, occurred *c.* 4000 cal. yr BP. This is consistent with archaeological evidence for the expansion of human activity from the chalkland into the Weald during the late Neolithic/early Bronze Age (Drewett *et al.* 1988). In the Romney Marsh region, the first phase of the construction of the ring ditch at Playden (near Rye) has been dated to *c.* 4000 cal. yr BP (Barker *et al.* 1971). This site has been interpreted in a number of ways with Bradley (1978) suggesting it was used for livestock management. The pollen evidence from the Brede Valley indicates both pastoralism and cereal cultivation were occurring. In the Pannel Valley, the small quantities of later Neolithic/early Bronze Age flint reported by Holgate and Woodcock (1988; 1989) are said to be indicative of transitory activity. This agrees well with the pollen evidence for the rapid regeneration of woodland at Pannel Bridge.

The pollen diagrams from the Rother Valley and the northern edge of the marshland show persistence of *Tilia*-dominated woodland in these areas post *c.* 4000 cal. yr BP. In the lower Rother, the juxtaposition of islands, peninsulas and wetland, appears potentially attractive to human occupation (Long, D. *et al.* 1998). Nevertheless, a concomitant archaeological survey (Gardiner, personal communication) failed to reveal any signs of prehistoric human activity. The delay in human populations penetrating the lower Rother, and particularly the northern edge of the marshland, may be related to the proximity of these areas to the less tractable soils of the Weald Clay. Unfortunately, due to the early cessation of peat growth, the timing of the destruction of the *Tilia*-dominated forests of these areas has yet to be determined.

A second phase of woodland destruction during the middle Bronze Age (*c.* 3400 cal. yr BP) eliminated *Tilia* from the Pannel Valley. The subsequent low tree pollen values indicate the open areas created were maintained into the Iron Age (beyond *c.* 2700 cal. yr BP). However, the high *Pteridium aquilinum* values and the absence of archaeological finds argue against intensive human activity. The subsequent rise in tree pollen values in the Pannel Bridge diagram has not been directly dated, though it seems likely to have occurred as early as 2,000 years ago. It appears therefore contradictory to the expansion of arable farming in the valley, which Holgate and Woodcock (1989) infer from the presence of Roman pottery and traces of medieval ridge and furrow on the upper slopes. However, Poaceae and *Plantago lanceolata* values do not decline and Cereal-type pollen occurs regularly. The development of a vegetation mosaic (areas of woodland, pasture and arable) similar to that characterising the valley today, particularly if the woodland occurred close to Pannel Bridge, is probably indicated.

The increase in human activity from *c.* 2600 cal. yr BP indicated at Little Cheyne Court may relate to the development of the iron industry in the eastern Weald, which was active from the Iron Age onwards (Cleere and Crossley 1995). However, with *Betula* and *Quercus* continuing to be well represented at this site (to *c.* 950 cal. yr BP) and woodland regeneration occurring at Pannel Bridge (*c.* 2000 cal. yr BP), there is no evidence to support the suggestion of Cleere (1976) that the woodlands of the region were devastated to supply fuel for this industry in the Roman period. The latter view does not take into account attempts that may have been made to renew the resource through woodland management techniques such as coppicing and pollarding (Rackham 1980). Unfortunately, the effect such land-use practices have on pollen representation is poorly understood. Clearly a detailed assessment of the impact of the iron industry cannot be made from the evidence currently available.

The pollen data available shows that the post-Neolithic impact of humans on the vegetation of the Romney Marsh region was not uniform. It hints at, though is currently insufficient to fully substantiate, the traditional view of a strong geological control. The information obtained for the late Neolithic/early Bronze Age is extensive and demonstrates land-use strategies varied. Both cultivation and pastoralism were practiced, while elsewhere clearance was followed by regeneration and other areas remained unaffected. Although more limited, the data available for the later periods also suggest a lack of uniformity. This complexity needs to be emphasized as its implications go beyond studies of human and vegetation history. Woodland destruction and subsequent land-use will have had a major influence on the supply of water and sediment to the valleys and marshland (Waller *et al.* 1999). Differential vegetation cover needs therefore to be considered when developing holistic models of the evolution of depositional complex.

Spatial and Temporal Trends in the Development of Wetland Vegetation

Clear spatial trends have been identified in the wetland vegetation of the Romney Marsh depositional complex during the accumulation of the "main marsh peat". Eutrophic, *Alnus glutinosa*-dominated, fen carr communities prevailed in the valleys. Although similar communities initially became established on Walland Marsh these appear to be base-poor variants with frequencies of *Salix* and particularly *Betula* pollen increasing with distance from the upland. This pattern is likely to have become established as a consequence of a decline in the influence base-rich water, draining from the valleys, out across the marshland. The accumulating peat mass itself will subsequently have further inhibited the movement of eutrophic waters across the marshland. This additional isolation probably enabled poor fen communities to progressively develop on Walland Marsh (e.g. first at Little Cheyne Court and subsequently Brookland

and Hope Farm). However, both the maintenance of the *Alnus glutinosa* communities in the valleys and the eventual development of ombrotrophic vegetation at Little Cheyne Court require further explanation.

Alder carr is usually regarded as transitional, both due to the accumulation of organic material resulting in aeration and acidification and the lack of internal regeneration (Walker 1970; Grime *et al.* 1988; Bennett and Birks 1990). The apparent *c.* 3000 year persistence (from *c.* 6800 to 3900 cal. yr BP) of *Alnus glutinosa* dominated pollen assemblages in the Brede and Pannel valleys is therefore noteworthy. It is possible that the over-representation of *Alnus glutinosa* pollen masks local phases of fen carr degeneration and re-establishment. However, it seems more likely that alder carr was sustained in the valleys by a combination of eutrophic run-off from the uplands and rising groundwater levels (Waller *et al.* 1999). Relative sea level rose at a rate of *c.* 2–4 mm yr^{-1} over this period (Long and Innes 1993; Long *et al.* 1996). Short-term water-table variations may have been accommodated through changes in the production and decomposition of organic material, though this requires further investigation.

Climate change, a shift towards wetter conditions, at what is traditionally termed the Sub-Boreal/Sub-Atlantic boundary, appears to have been the trigger for the development of ombrotrophic vegetation at Little Cheyne Court. Similar vegetation changes to the shift from *Eriophorum* to *Sphagnum imbricatum* peat at the LCC6/7 boundary have been recorded at sites across north-western Europe (Godwin 1975; Overbeck 1975) and the date obtained at Little Cheyne Court (2619 cal. yr BP) approximates with the timing of this event (2800–2710 cal. yr BP) as recently determined by van Geel *et al.* (1996). However, although also exposed to the wetter conditions, other sites on Walland Marsh failed to develop into ombrotrophic bog at this time. This suggests an additional factor is required to explain the changes seen at Little Cheyne Court. Differences in the antecedent vegetation are likely to be important. The *Eriophorum* community at Little Cheyne Court may have been a necessary precursor, as peat formed by herb vegetation is apparently able to accommodate more vertical movement and consequently the peat surface is less prone to flooding with base-rich water. Giller and Wheeler (1988) suggest it is this mobility that underlies the development of areas of acidic vegetation in the modern fen systems of Broadland.

Concluding Remarks

Pollen-based reconstructions from the Romney Marsh region began almost 50 years after Sir Harry Godwin initiated such studies in the coastal lowlands of Britain (Godwin *et al.* 1935; Godwin and Clifford 1938; Godwin 1940). One advantage of this late start is that it has been possible to develop a research strategy informed by recent developments in pollen analytical theory. In addition, the Romney Marsh work has been driven more by specific goals relating to past vegetation, rather than the precepts of sea-level studies or by the chance location of archaeological finds. Consequently not only do we have a comprehensive understanding of the vegetation history of the Romney Marsh region, but the pitfall of attributing vegetation change only to the process under investigation has largely been avoided. The studies undertaken have a wider relevance, in terms of enhancing our knowledge of both Wealden vegetation history and trends in the development of peat-forming communities in coastal lowland areas.

In spite of the progress made over the last two decades, further studies are required to resolve a number of significant issues. These include:

1) Studies into the early Holocene vegetation history of the region, to clarify issues such as the presence of *Alnus glutinosa*. Although the Pannel Bridge pollen diagram provides important information, the presence of reworked material and poor temporal resolution impose limitations on additional work at this site. Further high altitude sites may not exist and any that do are likely to suffer from similar problems. The investigations at Tilling Green (Waller and Kirby 2002) demonstrate that early Holocene organic sediments also exist at great depth, though their retrieval is expensive. Engineering works probably offer the best hope of recovering organic sediments of early Holocene age in the future.

2) Studies into the late Holocene vegetation history of the Rother Valley and dryland areas adjacent to the northern edge of the marshland. Amongst the many issues to be illuminated are the timing of the destruction of the *Tilia*-dominated woodland and the impact of the iron industry. The major limitation on such studies is the early cessation of peat formation (pre *c.* 3300 cal. yr BP at the sites investigated to date).

3) Studies to establish sedimentary and hydrological responses to changes in dryland vegetation cover (particularly woodland clearance). Although often cited as influential, the role played by changes in catchment vegetation, in the evolution of coastal lowland areas such as Romney Marsh, remains poorly understood. Given the evidence for differential land-use, combined investigations into vegetation and sedimentary history need to be undertaken at an appropriate scale (Waller *et al.* 1999).

4) Studies into the conditions that promoted and sustained the *Alnus glutinosa* dominated fen carr vegetation in the valleys. The rates of base-level change required need to be quantified.

5) Studies to determine the spatial and temporal extent

frequencies of the main taxa represented (particularly *Corylus avellana*-type and *Quercus*) have been influenced by long-distance marine transportation/reworking cannot be determined and minor taxa (e.g. *Pinus sylvestris, Alnus glutinosa, Juniperus communis*) may owe their presence entirely to these processes.

The Intercalated Peats

The assemblages from the thin intercalated peats (Fig. 2.4) have not been sub-divided and have been given the notation TG11–1 (for the Tillingham Valley) and OP16–1 (for the Old Place site in the Brede Valley).

TG11–1 (12.74–12.68 m) Quercus, Corylus avellana-*type, Poaceae, Cyperaceae zone.*
Four taxa attain percentages of *c.* 20% TLP or above. *Quercus* and Poaceae pollen values decline slightly towards the top of the zone, while Cyperaceae values rise. *Corylus avellana*-type frequencies are more variable. *Ulmus, Tilia, Alnus glutinosa* and *Pteridium aquilinum* are also consistently well represented (up to *c.* 5% TLP). High basal *Pinus sylvestris* and Chenopodiaceae values are recorded.

OP16–1 (13.75–13.60 m) Corylus avellana-*type,* Quercus, *Poaceae, Cyperaceae zone.*
High basal Poaceae values (*c.* 32 % TLP) are replaced by rising *Corylus avellana*-type frequencies that attain a maximum 43% TLP at the top of the diagram. Cyperaceae values peak mid-zone (15% TLP) while *Quercus* percentages are more consistent (at *c.* 20% TLP). *Ulmus, Alnus glutinosa* and, towards the top of the zone, *Sparganium emersum*-type pollen, is also well represented (at *c.* 5% TLP and TLP+Aq.)

The TG11–1 and OP16–1 assemblages are remarkably similar. The tree pollen percentages, in particular the low *Corylus avellana*-type values (compared with early Holocene assemblages, see Waller 2002) and low *Tilia* and *Alnus glutinosa* frequencies (compared to mid-Holocene assemblages, see Waller 2002), indicate they are at the very least broadly contemporary.

During the formation of these layers the local environment was clearly dominated by reedswamp, as indicated by the presence of *Phragmites* macrofossils and high Poaceae pollen values, and the pollen of emergent aquatics (e.g. *Sparganium emersum*-type, Cyperaceae). Such vegetation would be expected to occur as fringe between upper saltmarsh and dryland woodland, promoted by freshwater seepage. The spread of these communities onto the floodplain is indicative of an increased freshwater influence. Such conditions should also have favoured *Alnus glutinosa*. With pollen values of 5% TLP, alder is likely to have been present. Its local failure to expand can probably be attributed to this episode being short-lived.

With the herb taxa likely to have been derived from freshwater or brackish environments, the adjacent dryland

areas seem to have been well wooded during TG11–1 and OP16–1. *Quercus* and *Corylus avellana*-type appear to be the main woodland components. However, *Tilia* is likely to have been more prominent than the pollen values suggest, as it is under-represented (see Waller 2002). For the same reason *Fraxinus* was probably also present regionally. The *Ulmus* values (*c.* 5% TLP) are typical for this region prior to the mid-Holocene decline in elm, and support suggestions that this taxon (it has a high pollen representation) was a relatively minor woodland constituent (Waller 1993, 1994).

Diatoms

Diatom analyses have been conducted from the top of the organic (Unit 4) and the immediately overlying sediments in TGC and from the intercalated organic layer (Unit 2) and its transitions in TG11 in order to provide detailed information on the local depositional environment and water level fluctuations.

TGC

Below 27.68 m no diatoms are preserved. Between 27.68 and 27.30 m diatom preservation is good with marine (60% TDV) and brackish (40% TDV) taxa dominating. The main species present are *Nitzschia granulata, Nitzschia navicularis* (marine/brackish benthic, epipelon) and *Paralia sulcata* (planktonic), and their relative frequencies are consistent throughout. Subordinate marine/brackish benthic epipelic species include *Diploneis didyma, Nitzschia punctata* and *Scoliopleura tumida*. Less common marine planktonic taxa include *Pseudopodosira westii, Thalassiosira eccentrica* and *Podosira stelliger*. Epiphytic taxa form *c.* <2% TDV.

This assemblage closely resembles the *Melosira sulcata* and *Navicula digitoradiata var. minima* group of Vos and de Wolf (1988). The dominance of planktonic taxa (likely to be inwashed) and benthonic epipelic species (probably the *in situ* mud dwelling population) along with few epiphytic forms suggests deposition within a low saltmarsh/intertidal mudflat environment, proximal to tidal channels. These results, (coupled with the pollen evidence for a marine/brackish influence from the base of TGC-2) indicate that the lithostratigraphic transition between Unit 4 and 5 (at -24.65 m OD) is a transgressive contact.

TG11

In TG11 shifts in the relative frequency of marine and freshwater diatoms mirror the changes in lithostratigraphy. In the minerogenic unit below 12.74 m marine and brackish diatoms predominate with *Paralia sulcata* (marine plankton) and *Diploneis didyma, Nitzschia navicularis,* and *Nitzschia punctata* (brackish epipelon) the main taxa. Between 12.73 and 12.70 m (Unit 2) the marine and

Table 2.1. The lithostratigraphy of the deeper sections of the TGB, TGC, TG 11 and Old Place 16 boreholes.

TGB

Unit	Depth m (below surface)	Depth m OD	Lithology
5	Above 22.00	Above -19.04	Soft blue-grey silty clay with sand, organic detritus and *Phragmites* rhizomes. Nig. 2, Strf. 0, Elas. 0, Sicc. 2; As3, Ag1, Ga+, Dg+, Th[1] (*Phrag.*)+
4	22.00 to 22.45	-19.04 to -19.49	Soft light-medium grey silty clay, with organic detritus and *Phragmites* rhizomes. Nig. 2, Strf. 0, Elas. 0, Sicc. 3, Lim. sup. 0; As3, Ag1, Dg+, Th[1](*Phrag.*)+
3	22.45 to 22.91	-19.49 to -19.95	Medium grey silty clay with faint layers of detrital organic material. Nig. 2+, Strf. 1, Elas. 0, Sicc. 3, Lim. sup. 0; As3, Ag1, Sh+, Dg+
2	22.91 to 23.05	-19.95 to -20.09	Stiff medium grey silty clay with woody organic detritus (including a *Corylus avellana* nut) and finely laminated (bands *c.* <1 mm) organic partings and olive green sandstone (bedrock) clasts. Nig. 2, Strf. 1, Elas. 1, Sicc. 3, Lim. sup. 0; As3, Ag1, Gg+, Dg+, Dh+, Sh+
1	23.05 to 24.00	-20.09 to -21.04	Stiff light-brown mottled grey sandstone (bedrock) Nig. 2, Strf. 0, Elas. 0, Sicc. 3, Lim. sup. 1; Ag2, As1, Ga1

TGC

Unit	Depth m (below surface)	Depth m OD	Lithology
8	Above 25	Above -22.01	Soft, grey silty clay with occasional organic fragments. Nig. 2, Strf. 0, Elas. 0, Sicc. 3; As3, Ag1, Ga+, Th[1]+
7	25 to 27.49	-22.01 to -24.5	Dark grey silty clay with occasional roots. Nig. 2, Strf. 1, Elas. 0, Sicc. 3, Lim. sup. 0; As3, Ag1, Ga+, Th[1]+
6	27.49 to 27.59	-24.5 to -24.6	Grey silt with abundant roots and some detrital organic material. Nig. 2, Strf. 0, Elas. 0, Sicc. 2, Lim. sup. 0; Ag4, As+, Th[1]+, Dg+
5	27.59 to 27.64	-24.6 to -24.65	Yellowish-grey, stiff silt with clay and sandstone fragments. Nig. 2, Strf. 0, Elas. 0, Sicc. 3, Lim. sup. 0; Ag3, As1, Ga+, Gg+
4	27.64 to 28	-24.65 to -25.01	Light grey organic silt containing abundant plant macrofossils; including *Corylus avellana* wood, *Phragmites* rhizomes, leaf fragments and *Corylus avellana* and *Cornus sanguinea* nuts. Nig. 2, Strf. 0, Elas. 0, Sicc. 2, Lim. sup. 0; Ag3, Sh1, As+, Th[1](*Phrag.*)+, Dh+, Dl+,
3	28 to 28.08	-25.01 to -25.09	Grey-brown slightly organic sandy silt with wood (*Corylus avellana*) at base. Nig. 2, Strf. 0, Elas. 0, Sicc. 2, Lim. sup. 0; Ga2, Ag2, Gg+, Dl+, Dh+, Sh+
2	28.08 to 28.80	-25.09 to -25.81	Dark grey wet gravel in loose silty/sandy matrix. Nig. 2, Strf. 0, Elas. 0, Sicc. 1, Lim. sup. 0; Gg2, Ga1, Ag1, Gs+
1	Below 28.80	Below -25.81	Stiff grey silt with sandstone concretions (bedrock). Nig. 2, Strf. 0, Elas. 0, Sicc. 3, Lim. sup. 0; Ag2, Ga1, As1, Gg+

TG 11

Unit	Depth m (below surface)	Depth m OD	Lithology
3	Above 12.69	Above -10.22	Soft blue-grey silty clay with occasional plant and shell fragments. Nig. 2, Strf. 0, Elas. 0, Sicc. 2; As2, Ag2, Th[1](*Phrag.*)+, test.(moll.)+
2	12.69 to 12.74	-10.22 to -10.27	Light brown organic clayey silt with *Phragmites* remains. Nig. 2, Strf. 0, Elas. 0, Sicc. 2, Lim. sup. 1; Ag2, As1, Sh1, Th[1](*Phrag.*)+
1	Below 12.74	Below -10.27	Blue-grey silty clay with occasional *Phragmites* rhizomes. Nig. 2, Strf. 0, Elas. 0, Sicc. 2, Lim. sup. 0; As2, Ag2, Th[1](*Phrag.*)+

Table 2.1. continued.

OLD PLACE 16

Unit	Depth m (below surface)	Depth m OD	Lithology
3	Above 13.60	Above -10.79	Grey sandy silty clay. Nig. 2, Strf. 0, Elas. 0, Sicc. 2; As 2, Ag2, Ga+
2	13.60 to 13.78	-10.79 to -10.97	Greyish-brown organic silty clay. Nig. 2, Strf. 0, Elas 0, Sicc 2, Lim. sup. 0; Dg2, As2, Ag+, Th[1](*Phrag.*)+
1	Below 13.78	Below -10.97	Grey sandy silty clay. Nig. 2, Strf. 0, Elas 0, Sicc. 2, Lim. sup 0; As2, Ag2, Ga+, Th[1](*Phrag.*)+

brackish influence declines and freshwater species domin-ate (maximum 55% TDV). The main species recorded here are *Fragilaria virescens, Fragilaria pinnata,* and *Fragilaria construens var. venter* (all freshwater plankton). From 12.68 m and into the overlying silty clay, marine (*c.* 45% TDV) and brackish diatoms (*c.* 55% TDV) resume dominance. The main marine planktonic species are *Paralia sulcata* and *Podosira stelliger* with *Nitzschia navicularis* and *Diploneis didyma* the predominant brackish epipelic taxa.

The assemblages recorded from the clastic units and transitions are mainly brackish epipelic taxa of the *Navicula digitoradiata var. minima* group (Vos and de Wolf 1988), while freshwater planktonic species from the *Fragilaria construens* group increase within the organic rich material. These shifts indicate a transition from an intertidal mudflat environment through to high supratidal saltmarsh/freshwater reedswamp (possibly also lagoonal) conditions, followed by the return to mudflat.

Chronology

Details of the three AMS radiocarbon dates (two from plant macrofossils and one bulk date) obtained from the lower Tillingham Valley as part of these investigations and the original (conventional assay) BGS Tilling Green date (Welin *et al.* 1974) are provided in Table 2.2.

The dates from TGC are compatible with the high *Corylus avellana*-type pollen values recorded in the TGC-1 assemblage. Such frequencies occur across southern England during the early Holocene lasting, for example, from *c.* 10200 to 8200 cal. yr BP at Pannel Bridge (Waller 1993; Waller 2002) and *c.* 10700 to 8400 cal. yr BP at Holywell Coombe Folkestone (Bennett and Preece 1998). Although not as temporally diagnostic, the TV11–1 assemblage (with *Tilia* and *Alnus glutinosa* both present) is compatible with a date of 7935–7674 cal. yr BP (Beta-153521).

Discussion

Landscape Evolution During the Late Pleistocene/Early Holocene

Boreholes drilled for commercial purposes have long demonstrated the existence of channels deeply incised into the bedrock of the river valleys that drain into the western side of the Romney Marsh depositional complex. Combining the investigations described in this paper with the KCC borehole information and data previously collated from boreholes sunk as part of road schemes (Waller 1987; Long *et al.* 1996), it is possible to identify the approximate location of the Tillingham bedrock channel in the vicinity of Rye (Fig. 2.1). Over much of Brede Levels and the western side of Walland Marsh the bedrock surface consistently lies at between -15 and -20 m OD. In the Tillingham Valley the deep (> -20 m OD) channel occurs close to the modern river along the line of the hand auger transect, before continuing east into the Tilling Green estate, cutting through the neck of the modern meander. The boreholes that record bedrock below -20 m OD immediately to the south and east of Rye, are likely to represent the eastward continuation of this system. The bedrock channel of the Brede probably runs east across the middle of the Brede Levels towards Camber Castle (Waller 1987).

The bedrock profile of the Tillingham Valley appears to contain several channels. The detailed sub-surface profiles constructed from the upper, shallower, parts of the valleys (e.g. at Brede Bridge, Waller 1994) also contain evidence for several phases of incision. Incision will have occurred during periods of high fluvial discharge and low sea level such as the last glacial maximum, or periods of low sediment supply. The buried channel between TG1 and 3 in the Tillingham Valley transect (Fig. 2.2) is also likely to be the product of a former course of a tributary emerging from the Leasam valley. In the base of most of the deep boreholes, a sand and gravel unit overlies bedrock. This change from erosion to sedimentation is likely to have been produced by a combination of declining discharge and increasing sediment supply (Rose *et al.* 1980). The colluvial sediments that mantle the lower slopes of both the Tillingham and Brede valleys demonstrate the

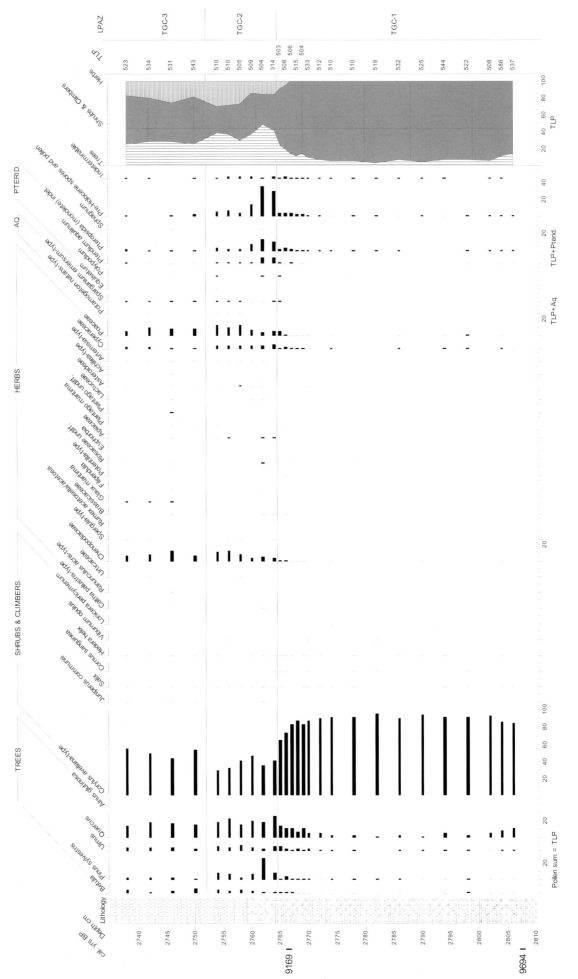

Fig. 2.3. Percentage pollen diagram from the basal units of TGC.

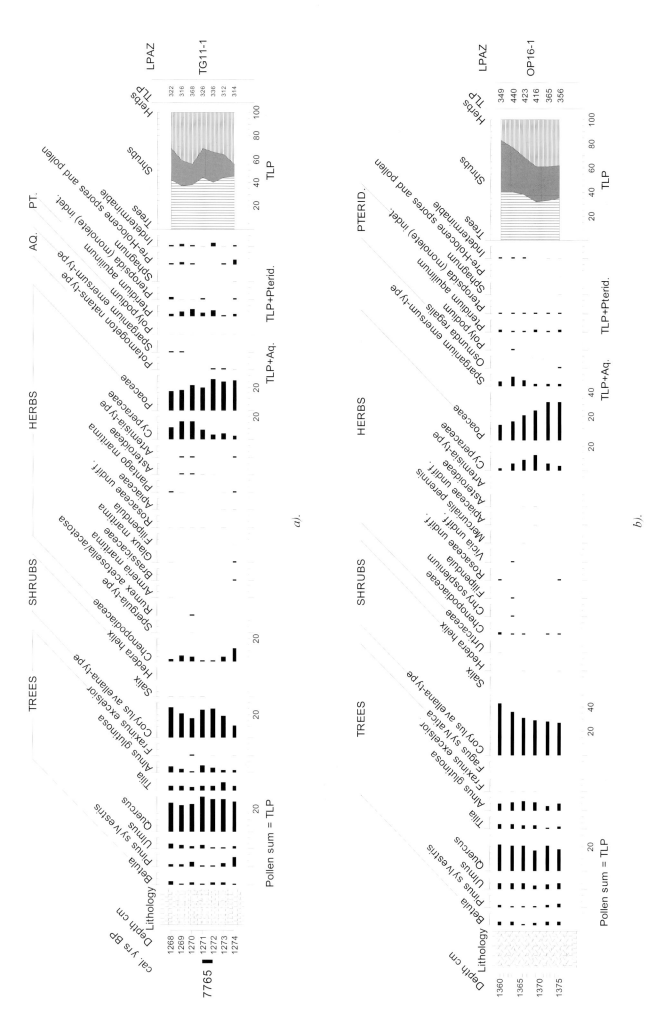

Fig. 2.4. Percentage pollen diagrams from the intercalated peats. a) Tillingham Valley (TG11) and b) Brede Valley (OP16).

Table 2.2. Radiocarbon dates from the lower Tillingham Valley.

Borehole	Depth (m)	Altitude (m OD)	Lab. Code	Material	Age ± 1σ error (^{14}C yr BP)	Mean calibrated age with 2σ range (cal. yr BP)
TG 11	12.71 to 12.72	-10.24 to -10.25	Beta-153521	*Phragmites* peat	6980±50	7765 (7935–7674)
TGC	27.66 to 27.67	-24.67 to -24.68	Beta-153522	*Cornus sanguinea* nut	8240±80	9169 (9470–9011)
TGC	28.07 to 28.08	-25.08 to -25.09	Beta-155394	*Corylus avellana* wood	8720±40	9694 (9905–9550)
TGA	c. 26.00	c. -22.65	IGS-C14/116	Laminated peat	9565±120	10, 950 (11200–10506)

capacity of the adjacent slopes to supply sediment in the pre-Holocene. These deposits appear not to interdigitate with the Holocene deposits, contain little or no organic matter or microfossils (Waller 1987) and are likely to have been produced by gelifluction during a cold climate. The replacement of sands and gravels by organic detritus mixed with fine grained clastic material indicates a further decline in discharge during a period of more extensive vegetation cover and hence a warmer climate (such as the early Holocene).

Both TGA and TGC contain these basic sediment types. However, correlation is difficult (Fig. 2.5). The deeper organic and overlying coarse clastic layer in TGA may represent the climatic fluctuations of the late-glacial as indicated in the introduction to this paper (with warmer conditions interrupted by the brief return of a cold climate prior to the opening of the Holocene). The cold conditions at the end of this period could have produced localised incision, thus allowing the organic sediments of TGC to accumulate at a similar altitude in the Holocene. However, it is difficult to reconcile the presence of an older Holocene organic layer in TGA (indicated by the date of 11,200–10,506 cal. yr BP) several metres higher than the younger Holocene organic layer in TGC. Possible explanations include a phase of incision during early Holocene, errors in the measurement of altitude and, with the radiocarbon dates in TGC supported by the biostratigraphy, either the upper organic layer in the BGS borehole not being *in situ* or incorporating older carbon. The uppermost coarse clastic layer, at least in TGC, can be shown through biostratigraphic evidence to be associated with the subsequent marine transgression (see below). Given this complexity and the cost of sinking boreholes to a depth of > -25 m OD it is unlikely that, in the absence of a substantial number of deep boreholes being sunk as part of a major engineering project, the sequence recorded in TGA can be recovered.

Early Holocene Sea-level Change

The record of RSL change in the Romney Marsh region is well documented for the period 6500–2000 cal. yrs BP (Long and Innes 1993; Long *et al.* 1996; Long *et al.* 1998; Waller *et al.* 1999) with 40 sea-level index points (SLIPs) providing a wide spatial coverage. However, there were no reliable pre c. 6500 cal. yr BP index points from the region prior to this study. With its value limited by the lack of supporting biostratigraphic information, the BGS date from Tilling Green (Welin *et al.* 1974) could only be used as a maximum value for RSL (Long *et al.* 1996). The new data from Tillingham Valley are presented here (Fig. 2.6), along with the pre-existing data from the mid and late Holocene, to provide the most complete record RSL change in the Romney Marsh region available to date.

With the errors associated with the altitude of these SLIPs likely to be over a metre (see below), neither the indicative meaning of the sample points (see Shennan 1986) nor the effects of palaeotidal change have been quantified. In this analysis, the OD sample heights of the transgressive and regressive samples used are assumed to approximate to MHWST (reference tide level) at the time of deposition (Tooley 1978; Shennan 1986). The height of MHWST varies along the coast. To enable comparison with other existing data (from the Romney Marsh region and Langley Point) all SLIPs have been reduced to MSL by subtracting the appropriate value for MHWST obtained from the nearest tide gauge station (Admiralty Tide Tables 2001). Recent work shows the reference water level for transgressive and regressive contacts varies between MHWST and MHWST+HAT/2 (see Horton *et al.* 2000). However, this difference in tide level is inconsequential in the context of millennial scale RSL change of tens of metres during the early Holocene. In addition, although the integrity of each SLIP has been verified using diatom analysis, no data set exists of modern diatom distributions from the Romney Marsh region that might enable more precise quantification of indicative meaning. The error bars assigned in this analysis (see below) are large enough to account for potential differences in reference water level between SLIPs.

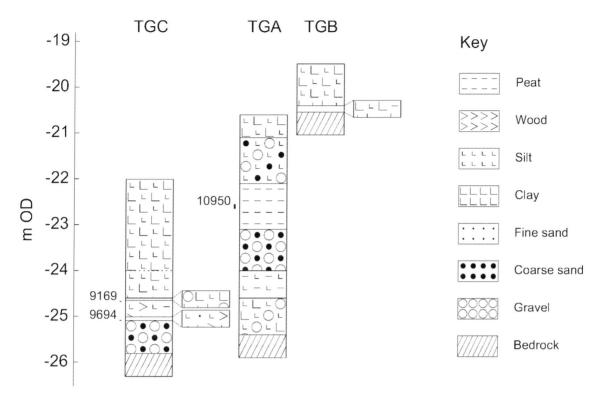

Fig. 2.5. Simplified lithostratigraphy of the three boreholes sunk to a depth of below -20 m OD in the vicinity of the Tilling Green estate. The radiocarbon data are the means of the calibrated date ranges in cal. yr BP.

The altitudinal error associated with SLIPs is usually assumed to be between 0.5 and 1.5 m (e.g. Long 1992; Shennan *et al.* 2000). Recent work suggests the effects of sediment compaction may be significantly greater (e.g. Haslett *et al.* 1998; Allen 1999; 2000). However, estimating this error is problematic. A geotechnical model capable of accurately decompacting stratigraphic sequences comprising the highly heterogeneous sediments recorded in the lower Tillingham has yet to be developed. The altitude of SLIPs can also be corrected for auto-compaction by comparing a basal peat chronology (where sediments directly overlie an undeformable substrate) with in-core dates (see Törnqvist *et al.* 1998; Gehrels 1999). However, no such chronology exits for the Romney Marsh area. The SLIPs points are therefore shown here with a vertical error band of +1.5/-0.5 m in accordance with previous studies from the region.

Due to compaction, SLIPs are likely to be lower than their original elevation (see Shennan *et al.* 2000) which is reflected by the greater upwards vertical error margin. Wider vertical errors have been assigned to the basal sample from TGC as it is from a freshwater context. This sample can be used as a limiting point, constraining the maximum altitude of MSL. The TG11 index point has clearly been affected by compaction as the altitude of the intercalated organic layer from which it derives deepens away from the valley side (Fig. 2.2). Assuming an approximately horizontal surface during deposition, rather

than the measured altitude at TG11 (-10.22 to -10.27 m OD) the altitude of *c.* -8.50 m OD (derived from TG9 where the layer overlies relatively uncompressible colluvium), has been used in Fig. 2.6 and in the calculation sea-level rise and sedimentation rates. When adjusted to MSL, the altitude of the intercalated organic layer is -12.04 m OD. The age uncertainty of the SLIPs is represented by the 2 sigma calibrated age range of the dated sample.

RSL in the Romney Marsh region was below -28.65 m OD prior to *c.* 9700 cal. yr BP (Fig. 2.6). The first reliable SLIP (from the trangressive contact in TGC) shows MSL *c.* 9200 cal. yr BP at an altitude of -28.24 m OD. Sea level then rose rapidly (*c.* 12 mm yr^{-1}) until *c.* 7800 cal. yr BP when MSL had reached -12.04 m OD. The rate of RSL rise subsequently (between *c.* 7800 and 6000 cal. yr BP) slows down to *c.* 4 mm yr^{-1}. A further deceleration follows, from *c.* 2–4 mm yr^{-1} between *c.* 6000 and 4000 cal. yr BP to less than 1 mm yr^{-1} thereafter (Long and Innes 1993; Long *et al.* 1996).

From this analysis the date derived from TGA (Welin *et al.* 1974) appears to be anomalous, occurring as a distinct outlier on the time/altitude graph. It now seems clear that, if *in situ*, this deposit represents an earlier phase of peat accumulation independent of sea-level rise. It is therefore recommended that this data point be no longer used in any discussion of early Holocene sea level history.

The only data available for the early Holocene from

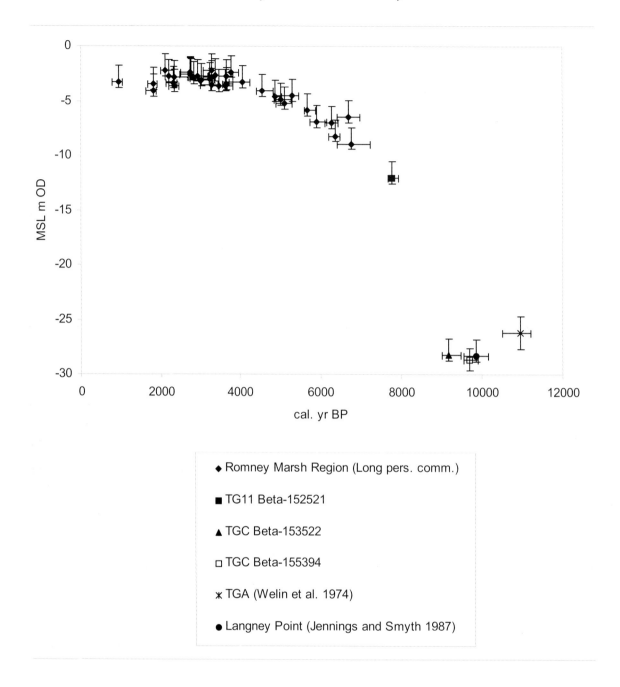

Fig. 2.6. Plot of sea-level index points for the Romney Marsh region. A single date from Langley Point, East Sussex, is included for comparison.

the East Sussex/Kent region with which the new data can be compared is the single SLIP (a transgressive contact) from Langney Point (Jennings and Smyth 1987). The latter shows MSL *c.* 10,000 cal. yr BP at -28.32 m OD and is thus in good agreement with the limiting date from TGC (Fig. 2.6). The similarity in altitude between transgressive contacts at Langney Point and TGC (given the *c.* 800 year age difference) during a period of rapid sea level rise can be attributed to effects of differential compaction.

Early Holocene Coastal Evolution

Organic material was clearly accumulating in the Romney Marsh region at inland localities independent of rising base levels during the very early Holocene (e.g. Pannel Bridge, Waller 1993). Given the absence of biostratigraphic evidence for marine/brackish conditions, organic sedimentation at base of the TGC sequence also appears to have commenced prior to any direct sea-level influence. However, it seems likely that, given the short interval over which the deposition of organic sediment occurred (*c*. 500 calendar years), the accumulation of the organic silts (Unit 4) at the base of TGC was promoted by rapidly rising sea level. Under such conditions seawards draining water is liable to pond up, resulting in the flooding of the channel at the base of the Tillingham Valley, the deposition of silt and the preservation of organic material.

The occurrence of the pollen of herb taxa associated with saltmarsh conditions (including the Chenopodiaceae) and marine-brackish diatoms towards the top of Unit 4 provides, at *c*. 9200 cal. yr BP, the first evidence for marine/brackish conditions in the Romney Marsh region. However, the initial inundation of the site is likely to be marked by the deposition of the clayey silt with sandstone fragments (Unit 5). The deposition of sandstone fragments can probably be attributed to the change from a fluvial to a tidal system. The ability of the river to transport locally derived catchment material would be reduced as tidal waters penetrated up river with this sediment deposited on the floodplain/emerging tidal flats and subsequently buried by fine clastic material. Erosional processes are also likely to be associated with this period of rapid flooding and shoreline retreat, with invasive tidal creek networks cutting into and reworking the organic deposits resting at the base of the Tillingham Valley. Such processes could also account for the presence of the sandstone fragments, the secondary and resistant pollen grains in TGC-2, and are likely to be responsible for the occurrence of eroded organic material at the base of the TGB borehole. With the coarse clastic material recorded in Unit 5 locally derived and associated with the initial stage of marine transgression it is unlikely to have formed part of a coastal barrier system. The influence of barriers on coastal evolution in East Sussex during the early Holocene has been stressed by Jennings and Smyth (1987; 1990) who used high values of *Juniperus communis* pollen in the Langney Point peat as evidence for the occurrence of sand barriers. In the Romney Marsh area, Dix *et al.* (1998), from offshore data, concluded that any early Holocene barrier is also likely to have been composed of sand rather than gravel and to have occurred at restricted localities close to the present shoreline. No evidence for the presence of such barriers in the vicinity of the lower Tillingham has been found. The lithostratigraphic (the predominance of fine-grained clastic sediments in the deep boreholes) and biostratigraphic (the diatoms, which suggest deposition within a low saltmarsh/mudflat environment) evidence, and the rapid landward advance of marine conditions during the early Holocene, argue against the local development of sand barriers during the initial stages of the marine transgression. The location and nature of any early Holocene barriers in the Romney Marsh area remains uncertain.

Between *c*. 9200 and 7800 cal. yr BP, with rising RSL providing the accommodation space, *c*. 16 m of fine clastic sediment was deposited at a rate of *c*. 12 mm yr^{-1}. The lack of lithostratigraphic information precludes discussion of the inundation of the lower Tillingham Valley, though with MHWST at *c*. -8.50 m OD by *c*. 7800 cal. yr BP tidal penetration is likely to have reached Brede Bridge in the Brede Valley (Waller 1987; 1994) and Bodiam in the Rother Valley (Burrin 1988).

The presence of the thin intercalated organic rich layer in TG11 indicates a brief interruption of intertidal marine/brackish conditions around 7800 cal. yr BP. From the biostratigraphic evidence it is clear that reedswamp expanded out across the Tillingham Valley. The absence of this layer from several boreholes suggests the maintenance of open water towards the centre of the valley. It is also possible that a localised system of erosive tidal creeks developed in the post-peat period. The upper contact of the organic material was irregular in TG11 though the consistency of the pollen assemblage argues against erosional truncation. The similarity between the pollen sequences (Fig. 2.4) and the comparable altitude of the peats supports the suggestion that this layer is contemporaneous with that reported by Waller (1987, 1994) from the Brede Valley. This brief increase in the freshwater influence may well therefore have registered widely in the valleys of the western marshland. The absence of evidence from other areas (e.g. the lower Rother Valley) is in part likely to reflect the scarcity of boreholes sunk to this depth for the purpose of palaeoenvironmental reconstruction (it is likely to have gone unrecorded in many commercial boreholes).

There are a number of possible explanations for the occurrence of this deposit. Such thin organic layers can arise through local processes including the interplay between the rate of RSL rise and the rate of sedimentation. If the rate of sediment supply outpaces the rate of RSL rise, the process of terrestrialisation will be initiated enabling freshwater vegetation to encroach upon areas of former mudflat (Wilks 1979). This process will be reversed when the rate of RSL rise exceeds the pace of organic sedimentation (see examples in Shennan *et al.* 1983; Gerrard *et al.* 1984). Any increase in freshwater discharge could also result in the seawards advance of peat forming communities.

Changes occurring in Rye Bay could have affected conditions within the river valleys. The contemporaneous deposition of large quantities of sand in Rye Bay creating extensive sand flats and banks may have reduced tidal penetration into the lower valleys and produced an increased freshwater influence. Long *et al.* (1996) report a coarsening upwards trend in borehole evidence southeast of Rye for which a shell date of 7930–7664 cal yr. BP provides a minimum age. This probably reflects an increase in tidal flow velocity related to rapid RSL rise and may also be associated with an increase in tidal amplitude following the opening of the Strait of Dover. The higher energy conditions resulted in the progressive influx of sediment (particularly sand) into Rye Bay from the east after *c*. 8000 cal. yr BP (Austin 1991; Long *et al.* 1996; Dix *et al.* 1998). Diatom evidence from Unit 2 possibly supports this suggestion as Vos and de Wolf (1988) state that the *Fragilaria construens* group is often associated with freshwater lagoonal environments.

The occurrence of organic deposits of similar age elsewhere along the south coast of England hints at a regional driving mechanism such as changes in RSL or sediment supply. Long (1992) reports a thin intercalated peat in the East Kent Fens dated to 7509–7169 cal. yr BP (at *c.* -8.65 m OD) and Godwin *et al.* (1958) a peat dated to 8377–7883 cal. yr BP (at -12.8 m OD, context unknown) from Poole Harbour. Altitudinal comparison is hampered by these deposits being deeply buried and therefore heavily compacted, and also by the large changes in tidal amplitude (up to 2 m) that occurred after the opening of the Dover Strait (Austin 1991). Any vertical fall in RSL cannot have been large or prolonged given the general rising trend of RSL from *c.* 9200 to 6500 cal. yr BP (see Fig. 2.6). However, it is possible that this deposit formed in response to a reduction in the rate of RSL rise. Topographic control may also be influential here as marginal valley sites, such as those noted above, are likely to be the most sensitive areas to small adjustments in RSL. Unfortunately the data presently available from the south coast of England are insufficient for this hypothesis to be fully tested.

Early Holocene Vegetation History

With the TGC pollen diagram spanning a time period covered in only two other radiocarbon dated profiles from the south-eastern corner of England it should contain important information on the arrival of tree taxa in this region during the early Holocene. The consistent presence of *Ulmus* in the TGC sequence does support the suggestion that this taxon was present in south-eastern England prior to *c.* 9500 cal. yr BP. In addition, the diagrams from the intercalated peats (particularly OP16–1) indicate *Fraxinus* was present by *c.* 7800 cal. yr BP. However, the TGC diagram in particular falls within a rather unfortunate time interval. It begins after the arrival of *Corylus avellana* and *Quercus* (*c.* 10,500 and 10,300 cal. yr BP respectively) and ends before the expansions in *Tilia* and *Alnus glutinosa* (*c.* 7800 cal. yr BP) at Pannel Bridge (Waller 1993), and thus adds little extra information. Given the controversy over its presence in the early Holocene (Bennett and Birks 1990; Waller 2002) this is particularly disappointing in the case of *Alnus glutinosa*. In contrast to the early Holocene record at Pannel Bridge only a few pollen grains of *Alnus glutinosa* were recorded from TGC (beginning at the top of TGC-1). However, the period covered by the Tilling Green diagram coincides with the lowest Holocene frequencies (and only gap in the record) of *Alnus glutinosa* recorded at Pannel Bridge. From the Pannel Bridge sequence more consistent frequencies of *Alnus glutinosa* and the presence of *Tilia* might be expected in the TGC profile from *c.* 9500 cal. yr BP. These discrepancies can, however, be attributed to the rapid inundation of the lower

Tillingham Valley and TGC-2 and 3 assemblages originating from marine/brackish sediment (in contrast to the slow accumulation of organic material at Pannel Bridge).

The assemblages from TGC are dominated by *Corylus avellana*-type pollen. High hazel pollen frequencies occur throughout Britain during the early Holocene (Godwin 1975). As noted previously, the dates from TGC (at between *c.* 9700–9200 cal. yr BP) are comparable to the other sites investigated in south-eastern England. Many hypotheses have been offered to account for this abundance of hazel (see Huntley 1993). The data from both Tilling Green and Pannel Bridge indicate that *Quercus* and *Ulmus* were present in the Romney Marsh region during the period of high *Corylus avellana*-type pollen frequencies. It is generally assumed that pollen production and dispersal by hazel is greater when this species occurs as a canopy forming species. Therefore any explanation for the high values has to account for hazel having a competitive advantage over these taxa. Amongst the more plausible hypotheses are that *Corylus avellana* was the most competitive species on certain (more fertile) soil types until the arrival and expansion of *Tilia* (Waller 1993), or that the climate (the relatively cold winters and cool summers) of the early Holocene favoured *Corylus avellana* (Huntley 1993). *Quercus* and *Ulmus* are likely to have been confined to the sandier and more acidic soils.

The occurrence (pollen and macrofossils) of the shrub *Cornus sanguinea* (formerly *Thelycrania sanguinea*) in the TGC diagram is also of interest. The species was recorded at Pannel Bridge during the early Holocene, but has not been noted in any of the mid or late Holocene pollen diagrams from the region. Today this species shows a preference for open stands and flowering is inhibited by shade. The *Corylus avellana* woodland of the early Holocene may therefore, even if canopy forming, have been of relatively low stature.

The formation of the intercalated peats *c.* 7800 cal. yr BP coincides with increases in the representation of *Tilia* and *Alnus glutinosa* at Pannel Bridge (Waller 1993; Waller 2002). The absence of any rise in *Tilia* during TG11–1 and OP16–1 may simply be a result of the short time-span these sequences cover. Unfortunately, this still leaves the relationship between the decline in *Corylus avellana* (from the very high values recorded in the early Holocene) and the rise in *Tilia* (with high frequencies recorded in the mid-Holocene) in need of clarification. Diagrams covering the period *c.* 9500–8000 cal. yr BP are required. The opportunity for the expansion of *Alnus glutinosa c.* 7800 cal. yr BP is likely to have been greater in the Pannel Valley than at the sites in the lower Brede and Tillingham valleys. With the Pannel Bridge site at a higher altitude and therefore not directly affected by the preceding period of very rapid sea-level rise, *Alnus glutinosa* was probably locally present and thus able take advantage of the favourable conditions. The subsequent replacement of *Alnus glutinosa* by Cyperaceae at Pannel Bridge is attributable to the further landward advance of marine/brackish conditions and associated increase in wetness after the deposition of the thin intercalated peat.

Conclusions

The KCC (TGA) borehole offered the prospect of extending detailed palaeoenvironmental reconstructions from the Romney Marsh region back to the earliest Holocene and possibly the late glacial. Unfortunately it has not proved possible either to replicate the TGA sequence or to establish correlation with the newly collected stratigraphic information. When exposed in section late glacial/early Holocene sediments from similar contexts can be seen to be locally highly complex reflecting several phases of aggradation and channel incision (e.g. Rose *et al.* 1980). Such intricacy, when combined with the logistical difficulties and expense of coring below -20 m OD, argues against further attempts to replicate the TGA sequence.

Despite these problems, the bedrock channel of the lower Tillingham Valley has now been much more closely defined and the sediments recovered have enhanced our understanding of aspects of the early Holocene environmental history of the region. Of particular importance is a phase of basal organic sedimentation lasting from *c.* 9700 to *c.* 9200 cal. yr BP. Pollen analysis from this layer confirms the dominance of *Corylus avellana* and the presence of *Quercus* and *Ulmus* in the early Holocene woodlands of the region. Biostratigraphic investigations have also demonstrated that the boundary between this layer and the overlying clastic sediments is a transgressive contact and is therefore the earliest record of marine/brackish conditions from the region. The landward advance of coast during the early Holocene was rapid and, as the presence of sandstone and peat fragments attest, accompanied by the erosion and reworking of locally derived material.

A second, thin intercalated, organic layer recovered from the lower Tillingham Valley and dated to *c.* 7800 cal. yr BP is also important in constraining the pattern of early Holocene sea-level rise. MSL rose from -28.24 m OD at *c.* 9200 cal. yr BP to -8.50 m OD at *c.* 7800 cal. yr BP at a rate of *c.* 12 mm yr^{-1}. Subsequently this rate declined to *c.* 4 mm yr^{-1} between *c.* 7800 and 6000 cal. yr BP and remained between 2–4 mm yr^{-1} from *c.* 6000 to 4000 cal. yr BP. Thereafter, the rate of RSL rose at less than 1 mm yr^{-1}.

The importance of these data is enhanced by the lack of information on early Holocene sea-level change from south coast of England as a whole. The dates derived from the basal organic layer in the Tillingham Valley are broadly comparable with a transgressive contact previously dated at Langney Point. The date from TGA is an outlier and now clearly of little value in this context. Organic layers dating close to *c.* 7800 cal. yr BP have previously been recorded from East Kent and Dorset, however, the processes underlying the formation of the thin intercalated peat found in the Tillingham Valley, and also the Brede Valley, are not fully understood. Given the rate at which sea level was still rising, alternative explanations including changes in the pattern of sediment influx, possibly as a consequence of the opening of the Strait of Dover, or purely local processes, may be required.

Acknowledgments

We are grateful to the Romney Marsh Research Trust for providing funds to support this project at various stages. JRK also received grants towards this work from the Quaternary Research Association and British Geomorphological Research Group. Simon Hayden at Gillshaw Farm is thanked for allowing vehicular access onto his land to enable the coring and drilling. Figures 2.1 and 2.2 were produced by the cartography units at Kingston, Hull and Plymouth Universities.

References

Admiralty Tide Tables 2001. UK and Ireland Volume 1. United Kingdom Hydrographic Office, Taunton.

Allen, J.R.L. 1999. Geological impacts on coastal wetland landscapes: some general effects of sediment autocompaction in the Holocene of northwest Europe, *The Holocene* 9, 1–12.

Allen, J.R.L. 2000. Holocene coastal lowlands in NW Europe: autocompaction and the uncertain ground, in K. Pye and J.R.L. Allen (eds) *Coastal and Estuarine Environments: Sedimentology, Geomorphology and Geoarchaeology* (Geological Society special publication 175), 229–52. London.

Austin, R.M. 1991. Modelling Holocene tides on the NW European continental shelf, *Terra Nova* 3, 276–88.

Barber, H.G. and Haworth, E.Y. 1981. *A Guide to the Morph-ology of the Diatom Frustule, With a Key to the British Freshwater Genera.* Freshwater Biological Association, Ambleside.

Bennett, K.D. 1994. Annotated catalogue of pollen and pteridophyte spore types of the British Isles. Unpublished manuscript. University of Cambridge: Department of Plant Sciences.

Bennett, K.D. 1995. Insularity and the Quaternary tree and shrub flora of the British Isles, in R.C. Preece (ed.) *Island Britain: a Quaternary Perspective* (Geological Society special publication 96), 173–80. London.

Bennett, K.D. and Birks, H.J.B. 1990. Postglacial history of alder (*Alnus glutinosa* (L.) Gaertn.) in the British Isles, *Journal of Quaternary Science* 5, 123–33.

Bennett, K.D. and Preece, R.C. 1998. Palaeobotany, in R.C.

Preece and D.R. Bridgland (eds), *Late Quaternary Environmental Change in North-west Europe,* 123–48, Chapman and Hall, London.

Birks, H.J.B. 1989. Holocene isochrone maps and patterns of tree spreading in the British Isles, *Journal of Biogeography* **16**, 503–40.

Burrin, P. 1988. The Holocene floodplain and alluvial deposits of the Rother valley and their bearing on the evolution of Romney Marsh, in J. Eddison, and C. Green (eds), *Romney Marsh: Evolution, Occupation, Reclamation* (Oxford University Committee for Archaeology Monograph **24**), 31–52. Oxford.

Denys, L. 1991. *A check-list of the diatoms in the Holocene deposits of the Western Belgian coastal plain with a survey of their apparent ecological requirements.* Belgische Geologische Dienst, Professional Paper No. **246**.

Denys, L. 1994. Diatom assemblages along a former intertidal gradient: a palaeoecological study of a sub-Boreal clay layer (Western coastal plain, Belgium), *Netherlands Journal of Aquatic Ecology* **28**, 85–96.

De Wolf, H. 1982. Method of coding of ecological data from diatoms for computer utilization, *Mededelingen Rijks Geologische Dienst* **36**, 95–98.

Dix, J., Long, A.J. and Cooke, R. 1998. The evolution of Rye Bay and Dungeness Foreland: New evidence from the offshore seismic record, in J. Eddison, M. Gardiner and A. Long (eds) *Romney Marsh: Environmental Change and Human Occupation in a Coastal Lowland* (Oxford University Committee for Archaeology Monograph **46**), 1–12. Oxford.

Gehrels, W.R. 1999. Middle and late Holocene sea-level changes in eastern Maine reconstructed from foraminiferal saltmarsh stratigraphy and AMS ^{14}C dates on basal peat, *Quaternary Research* **52**, 350–59.

Germain, H. 1981. *Flore des diatomées.* Société nouvelle des éditions boubée, Paris.

Gerrard, A.J., Adam, B.H. and Morris, L. 1984. Holocene coastal changes – methodological problems, *Quaternary Newsletter* **44**, 7–14.

Godwin, H. 1975. *History of the British Flora,* 2nd ed. Cambridge University Press, Cambridge.

Godwin, H., Suggate, R.P. and Willis, E.G. 1958. Radiocarbon dating the eustatic rise in ocean level, *Nature* **181**, 1518–19.

Grimm, E.C. 1987. CONISS: a fortran 77 program for stratigraphically constrained cluster analysis by the method of incremental sum of squares, *Computers and Geoscience* **13**, 13–35.

Grimm, E.C. 1993. *TILIA and TILIA*GRAPH. A Program for Analysis and Display.* Illinois State Museum, Springfield.

Hartley, B. 1986. A check-list of the freshwater, brackish and marine diatoms of the British Isles and adjoining coastal waters, *Journal of the Marine Biological Association* **66**, 531–610.

Haslett, S.K., Davies, P., Curr, R.H.F., Davies, C.F.C., Kennington, K., King, C.P. and Margetts, A.J. 1998. Evaluating late-Holocene sea-level change in the Somerset Levels, southwest Britain, *The Holocene* **8**, 197–207.

Hendey, N.I. 1964. *An Introductory Account of the Smaller Algae of British Coastal Waters. Part V: Bacillariophyceae (Diatoms).* MAFF Fishery Investigation Series IV. HMSO, London.

Horton, B.P., Edwards, R.J. and Lloyd, J.M. 2000. Implications of a microfossil based transfer function in Holocene sea-level studies, in I. Shennan and J.E. Andrews (eds) *Holocene Land-Ocean Interaction and Environmental Change Around the North Sea,* (Geological Society special publication **166**) 41–54. London.

Huntley, B. 1993. Rapid early-Holocene migration and high abundance of hazel (*Corylus avellana* L.): alternative hypotheses, in F.M. Chambers (ed.), *Climate Change and Human Impact on the Landscape* 205–16, Chapman and Hall. London.

Jennings S. and Smyth, C. 1987. Coastal sedimentation in East Sussex during the Holocene, *Progress in Oceanography* **18**, 205–41.

Jennings S. and Smyth, C. 1990. Holocene evolution of the gravel coastline of East Sussex, *Proceedings of the Geologists' Association* **101**, 213–24.

Long, A.J. 1992. Coastal responses to changes in sea-level in the East Kent Fens and southeast England, UK over the last 7500 years, *Proceedings of the Geologists' Association* **103**, 187–99.

Long A.J. and Innes, J.B. 1993. Holocene sea-level changes and coastal sedimentation in Romney Marsh, southeast England, UK, *Proceedings of the Geologists' Association* **104**, 223–37.

Long A.J. and Innes, J.B. 1995. The back-barrier and barrier depositional history of Romney Marsh, Walland Marsh and Dungeness, Kent, England, *Journal of Quaternary Science* **10**, 267–83.

Long, A.J., Plater, A.J., Waller, M.P. and Innes, J.B. 1996. Holocene coastal sedimentation in the Eastern English Channel: New data from the Romney Marsh region, United Kingdom, *Marine Geology* **136**, 97–120.

Long, A.J., Waller, M.P., Hughes, P. and Spencer, C. 1998. The Holocene depositional history of Romney Marsh proper, in J. Eddison, M. Gardiner and A. Long (eds) *Romney Marsh: Environmental Change and Human Occupation in a Coastal Lowland* (Oxford University Committee for Archaeology Monograph **46**), 45–63. Oxford.

Moore, P.D., Webb, J.A. and Collinson, M.E. 1991. *Pollen analysis,* 2nd ed. Blackwell, Oxford.

Palmer, A.J.M. and Abbott, W.H. 1986. Diatoms as indicators of sea-level change, in: Van de Plassche, O. (ed.) *Sea-Level Research: A Manual for the Collection and Evaluation of Data,* 457–87, Geo Books. Norwich.

Rose, J., Turner, C., Coope, G.R. and Bryan, M.D. 1980. Channel changes in a lowland river catchment over the last 13,000 years, in R.A. Cullingford, D.A. Davidson and J. Lewin (eds) *Timescales in Geomorphology,* 159–75, Wiley. Chicester.

Shennan, I. 1986. Flandrian sea-level changes in the Fenland II: Tendencies of sea-level movement, altitudinal changes, and local and regional factors, *Journal of Quaternary Science* **1**, 155–179.

Shennan, I., Lambeck, K., Horton, B.P., Innes, J.B., Lloyd, J.M., McArthur, J.J. and Rutherford, M.M. 2000. Holocene isostasy and relative sea-level on the east coast of England, in I. Shennan and J.E. Andrews (eds) *Holocene Land-Ocean Interaction and Environmental Change Around the North Sea* (Geological Society special publication **166**), 275–98. London.

Shennan, I., Tooley, M.J., Davies, M.J. and Haggart, B.A. 1983. Analysis and interpretation of Holocene sea-level data, *Nature* **302**, 404–06.

Shephard-Thorn, E.R. 1975. The Quaternary of the Weald: a review, *Proceedings of the Geologists' Association* **86**, 537–47.

Sims, P.A. (ed.) 1996. *An Atlas of British Diatoms*. Biopress. Bristol.

Stockmarr, J. 1971. Tablets with spores used in absolute pollen analysis, *Pollen et Spores* **13**, 615–21.

Stuiver, M. and Reimer, P.J. 1993. Extended C14 data base and revised CALIB 3.0 C14 age calibration program, *Radiocarbon* **35**, 215–30.

Tooley, M.J. 1978. *Sea-Level Changes in North-West England During the Flandrian Stage*. Clarendon Press. Oxford.

Törnqvist, T.E., van Ree, M.H.M., van 't Veer R. and van Geel, B. 1998. Improving methodology for high-resolution reconstruction of sea-level rise and neotectonics by palaeo-ecological analysis and AMS ^{14}C dating of basal peats, *Quaternary Research* **49**, 72–85.

Troels-Smith, J. 1955. Karakterisering af lose jordater, *Danmarks Geologiske Undersogelse*, Series IV, **3** (10): 73p.

Van der Werff, H. and Huls, H. 1958–74. *Diatomeenflora van Nederland. 8 Parts*. Published privately. De Hoef, The Netherlands.

Vos, P.C. and de Wolf, H. 1988. Methodological aspects of palaeoecological diatom research in coastal areas of The Netherlands, *Geologie en Mijnbouw* **67**, 31–40.

Vos, P.C. and de Wolf, H. 1993. Diatoms as a tool for reconstructing sedimentary environments in coastal wetlands: methodological aspects, *Hydrobiologia* **269/270**, 285–96.

Waller, M.P. 1987. The Flandrian vegetation history and environmental development of the Brede and Pannel valleys, East Sussex (unpublished Ph.D. thesis, The Polytechnic of North London).

Waller, M.P. 1993. Flandrian vegetational history of south-eastern England. Pollen data from Pannel Bridge, East Sussex, *New Phytologist* **124**, 345–69.

Waller, M.P. 1994. Flandrian vegetational history of south-eastern England. Stratigraphy of the Brede valley and pollen data from Brede Bridge, *New Phytologist* **126**, 369–92.

Waller, M.P. 2002. The Holocene vegetation history of the Romney Marsh region, in A. Long, S. Hipkins and H. Clarke (eds) *Romney Marsh: Coastal and Landscape Change Through the Ages* (Oxford University School for Archaeology 56), 1–21. Oxford.

Waller, M.P., Burrin, P.J. and Marlow, A. 1988. Flandrian sedimentation and palaeoenvironments in Pett Level, the Brede and Lower Rother valleys and Walland Marsh, in J. Eddison, and C. Green (eds) *Romney Marsh: Evolution, Occupation, Reclamation* (Oxford University Committee for Archaeology Monograph 24), 3–30. Oxford.

Waller, M.P., Long, A.J., Long, D. and Innes, J.B. 1999. Patterns and processes in the development of coastal mire vegetation: Multi site investigations from Walland Marsh, Southeast England, *Quaternary Science Reviews* **18**, 1419–44.

Welin, E., Engstrand, L. and Vaczy, S. 1974. Institute of Geological Sciences dates V, *Radiocarbon* **16**, 95–104.

Wilks, P.J. 1979. Mid-Holocene sea level and sedimentation interactions in the Dovey estuary area, Wales, *Palaeogeography, Palaeoclimatology, Palaeoecology* **26**, 17–36.

3. The Evidence for Late Holocene Foreland Progradation and Rapid Tidal Sedimentation from the Barrier and Marsh Sediments of Romney Marsh and Dungeness: A Geomorphological Perspective

Andy Plater, Paul Stupples, Helen Roberts and Caroline Owen

Three themes regarding the late Holocene evolution of Romney Marsh are addressed here, namely (i) episodic coastal change, (ii) marsh and barrier interdependence, and (iii) the sequence of foreland progradation and marsh sedimentation. Luminescence and ^{14}C ages in the region of the Holmstone gravel and Denge Marsh provide a chronology of tidal flat and sub-tidal shoreface progradation during the period of c. 3000–1000 cal. yr BP, which was a necessary precursor for the formation of Dungeness Foreland through rapid storm beach deposition from c. 1300 cal. yr BP. Statistical analyses of laminated tidal rhythmites in the former Wainway reveal a strong tidal control on marsh sedimentation, and enable the determination of rapid rates of accumulation c. 1m/y for this and other similarly laminated marshland facies. This sedimentary response to changing coastal or channel configuration is, therefore, rapid but vertically and spatially non-uniform, and is largely controlled by the operation of the tide rather than any simple balance between sea-level and sediment supply. It is proposed that rapid tidal flat aggradation and foreland progradation after c. 3000 cal. yr BP was achieved through high terrestrial sediment influx to the coastal zone coupled with destabilisation of the main gravel barrier complex in the region of Rye Bay.

These stones go through Man, straight to God,
if there is one.
What have they not gone through already?
Empires, civilisations, aeons. Only in them
If in anything, can His creation confront Him.
They came so far out of the water and halted forever.
That larking dallier, the sun, has only been able to play
With superficial by-products since;
The moon moves the waters backwards and forwards,
But the stones cannot be lured an inch farther
Either on this side of eternity or the other.
... from *On a Raised Beach*, Hugh MacDiarmid

Introduction

The gravel barriers and the uppermost minerogenic sediments of the Holocene stratigraphy of Romney Marsh, commonly known as the 'post-peat deposits' or Young Alluvium (Green 1968), possess an elusive record of environmental change. In the context of late Holocene relative sea-level change, the absence of intercalated organic horizons in the post-peat deposits means that the conventional sea-level index point approach to reconstructing relative sea-level is not applicable (Plater *et al.* 1999; Allen 2000). Similarly, whilst previous research has attempted to distill a record of relative sea-level change from the barrier complex of Dungeness (Lewis and Balchin 1940), these barrier features are controlled to a greater degree by high-energy events and their altitudinal record of storm tide level is affected greatly by their morphology and post-depositional reworking (Long and Hughes 1995; Plater and Long 1995). Recent research themes that have developed through detailed investigation of the gravel barrier and the post-peat deposits include the nature and timing of back-barrier flooding during the late Holocene (e.g. Long *et al.* 1996; 1998; Spencer *et al.* 1998a; 1998b); the location, pattern and relative chronology of the back-barrier drainage network (e.g. Green 1988; Eddison 1988; Wass 1995; Spencer *et al.* 1998b; Evans *et al.* 2001; Stupples 2002); palaeoecological and granulometric evidence of barrier progradation and integrity (e.g. Plater 1992; Long and Hughes 1995; Long and Innes 1995a; 1995b; Plater and Long 1995; Long *et al.* 1996; Spencer *et al.* 1998a; Plater *et al.* 1999; Lario *et al.* 2002); and sedimentological and morphological evidence of the history of land drainage, reclamation and settlement (e.g. Green 1968; Allen 1996).

Research into the palaeoenvironmental history of Romney Marsh and Dungeness during the late Holocene is made problematic because the sedimentary record has lost much of its palaeoenvironmental evidence through post-depositional alteration. As Green (1968) noted, much of the marshland has become decalcified in the surface layers due to pedological leaching (Old Marshland), but even in the Calcareous or New Marshland, where the post-peat deposits are generally thicker, preservation above the summer watertable level leads to either temporary (in the case of the zone affected by seasonal watertable movements) or permanent oxidation. Hence, soils and the upper parts of the post-peat deposits are mottled or variegated due to the oxidation of iron-organic complexes and the formation of hydrated iron oxides. Marshland drainage and reclamation has lowered the watertable in many areas and caused post-depositional oxidation of the upper metre or so of sediment. In these circumstances, diatoms that have been used in palaeoenvironmental reconstructions across the marsh (e.g. Long and Hughes 1995; Plater and Long 1995; Spencer *et al.* 1998a; Evans *et al.* 2001) are largely absent in these mottled facies as a result of dissolution in the presence of iron oxyhydroxides (Mayer *et al.* 1991). Furthermore, the detrital geochemical and magnetic characteristics of these sediments are likely to have been variably over-printed by pedogenesis (in their upper oxidised parts) and diagenesis (in the reduced region below the watertable) (Plater and Long 1995; Plater *et al.* 1999; Long *et al.* 1996). Despite these problems, the gravel barrier and marsh sediments are still able to provide information on coastal change, particularly on the relative importance of processes with contrasting magnitude and frequency characteristics.

Research Themes and Sites Investigated

The main research theme addressed in this paper is the significance of episodic coastal change during the Holocene, particularly the response of marsh sedimentation to aperiodic barrier emplacement. Although the tidal sediments of the marsh are generally regarded as the product of gradual change during the inter-storm period, research focuses on evidence for rapid response to changing boundary conditions. Similarly, the interdependence of the marsh and barrier environments is considered through the construction of a chronology for the progradation of

Dungeness Foreland and a debate on the potential influences on coastal change during the late Holocene.

In this study, chronological data on the early progradation of Dungeness has been obtained from ^{14}C and luminescence dating of shoreface sands beneath the Holmstone gravel complex on Lydd Ranges (Fig. 3.1). In addition, the timing and formation of Denge Marsh in relation to Dungeness Foreland has been established from ^{14}C dating of articulated shells preserved in the lower and upper laminated facies of the late Holocene stratigraphy (Plater and Long 1995; Plater *et al.* 1999), where the issue of barrier and marsh inter-dependence is addressed. Finally, investigation of potential rates of tidal infilling in environments where significant changes in morphology have had a marked impact on sedimentation, e.g. barrier emplacement or channel migration, has been undertaken in the region of the Wainway between East Guldeford Level and Camber. Although this phase of tidal deposition is one of the last to have occurred on Walland Marsh, the nature, rate of sedimentation and preservation of this sedimentary record provides information of significance to all phases of back-barrier marsh deposition in the region during the mid- to late Holocene.

Late Holocene Coastal Change

Foreland Progradation:
Holmstone to Dungeness

Recent investigations on the Lydd Ranges (Fig. 3.1) have sought to date the deposition of the Holmstone gravel ridge complex, and hence the onset of foreland progradation, by establishing the age of the transition between shoreface sands and storm gravels using optically-stimulated luminescence (OSL) dating. OSL dating (Aitken 1998) is applied to the minerogenic component of the sediment itself, rather than relying on the discovery and identification of suitable material which is *in-situ*, e.g. contained shell material that bears an equivocal relationship to the timing of deposition (Greensmith and Gutmanis 1990). The OSL technique is applied to naturally occurring minerals, such as quartz and feldspar, which record the exposure to ionising radiation in the natural environment. This luminescence signal is released on optical stimulation in the laboratory, or by exposure to sunlight. The technique relies on the principle that any pre-existing luminescence signal contained in the sediment grains is lost on exposure to sunlight during transport, prior to deposition. Once the sediments are deposited and become buried by successive layers of sediment, the luminescence signal builds up over time with exposure to naturally occurring alpha, beta, gamma and cosmic radiation. The luminescence signal determined in the laboratory is proportional to the period of time that has elapsed since the material was last exposed to sunlight. Thus, the OSL age determines the time of deposition of the sediments and, hence, gives the time of formation of the geomorphological feature in question.

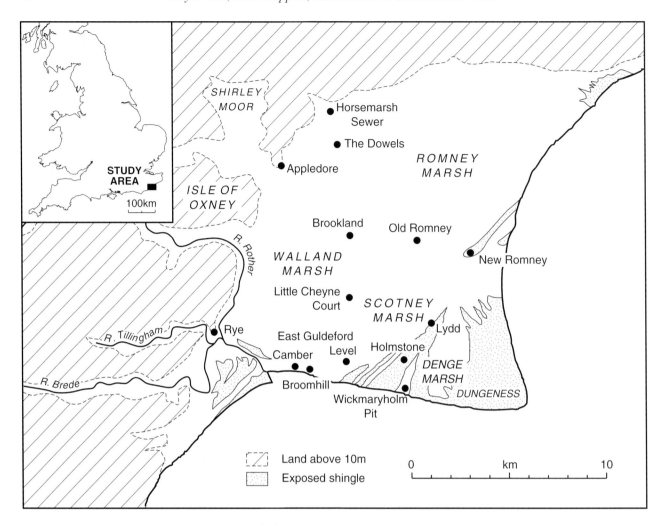

Fig. 3.1. Study areas and sites referred to in the text.

A 65 mm diameter core was collected from the north-eastern side of South Brooks Road on the Holmstone Shingle Beach (TR 02851893) using a shell and auger drilling rig. Approximately 2 m of well-rounded to sub-angular gravel (3–100 mm diam.) was observed overlying another 2 m of sub-rounded to sub-angular gravel (3–40 mm diam.) with sand. This passed downward into more than 2.3 m of sand with gravel lenses (often coarse gravel up to 120 mm in diam.). Core sections from 4.60–5.60 m and 5.60–6.33 m depth were sampled to represent the upper part of the shoreface sands that underlie the storm beach gravels (Greensmith and Gutmanis 1990). Core sections were sealed in plastic liners to maintain original water content, although the sediments from this depth were below the water table and, hence, saturated. A sample for OSL dating was taken from a depth of 5.00–5.15 m (-1.27 to -1.42 m OD). OSL measurements were made using the Single Aliquot Regenerative dose (SAR) protocol (Murray and Wintle 2000) applied to quartz grains of 180–212 μm diameter. Typical decay and growth curves are shown in Figure I Appendix 3.I. A total of 24 aliquots were examined, using preheats ranging from 160–300 °C

for 10 seconds, giving 24 independent determinations of equivalent dose (D_e). Of these 24 D_e values, 15 were used to generate the final OSL age, using preheats ranging from 160–240 °C (see Figure II, Appendix 3.I). The OSL age determined, based on these 15 independent estimates of the age, was 1390±80 years (see Table in Appendix 3.I).

The OSL age can be compared with a ^{14}C date of 9760–9010 cal. yr BP (Table 3.1) obtained on a shell fragment (possibly *Cerastoderma edule*) sampled from the adjacent gravely sands at a depth of 4.85–4.90 m (-1.12 to -1.17 m OD). Further corroborative ^{14}C dating was not possible due to the absence of any datable material (other than small shell fragments) in the shoreface sands. The disparity between the radiocarbon and luminescence ages can be attributed to the uncertain relationship between the ^{14}C age of the shell material and the timing of sand deposition, rather than the inaccuracy of the OSL age. Although not finely comminuted, the shell fragment preserved in these high-energy gravely sands must have been reworked from older material and transported some distance.

The apparent timing of storm beach formation to the south of Lydd, i.e. post-1350 years BP, may seem anomalous in the context of minimum ages obtained for gravel deposition from ^{14}C dates on peat beds preserved in gravel swales at Broomhill (3817–3622 cal. yr BP, Tooley and Switsur 1988) and Scotney Marsh (4060–4040 and 3990–3700 cal. yr BP; Spencer *et al.* 1998a; 1998b). The main Lydd gravel, i.e. the prominent barrier feature that runs south-west to north-east along the south-eastern flank of Walland Marsh, was, therefore, in place by *c.* 4000 cal. yr BP (Long and Innes 1993). However, the barrier is a complex landform made up of several phases of gravel deposition. Indeed, the orientation of successive gravel ridges attests to a sequence of 'shoreline welding' events that appear to focus in the region of Lydd, and the progressive change in orientation has been used to reconstruct the history of progradation for Dungeness Foreland (Gulliver 1897; Lewis 1932; 1937; Lewis and Balchin 1940; Cunliffe 1980; Eddison 1983).

From comparison with tidal levels from the Thames (Devoy 1979), Eddison (1983) dated the emplacement of the Midrips (see Fig. 3.1) to *c.* 3200 cal. yr BP, but sedimentation in this area may be more closely linked to the chronology of the main back-barrier depositional complex rather than to the period of foreland progradation during the late Holocene. Indeed, this age corresponds with the peat ages obtained for the inland flanks of the Lydd gravel barrier. Lewis and Balchin (1940) suggested that the gravel in the region of Denge Beach was deposited much later than the main barrier complex, i.e. some time between the Roman Period and AD 1300, and maybe even prior to AD 750. From this, Long and Innes (1993) proposed either a period of non-deposition, linked to a reduction in the rate of sea-level rise between 4050 and 1950 cal. yr BP, or continued eastward progradation of the foreland from Broomhill to Denge Beach during this period under the influence of factors such as the rate of relative sea-level rise, sediment supply, and wave/storm magnitude and frequency. Certainly, more continued deposition is favoured from the dating of a basal peat bed overlying gravel in Wickmaryholm Pit on Lydd Beach (Long and Hughes 1995), where a date of 2307–1737 cal. yr BP is indicative of significant progradation of Dungeness Foreland by *c.* 2000 cal. yr BP.

In their investigation of Dungeness in the region of the Power Station, Greensmith and Gutmanis (1990) established the general stratigraphy (for the 'Western' group of boreholes) of *c.* 25–30 m of offshore and lower shoreface sands and laminated sands and silts overlain, in turn, by *c.* 5 m of upper shoreface sands with gravel seams and *c.* 4–5 m of storm beach gravels with a sand matrix. Radiocarbon dates from the base of this sequence dated the onset of lower sandy facies deposition to *c.* 3100 cal. yr BP (assuming a 400 year marine reservoir correction, Stuiver *et al.* 1998), although it was acknowledged that dates on mixed megafaunal assemblages in shoreface, beach and intertidal zones were on mobilised shells that were probably moved inshore under the influence of wave and tidal activity. Hence, these dates are regarded as

maximum bracketing ages for the onset of nearshore sediment accretion. An additional ^{14}C date from shell material at *c.* -34 m OD in a borehole to the east of the lighthouse dated a sequence of channel sands beneath the storm beach gravel to 1069–735 cal. yr BP. Renewed aggradation of the gravel ridges was, therefore, interpreted to have commenced at *c.* 3100 cal. yr BP, with the latest event in the history of gravel deposition at Dungeness probably post-dating *c.* 1000 cal. yr BP. It is, therefore, of some significance that the OSL age beneath the Holmstone gravel corroborates the latter phase of storm beach deposition between *c.* 1400–1250 years BP.

In contrast to the above, the time range for gravel deposition between Jury's Gut and Wickmaryholm Pit is considered by Long and Hughes (1995) to be *c.* 4000–2000 cal. yr BP, and it is the timing of peat deposition on storm beach gravel in the Pit that conflicts with the chronology obtained from the Holmstone and Dungeness data. Whilst the upper part of the Wickmaryholm peat falls in the age range of AD 866 to 1396 (albeit with an age inversion), thus corroborating the emplacement of storm beaches in the region by *c.* 1250 cal. yr BP, the basal date of *c.* 2300–1700 cal. yr BP is indicative of gravel ridge emplacement by approximately 2000 cal. years BP. In this case, a series of gravel ridges will have had to have been deposited in the region of Lydd Beach whilst shoreface sands were still accumulating at Holmstone and Dungeness. Whilst the Lydd Beach may well have been deposited before the more eastern parts of Dungeness Foreland, it is difficult to envisage deposition prior to the Holmstone complex to the west. Hence, a second chronological model may be considered where the ^{14}C ages on shell material from Dungeness Foreland (Greensmith and Gutmanis 1990) provide only maximum ages for the onset of shoreface aggradation and, hence, easterly foreland progradation after *c.* 900 cal. years BP. This may then represent the closing stages of an earlier, and perhaps more continued phase of foreland progradation that had led to gravel ridge deposition in the region of Wickmaryholm by *c.* 2000 cal. years BP. In order to resolve this temporal enigma further dating must be carried out, but as peat deposits are so hard to come by and shell material bears such an equivocal relationship to the time of deposition, it is encouraging that OSL dating of sand beneath the gravel provides well-resolved ages.

Barrier and Marsh Interdependence: Denge Marsh

Additional chronological data for the progradation of Dungeness has been sought in the region of Denge Marsh, where continuing research has attempted to investigate the sequence of barrier formation and marsh infilling. With Dungeness Foreland being made up of a series of gravel recurves, there is limited evidence of alternate barrier and marsh sedimentation. Plater (1992) found evidence of differential marsh stratigraphy either side of the Brickwall

Farm gravel ridge (along which runs Dengemarsh Road), but not over the remainder of Denge Marsh (Plater and Long 1995; Plater *et al.* 1999). Here, the stratigraphy is largely a tri-partite sequence of a lower laminated facies of up to *c.* 3 m coarsely-laminated dark-grey shelly sands and black silts overlain by less than 0.3 m of laminated grey-brown sandy-silts with occasional detrital organic units, and capped by approximately 1 m of mottled (iron-stained) browny-grey and orange clayey-silts with occasional sandy-silts. Of these units, Plater *et al.* (1999) suggest that the lower laminated facies pre-date the main sequence of gravel recurves. Hence, the evolutionary model sees the gravel recurves of the foreland deposited on a basement of tidal sands and silts, followed by a period of quiet-water tidal lag deposition in the resulting back-barrier (Plater and Long 1995; Plater *et al.* 1999).

Attempts to date the marsh sediments in the Denge Marsh region have been largely unsuccessful, mainly due to the absence of distinct peat horizons or any *in situ* datable material. Indeed, thin peats in the upper laminated facies in the region of Boulderwall Farm do not offer the potential for dating as they possess a pollen assemblage akin to that of peats deposited between 3600 and 2200 cal. yr BP in the region of Midley Church Bank (Long and Innes 1993) and are, therefore, interpreted as detrital organic material eroded from the main marsh peat (Plater *et al.* 1999). Plater and Long (1995) and Plater *et al.* (1999) used the altitude of the marsh surface and that of the upper laminated tidal deposits to establish approximate ages for deposition from comparison with the relative sea-level curve for the region. The culmination of laminated facies deposition was dated to *c.* AD 630 whilst the present-day marsh surface dated from AD 1130, and perhaps from the well-documented period of severe storm events during the 13th century (Lewis and Balchin 1940; Green 1988). However, this approach makes reference to age data that are merely extrapolated from the youngest recorded sea-level index point in the region, i.e. *c.* 1800 cal. yr BP, to the present.

Evidence for the age of Denge Marsh is then based on archaeological and historical data. For example, the occurrence of Bronze Age artefacts to the north of Lydd has been documented by Needham (1988), and Cunliffe (1988) has recorded evidence of Roman occupation. Furthermore, according to Brooks (1988), the Denge Marsh estate was certainly in existence in the 10th century AD, and is even documented in an Anglo-Saxon charter dated to AD 774.

Recent stratigraphic work carried out for the RSPB and English Nature in the region of Manor Farm gravel pits (TR 05601830) (Fig. 3.1) recovered articulated *Cerastoderma edule* shells from a typical sequence of laminated silts and clays (with occasional sands) overlain by mottled silty-clay. The lower of these shells was located in core E14 at an altitude of +0.59 to -0.61 m OD in a sequence of laminated, mid- to dark-grey sandy-silt and silty-sand with traces of humified organic matter and shells,

and the upper one was in core D7 at an altitude of +0.90 to -0.92 m OD in some slightly laminated, mottled orange-brown and light browny-grey sandy, silty-clay. Radio-carbon dates on these shells of 1260–1080 and 1240–1050 cal. yr BP, respectively (Table 3.1), reveal that the lower part of the Denge Marsh stratigraphic sequence was, indeed, in place by *c.* AD 700–900. Hence, this phase of back-barrier tidal infilling appears to have been rapid and occurred some time between *c.* 1300 and 1000 years BP. Indeed, such rapid tidal infilling in response to changing boundary conditions, i.e. barrier emplacement, would be expected (see following section). Furthermore, it would seem that the laminated facies made up the earlier Denge Marsh estate and that the mottled facies are either the product of reclamation techniques or deposition from the 13th century storms (Plater and Long 1995).

In terms of marsh and barrier interdependence, if the lower laminated facies did indeed provide the substrate on which the complex of gravel recurves was deposited, this places the timing of eastern foreland deposition, or at least the distant extensions of the recurves, at *c.* 1300–1000 cal. yr BP. Chronologically, this provides further evidence for the rapid eastward progradation of Dungeness Foreland after *c.* 1300 cal. yr BP, and sedimentologically, can be linked with the seaward-prograding shelf sand body identified from the offshore record as a precursor of gravel barrier formation (Dix *et al.* 1998). Alternatively, the lower laminated facies may not pre-date the gravel recurves, and the fact that gravel is rarely encountered beneath these coarsely laminated silts and sands is because the saturated sands are so difficult to penetrate. Such an explanation denies the occasional presence of gravel recurve 'feather edges' in the upper laminated or the upper part of the lower laminated facies (Plater and Long 1995; Plater *et al.* 1999), and requires the presence of a deeper substrate on which foreland progradation took place. Of these, the former explanation is the more plausible, particularly given the surface expression of gravel in the Denge Marsh region.

Short-term Sediment Accretion Versus Long-term Marsh Evolution

Rapid Tidal Sedimentation: Evidence from the Wainway

Like Dungeness and Denge Marsh, the late Holocene evolution of the main back-barrier environment is characterised by major changes in coastal morphology driven by periods of barrier progradation. These broad-scale changes have brought about rapid tidal deposition in quiet-water conditions in the shelter of the barrier complex. The nature of deposition has, to some degree, been controlled by tidal level and changes in elevation due to relative sea-level rise, but the rate of deposition is, in the first instance, more related to sediment influx and accommodation space. Indeed, the early stages of barrier

Table 3.1. Radiocarbon data referred to in the text.

Site	Material	Context	Altitude (m OD)	Laboratory Code	Conventional ^{14}C Age BP (2σ uncertainty)	^{13}C/^{12}C Ratio	Calibrated Age (cal. yr BP)
East Guldeford Level/Camber Core TA1	Shell: *Cerastoderma edule*	Basal muddy sand beneath peat	-2.30	Beta-143342	870±40	+0.9%	535–445
Holmstone, Lydd Ranges	Shell Fragment: *Cerastoderma?*	Shoreface sand beneath gravel	-1.12 to -1.17	Beta-160062	8790±60	-6.6%	9760–9700 and 9640–9010
Denge Marsh Core E14	Shell: *Cerastoderma edule*	Upper part of lower laminated facies	+0.59 to 0.61	Beta-160061	1620±40	-1.1%	1260–1080
Denge Marsh Core D7	Shell: *Cerastoderma edule*	Upper laminated facies	+0.90 to 0.92	Beta-160060	1590±40	0.0%	1240–1050

progradation must create relatively deep water environments which infill rapidly. It is then only as the extent of deposition approaches the level of high tide that the rate of relative sea-level rise has any control over further tidal sedimentation or exposure and the encroachment of organic deposits (Spencer *et al.* 1998a; 1998b). However, even these apparently rapid rates of tidal deposition may have been vastly underestimated by using the limiting ages from intercalated peat deposits. Evidence for back-barrier tidal sedimentation in response to significant increases in accommodation space has recently been obtained in the vicinity of the former Wainway. Although this phase of marsh sedimentation during historic times took place under different rates of sea-level rise and sediment supply to those of the mid- to late Holocene, and arguably represents sedimentary response to very particular boundary conditions at a time of ongoing reclamation, the example serves as a convincing illustration of potential rates of tidal accretion following periodic changes in coastal morphology. The late Holocene deposits in the relict channel network of the Wainway between East Guldeford Level and Camber (see Fig. 3.1) are between 1 and 5 m thick. Core TA1 was located next to a surface expression of the silted Wainway channel, directly in front of the Wainway wall, and west of Guldeford sewer. The core was lithostratigraphically connected to an apparent channel fill sequence, incorporating up to several metres of brown to reddish-brown laminated sandy mud to muddy sand, with a lateral extent of the order of 100 m, and longitudinal extent of at least 2 km. Variations in the thickness of individual laminae were analysed using time series techniques to determine whether any cyclical control on sedimentation could be identified.

Within laminated sediments of tidal origin, variations in layer thickness through a core can be correlated to the changing state of the tide over time in terms of neap-spring, lunar monthly, seasonal and longer term cycles (Archer 1998; Nio and Yang 1991). The laminated deposits found in the Wainway comprise intercalated layers of sand and mud in which repeating cycles of thickening and thinning can be seen. Statistical analysis of these tidal rhythmites may reveal information regarding the tidal regime at the time of deposition, position within the intertidal zone, and deposition rates. In heterolithic rhythmites of this nature, a more complete record of tidal periodicities should be preserved in the sand rather than the mud layers. The latter are controlled by suspended sediment concentrations and slack water settling times, which are likely to be less sensitive to neap-spring (and other) cycles than the variations in current speed that control sand layer deposition (Dalrymple and Makino 1989; Dalrymple *et al.* 1991). It is the interpretation of the variation in sand layer thickness which receives most attention here.

In the laboratory, TA1 was split lengthways and lamination thickness recorded using a binocular microscope, with magnification up to 40x, mounted over a moving stage controlled by a micrometer. The stage was connected to an Atari PC running the *Input10* and *Dendro* data collection and manipulation software (Lageard *et al.* 1999). In an attempt to reduce noise in the tidal signal, the periodicity of which changes as the intertidal zone develops (Archer and Johnson 1997), the data were divided in half with top and bottom analysed separately. The periodicity of the tidal signal should change up-core because ongoing sedimentation leads to increased elevation within the tidal frame, which in turn reduces flooding frequency and, hence, fewer sand layers are deposited during each neap-spring period (Archer 1998, fig. 3, p.63; Archer and Johnson 1997, fig. 3, p.995). Analysing the entire dataset at once would decrease resolution of the principal tidal cycles due to interference from the temporal change in

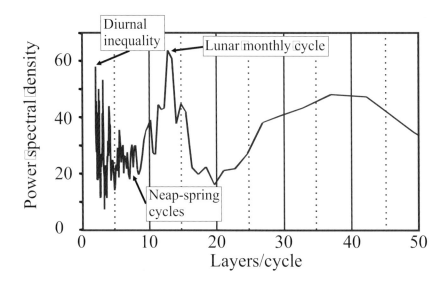

Fig. 3.2. Power spectra of sand laminae from the deeper half of core TA1 showing prominent cycles with periods of 2 and 13 layers suggesting diurnal inequality and lunar monthly cycle, respectively. The clusters of smaller peaks between 5 and 8 layers/cycle are interpreted as variations in the neap-spring cycle and possible interference from sub-ordinate lunar periodicities.

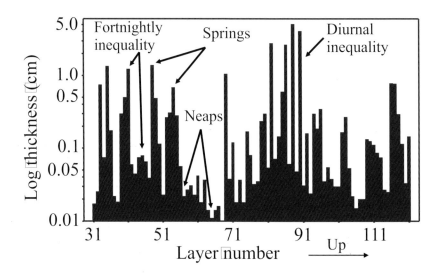

Fig. 3.3. Bar chart of the deepest sand layers from TA1 showing sinusoidal variability in layer thickness. The saw-tooth pattern of alternating thick and thin layers implies a diurnal inequality and, less clearly, an alternation between relatively greater and smaller peaks suggests a fortnightly inequality.

their periodicities. Division of the time series goes someway towards avoiding this effect. Fast Fourier transform (FFT) spectral analysis (Yang and Nio 1985; Davis 1986; Martino and Sanderson 1993; Archer 1994; 1998) of the resultant time series was completed using EXCEL and SPSS. Periodograms generated by the FFT were smoothed by the Tukey-Hamming window, with a span of five data points, to produce the spectral density plots (Fig. 3.2).

Several orders of repeating cycle were identified which correlated with the well-defined tide raising forces associated with the changing relationship between the earth, moon and sun over timescales ranging from days to fortnightly neap-spring and lunar monthly cycles as well as longer term seasonal and annual periodicities (Stupples in press). Lunar monthly cycles repeated approximately 11 to 13 layers, each composed of two sub-ordinate neap-spring periods with roughly half this number of layers (Figs 3.3 and 3.4). The number of layers per neap-spring cycle may seem unrealistically low but several factors support this interpretation. The Wainway is known to have been a sheltered, back-barrier tidal channel, that underwent a consistent period of siltation and reclamation over several hundred years (Eddison 1998), suggesting predominantly

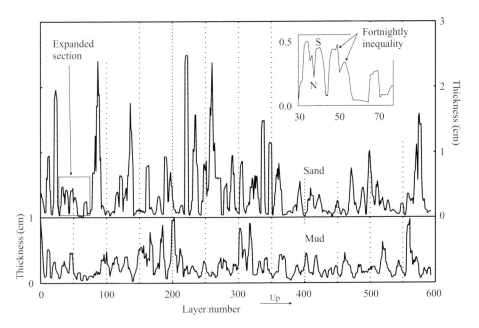

Fig. 3.4. Five-point moving average plot (roughly a neap-spring cycle) of sand and mud layer thickness of the entire laminated sequence from TA1. Fortnightly inequality in sand layers is well preserved, especially in the deepest third of the core, but mud layer cyclicity is more erratic.

low energy conditions (although periods of storm-induced high water are also recorded in the historical documents). Channels and flats towards the head of such an estuary tend to be flood-dominated as the incoming flood tide rises more quickly than the ebb falls, with the latter capable of little, if any, sediment transport (Kvale and Archer 1991; Dyer 1994; Archer *et al.* 1995; Choi and Park 2000). Consequently, the number of tidal events capable of depositing a sand layer would have been limited (Archer and Johnson 1997). In addition, the tidal range at Rye (the mouth of the estuary) is around 6.7 m at present. This is less than half that recorded at Mont Saint Michel and the Bay of Fundy, and even here complete neap-spring cycles are not preserved, or at least not consistently. Periodicities of 15–25 layers per fortnight are reported from the Bay of Fundy (Dalrymple and Makino 1989; Dalrymple *et al.* 1991) and 10–12 at Mont Saint Michel (Tessier *et al.* 1995; Tessier 1998). This suggests that the interpretation of the neap-spring and lunar monthly cycles from the Wainway is reasonable. Archer and Johnson (1997) predict that tidal rhythmites of this order may be expected if around one third of high tides were capable of inundating the site at the time of deposition. It may be more accurate to say that about one third of tides which flooded the area were capable of significant sand transport and so could record distinct tidal rhythmites.

Amalgamation must also be taken into account whereby, at springs, several sand layers can be deposited without intervening muds, the latter having been removed by the stronger spring tidal currents (Greb and Archer 1995; Choi and Park 2000). Similarly, at neaps, low energy conditions prevail and deposition of sand might not occur for several

tides, allowing the amalgamation of mud layers. Hence, the five to seven sand layers taken to represent a fortnight's deposition may, in fact, be due to flooding by a larger number of tides – the thickest layers being deposited by two or more consecutive tides.

Figure 3.5 indicates a repetitive longer term influence on deposition; a sense of these extended cycles is also seen in Figs 3.3 and 3.4. Assuming tidal control dominates, then two periods of relatively enhanced deposition might be expected each year coinciding with the convergence, and hence reinforcement, of the various tide raising astronomical cycles (Martino and Sanderson 1993; Kvale *et al.* 1994; 1999). This reinforcement should generate a period of peak deposition every six months. There are something like 16 to 17 broad, well-defined peaks in Fig. 3.5 where the 13 point moving average accentuates the trend in average layer thickness over (roughly) a lunar month. Periods of enhanced layer thickness recur every 30 to 50 layers which approximates to three to five months given 11 to 13 layers per lunar month. It would seem then that, given two peaks per year, only around six or seven months deposition was preserved each year, and around eight years deposition are recorded here in total. Figure 3.5 is closely comparable to examples from silty rhythmite sequences in the Brazil formation (Kvale *et al.* 1994, fig. 3c, p.333; 1999, fig. 6d, p.1160). No evidence of erosive, unconformable contacts was seen in TA1, but given the nature of the sediments and the scale of the cores, this is not sufficient to discount the possibility of their existence.

Average deposition rates may be estimated from these data. Taking an average of 12 couplets per lunar month, the 594 sand-mud couplets of TA1, having a total thickness

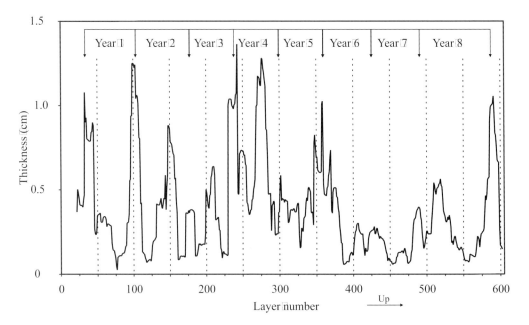

Fig. 3.5. Thirteen-point moving average (around one lunar month) of sand layer thickness in the laminated sequence from TA1. Peaks are interpreted as annual and semi-annual cycles caused by twice-yearly alignment and reinforcement of astronomical tide-raising forces.

of 3.87 m, gives an approximate deposition rate of 1 m/y. Whilst at first sight this appears unreasonably high, it is within the range reported in modern analogues for short term deposition rates of tidal rhythmites during the initial phase of, for example, channel infill (Dalrymple *et al.* 1991; Tessier *et al.* 1995; Allen and Duffy 1998; Li *et al.* 2000), prior to an equilibrium state where rates decline to the order of cm-mm per year as might be expected in such an environment. However, this calculation assumes that a complete record of deposition was preserved in the Wainway and also that deposition was continuous through-out the year. Archer (1991) finds a considerable disparity between the short-term deposition rates calculated from tidal rhythmites and the longer term rates derived from other sources in the Carboniferous of Colorado. He invokes periods of rapid short-term deposition of the cyclic sediments, perhaps when accommodation space is made available (e.g. channel infill), followed by long periods dominated by erosion or non-deposition. In addition, Li *et al.* (2000) noted from short-term monitoring (17 days) that only *c.* 9% of tidal laminae deposited on the open tidal flats of the southern Yangtze delta are preserved, mainly due to partial erosion or reworking by the following tidal cycle. Furthermore, in a 100-year period, the preservation potential of individual laminae is only of the order of 0.2% as a result of erosion and the impacts of high-energy storms. A similarly punctuated, discontinuous pattern of deposition is supported by the inferences drawn from Fig. 3.5 which implies that this sequence accumulated over about eight years. This time frame leads to an average deposition rate, or preservation rate, of around 0.5 m/y.

An indication of the chronology associated with this lithostratigraphy is provided by a radiocarbon date from the base of TA1, and the historical records of reclamation. All of transect TA was reclaimed between AD 1649 and AD 1685 (Eddison, personal communication 2002) with the end of sedimentation at TA1 probably being closer to AD 1649 than AD 1685. A minimum age for the onset of deposition of the sequence recorded at TA1 is provided by a radiocarbon date from a complete shell of *Cerastoderma edule* recovered from -2.30 m OD (5 m below the surface). This was below a thin, localised, detrital peat deposit and within the basal muddy sand, about 50 cm of which was recovered here. The shell gives a calibrated age of 535 to 445 cal. yr BP, and equates to a date of AD 1415 to AD 1505, the intercept date being AD 1455. This indicates that the 5 m of sediment recovered at TA1 accumulated in something like 200 years. The majority was deposited in less than ten years, infilling the channel, before a phase of more gradual accumulation with about 1 m deposited over tidal flats and eventually saltmarsh in the final *c.* 200 years before reclamation.

Accommodation space may have become available following changes in hydrodynamic conditions associated with reclamation towards the head of the Wainway in the 13th to 15th centuries (Gardiner, 1988; Eddison, 2000) which initiated the rapid infill of the deeply incised channel. Greb and Archer (1998) cite several examples of well preserved sequences of heterolithic rhythmites deposited in abandoned channels.

Rapid Tidal Deposition in Response to Changing Boundary Conditions.

In adopting a chronology based on stratigraphic transitions between minerogenic to biogenic sediments, by default the emphasis is placed on slow, gradual processes such as relative sea-level change and the time-averaged rate of terrestrial sediment influx to the coastal zone. Without additional chronological data, it is difficult to construct models other than those that assume linear progression from one data point to the other. Whilst it is acknowledged that aperiodic events such as storms are of considerable significance at the coast, it is difficult to distinguish low-frequency, high-magnitude events from high-frequency, low-magnitude processes in the sedimentary record and to find evidence of non-linear coastal change. In the approach presented here, even in the absence of a detailed chronology through the minerogenic sequence, a convincing case is made for episodes of rapid back-barrier sedimentation in response to changing boundary conditions. Furthermore, it is evident that much of the sedimentary response of the back-barrier to such changes may be achieved in a very short time period by cyclical tidal deposition, providing sediment supply is not a limiting factor. It is also apparent from this research that extended periods of sedimentation may not be the norm, and that back-barrier infilling may be achieved by rapid but localised accretion that, over the long term, makes its way over most of the back-barrier environment.

Whilst it is generally held that the pace of coastal change on Romney Marsh was predominantly gradual but punctuated by aperiodic high-energy storms, during which the morphology of the coast changed abruptly through barrier deposition or breakdown, it is clear that the response of tidal sedimentation to storm-induced change during the late Holocene may have been equally rapid. Under this scenario, rapid progradation of Dungeness Foreland through a combination of tidal sedimentation and gravel barrier emplacement is highly plausible.

Discussion

Late Holocene Back-Barrier Inundation: Post-Peat Deposition

The nature and cause of late Holocene inundation of the back-barrier marsh from *c.* 3200 years BP is the subject of some debate. A period of renewed sea-level rise provides a simple mechanism by which the outer parts of the back-barrier were inundated first, followed by the inner marsh as the marine influence progresses inland. Furthermore, temporal and spatial trends in replacement of peat by tidal muds in the back-barrier suggest that the tidal drainage pattern may have had some control over the nature of inundation (Long and Innes 1995a; Long *et al.* 1998), i.e. the oldest dates on peat inundation are found at Broomhill (3473–3217 cal. yr BP, Tooley and Switsur

1988) and Horsemarsh Sewer (3456–2993 cal. yr BP, Waller *et al.* 1999), but the main phase extends from 2456–2319 cal. yr BP at The Dowels (Waller *et al.* 1999) to 1811–1522 cal. yr BP at Rye (Long *et al.* 1996). In this case, any increase in the rate of sea-level rise exceeded the rate of organic sediment accumulation (Spencer *et al.* 1998a). The fact that the inner marsh peats give way to intertidal sediments at a lower altitude than the outer sites can be accounted for by a higher degree of compaction or shrinkage of these thicker sequences of peat, which continued beyond the time of initial inundation (Green 1968; Long and Innes 1995a; Allen 1996).

Inundation due to renewed sea-level rise may be called into question because the palaeoecological evidence for a gradual transgressive phase is spatially limited, particularly on Scotney Marsh and Romney Marsh proper where the transitional record from peat accumulation to back-barrier inundation is often missing due to widespread erosion of the pre-existing marsh sediments. Generally, vegetation response was insufficient to keep pace with the rising water level – there being some evidence of fen and emergent aquatic vegetation but not saltmarsh development (Waller *et al.* 1999). However, at Brookland (Long and Innes 1995), Scotney Marsh (Spencer 1997) and Little Cheyne Court (Waller *et al.* 1999) palaeoecological data reveal that the increase in the marine influence is heralded first by a rise in watertable and then the return of saltmarsh conditions. It is then of some significance that most of the peat-forming communities were unable to withstand the renewed sea-level rise at *c.* 3400–1500 cal. yr BP – particularly given their previous ability to survive relatively rapid sea-level rise in the mid Holocene (Long and Innes 1993). The coastal communities of the late Holocene were perhaps less robust than those of the mid Holocene. Indeed, it is only the more acidic raised bog communities that were able to develop through the late Holocene, and were amongst the last to be inundated (Waller *et al.* 1999). In this case, a small increase in the rate of sea-level rise led to the demise of the late Holocene reedswamp and fen communities that then collapsed under inundation and created accommodation space. A positive feedback may have then ensued where inundation led to compaction and increased incision, thus amplifying the initial small rate of relative sea-level rise.

The transition from peat to mineral-rich mudflat and/or saltmarsh is widespread throughout southern England and north-west Europe, implying a regional transgressive phase brought about by renewed sea-level rise at *c.* 4000–3000 cal. yr BP (Waller *et al.* 1999; Long *et al.* 2000). However, there is limited evidence of a renewed rise in relative sea-level at this time, or indeed any reliable evidence of sea-level trends during the late Holocene (Flemming 1982; Shennan 1983; 1989; Allen 2000). Indeed, Lamb (1982) notes that the drier conditions of the Bronze Age were followed *c.* 2800–2400 cal. yr BP by a period of increased wetness (the sub-Atlantic). By *c.* 2500 cal. yr BP, the cooling Arctic gave rise to a prevalence of cyclonic north-westerly winds in summer over the British Isles and across Europe. Sea-level rise driven by ocean volume change at this time seems improbable as the late Bronze/early Iron Age was a time of sharp climatic cooling and glacier growth in most parts of the world. Indeed, global sea level may even have been marginally lower, and did not recover until the Roman Period. Apparently higher seas in NW Europe may, therefore, have been due to exceptional high waters and flooding from storm surges.

A reduction in the integrity of the barrier has also been proposed as a mechanism for back-barrier inundation, particularly in the light of the stormy conditions of the sub-Atlantic period. For example, Long and Innes (1995a) note that abrupt changes in peat stratigraphy in the region of the Wainway reflect flooding, perhaps related to reduced sediment supply and/or changes in storm magnitude and frequency. However, Spencer *et al.* (1998a) and Lario *et al.* (2002) propose that little or no sedimentation occurred in the Scotney Marsh area as a result of either barrier breaching and/or overtopping. The relatively rapid ingress on marine water during breaching may well account for the abrupt transition from peat to intertidal silts and clays, but it must be emphasised that the back-barrier was always open to tidal inundation at this time (Long *et al.* 1998). Hence, there is no reason why a phase of barrier breaching would necessarily lead to renewed tidal deposition unless breaching lead to tidal ingress at a low-lying site well-removed from the normal influence of the sea, i.e. a back- or mid-marsh site that had become isolated from the tide due to continued accretion and progradation under the influence of sea-level rise.

In the absence of data on relative sea-level trends, a third hypothesis may account for an apparent rise in tidal level. Here, increased sediment supply from the Wealden rivers may have choked the tidal drainage channels and resulted in a plume of turbid water in the nearshore. Hence, the volume of the back-barrier embayment became restricted, and the incoming tide responded by rising higher and extending further inland. Indeed, this process is akin (albeit in reverse) to that which Pethick (1993) envisages as driving the response of estuarine systems to future sea-level rise. However, Vos and van Heeringen (1997) emphasise that as the cross-sectional area of inlets and channels decreases with sedimentation, the increase in bottom resistance acts to dampen tidal range. As a consequence, up-estuary tidal amplification may have been short-lived but of sufficient duration to initiate a sequence of deterioration in the peat-forming communities, thus increasing accommodation space. Equally, Long *et al.* (2000) note that increased sediment supply to the coastal zone would enhance tidal accretion and lead to emergence rather than submergence, unless compaction were lowering the substrate at a faster rate. Hence, the response of the back-barrier to any change in terrestrial sediment influx during the late Holocene may have been controlled to a significant degree by a series of inter-connected thresholds responding to only minor perturbations.

Increased input of terrestrial sediment to the coastal zone is likely at this time as the main phase of human-induced clearance in the Weald, and perhaps south-east England as a whole, dates from the later Neolithic to the late Bronze/early Iron Age (*c.* 4100–2200 cal. yr BP). Whilst this clearance is considered to have resulted in valley colluviation and alluviation in the lower reaches of some rivers in southern England (Bell 1982; Burrin and Scaife 1988), sediment supply to the coastal zone will also have increased due to greater catchment instability, higher runoff and higher river discharge. Indeed, Jennings *et al.* (1998) record an influx of minerogenic material into the back-barrier at Porlock related to human activity during the late Holocene, and Haslett *et al.* (1998) have used heavy metal concentrations to attribute increased sedimentation in the Somerset Levels to Roman lead mining in the catchment. Similarly, Plater *et al.* (2000) link marine inundation of peat deposits in the Tees estuary at *c.* 3200–2700 cal. yr BP to human- and climate-induced changes in terrestrial sediment flux to the coastal zone.

Despite the obvious human influences on soil erosion and sediment delivery, reviews of alluvial sediment records such as those by Starkel (1995), Macklin and Lewin (1993), Knox (1995) and Macklin (1999) have demonstrated that climate also has a significant regional, perhaps global, control on fluvial sedimentation. Indeed, many phases of late Holocene river alluviation date from *c.* 2800 cal. yr BP at the time of the sub-Boreal/sub-Atlantic transition. In southern Britain, for example, Macklin and Lewin (1993) note a major phase of lowland river alluviation at *c.* 2800–2400 cal. yr BP, later becoming focussed on *c.* 2900–2700 cal. yr BP in a subsequent review by Macklin (1999). The emergence of such regional signals implies a broader climatic rather than a local human influence on sediment flux. Van Geel *et al.* (1996) describe how the change from relatively warm, dry to humid and, at first, cold conditions between 2800–2710 cal. years BP (Kilian *et al.* 1995) impacted on the human populations of the Netherlands. In West Friesland, for example, the emergent estuarine lowlands colonised *c.* 3350 cal. yr BP began to experience increasing wetness *c.* 2760–2620 cal. yr BP due to climatic deterioration and impeded drainage, leading to their abandonment shortly after 2620 cal. yr BP. In contrast, only local inundation in the back-barrier environments of Zeeland is seen at this time due to barrier breaching, although the main phase of Holland Peat formation did come to an end *c.* 2600 cal. yr BP. In addition to increased wetness, associated increases in runoff and streamflow may have enhanced terrestrial sediment yield.

As noted previously, Macklin *et al.* (2000) question humans as the sole agent of river alluviation during the late Holocene, even though climate change during this period is not as extreme as that observed during glacial-interglacial cycles. Although late Bronze/early Iron Age alluviation is generally restricted to the more densely populated river valleys at that time in southern Britain, the periods of alluviation also coincide with a significant climatic shift at *c.* 2800 cal. yr BP. Macklin and Lewin (1993) therefore suggest that although disturbance may have been an important precursor to increased floodplain sedimentation, sediment delivery rates to streams and the valley floor were probably more closely related to climatic factors such as storms and floods. If this debate is applied to the Wealden rivers, there is a large body of evidence linking river alluviation to late Holocene clearance (e.g. Burrin and Scaife 1984; Scaife and Burrin 1983; 1985; Smyth and Jennings 1988; 1990; Waller 1994). However, Waller *et al.* (1988) and Waller (1993; 1994) note that the pollen record of the *Tilia* decline in the Brede and Pannel valleys is found in the upper part of the peat and there is some time lag before the deposition of the overlying minerogenic sediments. Although this may be attributed to storage within the river system or catchment physiography in relation to the site of deposition, the lag seen in the lower river reaches may be due to the time delay between clearance and the onset of a wetter climate. A scenario may therefore be envisaged, as described for Coombe Haven (Sussex) by Smyth and Jennings (1988), where increased erosion potential in cleared catchment areas was not translated into sediment removal and transport into the lowland river valleys and the back-barrier marsh until later. Sediment may well have accumulated at the bottom of cleared slopes almost immediately after clearance but transport further downstream, perhaps even bypassing the lower valley floodplain, may not have been accomplished until climate became wetter.

Clearly, the nature and extent of back-barrier inundation did not result in wholescale submergence of the marshland at *c.* 2800 cal. yr BP. Indeed, as noted above, the main phase of peat inundation dates from *c.* 2300 to 1700 cal. yr BP. In addition, Waller *et al.* (1999) describe evidence for the sub-Boreal/sub-Atlantic transition in the peat sequence at Little Cheyne Court, which was not inundated until *c.* 1000 cal. yr BP. Indeed, the pollen data also record increases in anthropogenic indicators in the region between *c.* 2600–950 cal. yr BP. Whilst not denying the persistence of some sites, and the later inundation of the back- and mid-marsh sites, the echos of clearance and climate change are expressed here in the foremarsh sites and beyond.

Shoreface Aggradation and Foreland Progradation

At the same time as the back-barrier distributary channels became more sediment-laden, terrestrially-derived sediment is likely to have been deposited seaward of the Lydd gravel barrier, leading to rapid aggradation of the shoreface during the period of *c.* 3000–1300 cal. yr BP. Indeed, Greensmith and Gutmanis (1990) identify the presence of detrital green clay minerals, i.e. glauconite, in the lower shoreface and offshore sand apron of Dungeness Foreland which they link, albeit tentatively, to the Holocene olive, green and greenish-grey silts and clays of the Rother Valley

(Burrin 1988). The new basement topography on the seaward flanks of the Lydd gravel, much like the seaward-prograding shelf sand body of Dix *et al.* (1998), provided an intertidal substrate for the storm beaches of Dungeness. However, whilst terrestrial sediment could vent into the sea *via* the New Romney outlet (Green 1988), it would be difficult for this material to make its way south against the overall drift pattern. Hence, a renewed influx of material up-drift, i.e. west of Dungeness Point, at *c.* 3000 years BP seems a necessary prerequisite for shoreface aggradation.

A further consideration to be made is that the temporary choking of the tidal system would have hampered the dispersal of the sediment-laden waters from the Wealden rivers. At this time, they may well have sought alternative pathways to the sea and began to disrupt the integrity of the gravel barrier in the region of Rye Bay on the outer banks of the southerly-arcing channel (Green 1988; Spencer *et al.* 1998b), especially if the competence and capacity of the Rother had increased with increasing runoff. Similarly the seaward flanks of the gravel barrier would have been influenced by the increased storm frequency of the sub-Atlantic (Lamb, 1982). The combined effects led to destabilisation of the gravel complex in the region of Rye Bay and aperiodic debouching of terrestrial drainage water along this route. Whilst the terrestrially-derived sands and silts aided the build-up of the tidal flat substrate on the seaward flank, destabilisation of the barrier complex produced a renewed influx of sand and gravel to the coastal zone (cf. Orford *et al.* 1991) that may have been necessary for the deposition of storm beaches on the shoreface in the region of Dungeness. Cannibalisation of the earlier barrier invigorated longshore supply of material and resulted in shoreface aggradation to the south of Lydd between *c.* 2800 and 1000 years BP which then, as a favourable basement topography developed, enabled rapid storm beach accretion of high level gravel from *c.* 1300 cal year BP.

Although this model is built on a contestable chronology for Dungeness Foreland and a series of inferences on sediment supply to the coastal zone in the late Holocene, an impersistent outlet of the Rother in the region of Rye Bay at *c.* 2800 provides some explanation for the pattern of late Holocene back-barrier inundation. This does not deny the catastrophic and permanent changes that took place in Rye Bay during the storms of the 13th century (Green 1988; Eddison 1998), and, in fact, provides a history for barrier destabilisation in the area that the later storms took advantage of. Furthermore, there must have been a significant change in coastal sediment processing at *c.* 3000 cal. yr BP to initiate the change in coastal geometry and the development of Dungeness Foreland from the earlier barrier.

Rapid shoreface and foreland progradation, together with the significant changes in coastal morphology brought about by the 13th century storms, led to marked shifts in boundary conditions and accommodation space. These shifts enabled tidal sedimentation in back-barrier settings that was both rapid (of the order of 1 m/y) and discontinuous (both vertically and spatially). Hence, the sedimentary response of the back-barrier has not been slow and gradual under the influences of incremental sea-level rise and sediment input, but episodic as tidal processes have acted to fill the void between the bed and the equilibrium conditions of high tide. Once equilibrium is approached, the balance between relative sea-level and sediment supply then controls the nature of further sediment accretion. It is, therefore, not surprising that diatom assemblages preserved in sedimentary records from these back-barrier settings are often dominated by open tidal channel conditions and show only limited evidence of shoaling (Plater 1992; Plater and Long 1995; Long *et al.* 1996; Spencer *et al.* 1998; 1998b; Plater *et al.* 1999; Evans *et al.* 2001).

Conclusions

The issue of marsh and barrier interdependence has been addressed through the acquisition of additional chronological data in the region of the Holmstone gravel and Denge Marsh using luminescence and ^{14}C techniques. It appears that tidal flat and sub-tidal shoreface progradation during the period of *c.* 3000–1000 cal. yr BP was a necessary precursor for the formation of Dungeness Foreland through rapid storm beach deposition from *c.* 1300 cal. yr BP. The onset of shoreface aggradation coincides with a period of significant terrestrial sediment influx driven by a combination of human-induced clearance and wetter climate. During this period, the main back-barrier may have become choked with sediment and the barrier became destabilised in the region of Rye Bay due to erosion of its inner flanks by enhanced stream discharge and its outer flanks by storm surges. Destabilisation provided renewed sediment input to the drift cell that then led to shoreface aggradation and subsequent foreland progradation.

Detailed analysis of laminated tidal rhythmites in the region of the Wainway has raised significant questions regarding timescales of deposition. Whilst chronologies based on intercalating peat beds give average rates of tidal deposition of the order of 1–5 mm/y, actual rates are probably of the order of 1 m/y. Statistical analysis of rhythmite thickness reveals several orders of repeating cycles that can be linked to cyclicity of the lunar and solar tides over timescales ranging from days to years. Hence, sedimentation rates may be determined in the absence of absolute dating. The results from the Wainway, that apply also to similar laminated sequences in the sediments beneath the main marsh peat and those on Denge Marsh, are indicative of rapid tidal sedimentation in response to changing boundary conditions such as barrier emplacement or breaching. In addition, it is evident that a great deal of the record may be absent due to the low preservation potential of individual laminae. The sedimentary response to changing coastal or channel morphology is, therefore, rapid but vertically and spatially non-uniform and is controlled by the operation of the tide rather than the balance between sea-level and sediment supply.

Acknowledgements
The authors should like to acknowledge the financial support of the Romney Marsh Research Trust, the Ministry of Defence, the RSPB and the BGRG. Thanks are also given to those individuals who have provided essential support in the planning, organisation and undertaking of the research described in this paper, in particular Antony Long, Brian Banks, Simon Busuttil, Pete Akers, Jill Eddison, Dorothy and Robert Beck, Larry Cooke, Peter Edwards, Jim Knowlton, Derek Howell, Mr. and Mrs. Goring, Chris Spencer, Wendy Woodland, Cathy Delaney, Nigel Crook, Anna Moran, Jayne Boygle, Jonathan Lageard, Dave Groom, Liz Maher, Hilda Hull, Irene Cooper, Bob Jude, Suzanne Yee, Sandra Mather and Peter C. Payne. Special thanks are given to Claire Mayers for her invaluable assistance in the field during that cold, wet week in early 2001 (A Space Odyssey).

References

Aitken, M.J. 1998. *An Introduction to Optical Dating*, Oxford University Press, Oxford.

Allen, J.R.L. 1996. The sequence of early land-claims on the Walland and Romney Marshes, southern Britain: a preliminary hypothesis and its implications, *Proceedings of the Geologists' Association* **107**, 271–80.

Allen, J.R.L. 2000. Morphodynamics of Holocene saltmarshes: a review sketch from the Atlantic and Southern North Sea coasts of Europe, *Quaternary Science Reviews* **19**, 1155–1231.

Allen, J.R.L. and Duffy, M.J. 1998. Temporal and spatial depositional patterns in the Severn Estuary, southwestern Britain, intertidal studies at spring-neap and seasonal scales, *Marine Geology* **145**, 147–71.

Archer, A.W. 1991. Modelling of tidal rhythmites using modern tidal periodicities and implications for short-term sedimentation rates, in E.K. Franseen, W.L. Watney, C.C. St. C. Kendall and W. Ross (eds) *Sedimentary Modelling, Computer Simulations and Methods for Improved Parameter Definition*, Kansas Geological Survey Bulletin **233**, 185–94. Lawrence, Kansas.

Archer, A.W. 1994. Extraction of sedimentological information via computer-based image analysis of gray shales in

Carboniferous coal-bearing sections of Indiana and Kansas, *Mathematical Geology* **26**, 47–65.

Archer, A.W. 1998. Hierarchy of controls on cyclic rhythmite deposition, Carboniferous basins of Eastern and Mid Continental U.S.A., in C.R. Alexander, R.A. Davis and V.J. Henry (eds) *Tidalites, Processes and Products*, SEPM Special Publication **61**, 59–68. Tulsa.

Archer, A.W. and Johnson, T.W. 1997. Modelling of cyclic tidal rhythmites (Carboniferous of Indiana and Kansas, Precambrian of Utah, USA) as a basis for reconstruction of intertidal positioning and palaeotidal regimes, *Sedimentology* **44**, 991–1010.

Archer, A.W., Kuecher, G.J. and Kvale, E.P. 1995. The role of tidal-velocity asymmetries in the deposition of silty tidal rhythmites (Carboniferous, eastern interior coal basin, USA), *Journal of Sedimentary Research* **A65**, 408–16.

Bell, M. 1982. The effects of land-use and climate on valley sedimentation, in A.F. Harding (ed.) *Climatic Change in Later Prehistory*, Edinburgh University Press, 127–42. Edinburgh.

Brooks, N. 1988. Romney Marsh in the Early Middle Ages, in J. Eddison and C. Green (eds) *Romney Marsh: Evolution, Occupation, Reclamation* (Oxford University Committee for Archaeology Monograph **24**), 90–104. Oxford.

Burrin, P.J. 1988. The Holocene floodplain and alluvial deposits of the Rother valley and their bearing on the evolution of Romney Marsh, in J. Eddison and C. Green (eds) *Romney Marsh: Evolution, Occupation, Reclamation* (Oxford University Committee for Archaeology Monograph **24**), 31–52. Oxford.

Burrin, P.J. and Scaife, R.G. 1984. Aspects of Holocene valley sedimentation and floodplain development in southern England, *Proceedings of the Geologists' Association* **95**, 81–96.

Burrin, P.J. and Scaife, R.G. 1988. Environmental thresholds, Catastrophe Theory and landscape sensitivity: their relevance to the impact of Man on valley alluviations, in J.L. Bintliff, D.A. Davidson and E.G. Grant (eds) *Conceptual Issues in Environmental Archaeology*, Edinburgh University Press, 211–32. Edinburgh.

Choi, K.S. and Park, Y.A. 2000. Late Pleistocene silty tidal rhythmites in the macrotidal flat between Youngjong and Yongyou Islands, west coast of Korea, *Marine Geology* **167**, 231–41.

Cunliffe, B.W. 1980. The evolution of Romney Marsh: a preliminary statement, in F.H. Thompson (ed.) *Archaeology and Coastal Change*, Society of Antiquaries Occasional Papers, New Series No.**1**, 37–55. London.

Cunliffe, B.W. 1988. Romney Marsh in the Roman Period, in J. Eddison and C. Green (eds) *Romney Marsh: Evolution, Occupation, Reclamation*. (Oxford University Committee for Archaeology Monograph **24**), 83–87. Oxford.

Dalrymple, R.W. and Makino, Y. 1989. Description and genesis of tidal bedding the Cobequid Bay-Salmon River Estuary, Bay of Fundy, Canada, in A. Taira and F. Masuda (eds) *Sedimentary Facies of the Active Plate Margin*, Terra Scientific, 151–77. Tokyo.

Dalrymple, R.W., Makino, Y. and Zaitlin, B.A. 1991. Temporal and spatial patterns of rhythmite deposition on mudflats in the macrotidal, Cobequid Bay – Salmon River Estuary, Bay of Fundy, Canada, in D.G. Smith, G.E. Reinson, B.A. Zaitlin and R.A. Rahmani (eds) *Clastic Tidal Sedimentology*,

Canadian Society of Petroleum Geologists, Memoir No.**16**, 137–60. Calgary.

Davis, J.C. 1986. *Statistics and Data Analysis in Geology*, 2nd ed. Wiley, New York.

Devoy, R.J.N. 1979. Flandrian sea level changes and vegetational history of the lower Thames Estuary. *Philosophical Transactions of the Royal Society*, Series B **285**, 355–407.

Dix, J., Long, A.J., Cooke, R. 1998. The evolution of Rye Bay and Dungeness Foreland, the offshore seismic record, in J. Eddison, M. Gardiner and A. Long (eds) *Romney Marsh: Environmental Change and Human Occupation in a Coastal Lowland* (Oxford University Committee for Archaeology Monograph **46**), 13–29. Oxford.

Dyer, K.R. 1994. Estuarine sediment transport and deposition, in K. Pye (ed.) *Sediment Transport and Depositional Processes*, Blackwell, 193–218. Oxford.

Eddison, J. 1983. The evolution of the barrier beaches between Fairlight and Hythe, *The Geographical Journal* **149**, 39–75

Eddison, J. 1988. 'Drowned Lands': changes in the course of the Rother and its estuary, and associated drainage problems, in J. Eddison and C. Green (eds) *Romney Marsh: Evolution, Occupation, Reclamation* (Oxford University Committee for Archaeology Monograph **24**), 142–62. Oxford.

Eddison, J. 1998. Catastrophic changes: the evolution of the barrier beaches of Rye Bay, in J. Eddison, M. Gardiner and A.J. Long (eds) *Romney Marsh: Environmental Change and Human Occupation in a Coastal Lowland* (Oxford University Committee for Archaeology Monograph **46**), 65–88. Oxford.

Eddison, J. 2000. *Romney Marsh: Survival on a Frontier*. Tempus, Stroud.

Evans, J.R., Kirby, J.R. and Long, A.J. 2001. The litho- and biostratigraphy of a late Holocene tidal channel in Romney Marsh, southern England, *Proceedings of the Geologists' Association* **112**, 111–30.

Flemming, N.C. 1982. Multiple regression analysis of earth movements and eustatic sea-level changes in the United Kingdom in the past 9000 years, *Proceedings of the Geologists' Association* **93**, 113–25.

Gardiner, M. 1988. Medieval settlement and society in the Broomhill area, and excavation at Broomhill church, in J. Eddison and C. Green (eds) *Romney Marsh: Evolution, Occupation, Reclamation* (Oxford University Committee for Archaeology Monograph **24**), 112–27. Oxford.

Greb, S.F. and Archer, A.W. 1998. Annual sedimentation cycles in rhythmites of Carboniferous tidal channels, in C.R. Alexander, R.A. Davis and V.J. Henry (eds) *Tidalites, Processes and Products*. SEPM Special Publication, **61**, 75–83. Tulsa.

Green, C.P. 1988. Palaeogeography of marine inlets in the Romney Marsh area, in J. Eddison and C. Green (eds) *Romney Marsh: Evolution, Occupation, Reclamation* (Oxford University Committee for Archaeology Monograph **24**), 167–74. Oxford.

Green, R.D. 1968. *Soils of Romney Marsh*. (Soil Survey of Great Britain, Bulletin No.**4**) Harpenden.

Greensmith, J.T. and Gutmanis, J.C. 1990. Aspects of the late Holocene depositional history of the Dungeness area, Kent, *Proceedings of the Geologists' Association* **101**, 225–37.

Gulliver, F.P. 1897. Dungeness Foreland, *The Geographical Journal* **9**, 536–46.

Haslett, S., Davies, P., Curr, R.H.F., Davies, C.F.C., Kennington, K., King, C.P. and Margetts, A.J. 1998.

Evaluating late-Holocene relative sea-level change in the Somerset Levels, southwest Britain, *The Holocene* **8**, 197–207.

Jennings, S., Orford, J.D., Canti, M., Devoy, R.J.N. and Straker, V. 1998. The role of relative sea-level rise and changing sediment supply on Holocene gravel barrier development: the example of Porlock, Somerset, UK, *The Holocene* **8**, 165–81.

Kilian, M.R., Van Der Plicht, J. and Van Geel, B. 1995. Dating raised bogs: new aspects of AMS ¹⁴C wiggle matching, a reservoir effect and climatic change, *Quaternary Science Reviews* **14**, 959–66.

Knox, J.C. 1995. Fluvial systems since 20,000 years BP, in K.J. Gregory, L. Starkel and V.R. Baker (eds) *Global Continental Palaeohydrology*, Wiley, 87–103. Chichester.

Kvale, E.P. and Archer, A.W. 1991. Characteristics of two, Pennsylvanian age, semidiurnal tidal deposits in the Illinois Basin, U.S.A., in D.G. Smith, G.E. Reinson, B.A. Zaitlin and R.A. Rahmani (eds) *Clastic Tidal Sedimentology*, Canadian Society of Petroleum Geologists, Memoir No.**16**, 179–88. Calgary.

Kvale, E.P., Fraser, G.S., Archer, A.W., Zawistoski, A., Kemp, N. and McGough, P. 1994. Evidence of seasonal precipitation in Pennsylvanian sediments of the Illinois Basin, *Geology* **22**, 331–334.

Kvale, E.P., Johnson, H.W., Sonett, C.P., Archer, A.W. and Zawistoski, A. 1999. Calculating lunar retreat rates using tidal rhythmites, *Journal of Sedimentary Research* **69**, 1154–68.

Lageard, J.G.A., Chambers, F.M. and Thomas, P.A. 1999. Climatic significance of the marginalization of Scots pine (*Pinus sylvestris L.*) c. 2500 BC at White Moss, south Cheshire, UK, *The Holocene* **9**, 321–31.

Lamb, H.H. 1982. *Climate, History and the Modern World*. Methuen, London.

Lario, J., Spencer, C., Plater, A.J., Zazo, C., Goy, J.L. and Dabrio, C.J. 2002. Particle size characterisation of Holocene back-barrier sequences from North Atlantic coasts (SW Spain and SE England), *Geomorphology* **42**, 25–42.

Lewis, W.V. 1932. The formation of Dungeness Foreland, *The Geographical Journal* **80**, 309–24.

Lewis, W.V. 1937. The formation of Dungeness and Romney Marsh, *Proceedings of the South Eastern Union of Scientific Societies* **49**, 65–70.

Lewis, W.V. and Balchin, W.G.V. 1940. Past sea-levels at Dungeness, *The Geographical Journal* **96**, 258–85.

Li, C., Wang, P., Daidu, F., Bing, D. and Tiesong, L. 2000. Open-coast intertidal deposits and the preservation potential of individual laminae: a case study from east-central China, *Sedimentology* **47**, 1039–51.

Long, A.J. and Hughes, P.D.M. 1995. Mid- to late-Holocene evolution of the Dungeness foreland, UK, *Marine Geology* **124**, 253–71.

Long, A.J. and Innes, J.B. 1993. Holocene sea-level changes and coastal sedimentation in Romney Marsh, southeast England, UK, *Proceedings of the Geologists' Association* **104**, 223–37.

Long, A.J. and Innes, J.B. 1995a. The back-barrier and barrier depositional history of Romney Marsh, Walland Marsh and Dungeness, Kent, England, *Journal of Quaternary Science* **10**, 267–83.

Long, A.J. and Innes, J.B. 1995b. A palaeoenvironmental investigation of the 'Midley Sand' and associated deposits at Midley Church Bank, Romney Marsh, in J. Eddison (ed.) *Romney Marsh: The Debatable Ground* (Oxford University Committee for Archaeology Monograph **41**), 37–50. Oxford.

Long, A.J., Plater, A.J., Waller, M.P. and Innes, J.B. 1996. Holocene coastal sedimentation in the Eastern English Channel: new data from the Romney Marsh region, United Kingdom, *Marine Geology* **136**, 97–120.

Long, A., Waller, M., Hughes, P. and Spencer, C. 1998. Holocene depositional history of Romney Marsh proper, in J. Eddison, M. Gardiner and A. Long (eds) *Romney Marsh: Environmental Change and Human Occupation in a Coastal Lowland* (Oxford University Committee for Archaeology Monograph **46**), 45–63. Oxford.

Long, A.J., Scaife, R.G. and Edwards, R.G. 2000. Stratigraphic architecture, relative sea level, and models of estuary development in southern England: New data from Southampton Water, in K. Pye and J.R.L. Allen (eds) *Coastal and Estuarine Environments: Sedimentology, Geomorphology and Geoarchaeology* (Geological Society special publication **175**), 253–79. London.

Macklin, M.G. 1999. Holocene river environments in Prehistoric Britain: human interaction and impact, *Quaternary Proceedings* **No.7**, 521–30.

Macklin, M.G. and Lewin, J. 1993. Holocene river alluviation in Britain, *Zeitschrift fur Geomorphologie Neue Folge – Supplementband* **88**, 109–22.

Macklin, M.G., Taylor, M.P., Hudson-Edwards, K.A. and Howard, A.J. 2000. Holocene environmental change in the Yorkshire Ouse basin and its influence on river dynamics and sediment fluxes to the coastal zone, in I. Shennan and J. Andrews (eds) *Holocene Land-Ocean Interaction and Environmental Change around the North Sea* (Geological Society special publication **166**), 87–96. London.

Martino, R.L. and Sanderson, D.D. 1993. Fourier and autocorrelation analysis of estuarine tidal rhythmites, lower Breathitt formation (Pennsylvanian), eastern Kentucky, USA, *Journal of Sedimentary Petrology* **63**, 105–19.

Mayer, L.M., Jorgensen, J. and Schnitker, D. 1991. Enhancement of diatom frustule dissolution by iron oxides, *Marine Geology* **99**, 263–66.

Murray, A.S. and Wintle, A.G. 2000. Luminescence dating of quartz using an improved single-aliquot regenerative-dose protocol, *Radiation Measurements* **32**, 57–73.

Murray-Wallace, C.V., Banerjee, D., Bourman, R.P., Olley, J.M. and Brooke, B.P. submitted. Optically stimulated luminescence dating of Holocene relict foredunes, Guichen Bay, South Australia, *Quaternary Science Reviews*.

Needham, S. 1988. A group of Early Bronze Age axes from Lydd, in J. Eddison and C. Green (eds) *Romney Marsh: Evolution, Occupation and Reclamation* (Oxford University Committee for Archaeology Monograph **24**), 77–82. Oxford.

Nio, S.D. and Yang, C.S. 1991. Diagnostic attributes of clastic tidal deposits: a review, in D.G. Smith, G.E. Reinson, B.A. Zaitlin and R.A. Rahmani (eds) *Clastic Tidal Sedimentology*, Canadian Society of Petroleum Geologists, Memoir No.**16**, 3–28. Calgary.

Orford, J.D., Carter, R.W.G. and Jennings, S.C. 1991. Coarse clastic barrier environments: evolution and implications for Quaternary sea level interpretation, *Quaternary International* **9**, 87–104.

Pethick, J. 1993. Shoreline adjustments and coastal management:

physical and biological processes under accelerated sea-level rise, *The Geographical Journal* **159**, 162–68.

Plater, A.J. 1992. The late Holocene evolution of Denge Marsh, southeast England: a stratigraphic, sedimentological and micropalaeontological approach, *The Holocene* **2**, 63–70.

Plater, A.J. and Long, A.J. 1995. The morphology and evolution of Denge Beach and Denge Marsh, in J. Eddison (ed.) *Romney Marsh: The Debatable Ground* (Oxford University Committee for Archaeology Monograph **41**), 8–36. Oxford.

Plater, A.J., Ridgway, J., Appleby, P.G., Berry, A. and Wright, M.R. 1998. Historical contaminant fluxes in the Tees estuary, UK: geochemical, magnetic and radionuclide evidence, *Marine Pollution Bulletin* **39**, 343–60.

Plater, A.J., Long, A.J., Spencer, C.D. and Delacour, R.A.P. 1999. The stratigraphic record of sea-level change and storms during the last 2000 years: Romney Marsh, southeast England, *Quaternary International* **55**, 17–27.

Plater, A.J., Ridgway, J., Rayner, B., Shennan, I., Horton, B.P., Haworth, E.Y., Wright, M.R., Rutherford, M.M. and Wintle, A.G. 2000. Sediment provenance and flux in the Tees Estuary: the record from the Late Devensian to the present, in I. Shennan and J. Andrews (eds) *Holocene Land-Ocean Interaction and Environmental Change around the North Sea*, (Geological Society special publications **166**), 171–95. London.

Scaife, R.G. and Burrin, P.J. 1983. Floodplain development in and the vegetational history of the Sussex High Weald and some archaeological implications, *Sussex Archaeological Collections* **121**, 1–10.

Scaife, R.G. and Burrin, P.J. 1985. The environmental impact of prehistoric man as recorded in the upper Cuckmere Valley at Stream Farm, Chiddingly, *Sussex Archaeological Collections* **123**, 27–34.

Shennan, I. 1983. Flandrian and Late Devensian sea-level changes and crustal movements in England and Wales, in D.E. Smith and A.G. Dawson (eds) *Shorelines and Isostasy*, Academic Press, 255–83. London.

Shennan, I. 1989. Holocene crustal movements and sea-level changes in Great Britain, *Journal of Quaternary Science* **4**, 77–89.

Smyth, C. and Jennings, S. 1988. Mid- to late-Holocene forest composition and the effects of clearances in the Coombe Haven valley, East Sussex, *Sussex Archaeological Collections* **126**, 1–20.

Smyth, C. and Jennings, S. 1990. Late Bronze Age – Iron Age valley sedimentation in East Sussex, Southern England, in J. Boardman, I.D.L. Foster, and J.A. Dearing (eds) *Soil Erosion on Agricultural Land*, John Wiley and Sons, 273–84. Chichester.

Spencer, C.D. 1997. The Holocene evolution of Romney Marsh: a record of sea-level change in a back-barrier environment, (unpublished Ph.D. thesis, University of Liverpool).

Spencer, C.D., Plater, A.J. and Long, A.J. 1998a. Rapid coastal change during the mid- to late-Holocene: the record of barrier estuary sedimentation in the Romney Marsh region, southeast England, *The Holocene* **8**, 143–63.

Spencer, C., Plater A.J. and Long, A. 1998b. Holocene barrier estuary evolution: the sedimentary record of the Walland Marsh region, in J. Eddison, M. Gardiner and A. Long (eds) *Romney Marsh: Environmental Change and Human Occupation in a Coastal Lowland* (Oxford University Committee for Archaeology Monograph **46**), 13–29. Oxford.

Starkel, L. 1995. Palaeohydrology of the temperate zone, in K.J. Gregory, L. Starkel and V.R. Baker (eds) *Global Continental Palaeohydrology*, Wiley, 233–49. Chichester.

Stupples, P. 2002. Late Holocene intertidal sedimentation: a lithostratigraphic approach to palaeoenvironmental reconstruction in the Wainway Channel, Romney Marsh, south east England (unpublished Ph.D. thesis, Manchester Metropolitan University).

Stupples, P. 2002. Tidal cycles preserved in late Holocene tidal rhythmites, the Wainway Channel, Romney Marsh, southeast England, *Marine Geology* **182**, 231–246.

Tessier, B. 1998. Tidal cycles, annual versus semi-lunar records, in C.R. Alexander, R.A. Davis and V.J. Henry (eds) *Tidalites, Processes and Products*, SEPM Special Publication, **61**, 69–74. Tulsa, USA.

Tessier, B., Archer, A.W., Lanier, W.P. and Feldman, H.R. 1995. Comparison of ancient tidal rhythmites (Carboniferous of Kansas and Indiana, USA) with modern analogues (the Bay of Mont-Saint-Michel, France), in B.W. Flemming and A. Bartholoma (eds) *Tidal Signatures in Modern and Ancient Sediments*, International Association of Sedimentologists, Special Publication **24**, 259–74.

Tooley, M.J. and Switsur, V.R. 1988. Water level changes and sedimentation during the Flandrian Age in the Romney Marsh area, in J. Eddison and C. Green (eds) *Romney Marsh: Evolution, Occupation, Reclamation* (Oxford University Committee for Archaeology Monograph **24**), 53–71. Oxford.

Van Geel, B., Buurman, J. and Waterbolk, H.T. 1996. Archaeological and palaeoecological indications of an abrupt climate change in The Netherlands, and evidence for climatological teleconnections around 2650 BP, *Journal of Quaternary Science* **11**, 451–60.

Vos, P.C. and van Heeringen, R.M. 1997. Holocene geology and occupation history of the Province of Zeeland, in M.M. Fischer (ed.) *Holocene Evolution of Zeeland (SW Netherlands)*, Netherlands Institute of Applied Geoscience TNO, Nr59, 5–110. Haarlem.

Waller, M.P. 1993. Flandrian vegetation history of south-eastern England. Pollen data from Pannel Bridge, East Sussex, *New Phytologist* **124**, 345–69.

Waller, M.P. 1994. Flandrian vegetational history of south-eastern England. Stratigraphy of the Brede valley and pollen data from Brede Bridge, *New Phytologist* **126**, 369–92.

Waller, M.P., Burrin, P.J. and Marlow, A. 1988. Flandrian sedimentation and palaeoenvironments in Pett Level, the Brede and lower Rother valleys and Walland Marsh, in J. Eddison and C. Green (eds) *Romney Marsh: Evolution, Occupation, Reclamation* (Oxford University Committee for Archaeology Monograph **24**), 3–30. Oxford.

Waller, M.P., Long, A.J., Long, D. and Innes, J.B. 1999. Patterns and processes in the development of coastal mire vegetation: multi-site investigations from Walland Marsh, Southeast England, *Quaternary Science Reviews* **18**, 1419–44.

Wass, M. 1995. The proposed Northern course of the Rother: a sedimentological and microfaunal investigation, in J. Eddison (ed.) *Romney Marsh: the Debatable Ground* (Oxford University Committee for Archaeology Monograph **41**), 51–78. Oxford.

Yang, C.S. and Nio, S.D. 1985. Estimation of palaeohydrodynamic processes from subtidal deposits using time series analysis methods, *Sedimentology* **32**, 41–57.

Appendix

Data on luminescence age obtained for sands under the Holmstone Shingle.

OSL age determination – Lydd Firing Ranges

- OSL measurements were made using a Single Aliquot Regenerative dose (SAR) protocol applied to 180–212 mm HF-etched quartz.

- A total of 24 aliquots were examined, using a pre-heat of 160–300°C for 10 s. Of these 24 discs, 15 were used to generate the final OSL age (preheats ranging from 160–240°C).

Field sample name	Lydd Ranges, Run 1
Aberystwyth Lab. number	**51 Lydd**
Depth (m)	5.07 ± 0.07
Material used for dating	Quartz
Grain size (μm)	180–212
Preparation method	Heavy liquid separation (Na polytungstate); 40% HF etch 45 mins
Measurement protocol	SAR; OSL 470 nm
Equivalent Dose, D_e (Gy)	**1.04 ± 0.04**
Number of aliquots, n	15
Water content (% dry mass)	25 ± 5
Unsealed α count rate (cts/ks.cm^2)	0.149 ± 0.003
U (ppm)	0.63 ± 0.08
Th (ppm)	2.10 ± 0.25
Sealed/Unsealed	0.98 ± 0.03
Calculated K (%)	0.51 ± 0.03
Layer removed by etching (μm)	10 ± 2
Infinite β dose rate (Gy/ka)	0.577 ± 0.018
External β dose rate 'wet' (Gy/ka)	0.394 ± 0.023
External γ dose rate 'wet' (Gy/ka)	0.237 ± 0.017
Cosmic (Gy/ka)	0.115 ± 0.004
Total dose rate (Gy/ka)	**0.75 ± 0.03**
OSL Age[#] (a)	**1390 ± 80**

[#] Ages are rounded to the nearest 10 and expressed as years before 2000 AD.

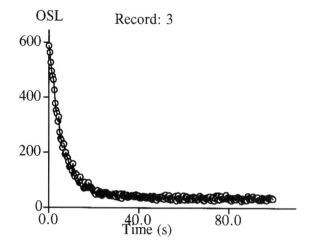

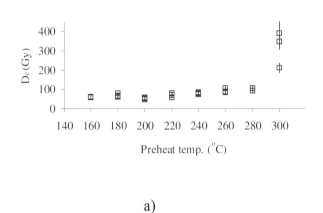

a)

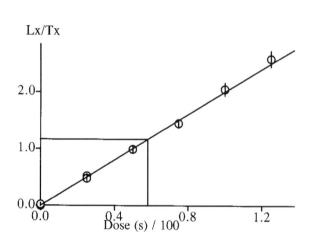

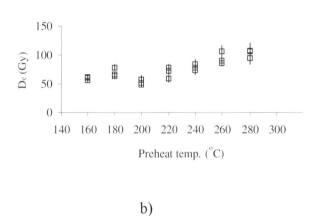

b)

Figure 3.I. Typical OSL a) decay curve and b) growth curve for sample Aber/51-Lydd, *taken from beneath the Holmstone gravel. The OSL signal used was taken from the initial 0.8 s of the decay curve, and the background subtraction was determined from the final 8.4 s of stimulation.*

Figure 3.II. Preheat plot for OSL sample Aber/51-Lydd, *taken from beneath the Holmstone gravel, showing the D_e values obtained for a) the full range of preheats, from 160–300°C/ 10s, and b) preheats from 160–280°C/10s on an enlarged vertical scale for clarity. D_e values obtained using preheats from 160–240°C/10s were used in the determination of the OSL age.*

4. Palaeoenvironmental Changes during the Last 4000 Years at Scotney Marsh, Romney Marsh, Kent: A Multiproxy Approach

Chris Spencer and Wendy Woodland

Lithostratigraphic and chronostratigraphic data from the Scotney Marsh trough, seaward of the main back-barrier environment, are combined in this paper with multi-proxy palaeoenvironmental indicators. Two new radiocarbon dates from organic sediments in the trough provide a detailed chronology for the evolution of the area immediately seaward of the main back-barrier. Detailed environmental reconstructions were completed on a stratotype core utilising diatoms and pollen, and for the first time in the Romney Marsh area, testate amoebae. These data provide a detailed reconstruction of salinity, past vegetation assemblages and, through testate amoebae, absolute water table depths in the freshwater peats. Good agreement exists between the three proxies, and a more detailed resolution of palaeoenvironmental change in the Scotney Marsh trough is achieved than hitherto possible

Two periods of peat formation are evident, separated by tidal channel conditions. The lower peat is contemporaneous with peat accumulation across much of southern Walland Marsh whereas the upper peat, investigated in detail here, demonstrates that peat forming communities were present in the Scotney Marsh trough between c. 2100–1660 cal. yr BP when the trough was isolated from the sea during the extension of the Lydd gravel complex. Eventual inundation of the peat sediments in the Scotney Marsh trough came from the north as rising sea level overtopped the protective barrier.

Introduction

This paper presents a detailed palaeoenvironmental reconstruction of events in the Scotney Marsh trough (Fig. 4.1) following the emplacement of gravel ridges in the locality. While much is known about the palaeoecological evolution of the north and west of the Romney Marsh region, little comparative information exists for the south-eastern area adjacent to the gravel ridges of the Lydd complex. The physical conditions that influenced the alternating sequences of gravel ridge complexes and gravel lows are known (Orford *et al.* 1991; Long and Hughes 1995), but the chronology and palaeoenvironmental character of events subsequent to gravel emplacement are less clear. This has resulted in an incomplete chronology for environmental change for the south-eastern area of the Romney Marsh depositional complex, particularly for the

area immediately seaward of the initial gravel barrier, referred to here as ridge 1 (Fig. 4.1). In this paper, we present palaeoecological information for this area from peats within the Scotney Marsh trough. Water chemistry reconstructions from diatoms and reconstructed vegetation communities from pollen are combined for the first time with reconstructions of water table depth from testate amoebae analysis. This enables the production of a multi-proxy palaeoecological reconstruction for this area of Scotney Marsh following gravel barrier emplacement. The additional proxy evidence from testate amoebae refine the history of infilling of the gravel lows at Scotney Marsh and facilitate a more detailed understanding of palaeo-environments in areas of Romney Marsh immediately seaward of ridge 1.

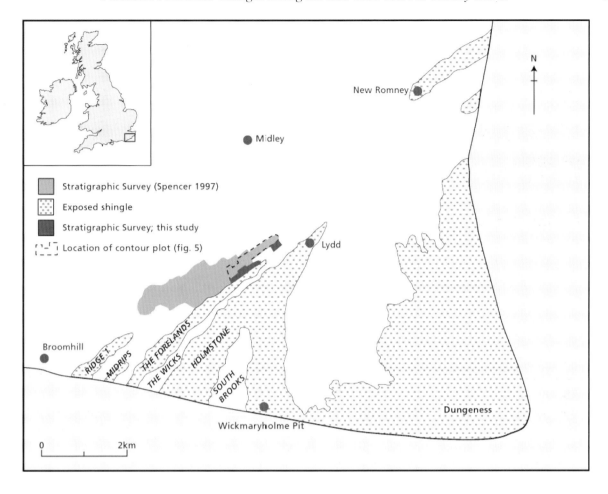

Fig. 4.1. Location map for the Scotney Marsh area.

Previous Work

Relatively little has been written of the chronology and palaeoenvironmental evolution of the back-barrier environments in the south-eastern area of Romney Marsh. This contrasts with sites further north and west (such as Walland Marsh) that provide a detailed palaeoenvironmental archive (Tooley and Switsur 1988; Waller *et al.* 1988; Long and Innes 1993; 1995a; Waller 1994; Long and Hughes 1995; Long *et al.* 1996; Spencer 1997; Spencer *et al.* 1998a; 1998b; Long *et al.* 1998; Evans *et al.* 2001). This discrepancy results from a paucity of datable organic sediments seaward (i.e. south and east) of a protective gravel barrier (ridge 1) that runs from Broomhill through the Scotney Marsh area (Spencer 1997; Spencer *et al.* 1998a; 1998b). This barrier marks a significant divide in marshland stratigraphy (Long and Innes 1993). Sites to the north and west of the barrier, on Walland Marsh, contain extensive mid-Holocene peats. Sites to the south and east, such as Denge Marsh (Plater 1992; Plater and Long 1995; Plater *et al.* 1999), The Midrips, The Wicks and South Brooks (Long and Hughes 1995) have yielded no organic material suitable for dating or multiproxy biostratigraphic analysis.

Organic sediments have been recorded and dated in the Scotney Marsh trough (Spencer 1997; Spencer *et al.* 1998a; 1998b) and also at Wickmaryholm Pit (Long and Hughes 1995), but palaeoenvironmental interpretations of the area immediately outside the initial protective gravel barrier remain speculative. In this paper, we present palaeoenvironmental data from Scotney Marsh that clarify the evolution of marsh sediments seaward of the main back-barrier environment. In particular, we detail the infilling of a lowland gravel swale, the Scotney Marsh trough, that lies immediately to the south and east of ridge 1.

Testate Amoebae Palaeoenvironmental Reconstruction at Scotney Marsh

Spencer (1997) produced a palaeoenvironmental reconstruction for Scotney Marsh that utilised pollen and diatoms to reconstruct vegetation communities and the degree of freshwater/marine influence in the locale. Limited extrapolations of soil moisture conditions were also made, based on the ratio of aquatic to terrestrial species within each vegetation assemblage. However, although vegetation provides information on the *relative* wetness of the environment it cannot, at present, provide *quantitative* reconstructions in terms of absolute water table depth below ground. Additionally, pollen can be dispersed over considerable distances, so the fossil pollen assemblage at a site may incorporate pollen from the surrounding region, and is therefore not site-specific. Consequently, pollen may not be a reliable quantitative indicator of hydrological conditions at a site. At Scotney Marsh, quantitative hydrological information is critical to a full understanding of *in situ* vegetation and sedimentological histories and the evolution of the marsh sediments within the gravel swales. For example, periods of standing fresh water in the Scotney Marsh trough may be indicative of a rise in the local water table during a marine transgression (Spencer 1997). Absolute measures of water table depth may detail the magnitude of this rise and allow an evaluation of its impact upon local landscape development.

In contrast to pollen, there is little lateral movement of testate amoebae, and assemblages tend to be locally distributed (Tolonen *et al.* 1992; Charman *et al.* 2000). Thus, regional inputs are minimal and the fossil assemblage can be considered to be site-specific. Testate amoebae are microscopic animals, typically 20 μm – 250 μm in size, which inhabit the surface layers of peatlands and other moist soils. Testate amoebae possess an outer shell (the 'test') that encloses the cytoplasm and which is preserved after the organism's death (Fig. 4.2). Tests are constructed either from the secretion of pre-formed siliceous plates or from agglutinated particles derived from the surrounding substrate (commonly diatom frustules, silica and organic remains). Testate amoebae depend on water to live because they use an unprotected cell membrane for feeding (Warner 1990). As a result, their distribution and abundance is controlled by the availability of moisture and they are confined to thin water films between soil particles, plant leaves and roots where they feed on other micro-organisms as well as upon each other. The relationship between testate amoebae and moisture (especially water table depth) in freshwater peatlands has long been recognised (Harnisch 1927; Jung 1936; De Graaf 1956; Schönborn 1962; Meisterfeld 1977; Tolonen *et al.* 1992; 1994). Some species are restricted to bog pools, while others may thrive on relatively dry bog hummocks. Testate amoebae therefore have considerable potential as palaeohydrological indicators. Theoretically, testate amoebae are sensitive to seasonal hydrological changes; they reproduce asexually and produce several generations per year, although these have yet to be fully quantified (Charman *et al.* 2000). However, their seasonal sensitivity is reduced by encystment of the organism during short-term fluctuations in moisture, temperature or food supply (Charman *et al.* 2000), so that an assemblage is probably more reflective of mean annual conditions (although this remains uncertain – see Charman *et al.* 2000). Furthermore, a fossil sediment sample represents several cycles of life and death in the testate community (Charman *et al.* 2000), thereby dampening a seasonal signal.

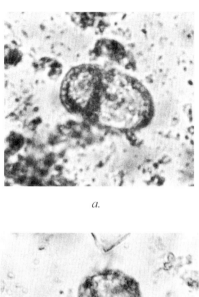

a.

b.

Fig. 4.2. Testate amoebae species recovered from core Q32. (a) Centropyxis platystoma (x 400 magnification) typical of wet conditions. (b) Cyclopyxix arcelloides (x 400 magnification), indicative of variable conditions from moderatley dry to shallow peatland pools.

Recently, transfer functions have been produced from testate amoebae to reconstruct fossil hydrological conditions on freshwater peatlands in terms of water table depth (Tolonen *et al.* 1985; Warner 1987; 1989; Woodland 1996; Woodland *et al.* 1998). A transfer function exemplifies the axiom 'the present is the key to the past'; it applies knowledge of modern species-environment relationships to reconstruct an environmental variable from the same species in a fossil assemblage. This study uses the transfer function of Woodland *et al.* (1998), which is based upon a strong relationship between testate amoebae taxa and water table depth below ground. The model is derived from 163 samples of testate amoebae collected from nine British mires. The hydrological relationship was modelled using a range of regression techniques and the model performance was tested for accuracy by comparing model-predicted water table depths with those measured at each sample location. The most accurate model was adopted for use in the transfer function. In terms of precision (or 'prediction error'), the transfer function used in this study allows the reconstruction of fossil water table depths with an error margin of ± 3.9 cm.

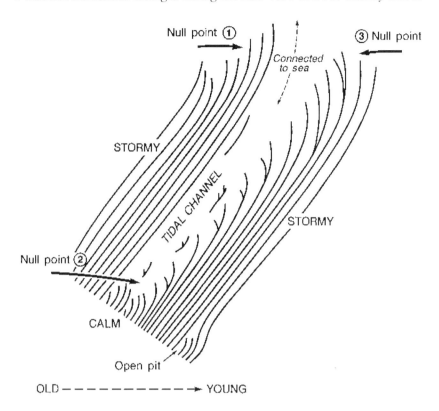

Fig. 4.3. Variable extension of gravel ridges (from Long and Hughes 1995).

The Chronology of Barrier Emplacement and the Evolution of Romney Marsh

The character, location and time of emplacement of ridge 1 (Fig. 4.1) was critical to the subsequent evolution of marsh sediments inland of the barrier. A consensus exists that ridge 1 extends north-eastward from Broomhill through Scotney Marsh (see Fig. 4.1). Minimum ages for the emplacement of this ridge are indicated by overlying peat deposits: at Broomhill, the base of the peat is dated to 3382–3345 cal. yr BP (Tooley and Switsur 1988) and at Scotney Marsh, *c.* 4000 cal. yr BP (Spencer 1997). However, the presence of salt marsh communities and the initiation of freshwater peat development at *c.* 6000 cal. yr BP on Walland Marsh would require barrier emplacement also at 6000 cal. yr BP (Waller *et al.* 1988; Long and Innes 1995a; 1995b; Long *et al.* 1996).

At Scotney Marsh a gravel trough separates ridge 1 from The Forelands ridge and the Lydd gravel complex (see Fig. 4.1). Seaward of ridge 1, deposition of alternating gravel and marsh sediments appears to relate to variable storm incidences (Long and Hughes 1995) and wave competence (Orford *et al.* 1991). Orford *et al.* (1991) explain how gravel entering a drift-aligned system moves down-drift until a reaching a null point where wave competence is insufficient to transport it further. During stormy periods, the null point migrates down-drift forming long gravel beaches; conversely, during periods of low storminess shorter beaches develop. Following a return to increased stormy conditions, longer gravel barriers then extend past the shorter ones, leaving a large gravel swale in their lee (Fig. 4.3). Long and Hughes (1995) use this model of variable distal extension to explain how the sequence of gravel ridges (e.g. The Forelands and Holmstone) and their intervening marsh sediments (e.g. The Midrips and South Brooks) evolved (Fig. 4.1).

Sedimentation in the intervening gravel swales occurred in conditions typical of tidal channels or inlets (Long and Hughes 1995; Spencer 1997; Spencer *et al.* 1998a; 1998b). Long and Hughes (1995) found no organic sediments present in these sequences. However, Spencer (1997) and Spencer *et al.* (1998a; 1998b) report organic sediments in the Scotney Marsh trough in core G60. These were interpreted as a buried 'open pit', dating to 3370–2970 cal. yr BP. Elsewhere within the Scotney Marsh trough, Spencer (1997) recorded organic sediments at *c.* +1.00 m OD, some 3 m above those recorded in G60. This paper reconstructs the palaeoenvironments of these upper peat deposits within the Scotney Marsh trough.

Study Area

The lithology for much of Scotney Marsh is presented in Spencer (1997) and Spencer *et al.* (1998a; 1998b), using information from 3400 boreholes arranged on a 25 m-interval grid. In the current study, the lithological map was extended south-eastward using data from a further

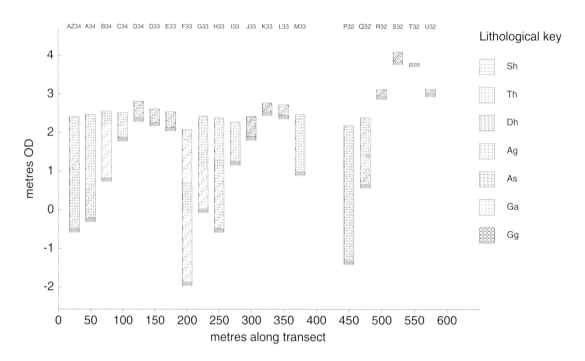

Fig. 4.4. *Stratigraphic transect across Scotney Marsh, incorporating the work of Spencer (1997).*

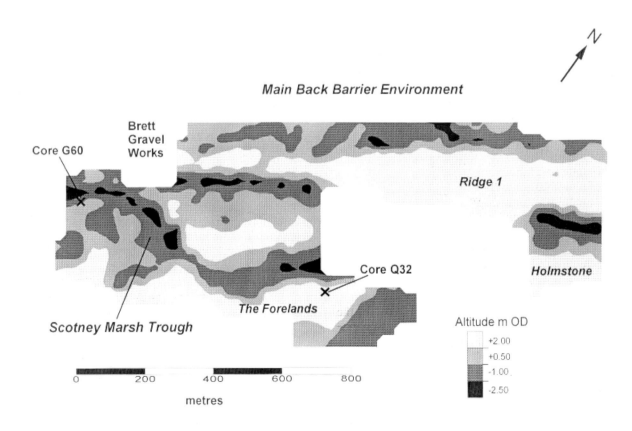

Fig. 4.5. *Contour plot of the gravel surface in the Scotney Marsh trough region, illustrating prominent ridges, troughs and stratotype cores (see Fig. 4.1 for location).*

200 boreholes arranged on the same grid in the region of Pigwell Farm (Fig. 4.1). By extending the stratigraphic information to the south and east of ridge 1, the upper peat units identified by Spencer (1997) can be investigated further to elucidate palaeoenvironmental evolution seaward of the main back-barrier environment.

Methodology

Stratigraphic data were collected using an Edelman auger and Eijkelkamp gouge corers, and sediments were described according to the classification scheme of Troels-Smith (1955). This scheme enables direct comparison to be made with sedimentological investigations completed by other workers in the Romney Marsh region. The altitudes of the boreholes were levelled to Ordnance Datum (equivalent to mean sea level, Newlyn) using a Sokkia optical level. The stratigraphic transect was created utilising TSPPlus (Waller *et al.* 1995) and the surface contour plots using SURFER.

A sample core was collected from Q32, where sediments typical of the stratigraphy of the Scotney Marsh trough were present. The core was collected using a modified piston corer and stored in plastic tubes to minimise disturbance to the sediments during transport. In the laboratory, the core was subsampled for diatom, pollen and testate amoebae analyses.

Samples for diatom and pollen analysis were prepared using standard techniques. Testate amoebae were prepared using Hendon and Charman (1997). Identifications of all microfossils were made at x400 and x600 magnifications under light microscopy. Diatom nomenclature follows Hartley (1986) and identifications were made using Van der Werff and Huls (1958–74) and Hendy (1964). Pollen identification is based on Moore *et al.* (1992), and testate amoebae identification follows Charman *et al.* (2000). A minimum of 200 pollen grains and 200 diatom valves were counted at each sample level and counts are expressed as a percentage of total land pollen (%TLP) and a percentage of total diatom valves (%TDV) respectively. The diatom and pollen diagrams (Figs. 4.6 and 4.7) were divided in to local assemblage zones using a visual inspection of the data, the basis for which was pronounced assemblage changes and ecological reasoning.

Testate amoebae are expressed as a percentage of the total tests counted. Normally, a minimum of 150 testate amoebae are counted at each level in freshwater peats (Woodland *et al.* 1998), but their low abundance at Scotney Marsh reduced the minimum count to 50 tests. Such impoverishment of the testate amoebae fauna has been encountered by other workers (Charman *et al.* 1998; Gehrels *et al.* 2001), where similarly low minima have been used. Low counts seem to impair quantitative reconstructions only if important indicator species are scarce (Woodland *et al.* 1998; Gehrels *et al.* 2001). This is not the case in the Scotney Marsh assemblage, where

rare species of <5% abundance (*Arcella catinus, Centropyxis aculeata, Pseudodifflugia fascicularis, Heleopera petricola*) are not strong hydrological indicators (Woodland *et al.* 1998; Charman *et al.* 2000). Only *Difflugia* species 1, for which no modern analogue exists, was excluded from the transfer function. This left 22 fossil species, from which the water table curve in Fig. 4.8 was derived.

The diagrams of diatom, pollen and testate amoebae assemblages were produced using the Tilia program of Grimm (1991); testate amoebae assemblage zones were derived from the CONISS computer program (Grimm 1987). Interpretation of the diatom assemblages was made following the schemes of Vos and de Wolf (1998; 1993) and Denys (1994). The diatom assemblages confirmed the freshwater provenance of the peats, allowing fossil water tables to be reconstructed from testate amoebae using the transfer function of Woodland *et al.* (1998). To produce a chronology for core Q32, two bulk samples of peat (5 cm thick) were removed from the undisturbed piston core and submitted to Beta Analytic for radiocarbon dating. The radiocarbon dates were calibrated to cal. yr BP using the CALIB3 program of Stuiver and Reimer (1993). They are presented in Table 4.1 alongside a summary of the contemporaneous sedimentary environment.

Results

Lithostratigraphy

A stratigraphic transect across Scotney Marsh is presented in Fig. 4.4. This combines Spencer's (1997) work (cores AZ34 – M33) with this study (cores P32 – U32). Each of the cores sampled in this study terminated at an impenetrable gravel unit. Fig. 4.5 shows the surface morphology of this unit, together with ridge 1 (cores C34 – E33), the north-eastern margin of The Forelands (cores R32 – U32) and another smaller, gravel feature (between cores J33 and L33). The Scotney Marsh trough forms a narrow topographic low between these two gravel ridges which widens to >500 m to the south-west (Spencer *et al.* 1998a).

A further gravel complex is present in the east of the study area (Fig. 4.5). This feature is the north-eastern margin of the Holmstone gravel complex, on which part of the town of Lydd is situated. Although not studied in detail here, fine grained sediments extending to *c.* -1.00 m OD are present between this gravel complex and The Forelands, suggesting the presence of another trough at the eastern margin of the study area. This sequence may relate to a later period of variable distal extension of the gravel beaches (Long and Hughes 1995).

Sediments overlying the gravel in the Scotney Marsh trough typically consist of four units, the local presence or absence of any of which is partially controlled by the underlying gravel morphology. The basal gravel (unit 1)

Table 4.1. Chronostratigraphic results for core Q32.

Site : Altitude *Laboratory Number* (Grid Reference)	Environment of deposition and the significance relative to sea-level and sediment type (Troels-Smith 1955)	^{14}C Age (Calibrated years BP±2 σ)	Uncalibrated radiocarbon age (± 1 σ)
Core Q32: +1.39 to +1.34 m OD *Beta-157460* (TR032204)	Salt marsh / freshwater reedswamp Transgressive contact (Sh2, Dh1, Th1, Dl+, As+)	1820 to 1510	1730 ± 70 BP
Core Q32: +0.79 to +0.74 m OD *Beta-157461* (TR032204)	Salt marsh / freshwater reedswamp Minimum age for gravel emplacement (Sh2, As1, Gg(maj)1, Dh+, Th^1+, Ag+)	2330 to 1900	2120 ± 80 BP

is overlain by unit 2: grey silty-clays, locally becoming sandy silts and occasionally containing gravel. Unit 2 occurs across the study area wherever the gravel morphology extends to sufficient depth. Unit 3 is a peat that typically passes transitionally into peaty-clay at both its upper and lower contacts. The unit encompasses peat deposits that vary between a well-humified peat and a peaty clay with localised gravel occurrences. The provenance of the gravels within the peaty clay remains unclear. However, gravel in similar sedimentary suites has been recorded in core G60 on Scotney Marsh (Spencer 1997; 1998a; 1998b) and at Wickmaryholm Pit (Long and Hughes 1995). At these sites it has been suggested that gravel may have slumped from the adjacent gravel outcrops, perhaps due to water percolation through the gravel under storm conditions or periods of high water level. Overlying unit 3 (where present), or unit 2 where the organic sediments are absent, is unit 4. The composition of this unit varies across the study area from an orange-grey oxidation mottled silty-clay, to a silty-sand. This unit passes transitionally into unit 5, a silty clayey topsoil which in places contains a significant gravel component where the gravel of unit 1 approaches the surface. The stratotype core, Q32, represents this four-fold stratigraphy and is described in Table 4.2.

Biostratigraphy

Diatoms

The diatoms show that the sediments in zone LDAZ Q32/1 (silts passing upwards into peaty-clays) were deposited under predominantly fresh to brackish water conditions. Upwards into LDAZ Q32/2, fresh to brackish diatoms continue to prevail, but the marine influence became increasingly prevalent towards the top of the zone. This is reflected by the transition from well-humified peat to silty gravel and silty clay. Clearly, fresh to brackish conditions dominated during the deposition of the peat sediments, and the presence of the *Melosira varians* diatom group of Vos and de Wolf (1988) indicates the presence of freshwater pools on the peat surface. During sediment

deposition in LDAZ Q32/1, the Scotney Marsh trough was isolated from marine influence, but during LDAZ Q32/2 a link to the open sea was established, introducing marine conditions.

Marine conditions increase throughout LDAZ Q32/3, as is demonstrated by significant increases in marine and brackish diatoms, and a corresponding fall in fresh and fresh-brackish taxa. In particular, increases in the *Melosira sulcata* group of Vos and de Wolf (1988) indicates that the silts and clays of this zone were deposited in a tidal channel / inlet. Similarly, high numbers of *Diploneis didyma*, of the *Navicular digitoradiata var. minima* group of Vos and de Wolf (1988), suggest that intertidal mudflats and creeks persisted during the deposition of these sediments, with fresh to brackish water inputs, perhaps at low tide.

Pollen

The assemblage in zone LPAZQ32/II (Fig. 4.7) records the replacement of a coastal reedswamp by a salt marsh during deposition of the peaty clay with gravels. The presence of aquatic taxa such as *Sparganium* suggest that pools of standing water were present on the salt marsh surface, and the diatoms indicate that these pools were fresh to brackish.

In zone LPAZQ32/III the reconstructed environment is of a coastal reedswamp, with wetland herb species in drier areas. Standing water at the site is indicated by high numbers of aquatic taxa. The environment became drier into zone LPAZQ32/IV this assemblage is interpreted as a sedge fen, although the presence of *Chenopodiaceae* and *Plantago maritima* indicate that a salt marsh community also persisted in the area.

Towards the top of the peat unit at a depth of 107.5 to 100.5 cm (+1.315 to +1.385 m OD) in zone LPAZQ32/V, *Poaceae* and *Cyperaceae* are dominant, and aquatic taxa increase upward. A corresponding decrease in herbs occurs as conditions become wetter. This probably reflects a rising water table in response to sea level rise, a relationship that has been demonstrated in other studies on Romney Marsh (Spencer 1997). Tidal inundation deposited silts

Table 4.2. Summary palaeoenvironmental history for Q32.

Altitude m (OD) (cm downcore)	Sediment type	Predominant diatoms	Predominant pollen	Predominant testate amoebae	Environment of deposition	Age cal. yr BP (^{14}C age)
+1.56 to +1.45 (83 to 94)	Orange-grey oxidation mottled silty-clay	Marine planktonic *Paralia sulcata* and *Pseudopodosira westii* are present throughout. High numbers of *Diploneis didyma*, *Eunotia monodon* and *Nitzschia punctata* are also present.	*Cyperaceae* dominate, with subordinate *Alnus*, *Corylus*, and *Poaceae*. Low but significant *Chenopodiaceae* and *Potamogeton*	Hygrophilous *Difflugia* sp. 1, *D. pristis* and *D. oblonga* dominate; *D. lucida* and *D.leidyi* significant. Low counts of drier taxa such as *Assulina muscorum*, *H. petricola*, *H. rosea*, *Corythion-Trinema* type.	Tidal mudflats dominated by marine to brackish conditions.	No data
+1.45 to +1.38 (94 to 101)	Gravel in a grey silty matrix	Fresh to fresh-brackish taxa (*Eunotia monodon*, *Gomphonema gracile*), dominate with subordinate numbers of brackish to marine taxa.	*Cyperaceae* and *Poaceae* strongly dominate with subordinate *Compositae* lig., *Chenopodiaceae* and *Potamogeton*	Hygrophilous *Difflugia* sp. 1 and *D. oblonga* dominant but declining to top of unit. *D. lucida*, *D. pristis* and *Amphitrema stenostoma* significant. Drier taxa absent, except for low counts of *A. muscorum*.	Increased marine influence, but still predominantly fresh-brackish conditions probably in a back-barrier lagoon.	No data
+1.38 to +1.08 (101 to 131)	Dark brown well-humified peat	Fresh to fresh-brackish taxa strongly dominate with very low numbers of brackish to brackish-marine taxa. A high value of *Melosira varians* is present in the middle of the unit.	*Cyperaceae* and *Poaceae* dominate. Aquatic taxa significant in upper and lower areas but low in the middle. *Chenopodiaceae* and *Plantago maritima* present throughout.	*D. pristis* dominant but declining to top of unit; *Centropyxis cassis* and *Cyclopyxis arcelloides* significant. *D. oblonga* increasing. Drier taxa absent except for sporadic counts of *Corythion-Trinema* type.	Coastal reedswamp gradually drying out becoming a sedge fen. An increase in aquatic taxa and salt marsh indicators demonstrating a rise in the water table.	1820 to 1510 (1730 ± 70 BP)
+1.08 to +0.95 (131 to 144)	Brown peaty-clay	Very strongly fresh to fresh-brackish, with *Eunotia monodon*, *Gomphonema gracile* and *Synedra ulna* the dominant species.	*Poaceae* and *Cyperaceae* dominate with high numbers of *Sparganium*.	Hygrophilous *D. pristis* dominant; increasing *D. oblonga* and *Centropyxis platystoma*. *C. arcelloides* and *C. cassis* declining. *Corythion-Trinema* type sporadic.	Fresh to fresh brackish conditions with coastal reedswamp vegetation.	No data
+0.95 to +0.74 (144 to 165)	Brown peaty-clay with some gravel	Very strongly fresh to fresh-brackish, with *Eunotia monodon*, *Gomphonema gracile* and *Synedra ulna* the dominant species.	*Poaceae* and *Cyperaceae* dominate with high numbers of *Chenopodiaceae* and *Sparganium*.	Hygrophilous *C. cassis* and *C. arcelloides* increasingly dominant. Sporadic counts of other species; drier taxa (*A. muscorum*, *H. rosea*, *Corythion-Trinema* type) rare.	Salt marsh conditions under fresh to fresh-brackish conditions.	2330 to 1900 (2120 ± 80 BP)
+0.74 to +0.66 (165 to 173)	Grey sandy silt with some clay	Very strongly fresh to fresh-brackish, with *Eunotia monodon*, *Gomphonema gracile* and *Synedra ulna* the dominant species.	No data	*D. pulex* significant. *D. pristis*, *Trigonopyxis arcula*, *Arcella discoides* and *C. platystoma* present in low counts.	Fresh to brackish conditions persisting at the margins of a tidal channel	No data
Below +0.66 (>173)	Gravel	No data	No data	No data	Storm beach	No data

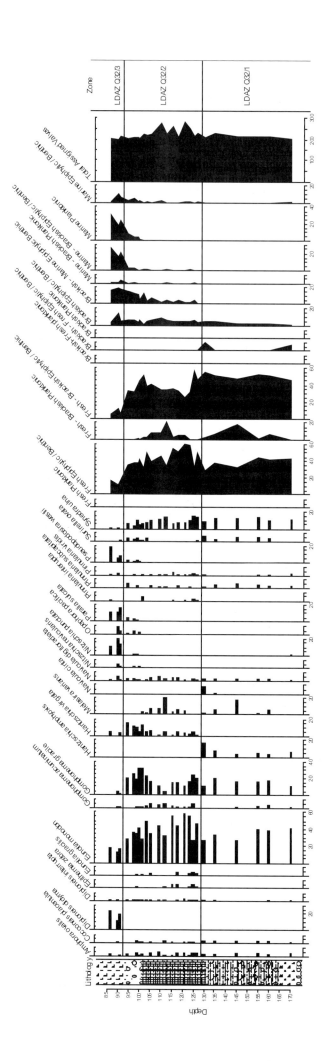

Fig. 4.6. Diatom diagram from core Q32 (see Fig. 4.4. for stratigraphic key).

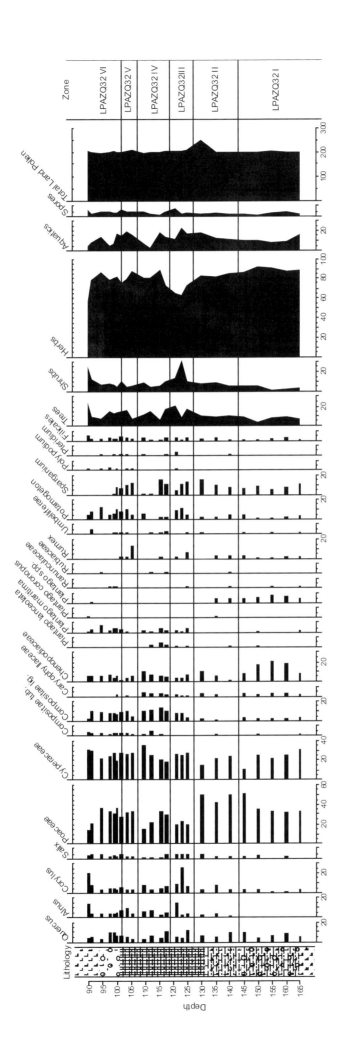

Fig. 4.7. Pollen diagram from core Q32 (see Fig. 4.4. for stratigraphic key).

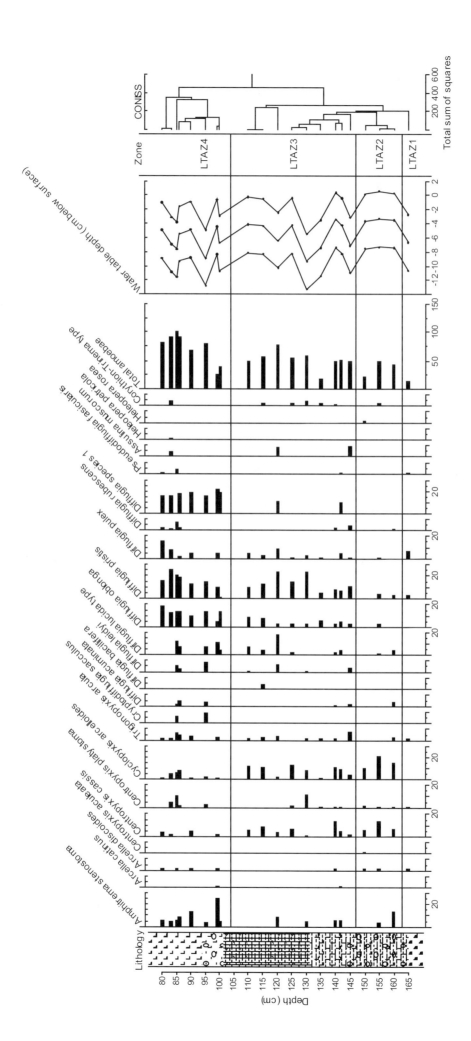

Fig. 4.8. Testate amoebae diagram from core Q32 (see Fig. 4.4. for stratigraphic key).

and gravels on top of the peat and this is evident with progression into zone LPAZQ32/VI. Relatively high levels of *Potamogeton* and salt marsh indicators suggest that where the vegetation persisted, environmental conditions were typical of a coastal reedswamp.

Testate Amoebae
Water table depths have been reconstructed to within ± 3.9 cm for the freshwater peat in core Q32, using the transfer function of Woodland *et al.* (1998). For the upper 20 cm of local testate amoebae assemblage zone, LTAZ4, 100 to 80 cm downcore (+1.39 to +1.59 m OD), the water table curve must be treated with caution, since the environment becomes increasingly marine, producing a poor match with the ombrotrophic peatlands from which the transfer functions were originally developed. Within marine environments, it is not known whether salinity exerts a stronger influence upon testate amoebae distribution and abundance than does moisture (Charman *et al.* 1998). A preliminary set of modern analogues exists for testate amoebae in salt marsh environments (Gehrels *et al.* 2001), but these relate to height above sea level and not to water table depth. This section of the water table curve must remain tentative, but good agreement does exist between the hydrological conditions derived from testate amoebae and the palaeoenvironment inferred from diatoms and pollen species (Table 4.2).

In Fig. 4.8, testate amoebae species are arranged according to water table depth, beginning with *Amphitrema stenostoma*, a species typical of bog pools, and ending with *Corythion-Trinema*, an indicator of dry or moderately dry conditions (Woodland *et al.* 1998; Charman *et al.* 2000). The basal zone, LTAZ1 between 173 and 165 cm downcore (+0.66 to +0.74 m OD), *contains Arcella discoides, Centropyxis platystoma, Difflugia pristis, D. pulex* and *Trigonopyxis arcula*. The reconstructed water table is 7 cm deep (i.e. 7 cm below ground surface), rising to –5.8 cm towards the top of LTAZ1.

LTAZ2, 165 to 209 cm (+0.74 to +0.93 m OD), is dominated by *Centropyxis cassis* and *C. arcelloides*, with occurrences of *Amphitrema stenostoma, Arcella catinus* and *A. discoides*. This suggests relatively wet conditions, with reconstructed water tables 3.5–5.8 cm deep. Drier taxa such as *Assulina muscorum, Heleopera rosea* and *Corythion-Trinema* type are rare. Species average eleven per sample, but test concentrations are comparatively low. This may be explained by episodes of higher energy in this zone (indicted by gravels within the peaty clay), which may have dislodged existing testate amoebae from substrates and prevented colonisation by others.

Zone LTAZ3 extends from 146 to 104 cm downcore (+0.93 to +1.35 m OD) and contains a marginally more diverse fauna of up to 12 species per sample, with higher counts of 50–100 individuals per sample. Within LTAZ3, species typical of wet conditions, such as *Amphitrema stenostoma, Difflugia pristis, Centropyxis cassis* and *Cyclopyxis arcelloides* are joined by intermediate species

such as *D. lucida;* drier taxa are again rare. Reconstructed water tables at the base of LTAZ3 average 4 cm deep, but the upper estimate indicates that surface water may be present (Fig. 4.8). This concurs with aquatic species in the pollen record and with the *Melosira varians* group of diatoms (Vos and de Wolf 1988). Between 140 and 130 cm downcore (+0.99 and +1.09 m OD), the water table deepens and this coincides with the replacement of a coastal reedswamp with a salt marsh. From 130 to 100 cm downcore (+1.09 to +1.39 m OD), the water table rises to approximately -4 cm and this is confirmed by high counts of aquatic pollen taxa (such as *Sparganium* and *Potamogeton*), and the diatom group *Melosira varians* (Vos and de Wolf 1988).

Zone LTAZ4, 104 to 80 cm downcore (+1.35 to -1.59 m OD) is dominated by *Difflugia pristis, D. oblonga* and '*Difflugia* species 1', which appears for the first time at 100 cm downcore (+1.39 m OD) and persists, albeit in declining numbers, to the top of the zone. *Amphitrema stenostoma* is also present, but decreases towards the top of the zone as the water table gradually deepens.

Overall, the testate amoebae of LTAZ4 indicate moderately wet conditions, during which the water table fluctuates around a depth of 5 cm. However, the assemblages and reconstructed water table within the uppermost 20 cm of LTAZ4 must be interpreted with caution in view of the increasing marine influence identified above. Within LTAZ4, a tentative exploration can be made of testate amoebae as indicators in salt marsh environments, following Charman *et al.* (1998) and Gehrels *et al.* (2001) and comparing the results with reconstructed vegetation and water chemistry. *Assulina muscorum* appears for the first time in core Q32 within LTAZ4. Charman *et al.* (1998) recorded this species on the highest parts of a salt marsh, and it may have occupied a similar position at Scotney Marsh. *D. pristis*, abundant in LTAZ4, occurs at intermediate elevations on a salt marsh (Charman *et al.* 1998; Gehrels *et al.* 2000). Evidence from testate amoebae therefore indicates a developing salt marsh within LTAZ4. This concurs with the marine influence recorded by the diatoms, and salt marsh taxa in the pollen record.

Comparability of Proxy Records
A number of general observations can be drawn from the detailed accounts presented above.

1. The match between all three proxy records is good in terms of the relative timing of shifts to wetter and drier conditions. The wetness peaks observed in the testate amoebae data match those recorded by the pollen and diatoms, notably during LPAZQ32 II and III, where the rising water table is matched by increases in aquatic pollen.

2. With the exception of the upper 20 cm of zone LTAZ4, water table fluctuations can be quantified and their fluctuation resolved more clearly in the testate amoebae

record than in the pollen and diatom records. In particular, the testate amoebae provide a site-specific reconstruction, compared to the regionally dampened pollen signature.

3. Even within the upper 20 cm of zone LTAZ4, where the marine influence becomes greater and where a cautionary interpretation of the reconstructed water table is advised, the match between all three proxies is good. In some cases, the testate amoebae may provide additional information regarding the salt marsh environment. For example, the pollen in LPAZQ32 VI records a developing salt marsh, and the testate amoebae further suggest that the sediments are from the middle or upper reaches of that salt marsh.

Discussion

The Palaeoenvironmental History of the Scotney Marsh Trough

A minimum age for gravel emplacement of 3370–2970 cal. yr BP in the Scotney Marsh trough is provided by the buried open pit sediments described by Spencer *et al.* (1998a). Within the trough, there existed an open pit with a shallow freshwater pond, fringed by salt marsh and reedswamp (Spencer 1997; Spencer *et al.* 1998a; 1998b). Elsewhere within the trough, conditions must have been relatively dry to allow peat forming communities to persist at one of the lowest points in the Scotney Marsh trough. The peats were eventually inundated and silts and gravels deposited as the trough became an environment typical of a tidal inlet. This event is dated to 3375–3070 cal. yr BP. This period of tidal inlet sedimentation in the trough appears to have been of short duration, as peat forming communities briefly returned before again being replaced by tidal inlet sedimentation (Spencer 1998a). Within the trough silts were deposited close to the tidal limit, with access to the open sea indicated by the dominance of the marine diatom *Paralia sulcata* (Spencer 1998a).

Tidal inlet deposits gradually infilled the gravel swale of the Scotney Marsh trough. Eventually the trough became cut off from the marine influence and became increasingly fresh to fresh-brackish (LDAZ Q32/1). This may have been due to continued barrier development to the south and east that isolated the Scotney Marsh trough from direct marine influence, probably the deposition of the Lydd gravel complex abutting ridge 1. This isolation allowed colonisation of peat forming communities along the margins. The onset of peat accumulation is dated here at 2330–1900 cal. yr BP at a depth of +0.74 to +0.79 m OD, the sediments being deposited on a salt marsh (LPAZQ32 I). As deposition continued, coastal reedswamp developed, characterised by grasses, sedges and aquatic taxa (LPAZQ32 II). Coastal reedswamp persisted at the site as peaty-clay gave way to peat. The testate amoebae confirm a relatively high water table (-4 cm) at the base of this zone, after which the water table deepened to -9 cm, and

recovered quickly to -4 cm. The slight drying of the ground surface may account for the increased occurrences of wetland herbs (as distinct from aquatic taxa indicative of standing water) at the site during LPAZQ32 III. Fresh to fresh-brackish conditions prevailed, demonstrating that the area was largely isolated from direct marine influence. In LPAZQ32 IV, an assemblage typical of a sedge fen is recorded at +1.315 to +1.25 m OD. The testate amoebae record a relatively stable water table depth of -4 cm.

A rising water table, in response to sea level rise, is indicated by aquatic pollen taxa in LPAZQ32 V. A slight rise in water table to -3.5 cm is indicated by the testate amoebae, before the marine inundation clouds the re-constructed water tables. Increases in marine-brackish and marine diatoms are also recorded at this level. By 1820–1510 cal. yr BP, at an altitude of +1.34 to +1.39 m OD, peat forming communities were inundated and a silty gravel was deposited in predominantly fresh to brackish conditions, although the marine input gradually increases into LDAZ Q32/2. Elsewhere in the locality, salt marsh and coastal reedswamp vegetation prevailed (as demonstrated by salt marsh indicators and aquatic species in the pollen assemblage), whilst minerogenic sediment persisted at this site. Into LDAZ Q32/3 silts and clays were deposited in predominantly marine to brackish conditions.

This record demonstrates a negligible marine influence during peat deposition, after which the marine influence progressively increased to such a point that a protective barrier was overtopped, allowing brackish water to inundate the site. It is unlikely that inundation was as a result of a catastrophic storm overtopping the protective gravel barrier, because a gradual increase in marine influence is recorded in the diatom record. Sea-level continued to rise as the upper silts and clays were deposited.

Wider Landscape Evolution

Research into the evolution of the main back-barrier environment to the north and west of ridge 1 has demonstrated that, following the initial gravel barrier emplacement, the area was gradually infilled with sediments deposited under tidal conditions (Tooley and Switsur 1988; Long and Innes 1995a). Eventually, these sediments became sub-aerially exposed and peat forming communities were able to establish and spread across the marsh, firstly in the back-marsh (Brede Valley, 7180–6445 cal. yr BP; Waller *et al.* (1988)) and then at Rye (6503–6213 cal. yr BP, Long *et al.* (1996)). Tidal sedimentation continued throughout this time in the mid-marsh and fore-marsh until the landscape here became sub-aerially exposed and colonised by saltmarsh and then freshwater peat forming communities (e.g. at Brookland, 5046–4861 cal. yr BP; Long and Innes (1995a)) and at Midley (4143–3896 cal. yr BP; Long and Innes (1993)). In the main back-barrier environment, peat forming communities did not colonise the tidal mudflats abutting ridge 1 until *c.* 4000 cal. yr BP in the Scotney Marsh area (Spencer 1997; Spencer *et al.* 1998a; 1998b) and 3817–3622 cal. yr BP at Broomhill (Tooley and Switsur 1988).

The emplacement of ridge 1 is dated to *c.* 6000 cal. yr BP. After this, a period of relatively low intensity storms (and consequently low competence waves) led to the accumulation of gravel beaches with significantly less distal extension relative to ridge 1; these ridges may be currently exposed in the region of the Midrips. Wave competence apparently increased, probably as a result of increased storm intensity, leading to the increased distal extension of gravel beaches and the deposition of The Forelands gravel complex. The succeeding gravel ridges extend past the shorter ones and are, therefore, wrapped around them; this had the effect of changing the orientation of the gravel ridges.

Eddison (1983) noted that each of the gravel ridge complexes is orientated 10° nearer to the north than the previous group (see Fig. 4.1) and suggested that this rotation must have started offshore in Rye Bay, but that evidence of this has subsequently been removed. Eddison (1983) also suggested that this altered orientation reflects the origin of the ness shape. Therefore, it is suggested here that the origin of the ness shape was a result of variable storm incidences that caused succeeding areas of shorter and longer distal extension of the gravel beaches. Each period of distal extension would have wrapped beaches around the preceding shorter beaches, thus bringing the orientation of the longer beaches nearer to the north.

The timing of these changes is uncertain, although minimum ages are available, either by the dating of overlying organic sediments (*e.g.* at Wickmaryholm Pit, Long and Hughes (1995)) or via archaeological evidence (Needham 1988). In Scotney Marsh trough, lying immediately seaward of ridge 1, the buried open pit sediments provide a minimum age for the emplacement of The Forelands gravel complex (see Fig. 4.9). The fact that peat forming communities existed here, dating to 3370–2970 cal. yr BP (Spencer 1997; Spencer *et al.* 1998a; 1998b), implies that The Forelands gravel complex was already in place by *c.* 3300 cal. yr BP, if not before this date. Sediments deposited under tidal conditions subsequently inundated the peat communities. The inundation of this (now buried) open pit may have been the result of continued sea-level rise sufficient to overtop the barrier that had isolated the Scotney Marsh trough from the open sea.

Throughout peat development in the open pit and its subsequent inundation, peat forming vegetation proliferated immediately to the north of ridge 1 in the main back-barrier environment. These sediments record a succession from salt marsh, coastal reedswamp and freshwater pools to sedge fen with localised alder carr (Waller *et al.* 1999). Subsequently salt marsh, and eventually tidal conditions, replaced the freshwater peat forming communities; this transgressive contact is dated to some time after 2710–2585 or 2510–2320 cal. yr BP (Spencer 1997; Spencer *et al.* 1998a; 1998b). Two separate periods of inundation are, therefore, recorded; firstly of the open pit sediments in the Scotney Marsh trough and, some *c.* 1000 to 600 years later, of the peats immediately north of ridge 1 in the main back-barrier environment. This may reflect continued sea-level rise throughout this time, initially to a level where tidal conditions reached the Scotney Marsh trough, then inundating the peat forming communities adjacent to ridge 1 in the main back-barrier environment.

The sediments that overlie the peat immediately north of ridge 1 were deposited in fresh-brackish to brackish conditions (Spencer 1997; Spencer *et al.* 1998a; 1998b). Similar conditions are recorded in the Scotney Marsh trough in the lowermost sediments of core Q32, where salt marsh and coastal reedswamp prevailed at 2330–1900 cal. yr BP. Throughout the deposition of the upper peats in the Scotney Marsh trough, minerogenic sedimentation prevailed immediately to the north of ridge 1 in the main back-barrier environment. The palaeoenvironmental reconstruction of these sediments is problematical because diatoms are absent (Spencer *et al.* 1998b). This could be due either to non-deposition or to post-depositional dissolution of biogenic silica (Mayer *et al.* 1991). The development of peat in the Scotney Marsh trough at this time demonstrates that certain locations, typically at the margins, were now sub-aerially exposed allowing peat forming communities to colonise. The Scotney Marsh trough was cut off from the influence of the sea, as demonstrated by the lack of marine diatoms, probably as a result of continued barrier emplacement to the south and east.

It is suggested here that the geomorphological characteristics of the Scotney Marsh trough altered throughout the development of these upper sediments. During, and for some time following the emplacement of ridge 1, marine conditions gained access to the Scotney Marsh trough from the south and east, around the distal end of the Forelands gravel complex (see Fig. 4.5). However, by the time the upper peat was deposited in the Scotney Marsh trough (2330–1900 cal. yr BP) additional gravel ridges had been deposited to the south east (perhaps even the Lydd gravel complexes of Holmstone and West Ripe) providing a considerable barrier to the sea from this direction. Any access to the sea must, therefore, have been from the north to north-west over ridge 1. Ridge 1 was, therefore, providing protection from marine influences and it enabled succession from coastal reedswamp to sedge fen to occur at site Q32 (Fig. 4.9).

Peat accumulation eventually ended at 1820–1510 cal. yr BP due to a marine incursion that overtopped ridge 1 and caused minerogenic sedimentation to resume in the Scotney Marsh trough. Variable dates exist for peat inundation. Mid- to fore-marsh sites were inundated relatively early, for example 2569–2474 cal. yr BP at Midley (Long and Innes 1993) and *c.* 2700 cal yrs BP in Scotney Marsh (Spencer 1997; Spencer *et al.* 1998a; 1998b). Somewhat later, sites in the back-marsh such as

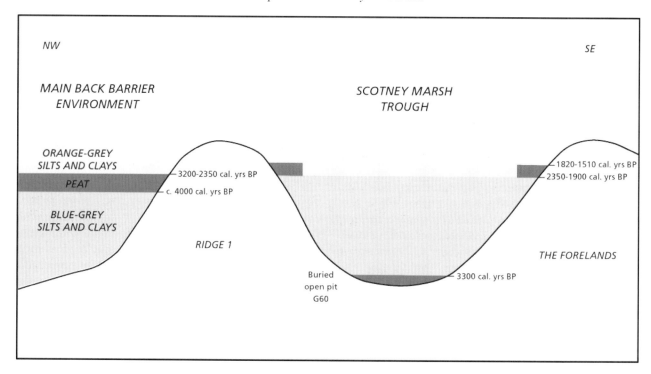

Fig. 4.9. Representation of the Scotney Marsh sedimentary succession.

Brookland (1890–1630 cal. yr BP, Long and Innes (1995a)) and the Brede valley (1938–1543 cal. yr BP, Waller *et al.* (1988)) were inundated. The overtopping of ridge 1 corresponds well with these later dates (1820–1510 cal. yr BP).

This process was not catastrophic; rather, a gradual increase in marine conditions is recorded in the trough. Brackish and brackish-marine diatoms gradually increase, as do aquatic pollen taxa; reconstructed water tables from testate amoebae are also in agreement. The presence of gravel within the silts that overly the peats further supports the hypothesis of barrier overtopping being responsible for peat inundation. The upper sediments record the transition from a fresh-brackish environment to a marine-brackish environment under increasingly marine conditions.

Application of Testate Amoebae to the Study Area

This paper presents the first application of testate amoebae in late Holocene sea level studies in the Romney Marsh region. Good agreement between moisture conditions reconstructed from testate amoebae and the changes recorded by pollen and diatoms suggest the technique has some potential for reconstructing palaeoenvironments here.

Improved resolution and a smaller margin of error in the water table reconstructions may be achieved through a better match between the modern species used to produce the transfer functions, and fossil species. The transfer functions applied in this paper, for example, were derived from oligotrophic, ombrotrophic peat (Woodland *et al.* 1998). Collection of hydrological data and modern species from modern environments analogous to the palaeoenvironments recorded in core Q32 is now necessary. Expanded knowledge of modern testate amoebae species' ecology on salt marshes (e.g. Charman *et al.* 1998; Gehrels *et al.* 2000) will go some way toward providing a better match between modern and fossil taxa in such environments.

Conclusions

The Scotney Marsh trough is situated immediately seaward of the main back-barrier environment and has existed for longer than, and has been sheltered by, sediments subsequently deposited to the south and east. As a result, this site preserves a record of palaeoenvironmental changes immediately seaward of the main back-barrier environment. It also contains datable organic sediments that provide a chronology for geomorphological change in this area. The alternating sequences of marsh sediments and gravel ridges have been linked to variable distal extension as a result of changes in wave competence. It is proposed here that this process also led to the origin of the ness shape described by Eddison (1983).

Following gravel emplacement, two periods of peat accumulation are recorded in the Scotney Marsh trough, separated by sediments deposited under tidal channel conditions. Deposition of the basal peats in the Scotney Marsh trough would have required protection from marine incursions by The Forelands gravel complex. The date of the basal peat (*c.* 3300 cal. yr BP) provides a minimum age for emplacement of this gravel complex.

Throughout the deposition of the basal peat and the overlying tidal channel sediments, marine access to the trough was from the south and east. However, the site eventually became isolated from the open sea, probably as a result of continued ridge accumulation, perhaps even of the Lydd Gravel complex. This allowed fresh to fresh-brackish conditions to persist in the Scotney Marsh trough and peat forming communities began to colonise the margins at 2330–1900 cal. yr BP. These were eventually replaced by minerogenic sedimentation at 1820–1510 cal. yr BP. Inundation is thought to be a result of sea-level rise

such that ridge 1 was overtopped, allowing brackish and eventually marine-brackish conditions to dominate the Scotney Marsh trough.

Acknowledgements
The authors wish to acknowledge the support of the Romney Marsh Research Trust both for the financial and logistical support enabling this work to be completed. Special thanks are also extended to Dorothy and Robert Beck for their invaluable local knowledge in gaining access to field areas, and to Richard Mourne and Richard Delacour who assisted in the initial stratigraphic surveys and Andy Plater and Claire Meyers who assisted in the collection of the sample core.

References

Charman, D.J., Roe, H.M. and Gehrels, W.R. 1998. The use of testate amoebae in studies of sea-level change: a case study from the Taff estuary, South Wales, UK, *The Holocene* **8**, 209–18.

Charman, D.J., Hendon, D. and Woodland, W.A. 2000. The identification of testate amoebae (Protozoa:Rhizopoda) in peats, *Quaternary Research Association Technical Guide no. 9*. Quaternary Research Association.

Chiverell, R.C. 2000. A proxy record of late Holocene climate change from May Moss, northeast England, *The Holocene* **16**, 9–29.

De Graaf, F. 1956. Studies on Rotaria and Rhizopoda from the Netherlands, *Biologisch Jaarboek Dodonea* **23**, 145–217.

Denys, L. 1994. Diatom assemblages along a former intertidal gradient: a palaeoecological study of a subboreal clay layer (Western Coastal Plain, Belgium), *Netherlands Journal of Aquatic Ecology* **28**, 85–96.

Eddison, J. 1983. The evolution of barrier beaches between Fairlight and Hythe, *Geographical Journal* **149**, 39–75.

Eddison, J. (ed.) 1995. *Romney Marsh: The Debatable Ground* (Oxford University Committee for Archaeology Monograph **41**), Oxford.

Eddison, J. and Green, C. (eds) 1988. *Romney Marsh: Evolution, Occupation, Reclamation* (Oxford University Committee for Archaeology Monograph **24**). Oxford.

Evans, J.R., Kirkby, J.R. and Long, A.J. 2001. The litho- and biostratigraphy of a late Holocene tidal channel in Romney Marsh, southern England, *Proceedings of the Geologists' Association* **112**, 111–30.

Gehrels, W.R., Roe, H.M. and Charman, D.J. 2001. Foraminifera, testate amoebae and diatoms as sea-level indicators in UK saltmarshes: a quantitative multi-proxy approach, *Journal of Quaternary Science* **16**, 201–20.

Grimm, E.C. 1987. CONISS: a Fortran 77 program for stratigraphically constrained cluster analysis by the method of incremental sum of squares, *Computers and Geoscience* **13**, 13–55.

Grimm, E.C. 1991. *TILIA and TILIAGRAPH Software*. Illinois State Museum.

Harnisch, O. 1927. Einigie Daten zur rezenten und fossil testacean Rhizopden-Fauna der Sphagnen, *Archiv fur Hyrobiologie* **18**, 246–360.

Hartley, B. 1986. A checklist of the freshwater, brackish and marine diatoms of the British Isles and adjoining coastal waters, *Journal of the Marine Biological Association* **66**, 531–610.

Hendon, D. and Charman, D.J. 1997. The preparation of testate amoebae (Protozoa:Rhizopoda) samples from peat, *The Holocene* **7**, 199–205.

Hendy, N.I. 1964. *An Introductory Account of the Smaller Algae of British Coastal Waters. Part V: Bacillariophyceae (Diatoms)*. Fisheries Investigation Series, **I**. H.M.S.O., London.

Jung, W. 1936. Thekamöben ursprünlicher, lebender deutscher Hochmoore, *Abhandlungen Landesmuseum der Provinz Westfalen Museum für Naturkunde* **7**, 1–87.

Long, A.J. and Innes, J.B. 1993. Holocene sea-level changes and coastal sedimentation in Romney Marsh, southeast England, UK, *Proceedings of the Geologists' Association* **104**, 223–37.

Long, A.J. and Hughes, P.D.M. 1995. Mid- and Late-Holocene evolution of the Dungeness Foreland, United Kingdom, *Marine Geology* **124**, 253–71.

Long, A.J. and Innes, J.B. 1995a. The back-barrier and barrier depositional history of Romney Marsh and Dungeness, Kent, *Journal of Quaternary Science* **10**, 267–83.

Long, A.J. and Innes, J.B. 1995b. A palaeoenvironmental investigation of the 'Midley Sand' and associated deposits at the Midley Church Bank, Romney Marsh, in J. Eddison (ed.) *Romney Marsh: The Debatable Ground* (Oxford University Committee for Archaeology **41**), 37–50. Oxford.

Long, A.J., Plater, A.J., Waller, M.P. and Innes, J.B. 1996. Holocene coastal sedimentation in the Eastern English Channel: new data from the Romney Marsh region, United Kingdom, *Marine Geology* **136**, 97–120.

Long, A.J., Waller, M., Hughes, P. and Spencer, C.D. 1998. The Holocene depositional history of Romney Marsh proper, in J. Eddison, M. Gardiner and A. Long (eds) *Romney Marsh: Environmental Change and Human Occupation in a Coastal*

Lowland (Oxford University Committee for Archaeology **46**), 45–63. Oxford

Mayer, L.M., Jorgensen, J. and Schnitker, D. 1991. Enhancement of diatom frustule dissolution by iron oxides, *Marine Geology* **99**, 263–66.

Meisterfeld, R. 1977. Die horizontale und vertikale Verteilung der Testaceen (Rhizopoden, Testacea) in Sphagnum, *Archive für Hydrobiologie* **79**, 319–56.

Moore, P.D., Webb, J.A. and Collinson, M.E. 1992. *Pollen Analysis*. Oxford.

Needham, S. 1988. A group of Early Bronze Age axes from Lydd, in Eddison J. and C. Green (eds), *Romney Marsh: Evolution, Occupation, Reclamation*, (Oxford University Committee for Archaeology **24**), 77–82. Oxford.

Orford, J.D., Carter, R.W.G. and Jennings, S.C. 1991. Coarse clastic barrier environments: evolution and implications for Quaternary sea-level interpretation, *Quaternary International* **9**, 87–104.

Plater, A.J. 1992. The late Holocene evolution of Denge Marsh, south-east England: a stratigraphic, sedimentological and micropalaeontological approach, *The Holocene* **2**, 63–70.

Plater, A.J. and Long, A.J. 1995. The morphology and evolution of Denge Beach and Denge Marsh, in J. Eddison (ed.) *Romney Marsh: The Debatable Ground* (Oxford University Committee for Archaeology **41**), 8–36. Oxford.

Plater, A.J., Long A.J., Spencer, C.D. and Delacour, R.A.P. 1999. The stratigraphic record of sea-level change and storms during the last 2000 years: Romney Marsh southeast England, *Quaternary International* **55**, 17–27.

Shennan, I. 1980. Flandrian sea-level changes in Fenland (unpublished Ph.D. thesis, University of Durham).

Shennan, I. 1986a. Flandrian sea-level change in the Fenland I: The geographical setting and evidence of relative sea-level changes, *Journal of Quaternary Science* **1**, 119–54.

Shennan, I. 1986b. Flandrian sea-level changes in the Fenland. II. Tendencies of sea-level movement, altitudinal changes, and local and regional factors, *Journal of Quaternary Science* **1**, 155–79.

Schonborn, W. 1962. Zur Ökologie der sphagnikolen, bryokolen un terrikolen Testaceen, *Limnologica* **1**, 231–54.

Spencer, C.D. 1997. The Holocene evolution of Romney Marsh: a record of sea-level change (unpublished Ph.D. thesis, University of Liverpool).

Spencer, C.D., Plater, A.J. and Long, A.J. 1998a. Rapid coastal change during the mid- to late-Holocene: the record of barrier estuary sedimentation in the Romney Marsh region, southeast England, *The Holocene* **8**, 143–63.

Spencer, C.D., Plater, A.J. and Long, A.J. 1998b. Holocene barrier estuary formation: the sedimentary record of the Walland Marsh region, in J. Eddison, M. Gardiner and A. Long (eds) *Romney Marsh: Environmental Change and Human Occupation in a Coastal Lowland* (Oxford University Committee for Archaeology **46**), 13–29. Oxford.

Stuiver, M. and Reimer, P.J. 1993. Extended C^{14} data base and revised CALIB 3.0 C^{14} age calibration program, *Radiocarbon* **35**, 215–30.

Tolonen, K. 1986. Rhizopod analysis, in Berglund, B.E. (ed.), *Handbook of Holocene Palaeoecology and Palaeohydrology*. John Wiley, 645–666. Chichester.

Tolonen, K., Warner, B.G. and Vasander, H. 1992. Ecology of testaceans (Protozoa:Rhizopoda) in mires in southern

Finland: I. Autecology, *Archiv für Protistenkunde* **142**, 119–38.

Tolonen, K., Warner, B.G. and Vasander, H. 1994. Ecology of testaceans (Protozoa:Rhizopoda) in mires in southern Finland: II. Multivariate analysis, *Archiv für Protistenkunde* **144**, 97–112.

Tooley, M.J. 1978. *Sea-level Changes: North-west England During the Flandrian Stage*. Clarendon Press, Oxford.

Tooley, M.J. and Switsur, R. 1988. Water level changes and sedimentation during the Flandrian Age in the Romney Marsh area, in J. Eddison and C. Green (eds) *Romney Marsh: Evolution, Occupation, Reclamation* (Oxford University Committee for Archaeology **24**), 53–71. Oxford.

Troels-Smith, J. 1955. Characteristics of Unconsolidated Sediments, *Geological Survey of Denmark, IV Series*, **3** (1–71).

Van der Werff, H. and Huls, H. 1958–74. *Diatomeenflora van Nederland*. 8 parts. Published privately: De Hoef, The Netherlands.

Vos, P.C. and de Wolf, H. 1988. Methodological aspects of palaeo-ecological diatom research in coastal areas of the Netherlands, *Geologie en Mijnbouw* **67**, 31–40.

Vos, P.C and de Wolf, H 1993. Diatoms as a tool for reconstructing sedimentary environments in coastal wetlands: methodological aspects, *Hydrobiologia* **269/79**, 285–96.

Waller, M.P. 1994. Flandrian vegetational history of southeastern England. Stratigraphy of the Brede valley and pollen data from Brede Bridge, *New Phytologist* **126**, 369–92.

Waller, M.P. 1994b. The Fenland Project, Number 9: Flandrian Environmental Change in Fenland. *East Anglian Archaeological Monograph* **70**, 1–353.

Waller, M.P., Long, A.J., Long, D. and Innes, J. 1999. Patterns and processes in the development of coastal mire vegetation: Multi-site investigations from Walland Marsh, Southeast England, *Quaternary Science Reviews* **18**, 1419–44.

Waller, M., Burrin, P.J. and Marlow, A. 1988. Flandrian sedimentation and palaeoenvironments in Pett Level, the Brede and lower Rother valleys and Walland Marsh, in J. Eddison and C. Green (eds) *Romney Marsh: Evolution, Occupation, Reclamation* (Oxford University Committee for Archaeology **24**), 3–30. Oxford.

Waller, M., Entwistle, J.A. and Duller, G.A.T. 1995 TSPPlus – A menu driven program for the display of stratigraphic data, *Quaternary Newsletter* **99**, 32–39.

Warner, B.G. 1987. Abundance and diversity of testate amoebae (Rhizopoda, Testacea) in *Sphagnum* peatlands in southwestern Ontario, Canada, *Archiv für Protistenkunde* **133**, 173–89.

Warner, B.G. 1989. Fossil testate amoebae (Protozoa) and hydrological history of an ombrotrophic bog in northwestern Ontario, Canada. *Proceedings of the International Symposium on Peat / Peatland Characteristics and Uses*. Bemidjii State Univeristy, Bemidjii, Minnesota, 5–14.

Warner, B.G. 1990. Testate amoebae (Protozoa). Methods in Quaternary ecology no.5, *Geoscience Canada* **5**, 65–74.

Woodland, W.A. 1996. Holocene palaeohydrology from testate amoebae: developing a model for British peatlands (unpublished Ph.D. thesis, University of Plymouth).

Woodland, W.A., Charman, D.J. and Sims, P.C. 1998. Quantitative estimates of water tables and soil moisture in Holocene peatlands from testate amoebae, *The Holocene* **8**, 261–73.

Romney Marsh: Coastal and Landscape Change through the Ages
(ed. A. Long, S. Hipkin and H. Clarke), OUSA Monograph 56, 2002, 75–83

5. Reconstructing Late Holocene Intertidal Environments and Channel Networks: A Review of the Role of Benthic Foraminifera Biostratigraphy on Romney Marsh

John Evans and Jason Kirby

Diatom and pollen data form the basis for most palaeoenvironmental reconstructions of late Holocene depositional environments on Romney Marsh, southern England. In comparison, benthic foraminifera, a fully and marginal marine meiofaunal group, are seldomly used. This short review evaluates the palaeoenvironmental use of benthic foraminifera retrieved from channel, mudflat and saltmarsh facies from Romney Marsh. These records are compared with the more established reconstructions, in particular those based on diatom data. We argue that benthic foraminiferal-based interpretations correlate only broadly with these other reconstructions. Moreover, improved preservation and greater palaeoenvironmental sensitivity, mean that foraminifera offer great potential in late Holocene palaeogeographic and sea-level studies. In particular, we advocate the use of a combination of benthic foraminiferal analyses, diatom, pollen and other techniques, to provide more precise and robust palaeoenvironmental reconstructions from the region.

Introduction

Tidal channels have long been recognised as central elements of the past coastal landscapes of Romney Marsh. Indeed, the fields of sedimentology (e.g. Wass 1995; Evans *et al.* 2001), biostratigraphy (e.g. Spencer *et al.* 1998a; 1998b), lithostratigraphy (e.g. Tooley and Switsur 1988; Long and Innes 1993; 1995; Spencer *et al.* 1998a; 1998b), geoarchaeology, (Allen and Rippon 1997) and history (Gardiner 1988; Eddison 1983; 1998) have all endeavoured to provide information relating to the evolutionary history of coastal channels in wetland and estuarine environments. Despite this work, there has been only a limited use of biostratigraphic data (especially foraminifera) to reconstruct the depositional history of former drainage and tidal channels in Romney Marsh (Tooley and Switsur 1988; Waller *et al.* 1988; Waller 1994, Wass 1995; Evans *et al.* 2001).

The potential of foramainifera for reconstructing past coastal environments is now well established, both in the U.K. and abroad, either in conjunction with or as an alternative to diatoms (e.g. Haslett *et al.* 1998a; 1998b;

Horton *et al.* 1999; Gehrels *et al.* 2001; Scott and Medioli 1978; 1986). As demonstrated by Scott and Medioli (1978; 1986), foraminifera can be used as indicators of past sea-level owing to their occurrence in vertical zones representing particular tide levels on modern saltmarshes. Thus, Haslett *et al.* (1998a) used foraminifera to reconstruct Holocene sea-level change in the Severn Estuary and Somerset Levels, based on a knowledge of modern saltmarsh foraminifera distributions in the Severn Estuary (Haslett *et al.* 1998b). In addition, Horton *et al.* (1999) provided a quantitative assessment of intertidal foraminiferal data around the U.K. for sea-level studies. Using relative data from ten sites in the U.K., Horton *et al.* (1999) identified a strong relationship between the distribution of foraminifera in the intertidal environments and the altitude and frequency of intertidal exposure. Horton *et al.* (1999) divided the foraminiferal distributions into a high and middle marsh zone (e.g. *Jadammina macrescens* (Brady), *Trochammina inflata* (Montagu) and *Miliammina fusca* (Brady), and a low-marsh and tidal flat zone dominated by calcareous species (e.g. *Elphidium*

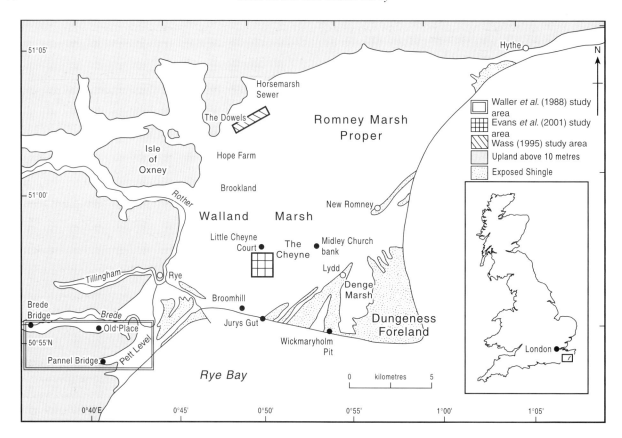

Fig. 5.1. Location map showing Romney and Walland Marsh region. Locations reviewed in text are denoted by boxes.

williamsoni Haynes, *Haynesina germanica* (Ehrenberg)). More recently, Gehrels *et al.* (2001) assessed the use of foraminifera, testate amoebae and diatoms as sea-level indicators at three sites in the U.K. Although this study concluded that diatoms and testate amoebae were the most precise sea-level indicators, the results of this, and the other studies referred to above, show that foraminifera offer much potential for the reconstruction of landscape evolution and sea-level change on Romney Marsh. Accordingly, in this paper we aim to:

- Review and compare reconstructions of intertidal environments and former tidal channels on Romney Marsh based on benthic foraminifera.
- Evaluate the use of benthic foraminifera in these contexts compared to other microfossil groups, notably diatoms on Romney Marsh.
- Identify future areas in which the application of benthic foraminiferal studies could lead to a better understanding of the evolution of Romney Marsh.

Study Area

Romney Marsh is located in the eastern English Channel and is divided into Romney Marsh proper and Walland Marsh (Fig. 5.1). Drainage, river and tidal channels are common in both regions and detailed biostratigraphic study

of one of the former channels (the Wainway) is outlined in Evans *et al.* (2001). The distribution and drainage patterns of tidal channels on Walland Marsh are summarised by Spencer *et al.* (1998b).

Review of Studies Based on Benthic Foraminifera Biostratigraphy

Waller *et al.* (1988) employed benthic foraminifera accompanied with sedimentological, lithostratigraphic and pollen/plant macrofossil data, to reconstruct the depositional history at sites on Pett Level and in the Brede Valley (Waller 1994) (Fig. 5.1). Foraminiferal analyses were applied to the minerogenic sediments above and below the main peat to determine depositional conditions during the pre- and post-peat environment (see Table 5.1a and 5.1b). On Pett Level, the pre-peat sediments comprise a lower blue-grey sand overlain by a blue-grey silty clay prior to the transition to the peat. Foraminiferal analysis from the sand revealed an assemblage dominated by open marine benthic species (e.g. *Ammonia batavus* Hofker, *Miliolinella subrotunda* (Montagu)) mixed with intertidal species (e.g. *Protelphidium germanicum*, *Elphidium williamsoni*). The frequency of these intertidal species increases within the silty clay whilst the marine taxa decline. The upward fining of sediment and the decrease of open marine species indicates a decline in energy and a reduction in marine conditions in the region with deposition occurring initially within a sand flat, through a transitional sand/mudflat environment to mudflat (Waller *et al.* 1988). This regressive trend continues prior to the transition to peat where a range of intertidal and marsh dwelling species are recorded (e.g. *Jadammina macrescens, Trochammina inflata*) indicating development of saltmarsh conditions. Foraminiferal evidence also indicates saltmarsh conditions prevailed during the end of peat formation and that the subsequent deposition of the overlying silty clays occurred within a sand or mudflat environment.

At the Brede Valley sites (e.g. Old Place), depositional conditions inferred from foraminiferal analyses are very similar to those recorded at Pett Level. The blue-grey clays underlying the peat were deposited within an intertidal mud or sand flat environment. Marine influence declines up-core and intertidal marsh develops prior to peat formation. In the post-peat sediments, a transgressive sequence is recorded with saltmarsh being replaced by mudflat conditions and progressively more brackish and marine influence. Mudflat conditions are interrupted at Old Place by an influx of marine inner shelf species (e.g. *Quinqueloculina seminulum*) which probably records deposition in a higher energy sand/mudflat environment. Finally, Waller *et al.* (1998) identified that marine conditions and environmental energy declined suggesting the return to a mudflat environment.

Biostratigraphic Approaches to Channel Reconstruction Using Benthic Foraminfera

Wass (1995) examined evidence for a possible northern course for the former River Rother, (originally identified and mapped by Green (1968)) between Appledore and Hythe using foraminifera and ostracods. Four sampling sites were used to characterise the channel deposits. Ostracod species indicated that the marine fauna decreased towards the west, i.e. away from the channel opening. In contrast, benthic foraminifera indicated that marine conditions existed towards the east of the channel (see Table 5.1b). Estuarine and tidal flat species (e.g. *Protelphidium germanicum* (Ehrenberg), *E. williamsoni*), were most frequent although there were also a wide range of marine species (e.g. *A. batavus* (defined by Wass 1995 as marine)) present in lower numbers. Wass' (1995) detailed microfaunal study compliments his lithostratigraphic and sedimentological data. However, it did not identify the northern course of the River Rother identified by Green (1968). Wass (1995) concluded that the channel sampled was the upper end of a sheltered arm of a tidal inlet that opened towards the east.

Perhaps the most important late Holocene channel on Romney Marsh is the Wainway Channel (Green 1968; Tooley and Switsur 1988; Long and Innes 1995; Spencer *et al.* 1998b). This can be traced from Rye towards the south coast and then northeast towards Lydd and New Romney. The late Holocene evolution of this channel in the Little Cheyne Court landscape is described by Evans *et al.* (2001). This study used litho-, bio- and chronostratigraphic analyses with historical data to reconstruct the depositional history of the Wainway Channel and surrounding sedimentary sequences. Benthic foraminifera and diatoms were used for the microfossil analyses, which enabled a direct comparison of the palaeoenvironmental potential of each technique (see Table 5.1b and Fig. 5.2).

Two cores were selected for analysis, one from a channel centre position (core WA1) and a second from a channel margin location (core LCC). At the former the stratigraphy comprises a thick (5 m or more) sequence of laminated sands and silts, which fines upwards and becomes more clay and silt rich towards ground surface. In the latter, the main marsh peat is abruptly overlain by a 2 m thick sediment sequence which extends to ground surface. A radiocarbon date from the top of the peat in LCC of 1057–912 cal. yr BP provides a maximum age for the overlying sediment sequence.

In core WA1, benthic foraminifera fauna and diatom flora (e.g. *A. batavus*/*Paralia sulcata*) indicate initially relatively high energy marine conditions, with much of the sediment and fauna/flora being washed in from the inner shelf (Table 5.1b). These marine conditions then gave way to brackish water and estuarine conditions. This is indicated by foraminifera and diatoms such as *H. germanica* and *Caloneis westii* (W. Sm.), and also by a change in particle size distributions which also reveal a fall in tidal energy. Diatoms are absent in the uppermost part of the core. However, benthic foraminifera are preserved (Fig. 5.2) and provide the only evidence for the final stage of the depositional history. An increase in the frequencies of saltmarsh dwelling species *J. macrescens* at the core top confirms the further removal of marine conditions, and historical and stratigraphic data point towards inning in the late 16th century. The absence of diatoms in the top of WA1 probably records post-depositional dissolution due to water table fluctuations causing changes in the redox status of the uppermost sediments (e.g. Mayer *et al.* 1991).

The main marsh peat in core LCC is overlain by minerogenic sediment and the diatom data from this core suggest a rapid switch from freshwater to tidal channel conditions accompanying this lithostratigraphic change. Such a sudden change in depositional environment may record erosion of the upper peat surface; indeed the stratigraphic contact between the top of the peat and the overlying sediment is relatively sharp and perhaps erosive. However, the foraminifera tell a rather different story. The abundance of saltmarsh taxa, notably *J. macrescens*, in the immediate post-peat sediments provides strong evidence that a saltmarsh became established between the end of freshwater conditions and the onset of tidal channel sedimentation. This is an important palaeoenvironmental revision. Above this level, marine inner shelf taxa (e.g.

Table 5.1a. Summary of main previous benthic foraminifera studies from pre-peat sediments on Romney Marsh (see Waller et al. 1988; Waller 1994).

Pett Level	Old Place	Brede Bridge
Peat	Peat	Peat
Saltmarsh J. macrescens	Intertidal marsh P. germanicum, J. macrescens	Intertidal marsh T. inflata, J. macrescens
Intertidal sand/mudflat E. williamsoni	Intertidal mud/sand flat E. williamsoni, P. germanicum	
Intertidal sandflat E. williamsoni, P. germanicum		
Open marine A. batavus, M. subrotunda		

Nonion depressulus (Walker and Jacob) and estuarine/ tidal flat taxa, (*E. williamsoni, H. germanica*) become dominant. This suggests that the Wainway Channel was periodically flooding, washing inner shelf species across the channel margins (Fig. 5.2). An up-core decline in marine taxa and the dominance of *H. germanica* within the top of the sequences occurs. Diatoms from LCC suggest tidal channel conditions persisted throughout the core, with high frequencies of marine planktonic forms. The apparent ecological insensitivity of the diatoms, accompanied with dissolutional problems best explain this contrast and highlights the strength of multiproxy work and the inclusion of benthic foraminifera in palaeoenvironmental reconstruction.

Discussion

Comparison of Palaeoenvironmental Reconstructions Based on Benthic Foraminfera Faunal Data

The studies summarised above mostly adopt multidisciplinary techniques with the overall aim of palaeoenvironmental reconstruction of local sedimentary sequences in both Walland and Romney Marsh. In order that a broader understanding is achieved, these palaeoenvironmental interpretations need to be integrated within the Holocene landscape of Romney Marsh as a whole. However, there are potential problems with this approach. Most significantly, some of the previous studies that used benthic foraminifera (e.g. Wass 1995) lack a chronostratigraphic framework, and this hinders direct correlation between sites across the study area.

Although the timing for the deposition of the sedimentary sequences is not always comparable, nevertheless the broad palaeoenvironmental interpretation can be evaluated and compared. The simplest model to explain the foraminiferal sequences found at all sites is gradual channel infilling, with up-core changes from open marine, to channel and then mudflat and saltmarsh depositional environments. This contrasts the diatom records, which tend only to record tidal channel depositional conditions and limited up-core changes in palaeoenvironment.

The pre-peat palaeoenvironmental groupings identified by Waller *et al.* (1988) at Pett Level, can be summarised into three main stages from the core base: (1) an early depositional sequence dominated by open marine benthic foraminifera; (2) an intertidal sequence; (3) a saltmarsh sequence. This three-stage model broadly corresponds with the interpretation provided by Evans *et al.* (2001) for core WA1 from the Wainway Channel. Post-peat sedimentary sequences from the Brede Valley sites studied by Waller *et al.* (1988) and Waller (1994) also show some similarities to the channel edge core (core LCC) investigated by Evans *et al.* (2001). For example an initial saltmarsh sequence was encountered at both sites. In core LCC this was replaced by marine inner shelf and estuarine / tidal flat conditions through the remainder of the core, with a decline of the marine taxa towards the core top. Waller *et al.* (1988) also identified an increase of marine species above the saltmarsh sequence, with mud flat above. These sedimentary sequences represent transgressive contacts associated with the fluctuating Holocene sea-level rise in Northwest Europe (see Long *et al.* 1998; Shennan *et al.* 2000), and are broadly comparable with other locations within the U.K. (e.g. Lloyd 2000).

Improved Palaeogeographic Reconstruction of Romney Marsh Through the Holocene

Palaeoenvironmental reconstructions based on benthic foraminifera data are available for only a few sites on Romney Marsh. To achieve directly comparable data sets, and in turn palaeoenvironmental reconstructions for sedimentary sequences, where possible biostratigraphic

Table 5.1b. Summary of main previous benthic foraminifera and diatom studies from post-peat sediments on Romney Marsh.

Waller et al. (1988); Waller (1994)		Wass (1995)	Evans et al. (2001)			
Pett Level	Old Place	River Rother 4 sites (W-E)	Wainway Channel		Little Cheyne Court	
			Foraminifera	Diatoms	Foraminifera	Diatoms
	Intertidal mudflat P. germanicum, E. williamsoni	Saltmarsh J. macrescens, T. inflata, H. wilberti	Saltmarsh J. macrescens	Mudflat/ low saltmarsh C. westii, P. westii, S. tumida	Estuarine/tidal flat A. batavus var. limnetes	No diatoms present
	Intertidal sand/mudflat Q. seminulum, M. secans	Tidal flats P. germanicum E. williamsoni	Brackish water/estuarine H.germanica, B. frigida	Marine tidal channel D. surirella, P. westii, C. belgica	Estuarine/tidal flat N. depressulus, H. germanica, E. williamsoni	No diatoms present
Intertidal mudflat P. germanicum E. williamsoni	Intertidal mudflat P. germanicum E. williamsoni	Marine M. subrotunda	Open marine A. batavus, N. depressulus	High energy tidal channel Paralia sulcata	Open marine N. depressulus, H. germanica.	No diatoms present
Saltmarsh J. macrescens	Intertidal marsh P. germanicum, J. macrescens				Saltmarsh J. macrescens.	Marine planktonic C. belgica, D. surirella, D. smithii, P. sulcata
Peat	Peat				Peat	

**Wainway Channel
Core WA1**

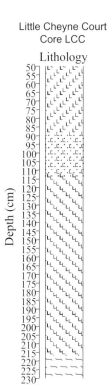

Indicative Environment	Foraminifera	Core Depth (cm)	Diatoms	Indicative Environment
Saltmarsh	J. macrescens	50	Not present	
		85 / 100	C. westii, P. westii, S. tumida	Mudflat/possibly low saltmarsh
Brackish water /estuarine	H.germanica, M. subrotunda N.depressulus B. frigida	140 / 180 / 220 / 260 / 300 / 340	D. surirella, P. westii C. belgica	Marine taxa, tidal channel
		380 / 390	Paralia sulcata	High energy tidal channel, open marine conditions
High energy tidal channel open marine conditions	A. batavus N. depressulus	420 / 445	Not present	

**Little Cheyne Court
Core LCC**

Indicative Environment	Foraminifera	Core Depth (cm)	Diatoms	Indicative Environment
Estuarine/ tidal flat	A. becarri var. limnetes, H.germanica	55	Not present	
Estuarine/ tidal flat + Open marine	N.depressulus H.germanica,	80 / 100	Not present	
		120	Not present	
Estuarine/ tidal flat + Open marine	E. williamsoni, N.depressulus H.germanica	140 / 160 / 180	C. belgica, D. surirella, D. smithii, P. sulcata (planktonic taxa)	Marine conditions, tidal channel
Saltmarsh	J. macrescens	200		
Peat	No Foraminifera	220	Peat	No Diatoms

Fig. 5.2. Comparison of benthic foraminifera and diatom data from the Wainway Channel (Core WA1) and Little Cheyne Court (Core LCC). Diatoms record little ecological variation or are not present in the core at certain horizons, whereas benthic foraminifera occur throughout the cores and can be used for palaeoenvironmental interpretation.

analyses should include the interpretation of more than one fossil group (e.g. diatom, benthic foraminifera, ostracod, and pollen data sets). This will help overcome the problems of differential preservation and the sensitivity of different groups to ecological change. The value of this approach is clear at the Wainway Channel, where the diatoms appear relatively blunt palaeoenvironmental indicies and are only partially preserved, whereas the foraminifera record more subtle changes in environment and are recorded more continuously. As highlighted in Evans *et al.* (2001) it may be beneficial to improve the understanding of the evolution of Romney Marsh, to revisit core sites with marginal marine/estuarine/channel sequences that have already received microfossil (especially only diatom) analyses.

Conclusions

The reconstruction of late Holocene intertidal environments, particularly tidal channels is essential to any study of former coastal landscapes. Palaeoenvironmental reconstructions of these features that result from the analyses of sedimentological, biostratigraphic and litho-/chronostratigraphic data are not only valuable to those studying the processes responsible for the channel's evolution, but also to the historian and geoarchaeologist. If multidisciplinary methodologies are applied to reconstructing the late Holocene landscape of Romney Marsh and other lowland coastal environments, the resultant findings become more widely appreciated and accessible. The biostratigraphic studies reviewed here all adopt the use of benthic foraminifera, accompanied with other proxies, to reconstruct the depositional history of different intertidal and channel environments within Romney Marsh. Valuable palaeoenvironmental reconstructions are provided which contribute to our understanding of the overall late Holocene evolution of the Romney Marsh landscape. Differences are identified between the studies, although the broad patterns are similar. In particular, the post-peat sediments record an initial saltmarsh phase, followed by an increase in water depth and tidal current. This is followed by an up-core reduction in grain size and a fall in the frequencies of fully marine foraminifera as tidal energy decreases and the marine influence falls. This is a prelude to reclamation.

Recommendations for Further Work

1. To improve our understanding of the Holocene landscape and drainage networks of Romney Marsh more extensive coring programmes need to be planned. One such avenue for further research could be the stratigraphic mapping of the Wainway Channel along its length accompanied by palaeoenvironmental investigation. This is important because it would result in enhanced understanding of one of the most significant late Holocene geographical features within Romney Marsh.

2. This could be further developed by sampling a range of sedimentary channels both contemporary and fossil in the region. Interpretations are at present qualitative, based on broad ecological reasoning. The study of modern distributions of foraminifera and diatoms in tidal channel environments from the region would enable more rigorous reconstructions of the Holocene record. Both benthic foraminifera and sedimentological data have the potential to resolve variations in tidal strength as well as the sea-level signal, based on the abundance/presence of species in fossil sediments that represent open marine conditions compared with estuarine/brackish water and saltmarsh conditions in contemporary environments.

3. Another approach, as discussed above, would be to revisit already existing sedimentary and palaeoenvironmental records and apply benthic foraminiferal analyses to enhance the existing palaeoenvironmental record.

4. Benthic foraminifera should also be applied more extensively to the pre-peat sedimentary sequences on Walland Marsh. In particular, they could be used to identify whether sediments were deposited in a back barrier or more open marine environment based on the abundance of inner shelf species benthic and open marine planktonic species compared with estuarine and intertidal species.

5. Short-lived increases in the frequencies of benthic foraminifera may also be used to reconstruct temporary inundation episodes, associated with either storm floods or changes in coastal configuration.

6. Benthic foraminifera have the potential to clarify environmental changes associated with the end of peat formation, and the processes operating during the post-peat period. Thus, pollen data from several sites suggest a rise in the watertable prior to the inundation of the main marsh peat. This implies a relatively gradual inundation. However, the top of the peat is often abrupt and perhaps eroded, whilst the diatom records from these sites rarely record the development of saltmarsh communities between the end of freshwater peat formation and the deposition of the overlying clastic sediments. In the light of the Evans *et al.* (2001) findings, the application of foraminifera in this context is likely to provide a clearer picture of the nature of environmental change during this period. For example, it would be possible to identify whether water tables rose rapidly, followed by a swift breaching and erosion of the peat in places, or whether the lack of saltmarsh is simply a reflection of the noted problems with diatoms as indicators of salinity and palaeoenvironment.

7. Lastly, careful study of benthic foraminifera from the uppermost sedimentary sequences would help define what environments were being reclaimed. Our under-

standing of the contemporary distribution of marsh species is now sufficiently advanced to provide a more precise answer to whether the land being reclaimed on Romney Marsh was low, mid or high marsh. However, precise sampling would be necessary to record the subtle changes within the benthic foraminifera assemblages. Moreover, in post-peat sediments, if sufficient geographical coverage was obtained of benthic foraminifera records, this altitudinal precision in identifying specific saltmarsh zones may make it possible to resolve whether oscillations in late Holo-

cene sea-level took place (as suggested by Plater *et al.* (1999) and Spencer *et al.* (1998b)) or whether a more continuous inundation occurred (Long *et al.* 1998). Benthic foraminifera data of post-peat and pre-reclamation environmental changes could then be linked in with the rich historical evidence that is available for Romney Marsh and also wider studies from elsewhere along the south coast where late Holocene sea-level changes have been identified (Edwards, 2001).

References

Allen, J.R.L. and Rippon, S.J. 1997. Iron Age to Early Modern activity and palaeochannels at Magor Pill, Gwent: An exercise in lowland coastal-zone geoarchaeology, *The Antiquaries Journal* **77**, 327–70.

Eddison, J. 1983. The evolution of the barrier beaches between Fairlight and Hythe, *The Geographical Journal* **149**, 39–75.

Eddison, J. 1998. Catastrophic changes: A multidisciplinary study of the evolution of the barrier beaches of Rye Bay, in J. Eddison, M. Gardiner, and A. Long (eds) *Romney Marsh: Environmental Change and Human Occupation in a Coastal Lowland* (Oxford University Committee for Archaeology Monograph **46**), 65–87. Oxford.

Edwards, R.J. 2001. Mid-to late Holocene relative sea-level change in Poole Harbour, southern England, *Journal of Quaternary Science* **16**, 221–36.

Evans, J.R., Kirby, J.R. and Long, A.J. 2001. The litho- and biostratigraphy of a late Holocene tidal channel Romney Marsh, Southern England, *Proceedings of the Geologists' Association* **112**, 111–30.

Gardiner, M. 1988. Medieval settlement and society in the Broomhill area and excavations at Broomhill Church, in J. Eddison, and C. Green (eds) *Romney Marsh. Evolution, Occupation, Reclamation* (Oxford University Committee for Archaeology Monograph **24**), 112–28. Oxford.

Gehrels, R.W., Roe, H.M. and Charman, D.J. 2001. Foraminifera, testate amoebae and diatoms as sea-level indicators in UK saltmarshes: a quantitative multiproxy approach, *Journal of Quaternary Science* **16**, 201–20.

Green, R.D. 1968. *Soils of Romney Marsh.* (Soil Survey of Great Britain, Bulletin **4**). Harpenden.

Green, C.P. 1988. Palaeogeography of marine inlets of the Romney Marsh area, in J. Eddison and C. Green (eds) *Romney Marsh: Evolution, Occupation, Reclamation* (Oxford University Committee for Archaeology Monograph **24**), 167–74. Oxford.

Haslett, S.K., Davies, P., Curr, R.H.F., Davies, C.F.C., Kennington, K., King, C.P. and Margetts, A.J. 1998a. Evaluating Late Holocene relative sea-level change in the Somerset Levels, southwest Britain, *The Holocene* **8**, 197–207.

Haslett, S.K., Davies, P. and Strawbridge, F. 1998b. Reconstructing Holocene sea-level change in the Severn Estuary and Somerset Levels: the Foraminifera connection, *Archaeology in the Severn Estuary* **8** (1997), 29–40.

Horton, B.P., Edwards, R.J. and Lloyd, J.M. 1999. UK intertidal foraminiferal distributions: implications for sea-level studies, *Marine Micropaleontology* **36**, 205–23.

Lloyd, J. 2000. Combined foraminiferal and thecamoebian environmental reconstruction from an isolation basin in NW Scotland: implications for sea-level studies, *Journal of Foraminiferal Research* **30**, 294–305.

Long, A.J. and Innes J.B. 1993. Holocene sea-level changes and coastal sedimentation in Romney Marsh, southeast England, U.K., *Proceedings of the Geologists' Association* **104**, 223–37.

Long, A.J. and Innes J.B. 1995. The back-barrier and barrier depositional history of Romney Marsh, Walland Marsh and Dungeness, Kent, England, *Journal of Quaternary Science* **10**, 267–83.

Long, A.J., Plater, A.J., Waller, M.P., Hughes, P.D.M. and Spencer, C. 1998. The Holocene depositional history of Romney Marsh Proper, in J. Eddison, M. Gardiner, and A. Long (eds) *Romney Marsh: Environmental Change and Human Occupation in a Coastal Lowland* (Oxford University Committee for Archaeology Monograph **46**), 45–63. Oxford.

Mayer, L.M., Jorgensen, J. and Schnitker, D. 1991. Enhancement of diatom frustule dissolution by iron oxides, *Marine Geology* **99**, 263–66.

Plater, A.J., Long, A.J., Spencer, C.D. and Delacour, R.A.P. 1999. The stratigraphic record of sea-level change and storms during the last 2000 years: Romney Marsh, southeast England, *Quaternary International* **55**, 17–27.

Scott, D.B. and Medioli, F.S. 1978. Vertical zonations of marsh foraminifera as accurate indicators of former sea-levels, *Nature* **272**, 528–31.

Scott, D.B. and Medioli, F.S. 1986. Foraminifera as sea-level indicators, in O. van de Plassche (ed.) *Sea-level Research: A Manual for the Collection and Evaluation of Data.* Geobooks, 435–56. Norwich.

Shennan, I., Lambeck, K., Flather, R., Horton, B., McArthur, J., Innes, J., Lloyd, J., Rutherford, M. and Wingfield, R. 2000. Modelling western North Sea palaeogeographies and tidal changes during the Holocene, in I. Shennan, and J. Andrews (eds) *Holocene Land-Ocean Interaction and Environmental Change around the North Sea* (Geological Society special publication **166**), 299–319. London

Spencer, C.D., Plater, A.J. and Long, A.J. 1998a. Rapid coastal change during the mid- to late Holocene: the record of barrier estuary sedimentation in the Romney Marsh region, southeast England, *The Holocene* **8**, 143–63.

Spencer, C.D., Plater, A.J. and Long, A.J. 1998b. Holocene barrier estuary evolution: The sedimentary record of the Walland Marsh region, in J. Eddison, M. Gardiner and A. Long (eds) *Romney Marsh: Environmental Change and Human Occupation in a Coastal Lowland* (Oxford University Committee for Archaeology Monograph **46**), 13–29. Oxford.

Tooley, M.J. and Switsur, V.R. 1988. Water level changes and sedimentation during the Flandrian Age in the Romney Marsh area, in J. Eddison, and C. Green (eds) *Romney Marsh. Evolution, Occupation, Reclamation* (Oxford University Committee for Archaeology Monograph **24**), 53–71.Oxford.

Waller, M.P. 1994. Flandrian vegetational history of south-eastern England. Stratigraphy of the Brede valley and pollen data from Brede Bridge, *New Phytologist* **126**, 369–92.

Waller, M.P., Burrin, P.J. and Marlow, A. 1988. Flandrian sedimentation and palaeoenvironments in Pett Level, the Brede and lower Rother valleys and Walland Marsh, in J. Eddison and C. Green (eds) *Romney Marsh: Evolution, Occupation, Reclamation* (Oxford University Committee for Archaeology Monograph **24**), 3–30. Oxford.

Wass, M. 1995. The proposed Northern course of the Rother: a sedimentological and microfaunal investigation, in J. Eddison, (ed.) *Romney Marsh: the Debatable Ground* (Oxford University Committee for Archaeology Monograph **41**), 51–78. Oxford.

Romney Marsh: Coastal and Landscape Change through the Ages
(ed. A. Long, S. Hipkin and H. Clarke), OUSA Monograph 56, 2002, 84–100

6. Romney Marsh: Evolution of the Historic Landscape and its Wider Significance

Stephen Rippon

Romney Marsh is one of the largest coastal wetlands in Britain, and has seen a long history of archaeological, documentary and geomorphological research. Recently, this has been complemented by interdisciplinary work of the Romney Marsh Research Trust's members, and we now have an extensive body of data relating to this remarkable landscape. In the first monograph produced by the Romney Marsh Research Trust, Christopher Green attempted a broad palaeogeographical reconstruction of how the Marsh may have evolved over the past 2,000 years, and this paper is an attempt to expand upon the model put forward. Some aspects of the wider significance of the history of Romney Marsh are then considered, including the importance of breaches in coastal barriers in affecting human utilisation of marshland landscapes, the significance of the associated estuaries for integrating coastal and inland economies, and the role of marshland within complex medieval estate structures.

Introduction

Romney Marsh is the third largest coastal wetland in Britain, and during the 19th and 20th centuries it saw a remarkably long history of archaeological, documentary and geomorphological/palaeoenvironmental research (e.g. Holloway 1849; Lewin 1862; Furley 1874; Teichman Derville 1936; Smith 1943; Ward 1952; Green 1968; Eddison and Green 1988; Eddison et al. 1998; Eddison 1995; 2000). Several attempts have previously been made to reconstruct its palaeogeography, and this paper endeavours to weave together a wide range of data to take this mapping further, in order to develop a hypothetical model for the Marsh's evolution that may provide a stimulus for further research. As a non-Romney Marsher, an attempt will also be made to reflect on the significance of both the Marsh itself, and the research that has been carried out there.

For those readers who are not familiar with wetland research it may be useful to place the work on Romney Marsh in a wider context. Since the 1970s the significance of wetland landscapes as records of environmental change and human endeavour has become widely recognised following John and Bryony Coles' pioneering work in the Somerset Levels (Coles and Coles 1986; Coles 1989). English Heritage followed up the 'Somerset Levels Project' with major programmes of survey and limited excavation in Fenland (Hall and Coles 1994; Crowson *et al.* 2000), North West England (e.g. Hodgkinson *et al.* 2000), and around the Humber Estuary (e.g. Ellis *et al.* 2001). Other areas saw more local initiatives focussing upon intertidal areas, such as the 'Hullbridge Survey' in Essex (Wilkinson and Murphy 1995), Goldcliff in the former county of Gwent (Bell *et al.* 2000), the Isle of Wight (Tomalin 2000) and Langstone Harbour in Hampshire (Allen and Gardiner 2000). Further work is also now proposed around the Thames Estuary (Williams and Brown 1999). These mostly state-funded projects have done much to improve our understanding of those dynamic coastal zones, but all too often their scope has been understandably limited to specific wetland environments that are under threat from drainage or erosion. They have also concentrated on archaeological and palaeoenvironmental investigation, resulting in a tendency for the medieval period, documentary sources, and the historic landscape itself to be rather neglected (though with notable exceptions: e.g. Silvester 1988; Hall 1996; Hodgkinson *et al.* 2000).

Two areas – Romney Marsh and the Severn Estuary – have seen a different approach, with the absence of a large-scale state-funded survey encouraging a series of imaginative and collaborative programmes of research. Around the Severn, the *Severn Estuary Levels Research Committee* has acted as a forum for debate, co-operation, and a means for establishing projects that have seen the close collaboration of archaeologists, sedimentologists, palaeoenvironmentalists and historians (see the annual reports of the Committee *Archaeology in the Severn Estuary*, and Rippon 2001a).

A very similar approach has emerged through the *Romney Marsh Research Trust*, and this is now the fourth in their series of monographs (Eddison and Green 1988; Eddison 1995; Eddison *et al.* 1998). In the early volumes (and indeed a series of other academic papers), the emphasis was on publishing the results of individual research projects, though Eddison (2000) has recently produced a much needed overview of the area's history.

There have been several attempts to reconstruct the sequence of reclamation, mostly in the eastern part of Walland Marsh (Furley 1874; Lewin 1862; Tatton-Brown 1988; Allen 1996; 1999; Eddison and Draper 1997), along with a number of attempts at broader palaeogeographical mapping of the whole Romney/Walland Marsh landscape. Notable examples include Holloway's (1849), Homan's (1938) and Ward's (1952) somewhat schematic reconstructions based upon documentary material, Green's (1988) sequence of three maps covering the Roman to medieval period (being based partly on the results of Green's (1968) soil survey), Spencer *et al.*'s (1998a; and see Spencer 1996; Spencer *et al.* 1998b) work on the buried Wainway palaeochannel, and Long *et al.*'s (1998) mapping of the start and end of peat formation. With the exception of the latter and Green's (1988) maps, however, each of these earlier palaeogeographical reconstructions only consider the landscape at one period, and even Green's (1988) study only mapped the changing course of the river Rother and contained little reference to the development of the cultural landscape (as has since been studied by Allen, Draper, Eddison and Tatton-Brown: see above). This paper therefore presents an attempt to integrate the results of all this research into both the natural and cultural landscape in order to improve upon these early attempts at palaeogeographical mapping.

A Wealth of Opportunities

The dynamic environment that is a coastal wetland offers human communities a range of potential resource-utilisation strategies (Rippon 2000). The rich ecological mosaics contain an abundance of natural resources that could be *exploited* by human communities. These resources would have included fishing, wildfowling, the grazing of livestock and the opportunity for producing salt by boiling sea water, and could be exploited without significantly changing the natural environment. Experiments on modern marshes, along with palaeoenvironmental evidence from both Britain and the continent, have shown that it is possible to grow a limited range of crops on a high intertidal marsh, though such environments are not ideally suited to agriculture due to the risk of flooding (Van Zeist 1974; Van Zeist *et al.* 1976; Bottema *et al.* 1980; Behre and Jacomet 1991; Rhoades *et al.* 1992; Crowson *et al.* 2000). One solution to the problem of flooding is to *modify* the landscape, for example through the construction of low embankments to protect crops from the occasional summer inundations but without the intention of providing year-round flood defence (Bazelmans *et al.* 1999; Rippon 2001c). While such 'summer dikes' will provide some protection, they existed in what remained an intertidal environment. In order to realise the full agricultural potential of coastal wetlands the landscape needed to be *transformed* through reclamation, by which the construction of a sea wall to keep the tides permanently at bay leads to an intertidal environment becoming wholly freshwater and with a managed water table. This reclamation could occur in an unsystematic, piecemeal fashion with individual parcels of land being enclosed as required, or as part of a systematic programme of drainage in which a large area was dealt with simultaneously.

Although a logical development, reclamation is a *high cost* undertaking in terms of the initial capital outlay, the recurrent cost of maintenance, and the loss of the rich natural resources of coastal wetlands. Reclamation is also a *high risk* undertaking, with the threat of flooding ever present. Considering these high costs and high risks, one might ask why anyone bothered to reclaim wetlands: the answer is that they offered a *high return* on that investment in terms of increased agricultural productivity. It is in this context, of a high cost, high risk, but high return strategy, that the decision taken by landowners and communities reclaim, or not to reclaim, their coastal marshes, can be seen (and see Rippon 2001d).

High Risk, High Investment, High Return

As described above, reclamation entails the investment of considerable resources in an area that remained at risk of flooding. The scale of expenditure was remarkable: in 1293/4, for example, Canterbury Cathedral Priory ran up a bill for £128 14s. 9d. for drainage and flood defence on its manor of Appledore, compared to an income of just £74 3s. 0d. (Smith 1943, 173). The motivation behind this huge investment of resources was clearly agricultural improvement. In the Pevensey Levels, for example, upland ground within Battle Abbey's Barnhorne estate was valued at between 3–6 pence per acre, whereas reclaimed marshland was worth 12 pence; unreclaimed marsh was valued at 4 pence rising to 10 pence if properly drained (Dulley 1966, 37).

Where good estate records survive, it appears at first sight that arable dominated the agricultural regimes, and there were indeed profits to be made from the sale of cereals (e.g. Udimore in the Brede Valley: Gardiner 1995, 133). However, a closer examination reveals that in certain areas a significant proportion of arable was sown with legumes, notably beans. At Agney, for example, around a third of the demesne arable was put down to leguminous crops (Smith 1943, 140; Gross and Butcher 1995, 109). This figure is in keeping with other coastal wetlands, such as Glastonbury Abbey's Brent estate on the Somerset Levels, where *c.* AD 1300 around 84% of the demesne was arable (Keil 1964, table 4), of which 43% was sown with beans. In contrast, Overton and Campbell (1999, table 7.4) estimate that nationally, in AD 1300 4.9% of arable was sown with legumes (all pulses). So what does the extent of bean cultivation on reclaimed coastal marshlands mean? Gross and Butcher (1995, 109) suggest that it was part of a wider strategy towards improving soil that also included the application of lime and marl, though evidence from other medieval estates suggests that the cultivation of beans was part of the animal husbandry economy, notably the rearing of pigs, cattle and possibly horses (e.g. Battle Abbey, Sussex: Searle and Ross 1967, 44; Chalvington in Sussex: Mate 1991, 82; Glastonbury Abbey: Keil 1964, 79, 81, 125; Forncett in Norfolk: Davenport 1967, 31; Milton in Essex: Nichols 1932, 122–3, 149; and see Rippon forthcoming a).

From the discussion above, it appears that reclaimed marshland was highly valued as agricultural land, but that although large areas are recorded as arable, when detailed data on cropping is available beans were a major crop, forming part of a livestock-based economy. Medieval estate managers were clearly making careful choices as to how they could most effectively utilise these distinctive environments, and the perception of landlords was that the high, particular pastoral, productivity of their marshland estates justified the costs and risks of maintaining flood defences.

The Wealth of Evidence

Romney Marsh is fortunate in having a wealth of evidence for palaeogeographical reconstruction, in terms of geomorphological, sedimentological and paleoenvironmental studies, documentary research, and to a lesser extent archaeological investigations. The palaeoenvironmental work initially focussed on the coastal barrier (Eddison 1983), then the valleys that join the Marsh from the west (e.g. Waller *et al.* 1988), and latterly in Walland Marsh (Spencer *et al.* 1998a; 1998b) and Romney Marsh proper (Long *et al.* 1998). This work concentrated on establishing

the major phases of wetland development, and is now being extended to specific issues concerning the evolution of the cultural landscape, such as the development of the Wainway Channel, and the nature/extent of late 13th/14th century flooding (see below; and other papers in this volume).

One key piece of research was Green's (1968) soil survey which remains an important resource in any attempt at palaeogeographical reconstruction of the recent landscape (Fig. 6.1). Its value is that variations in soil character can be linked to features within the historic landscape (such as sea walls), that in turn can be dated through the careful analysis of historical records. Romney Marsh is fortunate in having historical sources of exceptional quality, notably a series of early medieval charters, many referring to a series of landscape features in the boundaries of those estates, such as rivers (Fig. 6.2; Brooks 1988). Most of these charters relate to grants of land to various ecclesiastical institutions, and the survival of extensive records relating to the subsequent management of these estates in the post-Conquest period has allowed a very detailed picture to be painted of medieval agriculture on the Marsh (e.g. Smith 1943; Gardiner 1995; 1998; Gross and Butcher 1995; Draper 1998). The records of the major port towns also survive (e.g. Riley 1874a; 1874b; 1876a; 1876b; 1876c), which along with the calendars of state papers, contain a wealth of information about the rapidly evolving estuaries and coast.

There have also been a number of important archaeological investigations, including fieldwalking (Gardiner 1994; Reeves 1995; Allen 1999) and excavations (Barber 1998), though there is a desperate need for more such work. Until recent agricultural intensification Romney Marsh also had a remarkable set of earthworks, notably sea walls, relating to abandoned phases of reclamation, partly plotted by Green (1968) and since studied through early air photographs and the surviving field evidence (Fig. 6.3; Tatton-Brown 1988; Vollans 1988; Allen 1996; 1999; Eddison and Draper 1997; Rippon 2000). A key aspect of these earthworks is their potential for being linked with documented features (e.g. sea walls) and areas of reclamation, as has been attempted for the eastern part of Walland Marsh (Lewin 1862; Furley 1874; Tatton-Brown 1988; Vollans 1988; Allen 1996; Eddison and Draper 1997) and the Broomhill area (Gardiner 1988). Allen (1996; 1999) has also shown how the elevation differences that develop either side of an active sea wall can be used to locate embankments that have long been demolished. Some analysis has also been made of field boundary patterns (e.g. Eddison and Draper 1997; Tatton-Brown 1988), though the historic landscape of the Romney/Walland Marsh area *as a whole* – that is the overall pattern of roads, fields and settlements – has not been studied in any great depth. Work in other reclaimed wetland landscapes has shown the enormous potential for historic landscape analysis in establishing the history of reclamation (e.g. Silvester 1988; Hall 1996; Rippon 1996;

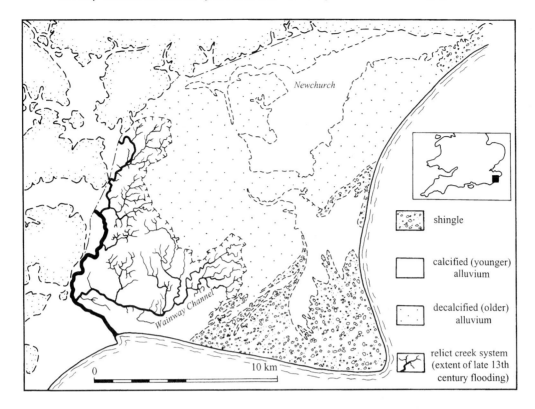

Fig. 6.1. Simplified soils map, distinguishing older 'decalcified' and younger 'calcified' alluvium, and the surviving shingle ridges (after Green 1968).

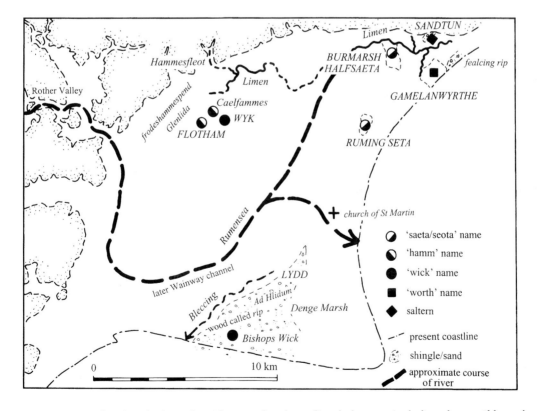

Fig. 6.2. Evidence contained within the boundary clauses of early medieval charters, including the possible early course of the Limen *via an estuary by* Sandtun, *and its later diversion through a breach in the shingle barrier by the church of St Martin (Romney). The names of estates are in capitals, and places mentioned in the boundary clauses in lower case (after Brooks 1988; Rippon 2000).*

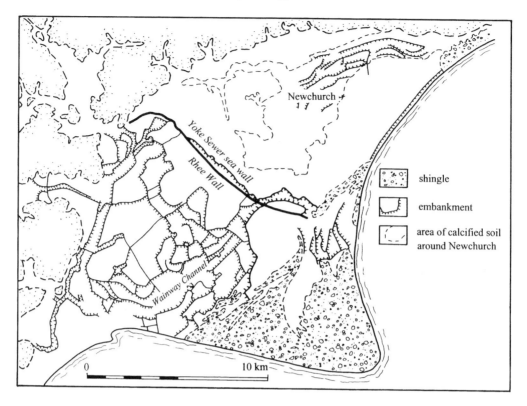

Fig. 6.3. Relict sea walls and flood banks (both extant and from early air photographs), including the former course of the Rother via the Wainway Channel, the sea wall along Yoke Sewer, and the later Rhee Wall (from Ordnance Survey 1st edition Ordnance Survey Six Inch map, and air photographs in the National Monuments Record).

Williamson 1997) and this paper is an attempt to make some progress in Romney Marsh.

The Historic Landscape: The Richest of all Historic Records?

It was probably W.G. Hoskins (1955) who first recognised the value of interrogating the historic landscape for it contains within it a wealth of information regarding how that landscape came into being (e.g. Fig. 6.4). This is perhaps particularly so within a reclaimed wetland, for once a field boundary is created it performs a vital drainage function which makes it less expendable than equivalent boundaries in dryland landscapes. The lines of sea walls that are no longer needed due to further reclamation, are still preserved as they had become field, and often estate, boundaries. The layout of fields and roads will also reflect the process of reclamation. For example, saltmarshes are naturally drained by a network of meandering creeks, and following embanking, if such a marsh is enclosed in a gradual and piecemeal fashion (perhaps by numerous individual tenants within a community), these creeks will often be exploited as field boundaries. In this way, the broad loops of meandering creeks come to be fossilised within the post-reclamation pattern of fields (e.g. Fig. 6.4: Snave and Ivychurch to the north east of the 'Yoke Sewer'

sea wall). In contrast, if the process of enclosure and drainage following reclamation was carried out in a single episode (perhaps under the control of a single individual), then these creeks might be ignored, as a geometrically-arranged system of fields is imposed over a very large area (e.g. Fig. 6.4: Brookland). Landuse might also affect the pattern of fields: arable fields, for example, tend to be smaller than those created for pasture (particularly sheep pasture; e.g. Fig. 6.4: the area south east of Brookland).

The pattern of parish boundaries can also be informative. Romney Marsh proper, to the north east of an early sea wall along the line of Yoke Sewer (marked with arrows on Fig. 6.4; Allen's (1996; 1999) 'Rumenesea Wall'), was the earliest area to be colonised in the medieval period, and the parishes there tend to be compact, though with very irregular boundaries (e.g. Newchurch and Snave: Fig. 6.5). Some areas of the Marsh were part of estates centred on the fen-edge (the upland/wetland interface) or even further inland, and detached parcels of the latter sometimes became detached parts of the parishes (e.g. parcels of Ebony, Appledore, Kenardington, and Bilsington). When Walland Marsh came to be reclaimed the existing parishes were often simply extended across the old sea wall along Yoke Sewer (e.g. Brenzett and Ivychurch: Fig. 6.5). In other cases, these newly reclaimed areas came to support their own communities and became parishes in their own right (e.g. Brookland and Fairfield). In both cases, the

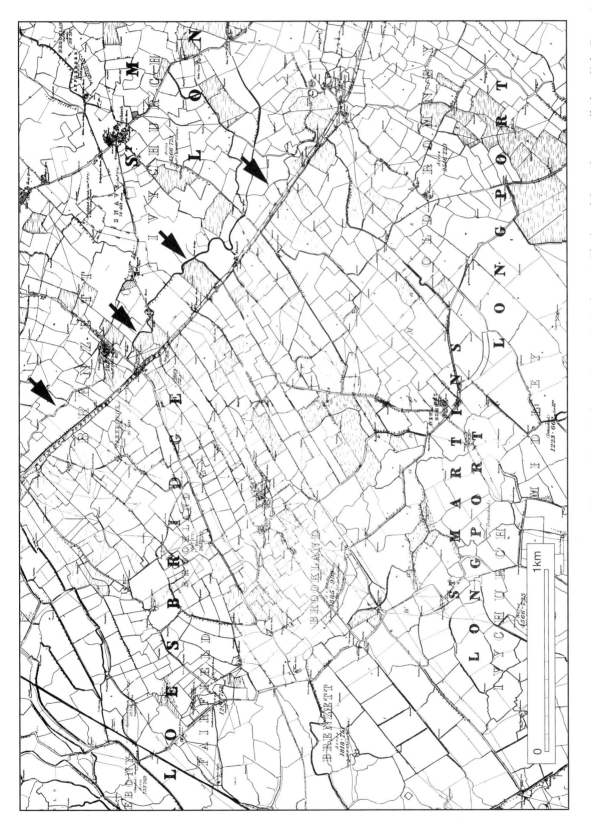

Fig. 6.4. The historic landscape in Ivychurch and Brookland (extract of the 1st edition Ordnance Survey Six Inch map). The line of the early sea wall along Yoke Sewer is marked with arrows. The highly irregular pattern of fields in that part of Ivychurch north east of the Yoke Sewer was created through piecemeal enclosure and drainage, incorporating the lines of naturally meandering former saltmarsh creeks. In contrast, the carefully planned landscape in Brookland reflects a more systematic approach to reclamation.

Walland Marsh parishes/parish-extensions were long, thin and relatively straight sided, reflecting the creation of landscape features on a larger scale, and on a more planned fashion, than was the case in Romney Marsh proper.

Figure 6.4 shows the complexity of the historic landscape in one small part of Romney Marsh. As described above, the various patterns of fields, roads and settlements reflect the history of drainage, enclosure and landuse, and on the Severn Estuary wetlands, for example, a detailed characterisation of the historic landscape demonstrates that surprisingly fine levels of detail can be achieved in writing a landscape history of that area (e.g. Rippon 1996, figs. 29, 33–4; 2001b). Such detailed work is yet to be attempted for Romney Marsh, though a very basic characterisation is shown in Figure 6.6. Nine broad character areas can be provisionally identified, based upon the Ordnance Survey First Edition Six Inch maps, chosen as they represent the earliest accurate field-scale mapping of this entire landscape (other than the Tithe maps that inherently only cover individual parishes). It should be stressed that this is, therefore, a characterisation of the 19th century landscape, and that there will have been many important changes since the medieval period, for example in the extent of settlement (there having been considerable settlement desertion in certain areas: e.g. Gardiner 1994; 1998; Reeves 1995; Allen 1999).

1. Romney Marsh proper is broadly of a similar character with mainly small, irregular shaped fields, highly sinuous roads, and a dispersed settlement pattern. Some of the gently curving field boundaries appear to incorporate the lines of naturally meandering creeks. This landscape appears to have been created around the 9th to 11th century, as the extensive area of marsh protected from flooding by the Yoke Sewer sea wall was gradually enclosed and drained. There are, however, significant variations, such as areas of more regularly arranged fields between Burmarsh and Newchurch that suggest a somewhat different process of landscape evolution. Further, more detailed characterisation is required.

2. The 12th century innings in the east of Walland Marsh have a very different character, with a greater degree of planning evident in the series of parallel boundaries laid out from the Yoke Sewer sea wall (Fig. 6.4). A series of discrete reclamations can in fact be identified in the area (Fig. 6.9). Some settlement is more nucleated, whilst there is also a scatter of isolated farms.

3. The Broomhill-Old Romney area comprises a series of discrete reclamations that further work could disentangle. Regularity in the fields once again suggests some degree of planning, associated with a dispersed settlement pattern.

4. Denge Marsh has a highly distinctive field boundary pattern, though whether the regularity is due to deliberate planning or simply constraints imposed by the roughly parallel beach ridges, is unclear. This ill-drained

area was without settlement in the 19th century (though this has not always been the case: Gardiner 1998).

5. Area of large fields on Walland Marsh, created in the late medieval period probably as sheep pastures. Not settled.

6. East Guldeford: a relatively discrete series of reclamations, with some coherence in the core area. One loosely nucleated settlement created in the late 15th century.

7. A very diverse character area relating to successive innings in the Rother Valley and along its former course to New Romney (the Wainway Channel).

8. Recent reclamation of the estuary at New Romney.

9. Shingle ridges.

It must be stressed that this is a very basic characterisation, and there is certainly scope for far more detailed work, integrating information contained within the historic landscape, archaeological and sedimentological investigations, and documentary research.

A Model for the Reclamation of Romney Marsh

What follows is a hypothetical model for the reclamation of Romney Marsh, based upon the integration of the diverse sources of data introduced above (and see Rippon 2000). It should not be regarded as a definitive statement, for there remain many gaps in our knowledge and it has not been possible to check all the evidence on the ground. In fact, what follows will hopefully illustrate *an* approach to understanding this complex landscape, and present a set of hypotheses which others can then pursue through further research.

There has been much debate over the broad phases in the evolution of Romney Marsh, notably the former course of the River Rother, and the River *Limen* recorded in the bounds of several early medieval charters (Brooks 1988; Wass 1995; Rippon 2000, 160–1, 191–5). Ward (1952) showed two rivers leaving the Rother Valley at Appledore, one flowing directly east towards Hythe, the other flowing south towards Rye and then turning north east to an estuary at New Romney. The northern, minor, course has been equated with an area of calcified alluvium mapped by Green (1968, figs. 14, 16; and see Homan 1938; Brooks 1988, 95–6), and interpreted as a palaeochannel. It is referred to in several charter bounds as the *Limen*, but *west of Newchurch* was shown by Wass (1995) to be a sheltered arm of a tidal creek without significant freshwater input; this northern *Limen* was not a course of the Rother.

So where did the Rother flow? Brooks (1988) argues that it flowed out of the Rother Valley south eastwards down a palaeochannel identified by Green (1968, fig. 16), and later followed by the Yoke Sewer. Brooks (1988) and Allen (1996; 1999) argued that this was the river *Rumenesea* documented in a charter of 920. This minor channel cannot, however, have taken all the waters of the Rother, and Allen (1996; 1999) followed Ward (1952) in arguing that the main course of the Rother flowed south from Appledore towards Old Winchelsea where it was deflected north east as far as Old Romney, then turning abruptly east to discharge its water into an estuary at New Romney. Green (1988), however, had proposed that the Rother originally flowed north-east past Old Romney to an estuary at Hythe (also identified by Cunliffe 1988 in the Roman period). This route has been explicitly rejected by Allen (1996; 1999) and Long *et al.* (1998), but it is the contention here is that Green (1988) was correct.

Palaeoenvironmental investigations on Walland Marsh 'neither confirm nor refute this hypothesis' that the Rother originally flowed into an estuary at Hythe (Spencer 1996, 336; and see Spencer *et al.* 1998a, 26), and although work by Long *et al.* (1998, 57) failed to locate a discrete palaeochannel south of Newchurch, the distribution, depth and composition of sediments in several boreholes are suggestive of a 'wide intertidal sandflat and mudflat'. The presence of an estuary at Hythe is supported by the extensive area of calcified alluvium (Fig. 6.1; Green 1968), and the possible lines of flood banks preserved as earthworks and in the line of field boundaries (Fig. 6.3). The location of the Roman fortress at Stutfall also strongly implies a substantial tidal inlet, as was the case with other forts of the 'Saxon Shore' (e.g. Bradwell in Essex: Wilkinson and Murphy 1995, fig. 119). Had the Hythe inlet not had a major river flowing into it, washing out the tidally deposited silts, it would not have remained open (as was the problem with the estuary at New Romney: Vollans 1988; and see Allen 1985). It is therefore argued here that Green (1988) was correct in suggesting that the Rother originally flowed south towards Rye where it was deflected by the shingle barrier north east all the way to Hythe. This is referred to here as the 'proto-Rother' on Figure 6.7.

In the Roman period, therefore, Romney Marsh appears to have been an extensive saltmarsh protected by a shingle barrier running from Fairlight, past Lydd, to Dymchurch, with a tidal inlet below the Roman fortress at Stutfall Castle near Hythe (Fig. 6.7). The marshes were certainly used for salt production and presumably seasonal grazing, though there is no evidence that the natural environment was in anyway modified through reclamation.

During the late/early-post Roman period the Marsh was flooded, probably due to a rise in relative sea level seen all around North West Europe (Rippon 2000, 138–51), and which buried the Romano-British landscape under variable amounts of alluvium. Early medieval charters, Domesday, and a series of probably related documents (the *Domesday Monachorum* and *Excerpta*: Neilson 1932; Morgan 1983) indicate that by the 11th century Romney Marsh proper (north east of the Yoke Sewer sea wall) was extensively occupied, while the existence of three 10th century administrative units ('Hundreds') wholly located on the Marsh suggests that this was a stable, well-settled landscape by that date (Fig. 6.8). References in the boundary descriptions of the charters, including indicators of arable cultivation, a complex pattern of land-holding, and possible artificial drainage features, imply that reclamation was well underway by the 9th century. What may have made this possible was a breach in the shingle barrier at New Romney, some 10 km south of the 'proto-Rother's' old estuary near Hythe. This left Romney Marsh proper relatively flood-free, there being few substantial freshwater streams flowing off the uplands to the north (Fig. 6.6), and the coast largely protected by a shingle barrier (Rippon 2000, 157–67).

As population and the profits from agriculture increased, so did the demand for more land, and by the mid 12th century there were a series of reclamations to the south west of the Yoke Sewer sea wall, on what become known as Walland Marsh (e.g. Turcoples Land, More Court/St Thomas' Inning, Miselham/Brookland, and Fairfield: Fig. 6.9). Following Elliott (in Lewin 1862), these innings have been erroneously equated with the work of a series of archbishops, though in practice it was probably the work of groups of tenants encouraged to improve large areas of the lords' waste with low rents. Possibly as early as the 11th century another breach in the shingle barrier occurred at what was to become (Old) Winchelsea, and over time the Rother took this shorter route into the English Channel (Fig. 6.9; Eddison 1998). This resulted in the silting-up of the old estuary at New Romney which by that date had become a major port. Since there was no longer sufficient freshwater discharge from the Rother to keep the estuary clear of silt, the port authorities constructed a major artificial watercourse, the Rhee Wall, to takes water from the Rother at Appledore, straight across the new innings on Walland Marsh, to Old Romney Bridge (Fig. 6.10; Vollans 1988). Meanwhile, the old course of the Rother was abandoned and reclaimed, becoming the estate of Agney.

The Late Medieval Period: Responses to Crisis

The full extent of reclamation on Walland Marsh is unclear for in the late 13th and 14th centuries a series of storms led to extensive flooding, the extent of which can be gauged through the deposition of relatively recent 'calcified' alluvium (Fig. 6.11). Initially the response of estate owners was to invest considerable sums in restoring flood defences (Smith 1943; Gross and Butcher 1995; Rippon forthcoming b), though an unknown area of formerly reclaimed land was lost. Some areas were recovered during the 14th century, though the recolonisation of Walland Marsh was largely achieved in the late 15th century in an area which came to be known as the Guldeford Level (Fig. 6.12). In 1478 the Abbot of Robertsbridge granted Richard Guldeford 1,300 acres of saltmarsh in the parishes of Playden, Iden and Broomhill in Sussex. In 1497, Guldeford

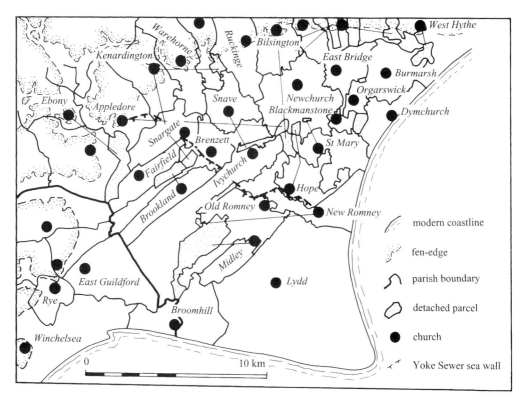

Fig. 6.5. Parish boundaries on Romney Marsh, with larger detached parcels (based on Tithe Maps, after Brooks 1988).

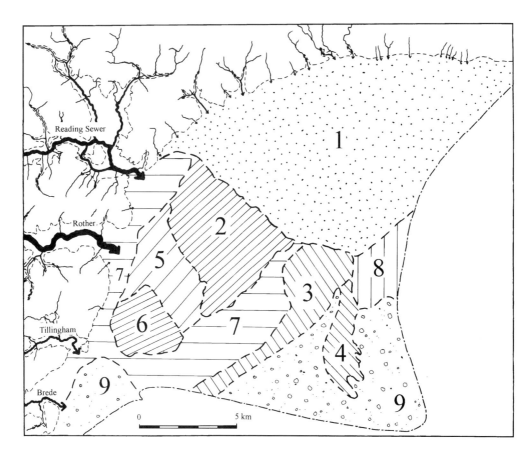

Fig. 6.6. A basic characterisation of the historic landscape of Romney Marsh. 1: highly irregular landscape created through piecemeal enclosure and drainage on Romney Marsh proper; 2–4: systematic reclamation, characterised by a degree of overall planning on Walland and Denge Marshes; 5: area of larger fields created for sheep pasture in Walland Marsh; 6: Guldeford Level, partly reclaimed during the late medieval period; 7: reclamation of the Rother Estuaries; 8: late reclamation south of New Romney; 9: shingle ridges. The scale of rivers flowing in the Marsh is shown schematically.

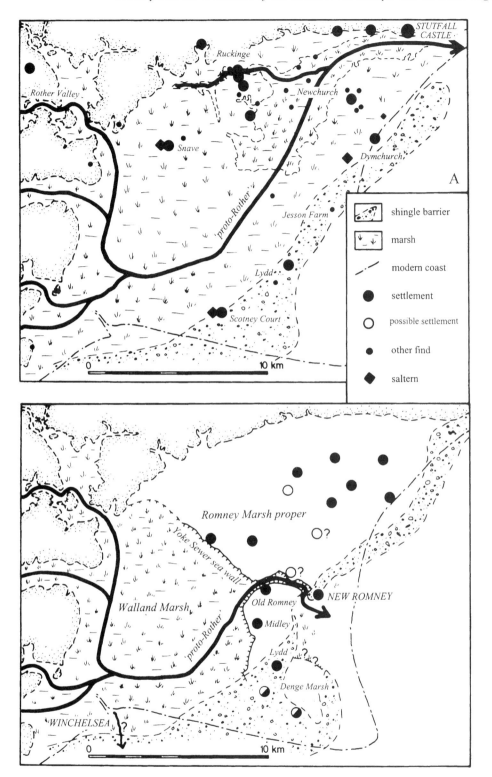

Fig. 6.7. The earlier Romano-British period (1st to 3rd centuries): the whole of Romney Marsh appears to have been an intertidal wetland, exploited for its rich natural resources, including the production of salt. The Roman fortress of the 'Saxon Shore' at Stutfall Castle overlooked the estuary of the 'proto-Rother'.

Fig. 6.8. c.11th century: Romney Marsh proper had been abandoned by the 'proto-Rother' as it now flowed into its new estuary at New Romney. A sea wall along the line of the modern Yoke Sewer protected the reclaimed and settled area from tidal inundation. Domesday and the Domesday Monachorum *suggest it was extensively settled. A new breach in the natural shingle barrier at Winchelsea may have occurred by this time (after Brooks 1988; Eddison 1998; Allen 1999).*

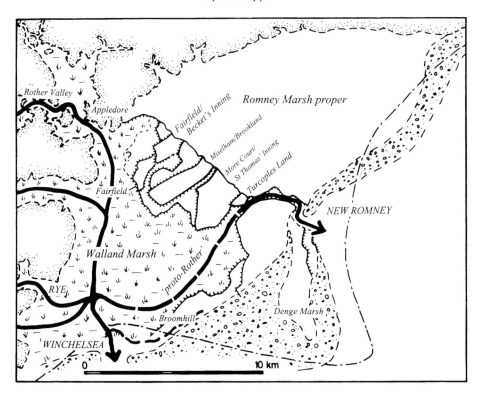

Fig. 6.9. Twelth century inning in Walland Marsh, rooted on the Yoke Sewer sea wall. Some waters of the 'proto-Rother' still flowed into the estuary at New Romney, though they were increasingly being diverted to the new inlet at Winchelsea (after Gardiner 1988; Tatton-Brown 1988; Eddison and Draper 1997).

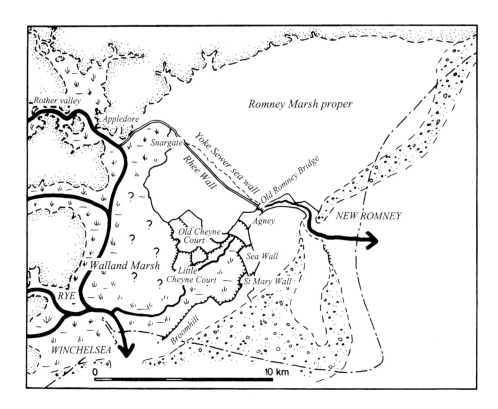

Fig. 6.10. Thirteenth century: further reclamation on Walland Marsh, notably along the now abandoned line of the 'proto-Rother' at Agney. The full extent of reclamation is unknown due to later flooding. The Rhee Wall was constructed across the earlier innings to try and flush out the harbour at New Romney (after Vollans 1988; Allen 1996; Eddison and Draper 1997).

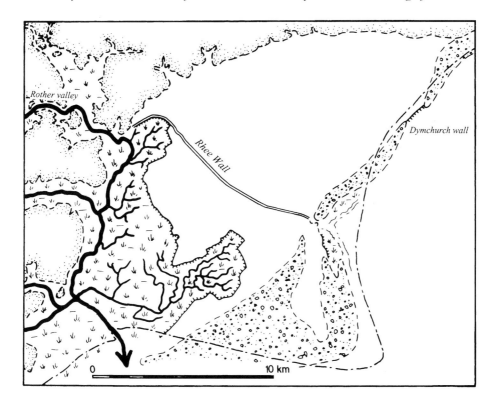

Fig. 6.11. The approximate extent of late 13th/14th century flooding (based on Green's 1968 soil survey).

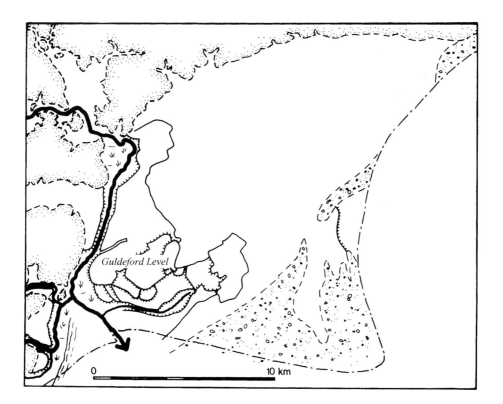

Fig. 6.12. Late 15th century and subsequent reclamation of the Guldeford Level.

acquired further land, and in 1499 he was given permission to build a church in 'Guylforde Innynge, formerly Brunchings, which had been submerged for 300 years and lately recovered by him at great expense'. By his death in 1506 this area had become the parish of 'New Guldeford', with six messuages, a church, and a mill (Salzman 1937, 151). The motivation for reclamation now, at a time of relatively low population and grain prices, was clearly the raising of sheep, reflected in the large size of the fields that were created at this time (and see Gardiner 1998).

Romney Marsh in Context

The hypothetical palaeogeographical reconstruction outlined above is an attempt to draw back from the wealth of detailed research that has been achieved over recent decades in an attempt to see the wider picture. We can in fact pull back even further and see how Romney Marsh fits in with the development of comparable wetland landscapes. Several themes will be briefly considered here: the significance of coastal barriers in the evolution of wetland landscapes, the importance of tidal estuaries as long-term foci for human activity, the early medieval expansion of settlement into such physically difficult environments, and the role of marshland within large-scale estates.

A large number of extensive coastal marshlands are, like Romney Marsh, sheltered behind a natural barrier of sand and shingle (e.g. the Somerset Levels, North Somerset Levels, Pevensey Levels, the Halvergate Marshes in Norfolk, and parts of the Lincolnshire Marshes in Britain, and Holland in the Netherlands). These barriers provide protection from tidal flooding, and in certain cases their creation, or migration, may have allowed the adjacent marshes to dry out, making them more amenable to human exploitation and even settlement (e.g. the Halvergate Marshes in the early medieval period: Williamson 1997, 12–14). These barriers, however, can also disrupt the discharge of freshwater if there are insufficient breaches through which rivers draining the hinterland can flow. In Holland, for example, it was only when the coastal sand dunes were breached in several places during the 10th century that drainage improved, making it possible for human communities to colonise the wetlands behind (Besteman 1990, 93–6). In Romney Marsh, it has been shown how successive breaches, first at New Romney and later at Old Winchelsea, led to the progressive shift westwards of the Rother which may have been a major factor in encouraging and then shaping the reclamation of first Romney Marsh proper and then Walland Marsh. Whilst old deterministic views that human behaviour is dictated by the natural environment have rightly been rejected, it is important to remember that coastal wetlands are landscapes whose character is more at the whim of nature than most.

The breaches in these natural barriers through which freshwater rivers discharged their waters inevitably became important long-term foci for human activity. On Romney Marsh, for example, the northernmost inlet was overlooked by the Roman fortress of the 'Saxon Shore' at Stutfall Castle (*Portus Lemanis*), and the early medieval trading settlement at 'Sandtun'. The inlet at New Romney, initially the site of a small fishing settlement, later became the site of a port engaged in international trade, as was the case at Wincheslsea. It was no doubt through these ports that much of the produce of Romney Marsh, and indeed its wider hinterland was shipped, so articulating the economy of this area with the wider region. The same may well have been true in the Roman period, as *Portus Lemanis* appears to have been linked with the exploitation of Wealden iron, where many iron-producing sites lay within easy reach of the rivers that flowed eastwards into Romney Marsh (Cunliffe 1988). Indeed, Allen and Fulford (1996; 1999) have shown that from the 2nd century there was increased navigation around the British coast, for example in stone, pottery and possibly grain, and the substantial tidal inlet on Romney Marsh was probably another element in this system of supply.

The same can be seen in other coastal wetlands. At Magor Pill, on the Gwent Levels, for example, occupation dates back to the Iron Age, and by the Romano-British period there was a substantial settlement probably engaging in coastal trade around the Severn Estuary (Allen 1998). During the medieval period it was similarly the site of small port or landing place, while a little upstream there was a watermill (Allen and Rippon 1997; Nayling 1998). The Severn Estuary as a whole was a focus for communications, not a barrier, being used for example in the shipping of Black Burnished Ware pottery from South East Dorset to the military establishment in South East Wales and on to the northern frontier (Allen and Fulford 1996). Other key rivers included the Axe, which may have been used to ship Mendip lead, and the Congresbury Yeo, beside which lay the kilns of the 'Congresbury Ware' pottery industry (Rippon 1997). During the Roman period it would appear that the existing network of rivers around the Severn was sufficient for this trade, though in Fenland it was necessary to improve communication through the construction of canals (Hall and Coles 1994, 105–9; Rippon 2000, 65–79). This must have entailed a huge investment of resources, and although the canals were built to allow goods to pass *through* the wetlands they still made these areas focal within the regional landscape. With its diversity of resources, it is not surprising that Fenland is ringed by small towns and a high density of fen-edge settlement, whilst the agricultural productivity of the marshes themselves is demonstrated by the remarkable density of settlement and the substantial estate centre at Stonea. Though physically a difficult (or even 'marginal') environment (Fenland was never reclaimed in the Roman period), locationally it was very central to the local economy. Romney Marsh, in contrast, although lying in South East Britain, was in fact locationally marginal and its hinterland lacked major centres of consumption or villa-based estates. Whilst relatively little is known of its use in the Roman period (apart from the presence of salt production) we probably should not expect such extensive settlement as seen in Fenland or the Severn wetlands.

The recolonisation of Romney Marsh appears to have been well underway by the 9th century, as was the case in the North Kent Marshes (Rippon 2000, 152–85). Compared to other coastal wetlands, this is relatively early, suggesting that it had now become a valued area. In the Norfolk Marshland, for example, whilst there was settlement of the coastal marshes by the 7th to 9th century these sites lay in an intertidal, as opposed to a reclaimed landscape (Crowson *et al.* 2000, 213–25). It was only around the 10th century that the area appears to have been embanked (Crowson *et al.* 2000, 225–30; Rippon 2000, 175). In areas such as South East Wales, the Pevensey Levels, Essex, the Havergate Marsh in Norfolk, along stretches of the Lincolnshire coast and around the Humber Estuary, reclamation was even later (Rippon 2000). The relatively early date of reclamation on Romney Marsh can be attributed to a number of factors. The early establishment of the Christian church led to the endowment of a series of wealthy monasteries in Kent, which had the inclination and resources to increase the productivity of their estates, especially on areas of underdeveloped land ripe for improvement. The marshland holdings of those monasteries were part of a complex estate structure that included land in the fertile agricultural 'core' regions of Kent, and the woodland of the Weald (e.g. Smith 1943; Everitt 1986). The holdings in Romney Marsh, in the very south of Kent, were physically remote and in an unreclaimed state that may be regarded as physically 'marginal'. In practice, however, they were to become a highly valued asset because of the diversity they brought to these medieval estates, initially as seasonal pasture, and later through the opportunity they provided for raising new revenue through improvement (reclamation). Far from being 'marginal', their proximity to a series of port towns, and the huge investment in reclamation, suggests that this was regarded as a valued region within the pattern of Kentish monastic estates.

Conclusions

Romney Marsh is fortunate in having a wide range of evidence that has been generated from its long history of academic research. This palaeoenvironmental, archaeological and documentary evidence has been integrated in the tentative model for how the historic landscape evolved that is outlined above. Perhaps the one resource that has yet to be exploited to its full is information locked within the historic landscape itself, though hopefully this paper will have shown its potential. It must be stressed that this palaeogeographical reconstruction is highly speculative, but it will hopefully provide a stimulus for further research. In particular, this paper has supported Green's model of the Rother originally discharging its water via a tidal estuary at Hythe. This hypothesis needs to be tested through a carefully targeted programme of palaeoenvironmental work focussed on the potential line of this palaeochannel.

The history of human exploitation of Romney Marsh shares many features in common with other coastal wetlands in Britain. The historic landscape evolved as human communities changed from simply exploiting the rich natural resources (as was the case in the Roman period), to transforming it through reclamation. This was a high cost strategy in terms of the initial investment of resources, and a high risk strategy as the shown by the widespread flooding during the late 13th and 14th centuries. Coastal wetlands are particularly dynamic landscapes, and as such are particularly prone to environmental changes, in this case the evolution of, and breaches in, the natural shingle barrier. Though constantly at risk from flooding, and with a high annual cost in terms of maintaining flood defences, the perception of estate owners and marshland communities was clearly that the returns from agriculture made that investment worthwhile. This high agricultural productivity, and proximity to nodal points in the coastal navigation network, made land on coastal levels and marshes highly desirable: far from being in any sense 'marginal', these were core regions for much of their recent history.

Acknowledgements
First and foremost I must thank members of the Romney Marsh Research Trust for shedding so much light on this remarkable landscape, and Antony Long for inviting me to present this paper, and his editorial advice. I first visited the Marsh with John Allen and Mike Fulford, two former colleagues from Reading University, and I take this opportunity to thank them for stimulating and encouraging my research into wetland landscapes.

References

Allen, J.R.L. 1985. Intertidal drainage and mass-movement processes in the Severn Estuary: rills and creeks (pills), *Journal of the Geological Society, London* **142**, 849–61.
Allen, J.R.L. 1996. The sequence of early land-claims on the Walland and Romney Marshes, southern Britain: a pre-liminary hypothesis and some implications, *Proceedings of the Geologists' Association* **107**, 271–80.
Allen, J.R.L. 1998. Magor Pill multiperiod site: the Romano-British pottery, and status as a port, *Archaeology in the Severn Estuary* **9**, 45–60.

Allen, J.R.L. 1999. The Rumenesea Wall and the early settled landscape of Romney Marsh (Kent), *Landscape History* **21**, 5–18.

Allen, J.R.L. and Fulford, M.G. 1996. The distribution of South East Dorset black burnished category 1 pottery in South West Britain, *Britannia* **27**, 223–81.

Allen, J.R.L. and Fulford, M.G. 1999. Fort building and military supply along Britain's eastern channel and North Sea coasts: the later second and third centuries, *Britannia* **XXX**, 163–84.

Allen, J.R.L. and Rippon, S.J. 1997. Iron Age to early modern activity and palaeochannels at Magor Pill, Gwent: an exercise in lowland coastal-zone archaeology, *Antiquaries Journal* **77**, 327–70.

Allen, M. and Gardiner, J. 2000. *Our Changing Coast: a Survey of the Intertidal Archaeology of Langstone Harbour, Hampshire*. Council for British Archaeology research report **124**.

Barber, L. 1998. Medieval Rural Settlement and Economy at Lydd, in J. Eddison, M. Gardiner and A. Long (eds) *Romney Marsh: Environmental Change and Human Occupation in a Coastal Lowland* (Oxford University Committee for Archaeology Monograph **46**), 89–108. Oxford.

Bazelmans, J., Gerrets, D., Koning, J. de, Vos, P. 1999. Zoden aan de dijk. Kleinschalige dijkbouw in de late prehistorie en protohistorie van noordelijk Westergo, *De Vrije Fries* **79**, 7–74.

Behre, K.-E. and Jacomet, S. 1991. The ecological interpretation of archaeobotanical data, in W. Van Zeist, K. Wasylikowa, and K.-E. Behre (eds) *Progress in Old World Palaeo-ethnobotany*, Balkema, 81–108. Rotterdam.

Bell, M., Caseldine, A. and Neumann, H. 2000. *Prehistoric Intertidal Archaeology in the Welsh Severn Estuary*. Council for British Archaeology research report **120**.

Besteman, J.C. 1990. North Holland AD 400-1200: turning tide or tide turned?, in J.C. Besteman, J.M. Bos and H.A. Heidinga (eds) *Medieval Archaeology in the Netherlands*, Van Gorcum, 91–120. Assen/Maastricht.

Bland, B.F. 1971. Crop production: cereals and legumes, in Summerfield, R.J. and Roberts, E.H. (eds) *Grain Legume Crops*, Collins, 269–303. London.

Bond, D.A., Lewis, D.A., G.C., Hawton, G.C., Saxena, M.C. and Stephens, J.H. 1985. Faba bean (*Vicia faba* L), in R.J. Summerfield and E.H. Roberts (eds) *Grain Legume Crops*, Collins, 199–265. London.

Bottema, S., Hoorn, T.C. Van, Woldring, H. and Gremmen, W.H.E. 1980. An agricultural experiment in the unprotected saltmarsh, part II, *Palaeohistoria* **XXII**, 127–40.

Brooks, N. 1988. Romney Marsh in the Early Middle Ages, in J. Eddison, and C. Green (eds), *Romney Marsh. Evolution, Occupation, Reclamation* (Oxford University Committee for Archaeology Monograph **24**), 90–104. Oxford.

Campbell, B.M.S. 1988. The diffusion of vetches in medieval England, *Economic History Review*, 2nd Ser. **XLI**, 193–208.

Coles, J. 1989. *Somerset Levels Papers* **15**, Somerset Levels Project. Exeter

Coles, B. and Coles, J. 1986. *Sweet Track to Glastonbury*. Thames and Hudson. London.

Crowson, A., Lane, T. and Reeve, J. 2000. *Fenland Management Project Excavations 1993–1995*, (Lincolnshire Archaeology and Heritage Reports Series **3**). Sleaford.

Cunliffe, B. 1988. Romney Marsh in the Roman Period, in J. Eddison, and C. Green (eds) *Romney Marsh. Evolution, Occupation, Reclamation* (Oxford University Committee for Archaeology Monograph **24**), 83–87. Oxford.

Currie, C.R.J. 1988. Early vetches: a note, *Economic History Review*, 2nd Ser. XLI, 114–6.

Davenport, F.G. 1967. *The Economic Development of a Norfolk Manor, 1086–1565*. Cambridge.

Draper, G. 1998. The farmers of Canterbury Cathedral Priory and All Soles College Oxford on Romney Marsh *c.* 1443–1545, in J. Eddison, M. Gardiner and A. Long (eds) *Romney Marsh: Environmental Change and Human Occupation in a Coastal Lowland* (Oxford University Committee for Archaeology Monograph **46**), 109–28. Oxford.

Dulley, A.J.F. 1966. The Level and Port of Pevensey in the Middle Ages, *Sussex Archaeological Collections* **104**, 26–45.

Dyer, C. 1989. *Standards of Living in the Later Middle Ages, c. 1200–1520*. Cambridge University Press. Cambridge.

Eddison, J. 1983. The evolution of the barrier beaches between Fairlight and Hythe, *Geographical Journal* **149**, 39–53.

Eddison, J. (ed.) 1995. *Romney Marsh: The Debatable Ground* (Oxford University Committee for Archaeology Monograph **41**). Oxford.

Eddison, J. 1998. Catastrophic Changes: a multidisciplinary study of the evolution of the barrier beaches of Rye Bay, J. Eddison, M. Gardiner, and A. Long (eds), *Romney Marsh: Environmental Change and Human Occupation in a Coastal Lowland* (Oxford University Committee for Archaeology Monograph **46**), 65–87. Oxford.

Eddison, J. 2000. *Romney Marsh: Survival on a Frontier*, Tempus. Stroud.

Eddison, J. and Draper, G. 1997. A landscape of medieval reclamation: Walland Marsh, Kent, *Landscape History* **19**, 75–88.

Eddison, J., Gardiner, M. and Long, A. (eds) 1998. *Romney Marsh: Environmental Change and Human Occupation in a Coastal Lowland* (Oxford University Committee for Archaeology Monograph **46**). Oxford.

Eddison, J., and Green, C. (eds) 1988. *Romney Marsh: Evolution, Occupation, Reclamation* (Oxford University Committee for Archaeology Monograph **24**). Oxford.

Ellis, S., Fenwick, H., Lillie, M. and Van de Noort, R. 2001. *Wetland Heritage of the Lincolnshire Marsh: An Archaeological Survey*. Humber Wetlands Project. Kingston upon Hull.

Everitt, A. 1986. *Continuity and Colonisation: the Evolution of Kentish Settlement*. Leicester University Press. Leicester.

Finberg, H.P.R. 1951. *Tavistock Abbey: a Study in the Social and Economic History of Devon*. Cambridge University Press. Cambridge.

Furley, R. 1874. *A History of the Weald of Kent* (volume **2**). Ashford and London.

Gardiner, M. 1988. Medieval settlement and society in the Broomhill area, and excavations at Broomhill church, in J. Eddison and C. Green (eds), *Romney Marsh: Evolution, Occupation, Reclamation* (Oxford University Committee for Archaeology Monograph **24**), 112–127. Oxford.

Gardiner, M. 1994. Old Romney: an examination of the evidence for a lost Saxo-Norman port, *Archaeologia Cantiana* **114**, 329–45.

Gardiner, M. 1995. Medieval farming and flooding in the Brede

Valley, in J. Eddison (ed.), *Romney Marsh: The Debatable Ground* (Oxford University Committee for Archaeology Monograph **41**), 127–37. Oxford.

Gardiner, M. 1998. Settlement Change on Walland and Denge Marshes, 1400–1550, in Eddison, M. Gardiner, and A. Long (eds) *Romney Marsh: Environmental Change and Human Occupation in a Coastal Lowland* (Oxford University Committee for Archaeology Monograph **46**), 129–46. Oxford.

Green, C. 1988. Palaeogeography of marine inlets of the Romney Marsh area, in J. Eddison, M. Gardiner, and A. Long (eds), *Romney Marsh: Environmental Change and Human Occupation in a Coastal Lowland* (Oxford University Committee for Archaeology Monograph **46**), 167–74. Oxford.

Green, R.D. 1968. *Soils of Romney Marsh,* (Soil Survey of Great Britain, Bulletin No. **4**), Harpenden.

Grieg, J. 1988. *Plant Resources,* in G. Astill and A. Grant (eds) *The Countryside of Medieval England,* Blackwells, 149–87. Oxford.

Gross, A. and Butcher, A. 1995. Adaptation and investment in the age of the Great Storms: agricultural policy on the manors of the principal lords of the Romney Marshes and the marshland fringe, *c.* 1250–1320, in J. Eddison (ed.) *Romney Marsh: The Debatable Ground* (Oxford University Committee for Archaeology Monograph **41**), 107–17. Oxford.

Hall, D. 1996. *The Fenland Project, Number 10: Cambridgeshire Survey, Isle of Ely and Wisbech.* East Anglian Archaeology **79**.

Hall, D.N. and Coles, J. 1994. *The Fenland Survey: An Essay in Landscape and Persistence* (English Heritage Archaeological Report **1**). London.

Hodgkinson, D., Huckerby, E., Middleton, R. and Wells, C.E. 2000. *The Lowland Wetlands of Cumbria.* (North West Wetlands Survey **6**). Lancaster.

Holloway, W. 1849. *The History of Romney Marsh.* London: John Russell Smith.

Homan, 1938. The Marshes between Hythe and Pett: an attempt at the reconstruction of their topography as it was in the Middle Ages, *Sussex Archaeological Collections* **LXXIX**, 199–223.

Hoskins, W.G. 1955. *The Making of the English Landscape.* London.

Howell, C. 1983. *Land, Family and Inheritance in Transition: Kibworth Harcourt 1280–1700.* Cambridge University Press. Cambridge.

Keil, I.J.E. 1964. The Estates of Glastonbury Abbey in the Later Middle Ages (unpublished Ph.D. thesis, University of Bristol).

Lewin, T. 1862. *The Invasion of Britain by Julius Caesar.* London: Longman, Green, Longman and Roberts.

Long, A., Waller, M., Hughes, P. and Spencer, C. 1998. The Holocene depositional history of Romney Marsh proper, in J. Eddison, M. Gardiner and A. Long (eds) *Romney Marsh: Environmental Change and Human Occupation in a Coastal Lowland* (Oxford University Committee for Archaeology Monograph **46**), 45–63. Oxford.

Mate, M. 1991. The agrarian economy of south-east England before the Black Death: degressed or bouyant?, in B.M.S. Campbell (ed.) *Before the Black Death: Studies in the 'Crisis' of the Early Fourteenth Century,* Manchester University Press, 78–109. Manchester.

Morgan, P. 1983. *Domesday Book: Kent.* Phillimore. Chichester.

Nayling, N. 1998. *The Magor Pill Medieval Wreck.* Council for British Archaeology research report **115**.

Neilson, N. 1932. The Domesday Monachorum, *Victoria County History of Kent* **3**, 253–69.

Nichols, J.F. 1932. Milton Hall: the compotus of 1299, *Transactions of the Southend-on-Sea Antiquarian and Historical Society* **II**, 113–67.

Overton, M. and Campbell, B.M.S. 1999: Statistics of production and productivity in English agriculture 1086-1871, in van Bavel, B.J.P. and Thoen, E. (eds) *Land Productivity and Agro-Systems in the North Sea Area (Middle Ages – 20th Century* (Brepols), 189–208.

Postan, M.M. 1966. *The Cambridge EconomicHistory of Europe. Volume 1: The Agrarian Life of the Middle Ages.* 2nd Ed. Cambridge University Press. Cambridge.

Reeves, A. 1995. Romney Marsh: the fieldwalking evidence, in J. Eddison (ed.) *Romney Marsh: The Debatable Ground* (Oxford University Committee for Archaeology Monograph **41**) 78–91. Oxford.

Rhoades, J.D., Kandiah, A. and Mashali, A.M. 1992. *The Use of Saline Waters for Crop Production.* F.A.O. Irrigation and Drainage papers 48.

Riley, H.T. 1874a. Manuscripts of the Corporation of Hythe, Kent, *Historic Manuscripts Commission, 4th report, part 1,* 429–39.

Riley, H.T. 1874b. Manuscripts of the Corporation of New Romney, Kent, *Historic Manuscripts Commission, 4th report, part 1,* 439–42.

Riley, H.T. 1876a. Manuscripts of the Corporation of Rye, Kent, *Historic Manuscripts Commission, 5th report, part 1,* 488–516.

Riley, H.T. 1876b. Manuscripts of the Corporation of Lydd, Kent, *Historic Manuscripts Commission, 5th report, part 1,* 516–33.

Riley, H.T. 1876c. Manuscripts of the Corporation of New Romney, Second Notice. *Historic Manuscripts Commission, 5th report, part 1,* 533–54.

Rippon, S. 1996. *The Gwent Levels; the Evolution of a Wetland Landscape.* Council for British Archaeology research report **105**.

Rippon, S 1997. *The Severn Estuary: Landscape Evolution and Wetland Reclamation* Leicester University Press. London.

Rippon, S. 2000. *The Transformation of Coastal Wetlands.* The British Academy. London.

Rippon, S. 2001a (ed.). *Estuarine Archaeology: the Severn and Beyond* (Archaeology in the Severn Estuary **11**, for 2000). Exeter: Severn Estuary Levels Research Committee.

Rippon, S. 2001b. The Historic Landscapes of the Severn Estuary. In Rippon, S. (ed.), *Estuarine Archaeology: the Severn and Beyond* (Archaeology in the Severn Estuary **11**, for 2000). Severn Estuary Levels Research Committee. 119–35. Exeter.

Rippon, S. 2001c. Infield and Outfield: the early stages of marshland colonisation and the evolution of medieval field systems. In Lane, T. (ed.) *Through Wet and Dry: Essays in Honour of David Hall,* Heritage Lincolnshire. 54–70. Sleaford.

Rippon, S. 2001d. Reclamation and regional economies of medieval Britain, in Raftery, B. and Hickey J. (eds) *Recent Developments in Wetland Research.* 139–59. Dublin.

Rippon, S. forthcoming a. Fields of beans and flocks of sheep:

the perception of wetland landscapes during the medieval period. In M. Bell and C. Boardman (eds) *Geoarchaeology: Landscape Change Over Archaeological Timescales.*

Rippon, S. forthcoming b. Adaptation to a changing environment: the response of marshland communities to the late medieval 'crisis'. *Journal of Wetland Archaeology* **1**.

Round, J.H. 1906. The Domesday Survey, *Victoria County History of Somerset* **1**.

Salzman, L.F. 1937. Broomhill, *Victorian County History of Kent* **9**, 148–50.

Searle, E. and Ross, B. 1967. *Accounts of the Cellarers of Battle Abbey 1275–1513.* Sydney University Press. Sydney.

Silvester, R.J. 1988. *The Fenland Project, Number 3: Norfolk Survey, Marshland and Nar Valley.* East Anglian Archaeology **45**.

Smith, R.A.L. 1943. *Canterbury Cathedral Priory: a Study in Monastic Administration.* Cambridge University Press. Cambridge.

Spencer, C.D. 1996. The Holocene Evolution of Romney Marsh: a record of sea level change in a back barrier environment (unpublished Ph.D. thesis, University of Liverpool).

Spencer, C., Plater, A. and Long, A. 1998a. Holocene barrier estuary evolution: The sedimentary record of Walland Marsh, in J. Eddison, M. Gardiner and A. Long (eds) *Romney Marsh: Environmental Change and Human Occupation in a Coastal Lowland* (Oxford University Committee for Archaeology Monograph **46**), 13–29. Oxford.

Spencer, C., Plater, A. and Long, A. 1998a. Rapid coastal change during the mid- to late Holocene: the record of barrier estuary sedimentation in the Romney Marsh region, southeast England, *The Holocene* **8**, 143–63.

Tatton-Brown, T. 1988. The topography of the Walland Marsh area between the eleventh and thirteenth centuries, in J. Eddison and C. Green (eds) *Romney Marsh: Evolution, Occupation, Reclamation* (Oxford University Committee for Archaeology Monograph No. **24**). 105–11. Oxford.

Teichman Derville, M. 1936. *The Level and Liberty of Romney Marsh in the County of Kent.* Headley Brothers. Ashford and London.

Thornton, C. 1991. The determinants of land productivity on the Bishop of Winchester's demesne at Rimpton, 1208 to 1403, in Campbell, B.M.S. and Overton, M. (eds) *Land, Labour and Livestock,* Manchester University Press, 183–210. Manchester.

Tomalin, D. 2000. Stress at the seams: assessing the terrestrial and submerged archaeological landscape on the shore of the Magnus Portus, in A. Aberg and C. Lewis (eds) *The Rising Tide: Archaeology and Coastal Landscapes,* Oxbow Books, 85–98. Oxford.

Tusser, T. 1557. *Five Hundred Points of Good Husbandry ....* Reprinted 1812, ed. William Mavor, London.

Vollans, E. 1988. New Romney and the 'river of Neweden' in the later Middle Ages, in J. Eddison and C. Green (eds) *Romney Marsh: Evolution, Occupation, Reclamation* (Oxford University Committee for Archaeology Monograph **24**), 128–41. Oxford.

Waller, M., Burrin, P. and Marlow, A. 1988. Flandrian sedimentation and palaeoenvironments in Pett Level, the Brede and lower Rother Valleys and Walland Marsh, in J. Eddison and C. Green (eds) *Romney Marsh: Evolution, Occupation, Reclamation* (Oxford University Committee for Archaeology Monograph **24**), 3–30. Oxford.

Ward, G. 1952. The Saxon history of the town and port of Romney, *Archaeologia Cantiana* **LXV**, 12–25.

Wass, M. 1995. Proposed northern course of the Rother: a sedimentological and microfaunal investigation, in J. Eddison (ed.) *Romney Marsh: The Debatable Ground* (Oxford University Committee for Archaeology Monograph **41**), 51–77. Oxford.

Wilkinson, T.J. and Murphy, P.L. 1995. *The Archaeology of the Essex Coast, Volume 1: The Hullbridge Survey,* East Anglian Archaeology **71**.

Williams, J. and Brown, N. 1999. *An Archaeological Research Framework for the Greater Thames Estuary.* Essex County Council. Chelmsford.

Williamson, T. 1997. *The Norfolk Broads: a Landscape History.* Manchester University Press. Manchester.

Wretts-Smith, M. 1931/32. Organisation of Farming at Croyland Abbey 1257–1321, *Journal of Economic and Business History* **IV**, 168–92.

Zeist, W. Van. 1974. Palaeobotanical studies of settlement sites in the coastal area of The Netherlands, *Palaeohistoria* **16**, 223–371.

Zeist, W. Van, Van Hoorn, T.C., Bottema, S. and Woldring, H. 1976. An agricultural experiment in the unprotected salt-marsh, *Palaeohistoria* **18**, 111–53.

Romney Marsh: Coastal and Landscape Change through the Ages
(ed. A. Long, S. Hipkin and H. Clarke), OUSA Monograph 56, 2002, 101–120

7. The Late Medieval 'Antediluvian' Landscape of Walland Marsh

Mark Gardiner

Flooding in the late 13th century led to the inundation of a large area of the south-west of Walland Marsh. Two major inlets were formed along the Wainway Channel and the line of the River Rother, and much of the flooded land became saltmarsh. Saltmarsh creeks seem to have formed along the lines of earlier drainage ditches preserving evidence of the pre-inundation or 'antediluvian' landscape. Part of the flooded land was reclaimed between the late 14th and late 15th centuries. Kent Ditch had been dug as a drainage channel by the early 15th century and formed the county boundary between Kent and Sussex. It probably ran along a similar line to its antediluvian predecessor. The reclaimed landscape of Walland Marsh reflects, therefore, not only the work of the 14th and 15th century, but also of the original enclosure a century or two earlier. Marsh landscapes elsewhere in England may also be the product, not of a single phase of enclosure, but include elements which survive from Roman and early medieval episodes of inning.

Medieval marshland should be an ideal environment for the application of landscape archaeology. The reclaimed landscape appears to have been a *tabula rasa* on which Roman and medieval communities laid out fields and ditches. These field patterns were long-lasting, because boundaries, usually marked by drainage ditches, could not readily be changed. It is possible, therefore, to dissect the field patterns and determine the sequence of reclamation, as Silvester has shown in the Norfolk Fens and Rippon has demonstrated in the Severn Estuary and Somerset Levels.[1] However, not all marshlands are the result of a single episode of reclamation. The Fens themselves display evidence for Roman as well as medieval settlement, raising the question whether the landscape of the earlier period may have influenced the later.[2] On the Wentlooge Levels in Gwent, for example, the Roman drainage channels survived as features and continued to be used in the medieval and modern periods.[3]

Questions of persistence and the remaking of the marshland landscape are particularly important for Walland Marsh where there were two distinct episodes of reclamation, both medieval. There is negligible evidence for Roman reclamation and limited evidence for settlement. The first took place during the 12th and early 13th centuries as settlement extended outwards in two directions, from the uplands in Sussex and from the already settled areas of Romney Marsh proper in Kent. A considerable part of the reclaimed land was subsequently lost in the flooding of the late 13th century. Some of the inundated areas were not again reclaimed until a second phase of inning a century or more later. It has been commonly assumed that the earlier landscape of Walland Marsh was largely erased by the late-13th-century flooding and deposition of sediment. That view, for example, is implicit in Cook's description of the drainage system of Guldeford Marsh.[4] But contemporary examples of set-back or managed retreat, considered further below, show that the reintroduction of tidal water into marshland does not result in sudden extreme change to the drainage pattern, but in the progressive development of a new hydraulic regime over a timescale of decades or even centuries. That raises the possibility that the pattern of fields and watercourses on

Walland Marsh is not only the product of 14th- and 15th-century activity, but may be based on an earlier, 'ante-diluvian' or pre-flood landscape dating to the 12th or early 13th century.

The present paper examines the evidence for an antediluvian landscape on the south and west sides of Walland Marsh. The documentary background to the early 13th-century enclosure, the flooding of 1287 and after, and the subsequent reclamation of the marshland are examined in the first part. The geomorphological evidence for the development of saltmarsh and the response to subsequent flooding is considered in the second section. The subsequent section examines in detail the archaeo-logical evidence for the antediluvian landscape on Walland Marsh and its implications for the 14th- and 15th-century reclamations (Fig. 7.1). The issue of the persistence of marshland landscapes more generally forms the subject of the conclusion.

Historical Evidence for Reclamation, Flooding and Recovery

The early history of the reclamation of Walland Marsh is largely undocumented. The work of constructing many kilometres of embankment and digging even greater lengths of drainage ditch within the enclosures must have been costly, but sources which might have recorded such activities rarely survive from the 12th and early 13th centuries when much of the work must have taken place. The exceptional records for the Broomhill area have been discussed elsewhere and these include a series of agree-ments made by the abbeys of Battle and Robertsbridge by which they contracted to enclose substantial areas and divide the land in the proportion 7/12ths and 5/12ths.[5]

The enclosure of Walland Marsh was made possible by the shingle barrier which protected the south-west side from the sea. The evidence suggests that there was a continuous route along the shingle even as late as 1200.[6] Administratively, the south-western part of Walland Marsh belonged to Sussex rather than Kent. Originally, the parish of Icklesham seems to have included the area of the later parish of St Thomas of Winchelsea and extended eastwards from the upland as far as the boundary with Kent.[7] The parishes of Playden and Iden likewise stretched onto the marsh.[8] The obvious line for the boundary between Kent and Sussex was the River Rother which formed the limit of the counties further west. The fact that this was not adopted across the marsh suggests, firstly, that it was not a major watercourse and, secondly, that estates in Sussex are likely to have established rights on the wetland at an early date.[9] The Rother may not have had a single river course, but could have consisted of a series of minor channels. One channel was known as the 'water of Rye' and was sufficiently narrow to be bridged at one point and possibly elsewhere. In the early 13th century the manor of Leigh in Iden held lands on both sides of the 'water of

Rye' and access to the marshlands was obtained over *Morbrigge*.[10] The 'water of Rye' was exposed to marine influence and in *c.* 1200 salt water was penetrating as far inland as Playden. Salt was being made there, perhaps near to Saltcot Street (*Salkote*: 1345), and the land at *Eures*, which may be identified with the place later called River (Playden), was described as salt marshland.[11]

There was apparently a gap in the shingle barrier by the early 13th century when West Winchelsea was evidently distinguished from a similar area on the east. A watermill mentioned there in 1220 is likely to have been a tide mill, since the flow of river water so near the sea would hardly have been sufficient to drive it.[12] The evidence for the progressive decay of the barrier beach has been traced elsewhere.[13] It is notable that clauses in deeds contingent upon the submergence of lands by the sea occur in the 1220s in the area of Old Winchelsea while enclosure continued confidently in the more distant marshland until the 1240s.[14] The flooding caused by the storms of 1250, 1252 and particularly of 1287 and 1288 is well known. In the last of those years, the floods of 4th February not only affected the coastal areas, but also the Brede Valley and up the Rother Valley to Iden and Ebony near Appledore.[15] Eddison and Draper have suggested that the flooded area extended east and north as far as a line of walls which they have named the 'great cordon', and which was called in some contemporary documents 'the Great Wall of Appledore' (Fig. 7.2).[16]

The impact of the flooding and the process of the recovery after the storms is difficult to trace. It is unlikely that it was simply a matter of restoring the embankments and clearing the drains. The storms wrought fundamental changes to the coastal topography, and the shingle barrier which had protected the south-west coast of Walland Marsh was still in retreat late in the 1330s. A commission *de walliis et fossatis* was empanelled in 1331 to examine the marshes between Rye and New Winchelsea, and another, which commenced work in 1333 and reported in 1336, was concerned with land further west near to Winchelsea, which was exposed as the breach in the shingle continued to increase.[17] Between 1337 and 1341 extensive works were undertaken to protect from the sea 128 acres at *Spadlond*, an area to the east of New Winchelsea. These were ultimately unsuccessful as the marsh was finally 'destroyed by the storms of the sea' in 1351.[18]

The breach in the shingle barrier created two large inlets which stretched inland up the west side of Walland Marsh and along the Wainway Channel on the south side (Fig. 7.1). Eddison has suggested that the breach extended as far eastwards as Broomhill Farm and is marked by the high-level shingle bank which can be traced running beneath the farm and Beach Banks Cottage.[19] Unpublished excavation undertaken in 1989 confirmed that the shingle at the point sectioned was about 0.95 m thick and lay on fine-grain sediments. That work confirmed that the shingle bank was unrelated to the low-level shingle mass which underlies the south-eastern part of Walland Marsh. It is

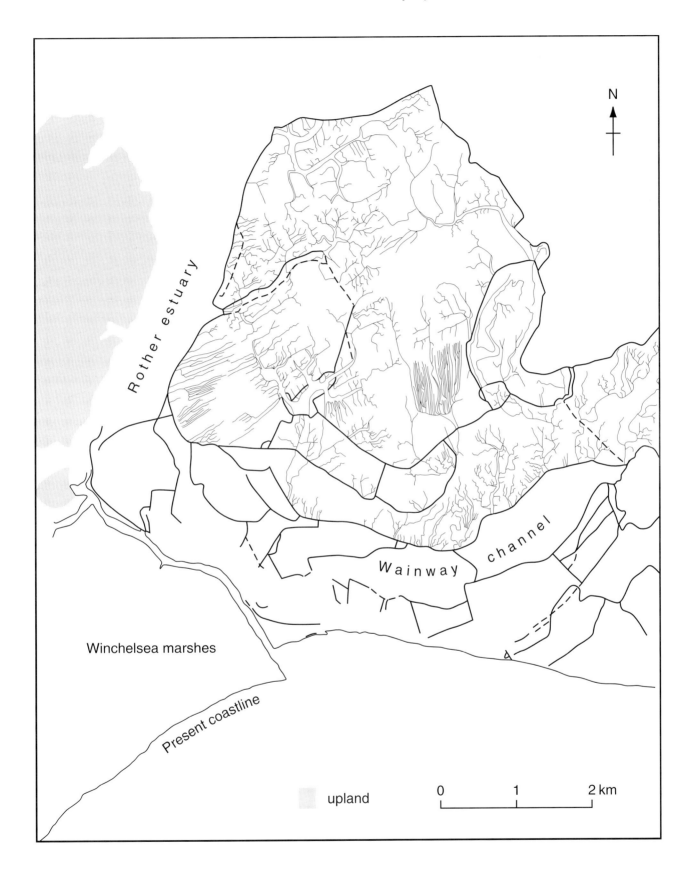

Fig. 7.1. The south-west side of Walland Marsh.

hard to reconcile such an enormous breach with the documentary evidence. In 1341 there was a protected anchorage at Winchelsea suitable for the mustering of a fleet of 200 or 250 ships intended for the invasion of Brittany.[20] It had became established as an important anchorage for English and foreign ships and since at least 1330 the area had been called the Camber, a name which implies a partially enclosed roadstead.[21] It seems difficult to accept that an extensive breach could have healed so rapidly in the first half of the 14th century and therefore the shingle bank north-east of Broomhill may represent a separate, local failure.

Some of the shingle from the breach in the barrier south of Rye was driven northwards into the estuary and on to the point between the estuarine channels of the Rother and the Wainway where it formed a bank which may be traced beneath Black House Farm, Moneypenny and Salts Farm. On the west side of the estuary shingle rolling northwards caused problems with access to Winchelsea. In 1336 the merchants of Winchelsea obtained permission to levy a charge on ships and goods coming into the harbour to pay for a breakwater to protect it from the sand and shingle which were choking the entrance. Measures were also made to encourage tidal flow up the Brede in the hope that it would help clear the obstruction.[22] In the longer term, it was not the sand and shingle which caused a problem, but fine-grain sediments which progressively choked the port. It was evidently in a bid to clear these that massive works were undertaken in the Brede Valley at some date between 1419 and 1442 to create a tidal inlet known as 'the Channel'. 'The Channel' was intended to permit the flow of tidal water up the Brede, encourage the scouring of the port at Winchelsea and so clear it of the sand and shingle which had been concerning the merchants for a century.[23]

The impact of the removal of the shingle barrier on Walland Marsh west and south of the Great Wall can only be speculated. It seems likely that any sea embankments in the area may have been breached but, unless they were near to the coast and exposed to the impact of waves, it is unlikely that very long lengths would have been removed. However, the reclamation of the marsh was evidently not a simple task and little work appears to have taken place for a century after the flooding. The work of reclaiming Appledore Marsh, the Becard and Kete Marsh on the north-west side of Walland Marsh was not begun until late in the 14th century. An area of 107 marsh acres (about 133 statute acres) was enclosed in 1390 at the cost of £220 13s. 8d., equivalent to 41s. 2d. for every marsh acre, and funded by the archbishop of Canterbury, the prior of Christ Church Canterbury and abbot of Robertsbridge.[24] In 1399 566 marsh acres were enclosed in Appledore Marsh at the lesser cost of 12s. 8d. an acre and the following year a further 128 acres in the Becard to the west of Fairfield church were also inned.[25] All those lands were drained and enclosed by monastic houses, but lay individuals were also active. A lease of 1391 was issued by a Rye merchant,

John Salerne, for 112 marsh acres he held to the south of Kete Fleet.[26] On the south side of Walland Marsh, the picture is probably indicated by an inquisition of 1397 into the lands of the archbishop of Canterbury which shows that he held innings at Roundmarsh and Baynham (near Cheney Court) in his manor of Cheney and also an area of unenclosed saltmarsh worth 40s.[27]

By the early 15th century much of the land as far as Kent Ditch had probably been brought back into use. Little more work appears to have been undertaken until the 1470s when there was a resurgence of interest. A contract of 1471 between the prior of Christ Church and Richard Clark of Appledore records the intended enclosure of an area of land of uncertain size called *Pikes*.[28] Two years later, the archbishop of Canterbury, the prior of Christ Church Canterbury and the abbot of Robertsbridge reached an agreement for further inning at Becard.[29] Other land remained to be inned on the south-west of Kent Ditch. In 1478 Richard Guldeford was granted an area of salt marsh by Robertsbridge Abbey and this marked the start of a new phase of inning. His new marsh seems to have lain south of More Fleet (Fig. 7.2: 6).[30] Not all the work of this period was enclosure of new land: work was also undertaken to reinforce the existing walls against the sea.[31] There was considerable concern about the flooding of Cowlese Marsh and a commission of sewers was established for the area.[32] At the same time a commission *de walliis et fossatis* was empanelled in 1477 to look at all the walls along the marsh from Appledore to Rye and a new scot-list was drawn up for the whole of Walland Marsh.[33] Concern extended to the area north of the Isle of Oxney, and a map showing that area may belong to this period.[34]

Walland Marsh had been substantially reclaimed by 1500, even as far as East Guldeford where a church was then under construction on land recently enclosed by Richard Guldeforde (Fig. 7.2: 6).[35] The only lands subsequently recovered were those in the Wainway Channel which are the subject of a separate investigation (Fig. 7.2: 4–5 and 7). Some areas had been salt marsh for 200 years between the flooding of the late 13th century and their final recovery, but much of the marsh immediately south and west of the Great Wall seems to have been brought into use, perhaps only as saltmarsh grazing, within a century or less of the flooding.

Geomorphological Approaches to Creek Patterns on Coastal Saltmarshes

Although considerable work has been undertaken on the development of saltmarshes, there has been relatively little study of the development of the plan of their creeks. This is a little surprising given the range of variation in creek pattern. Pethick, who has undertaken preliminary work on the problem, has emphasized the importance of two factors – wave energy and tidal energy – in the development of

Fig. 7.2. The saltmarsh creek system of south-west Walland Marsh after the late 13th-century inundation. The main creeks are labelled with upper-case letters; the enclosures are numbered. The area of ground between the creek systems is hatched and labelled 'a'.

creek form. Where the marshes are exposed to the open sea, wave action may be more important, but in sheltered situations tidal energy will be the dominant factor.[36] Saltmarsh creeks, in conjunction with the mudflats, are morphologically adapted to absorb the wave and tidal energy. The long parallel creeks found, for example, on the Dengie Peninsula (Essex) have not developed to respond to tidal energy which is relatively slight, but to

low-frequency, wind-wave energy which forces water up into the marshes. The resulting creek pattern may be classified as linear (Fig. 7.3: 1).[37] By contrast, at Scolt Head Island (Norfolk) and around the Tollesbury marshes (Essex), where the dominant force is tidal, the creeks form a dendritic pattern. In the former place, the breadth of the saltmarsh is considerable and the tidal energy is dissipated in a network of branching channels which do not stretch

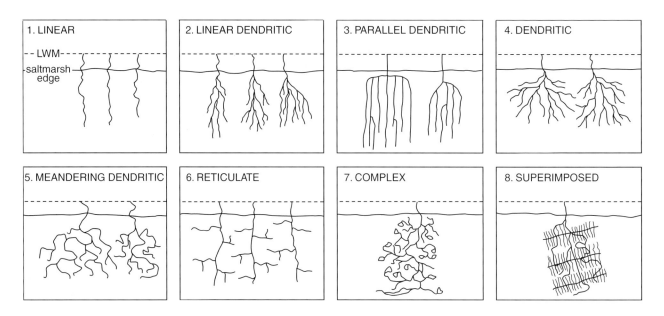

Fig. 7.3. Types of saltmarsh creek networks (modified from Pye (2000, fig. 3)).

to the back of the marsh (Fig. 7.3: 4). At Tollesbury, where the marsh is much narrower, the saltmarsh creeks have a meandering form to allow the energy to be dissipated in a more confined space (Fig. 7.3: 5).[38] Variations on the linear and dendritic plans may be found on other marshlands. The creeks at the mouth of the River Nene east of Gedney Drove End (Lincs), for example, have a linear dendritic form (Fig. 7.3: 2), while those at Kincardine on the Firth of Forth shown a parallel dendritic pattern (Fig. 7.3: 3).[39] Reticulate creek patterns are rare and Allen has commented that they could 'reflect antecedent forms' (Fig. 7.3: 6).[40] It is suggested below that reticulate and superimposed forms (Fig. 7.3: 8) are the results of the inundation of reclaimed marshland. The final type, the complex creek pattern is limited to places where the saltmarshes are being eroded. An example has been recorded at Tollesbury (Fig 7.3: 7).[41]

The differences in tidal and wave energy do not provide a complete explanation for variation in the form of creek systems. The nature of the underlying sediment or soil and the character of vegetation, which itself is related to the nature of the soil, are also important factors. Saltmarsh vegetation generally has a wide range of tolerance of local conditions, but the abundance of species is affected by the physical conditions which determine waterlogging and soil aeration.[42] Chapman distinguishes between three groups of creek system. The first occurs on sandy marshes where there are relatively few creeks and consequently their plan is simple. The second is found in muddy marshes which tend to have dendritic creek systems. The third is associated with marshes dominated by *Spartina* (Cord grass) found typically in southern England. These generally have a more complex system of branched, winding creeks,

partly because the vegetation grows in isolated clumps, but also because such saltmarshes lack a distinct slope.[43] A further influence on creek plan is the age of the system. As the saltmarsh develops, the pattern of drainage evolves from a simple system with low sinuosity to a more complex one with an elaborate network of channels formed by headward erosion, although in the final stages of maturation, lengths of channel may silt up and become abandoned.[44] The final factor in the development of marshland creek systems, and one which may be as important or more so than those already discussed in the form of reactivated marshlands, is the micromorphology of the surface. The headward development of tidal creeks on the Mary River in northern Australia, for example, was influenced by the presence of palaeochannels which were reactivated as the saltmarsh channels extended headward.[45]

The results of geomorphological studies of coastal saltmarsh elsewhere cannot be applied uncritically to the specific case of Walland Marsh. There are a number of significant differences between the saltmarshes of East Anglia, where many of the models have been developed, and the flooded area of Walland Marsh. The most basic of distinctions relates to the size and form. The saltmarshes at Walland after their inundation were contained within a restricted-entrance embayment and formed a triangle with a total area of about 35 km² with extensions to the eastern end of the Wainway Channel and in the Rother Valley. This is very much larger than most coastal- or estuarine-fringing marshes, and the drainage pattern was correspondingly different. The marshlands on coastal and estuary edges have an aligned pattern of drainage; on Walland Marsh it was radial in form.[46] The second major difference between most of the East Anglian saltmarshes and the inundated area of Walland Marsh is that the former had developed through progressive accretion of deposits. Such marshlands might be termed 'primary'. Walland Marsh in the 14th century was the product of inundation or reactivation of a former saltmarsh as a consequence of the breakdown of embankments and might be referred to as 'secondary marshland'. Work on similar, but more recently reactivated marshlands in Essex and north Kent has shown that they have experienced a prolonged period of adaption as ground levels and creek systems have changed to accommodate tidal water flows. Even a century after the marshes have been reactivated, considerable areas remain as mudflats and have not been colonized by vegetation and developed as saltmarsh.[47] This raises the further issue of the time-scales over which the development of marshland has been examined. Many studies have looked at relatively short-term changes, over a period years or decades. This may be appropriate for the development of natural marshes, although even these seem to have a longer period of change, but a greater time-frame is certainly necessary for reactivated marshland.[48]

Secondary marshes present, therefore, particular features only some of which will be common with developing or primary saltmarsh. The initial channels in secondary marshland tend to form on the lines of existing drainage ditches and may also develop in the low areas of former creek channels. The tendency for creeks to develop in palaeocreeks will be accentuated by the funnelling of tidal water through breaches in the embankment. Embankments are unlikely to be removed completely when marshes are inundated, but localized breaches will develop in the weakest parts which will tend to lie at the sites of former incised creeks. These can often be recognized, even where a breach has not occurred, in the profile of embankments. The embankments tend to dip above creek beds where greater compaction has occurred and, because of the lower altitude, these form areas of weakness at times of high water level. The initial pattern of saltmarsh creeks, where these have followed drainage ditches, is likely to be superseded by a more sinuous pattern representing an adaptation to the changed hydraulic regime. The process occurs more rapidly where the inundated marsh has a relatively low altitude. It has already been noted that, due to sea-level rise and compaction, earlier reclaimed marshes have a lower altitude than those reclaimed later, and both are lower than active saltmarsh. Secondary marshes thus tend to have a low altitude relative to the tidal range.[49]

The incorporation of earlier drainage features in secondary or reactivated marshes and their adaptation to the new conditions has been shown in Kent and Essex. Aerial photographs of Northey Island, Essex show that the saltmarsh, formed in 1897 when the sea wall was breached, has retained traces of the earlier grips (shallow open field drains), particularly on the higher land where less sediment has been deposited.[50] Similarly, at Groom's Farm, North Fambridge (Essex) which was reactivated at the same date, aerial photographs show that a large part of

the grips of the pre-inundation landscape still survive.[51] The persistence of earlier drainage systems in reactivated marshland will depend partly on their altitude and partly upon the soils through which they were cut. Many creeks in a secondary marsh will inherit just some of the features of the drained landscape, whether in the form of palaeo-creeks or field ditches, and these will be progressively modified as the saltmarsh develops.

This can be most clearly illustrated by comparing the antediluvian landscape at North Fambridge depicted on the first-edition six-inch map of 1880 with an aerial photograph of the same area taken in 1988. The aerial photograph, which has been transcribed here, shows two main areas. The flooded area is evident on the west and a reclaimed area to the south-east of Groom's Farm where a pattern of drainage ditches of grips is evident. The sea bank was breached during the flooding in two areas: to the south of Groom's Farm and to the south-west (Fig. 7.4: a, b). The flooding was constrained by a railway embankment on the north side. An attempt had been made to build a new embankment (c) across the former breach, not on the original alignment, but set back to avoid the scour pit. Work on the embankment proceeded from east to west, but was not completed and stopped short of the second breach which remains open. The completed piece of embankment did, however, prevent a major creek from developing behind the first breach (b), possibly on the line of an earlier palaeocreek.[52] The major creek (d) at the second breach is also evidently based on a palaeocreek which, like the first, had been straightened and used as a major field ditch. Lesser creeks (e, f) developed, in the case of the former along the delph or quarry ditch behind the embankment, and along a modified palaeocreek in case of the latter. It seems that the breach effectively rejuvenated the natural drainage system, which was much modified when the area had been embanked. Not all field ditches had developed into creeks, notably ditch (g) which appears to be progressively silting up, because it has been blocked by the partially completed embankment. The marsh at Groom's Farm should therefore be viewed as being in the midst of a transformation. Almost a hundred years after the marsh was reactivated, the pattern of grips survive as minor creeks (Fig. 7.4: i) and the natural pattern of drainage is reasserting itself, though in modified form.

The development at North Fambridge over a period of about 90 years provides a useful analogue for the processes which may have taken place on Walland Marsh. The lower parts of the rejuvenated creeks have become much wider and more sinuous than the field ditches which preceded them. The greater tidal flow has allowed the sides of the creeks to be cut away and new meanders to be incised. The low-order or more minor creeks, the grips and field ditches, have survived in only a slightly altered form, even close to the site of the breaches. In one case, what appears to have been a former ditch (Fig. 7.4: j), although one which was dry at the time of the 1880 map, has been reinvested with water as a result of the inundation. On the other hand, not

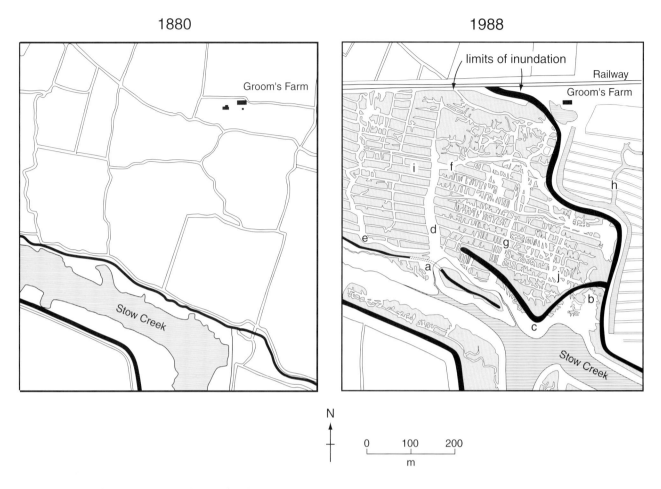

Fig. 7.4. Embanked and inundated marshland at Groom's Farm, North Fambridge, Essex (based on Ordnance Survey first-edition six-inch map, Essex 62 (1880) and Crooks and Pye (2000, fig. 4) (1988)).

all the palaeocreeks have been reactivated. The location of breaches within the earlier embankment and the partially reconstructed new embankment has had a profound effect on the way in which the saltmarsh creeks have developed. The creek to the north of (b) has not been reopened. All this suggests that the resulting inundated landscape is a product of the original unenclosed saltmarsh, the history of ditching and embankment, the location of breaches, and the subsequent modification of the drowned landscape.

Geomorphological Approaches applied to Walland Marsh

It is questionable whether any of the major marshlands in England was reclaimed from an entirely natural state. Rippon has suggested that reclamation is the final state of human intervention in wetlands and is often preceded by simple exploitation of the natural resources – for example grazing, fishing, fowling and reed-cutting – and then by modification in which summer embankments are constructed to prevent flooding during the growing season or ditches improved to speed the flow of water.[53] Reclamation

itself is usually a step-by-step task and each inning not only allows the land within it to be utilized more completely, but also influences the creeks and drainage pattern beyond the embankment. The system of creeks in the saltmarsh outside the embankment changes to accommodate the altered drainage regime by a narrowing of channels to reflect reduced tidal flow and the infilling of the creeks at the head of the system. At the same time the presence of the embankment wall leads to the increased deposition of sediment at its foot which in turn helps to prepare the way for subsequent enclosures.[54]

Reclamation does not erase the pattern of the former saltmarsh, though cultivation and changes in the drainage system will act over a period of time to obliterate most surface remains. Distinctive traces may survive in the sinuous pattern of drainage ditches reflecting the earlier line of saltmarsh creeks and also in the remaining water- and rush-filled creeks cut off by the construction of an embankment. These deeper creeks are truncated fragments of the former system and cannot be readily drained through the embankment because the marsh on the seaward side rapidly develops through sedimentation to a greater height than that on the landward (Fig. 7.5). The greatest sedi-

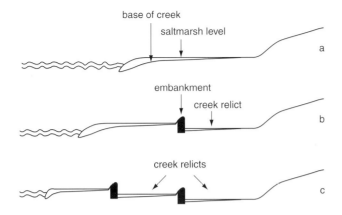

Fig. 7.5. The formation of creek relicts on reclaimed marshland.

mentation in a saltmarsh occurs towards the distal end of creeks during the period of slack highwater and at the edge of creek sides forming low levées. A mature saltmarsh, though broadly level, rises at the landward margin and falls on the seaward edge.[55] Rising sea-level and autocompaction of sediments also contribute to the problem of drainage of creek relics, and indeed of inned marshland generally. The consequence of progressive sea-level rise is that later innings have a higher level than the earlier, producing a stepped profile rising in the direction of the sea.[56]

The application of these principles to Walland Marsh allows a partial reconstruction of the form of the saltmarsh before its reclamation. There were two large inlets leading from the estuary mouth south of Rye which ran northwards along the line of the Rother and eastwards along the line of a major palaeochannel – the Water of Chene – forming the Wainway.[57] The impact of wave action within the flooded area of Walland Marsh was limited by the shingle on the south-west edge of Guldeford Level which by the late 16th century was held in place by groynes; there were further groynes on the opposite side of the Rother to protect the causeway which linked Rye to Playden. Waves were able to penetrate to the upper part of the Rother estuary and by the middle of the 15th century there were further groynes near Kete Marsh.[58] The plan based on Green's soil map suggests that the drainage of the inundated saltmarsh had a radial pattern with five major creeks conveying water into the Wainway and Rother channels. The form of those creeks differs considerably, reflecting their different exposure to wind and wave energy. Creek B (Fig. 7.2), for example, has a linear form suggesting that it has adapted to dissipate wind-wave energy in the Rother inlet. It contrasts with the branched and meandering form of Creek E which empties into the Wainway Channel and consequently was well protected from wave action from the open sea. The south-east corner of the marsh was not drained by a single creek, but by means of percolation through the shingle barrier.

The reconstructed pattern of creeks also allows the landscape of the 14th and 15th centuries to be examined. The creeks drained outwards from the centre of the reactivated marshland leaving a central 'watershed' which has no creek depressions (Fig. 7.2: a). The band is followed by a well-marked road shown on the 1592 map of Walland Marsh, the present A259 road from Whitehouse Farm to Guldeford Corner.[59] It can hardly be coincidental that the south-east side of the 'ridge', as picked out on Green's soil map, is followed by the boundary between Brookland and Ivychurch parishes which otherwise assumes a seemingly arbitrary line through the fields. It is likely that this area was among the first utilized after the late 13th-century flooding and the fields adjoining the road are notably regular. Immediately to the north are the groups of fields known as *Le Doolez* discussed by Eddison and Draper and dated by them to the late 14th century, which likewise have long parallel-sided ditches on the north-west and south-east.[60]

The discussion raises the issue of whether the use of Walland Marsh outside the Great Wall from the late 14th century was preceded by the construction of an embankment. Embankments had been built on the east side of the Rother inlet late in the 14th or early 15th centuries. The greatest danger of flooding came from that direction, since waves might be driven up into the inlet. Other areas of the marsh, however, may have been drained but not embanked.[61] Kent Ditch, which was certainly in place by 1416, may have been not only a boundary mark, but also an important drainage channel which emptied to the north-west into Creek B and in the south-east to the lower part of Creek D.[62] Unenclosed saltmarsh was commonly used for grazing in the medieval period and in some places the practice still persists. Part of the Fens on the north-west side of the Wash was held in common and the commoners had the duty of maintaining the drainage ditches, but it was not embanked. Other areas of that marsh were used in a similar manner, including land outside the sea embankments.[63] The central part of the south-west of Walland Marsh (Fig. 7.2: 1) seems to have been used in this way, because there is no evidence for embankments across the area.

Archaeological Evidence for an Antediluvian Landscape

Three stages of the later development of this southern area of Walland Marsh have been outlined based upon historical evidence and landscape evidence. These are the inundation of the late 13th century and the reactivation of the marshland, the modification of the saltmarsh through the construction of drainage ditches, including Kent Ditch, and finally the recovery of the marsh through the construction of embankments to exclude the salt water (Fig. 7.6: 4–6). The evidence for the stages of development of the marsh which preceded these is more complex and

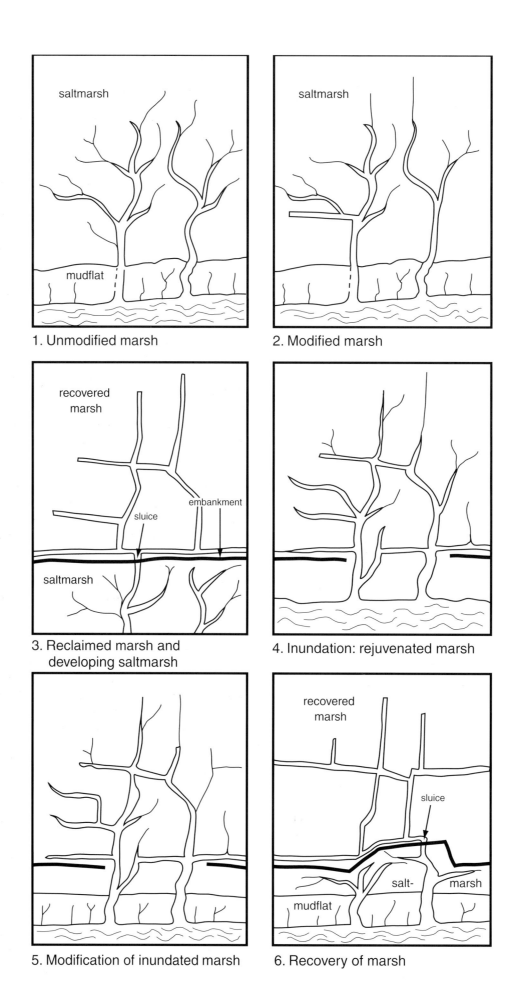

1. Unmodified marsh

2. Modified marsh

3. Reclaimed marsh and
   developing saltmarsh

4. Inundation: rejuvenated marsh

5. Modification of inundated marsh

6. Recovery of marsh

Fig. 7.6. Schematic model of marshland modification, reclamation and inundation.

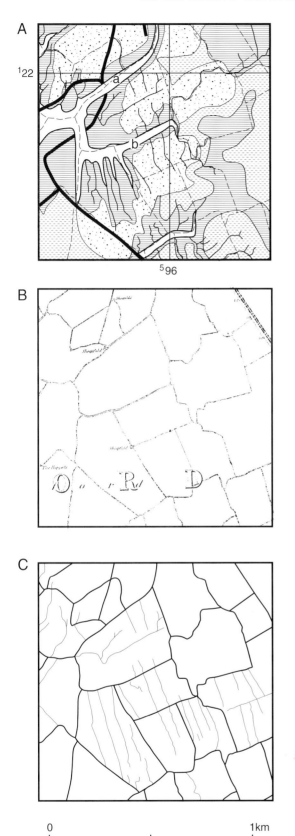

Fig. 7.7. The Hoppets: (A) soils (after Green (1968)), (B) late 19th-century landscape (Ordnance Survey first-edition six-inch map, Sussex sheet 45) and (C) landscapes features (from aerial photographs). For key to soils, see Fig. 7.8.

depends on the view that the creek system on the inundated marsh is likely to have inherited, at least in part, the antediluvian drainage system. However, the antediluvian system of drainage ditches was itself an adaptation of the natural creek system. It is thus possible to identify three earlier stages in the development of the marsh (Fig. 7.6: 1–3). The first is when the marsh was exploited by humans but was largely unaltered. The second stage is marked by the modification of the saltmarsh by means of grazing, ditch-digging and possibly the construction of summer dykes. These two phases of usage are hypothetical and no evidence is offered for them here, although excavations at Lydd Quarry have provided reasons for assuming a phase of modification which preceded a thorough transformation of the marsh.[64] It is the third stage, the inning of the marshland, which is considered in greater detail.

Using recently reactivated saltmarshes, it has been possible to show that a pre-flood landscape *might* have survived the inundation of Walland Marsh in the late thirteenth century. It needs to be shown that there are definite indications that it *did* do so. The analysis is based on three elements. Green's soil map provides an essential tool in the understanding of the evolution of the landscape. The map identifies soils of the Romney-Agney Complex which tend to occur on the edges of the main creek ridges and are found in the former Wainway Channel which remained open until the 17th century. The soils, therefore, are generally associated with areas of major and minor creeks, and often have distinct sedimentary laminations.[65] Green also records the creek relics, the rush-filled remnants of the former creeks, and creek depressions, lower areas in pasture which mark the line of the minor saltmarsh creeks. Aerial photographs provide a useful supplement to Green's map and allow some of the smallest creek depressions to be traced and creeks which have been ploughed out to be recorded. A variety of collections have been consulted, particularly the sets held by the County Councils in Kent and East Sussex. Aerial photographs taken by the Potato Marketing Board in 1979 and now in private hands have also been used. The third source for the study are historical maps which allow the identification of field boundaries, ditches, embankments and other landscape features. The key maps used are the Ordnance Survey first-edition six-inch maps published in the 1870s which may be supplemented by earlier estate and tithe maps.

It seems likely that the drainage system of the 12th or early 13th century in Walland Marsh was formed, at least in part, through the modification of natural saltmarsh creeks, as it clearly was elsewhere on Romney Marsh. In some cases the creeks will have been thoroughly straightened to speed the discharge of water and create more regularly shaped fields. Otherwise, the creeks may have been adapted to serve as drains and will retain substantially their original plan. These will be difficult or impossible to distinguish from creeks newly formed after

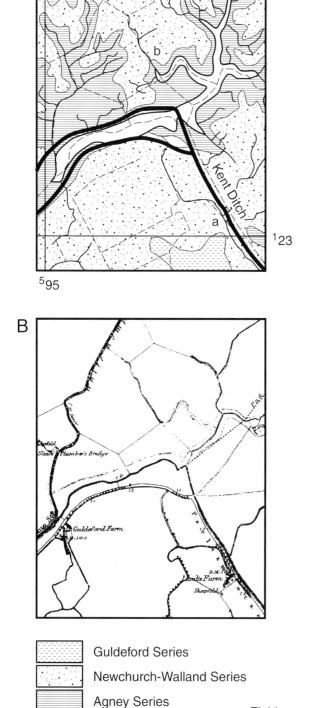

Guldeford Series

Newchurch-Walland Series

Agney Series

Shingle

– – – – Field boundaries

0 _____ 1km

Fig. 7.8. Offen's Farm: (A) soils (after Green (1968)) and (B) late 19th-century landscape (Ordnance Survey first-edition six-inch maps, Sussex sheets 32, 45).

the late 13th-century flooding. Traces of an antediluvian landscape should be apparent not in the straight ditches of the final reclamation, nor in the sinuous channels reflecting modified lines of natural channels, but from a pattern which has an underlying regularity which has been naturally modified. Antediluvian embankments may not be present, either because they have been removed in the inundation, or because they were incorporated into later sea defences, or because they were never built. Antediluvian sea defences on Walland Marsh may not have been necessary when the land was originally reclaimed since it was protected from the sea by the coastal shingle barrier. It is possible, however, that some defensive walls were constructed from the middle of the 13th century as the marsh was increasingly threatened by marine incursion.

Three areas have been chosen for detailed study, each one intended to illustrate a different approach to the identification of the antediluvian landscape.

The Hoppets

The Hoppets is the name given on the first-edition six-inch map to a sheepfold to the north-east of a large creek mapped by Green, an area now drained southwards by the Guldeford Sewer (Fig. 7.7). The evolution of the area is undoubtedly complex and is only partly understood. A large creek shown on the west edge of the map divides into two main arms (Fig. 7.7A: a and b). A series of parallel creek depressions extend outwards at right angles from the arms, running for up to 500 m. The whole pattern is notably rectilinear and its artificial character is emphasized by the way alignments run across the arms of the main creek. However, the depressions in their present form have been influenced by natural factors and the way in which they become wider and deeper as they approach the main creeks, suggests that they have functioned as creeks within the saltmarsh.

The system is interpreted as a reworked network of long narrow drainage ditches. When the area was submerged, the main ditches became more substantial creeks, while the tidal flow in the minor creeks modified their shape, but did not alter their fundamental pattern.

Offen's Farm

Offen's Farm, formerly called Guldeford Farm, lies just within East Sussex and close to the county boundary (Fig. 7.8). For a considerable part of its length the boundary follows a clearly artificial line marked by Kent Ditch (Fig. 7.2). The boundary had been established by 1416 since in that year witnesses reported that there was a ditch marking the boundary between the counties of Kent and Sussex called *Kent Mark* or *Kent Barr* which ran straight from a sea wall to Broomhill.[66] It is not clear which sea wall was intended, since the straight length of the county boundary marked by Kent Ditch in the 19th century, and very

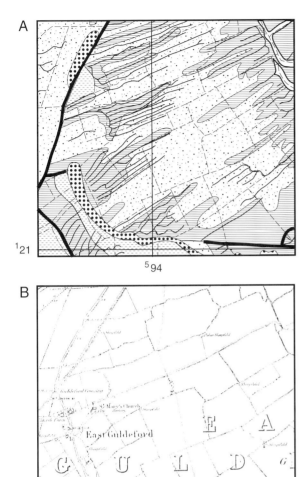

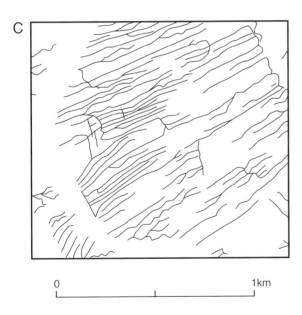

probably in the 15th century, terminated at an arm of a large creek called More Fleet to the north-west.[67] On the south-east the boundary turns at another major fleet, unsurprisingly called Kent Creek.[68] The 'straight' alignment of the county boundary is in reality made up of three distinct parts. That from the former More Fleet to Guldeford Lane Corner is slightly irregular and is shown by Green as lying at the foot of a possible embankment (Fig. 7.2: b-c). From Guldeford Lane Corner it runs south-eastwards until it crosses a sea wall about 400 m from Barn Farm, and changes alignment (Fig. 7.2: c-d). The third length runs straight to Kent Creek (Fig. 7.2: d-e).

Two features suggest that the boundary existing by the early 15th century may in fact have been re-established on the line of an earlier division. A small creek is mapped by Green at the foot of the possible embankment near to Lamb Farm (Fig. 7.8A: a). It is also shown on the six-inch map as a drainage ditch. The creek is slightly sinuous and appears to be of natural rather than artificial origin. If it is natural then it evidently developed at the foot of an existing embankment during the period of inundation. That would suggest that the embankment itself is of antediluvian origin. North-west of More Fleet is a small area of rectilinear creek depressions. One of the depressions is about 250 m long and is aligned with the straight length of the county boundary (Fig. 7.8A: b). The alignment of both these creeks tends to imply that there were earlier features on the line of Kent Ditch. It seems that when Kent Ditch was dug, perhaps in the late 14th century, it was established on the line of an existing drainage or boundary feature. However, in its later form its function was to drain the marshes and it was not extended north-west beyond More Fleet where the earlier feature ran.

East Guldeford

The area to the north-east of East Guldeford church has a remarkable pattern of sub-parallel creek depressions (Fig. 7.9). These drained both north-eastwards to a creek and south-westwards into the River Rother and the Wainway Channel. The post-medieval fields are orientated similarly, but not identically. However, it seems that the creek system is the earlier feature since some creek depressions continue across field-boundaries. Green maps a substantial number of creek depressions, but others are visible on aerial photographs. This area of the marsh was not recovered until the second half of the 15th century, but the system of channels does not date from that period as their irregularities suggest that they have a semi-natural origin. It seems improbable that they are wholly natural, because the two systems, draining south-westwards and north-eastwards, are aligned. The most likely interpretation is that the creek systems which developed behind the protection barrier of shingle derive from an antediluvian pattern of drainage ditches or grips.

Fig. 7.9. East Guldeford: (A) soils (after Green (1968)), (B) late 19th-century landscape (Ordnance Survey first-edition six-inch map, Sussex sheet 45) and (C) saltmarsh creeks (from aerial photographs and Cook (1994)). For key to soils, see Fig. 7.8.

Table 7.1. The morphological regions of the antediluvian landscape of Walland Marsh.

Area Ia
Area Ia is divided from Area Ib by a substantial creek aligned NW-SE. The creek depressions, however, lie at right angles to the creek and form a sub-parallel system. The pattern has been described in greater detail above.

Area Ib
The pattern is orthogonal rather than parallel, although it is aligned to, or at right angles to, the creek depression system in Area Ia. There is a definite regularity to the creek pattern on the south-west side of the area and it is notable that the creeks are parallel to the major creek to the north-west, More Flete. The north and north-eastern limits of the area are debatable, since traces of an orthogonal plan are also found in Area V.

Area II
The pattern of creek depressions in Area II is remarkable for the subparallel alignment. However, the creek pattern, if it is artificial in form, must pre-date the construction of Kent Ditch which cuts across the south-west corner of the area. If, as has been suggested, Kent Ditch is of antediluvian origin, then there are some problems in explaining the dating of the creek pattern. However, the creek pattern may be an example of a parallel dendritic form (Fig. 7.3: 3) and could be entirely natural.

Area III
The area includes The Hoppets which was discussed above. Traces of a possible antediluvian sea wall have been identified in the north part of the area. The land was drained by two arms of Creek C (Fig. 7.2) and the creek depressions reflect an orderly landscape.

Area IV
A small number of creek depressions are plotted by Green (1968) in this area, but they are notable for two pairs which form two parallel alignments running east-northeast and are clearly based on an antediluvian ditch system.

Area V
The complex pattern of creeks have a general east-northeast to west-southwesterly orientation which is reflected in one arm of the the major creek on the north side of the area. The creek pattern at the head of Moor Fleet is less clear and seems to be less artificial.

Area VI
Analysis of aerial photographs have suggested that not only the drainage ditches, but also other antedilvuian landscape features can be identified. A ditch can be traced for some distance as a soil mark, but it survives as a slight depression at the northern end. Two intersecting roads marked by field ditches are also identifiable as soil marks. The present ditch system and former creeks suggest a regular field pattern (Fig. 7.12).

A wider perspective

The three examples have used morphological analysis of the pattern of creeks and creek depressions to suggest that there is substantial evidence for an antediluvian landscape on Walland Marsh. Although not all creeks or depressions followed the line of earlier field ditches or sewers, the general arrangement was commonly determined by the antediluvian features. It should therefore be possible to recover evidence of the general landscape, not merely small areas of it, by analyzing the general morphology. Green's soil map provides a general view of the creek system as it developed during the course of reclamation. Although it does not show all the creek depressions visible on aerial photographs, it does indicate the general pattern.

Analysis of the pattern suggests the presence of a number of areas with distinctive features, which are listed in Table 7.1 (Fig. 7.10). Areas of parallel creeks, rectilinear patterns and dendritic systems can all be identified. In some places the underlying creek patterns are reflected in the later arrangement of field boundaries, but elsewhere the field ditches cut across the natural system. The map of creeks can be augmented by a small number of soilmarks shown on aerial photographs which are clearly artificial in origin. These are features which were buried by later sediments and were not reworked as saltmarsh creeks. It may be possible, therefore, with further detailed analysis of aerial photographs to reconstruct many further features of the antediluvian landscape.

Conclusion

The identification and study of the late 12th- and 13th-century landscape on Walland Marsh has implications for work on marshland elsewhere in Britain. Firstly, it raises a number of questions about areas of supposedly natural saltmarsh. A number of coastal areas of Britain have been inundated at some time in the past and some have not been recovered, remaining instead as saltmarsh. These may be mistakenly identified as marshland unaffected by human activity. One example is found in the north Norfolk marshes where the creek pattern east of Ship Lane at Thornham clearly picks out the line of a former embankment which continued that of the existing sea wall on the west of the lane. Likewise, an aerial photograph of 'typical

Fig. 7.10. Morphological areas of saltmarsh creeks in south-west Walland Marsh.

creek systems' on the Dengie Peninsula in Essex clearly shows evidence that the channels have been straightened and altered by human action.[69] Other marshes may have been modified rather than transformed by local communities for the purposes of hunting, grazing or fishing. Indeed, it is questionable whether any marsh in England is pristine, in the sense of entirely unaltered by human intervention. Studies of marsh development should not ignore the impact of human activity, but embrace it as one of the factors in the interaction between populations and their environment.

The second implication of the observations of the

Walland Marsh landscape is that many medieval enclosures will not have started with a *tabula rasa* of natural saltmarsh creeks. The medieval landscapes were influenced either by earlier enclosures of the Middle Ages, or indeed by Roman activity. The impact of Roman works on the medieval and later marshlands has not been widely recognized, although Rippon raised the possibility that the artificial line of the reens or streams in the Caldicot Level might date back to the early first millennium. He has also noted that some of the field-drains in Wentlooge Level were rehabilitated after post-Roman flooding.[70] The persistence of the pattern of Roman drainage at Wentlooge

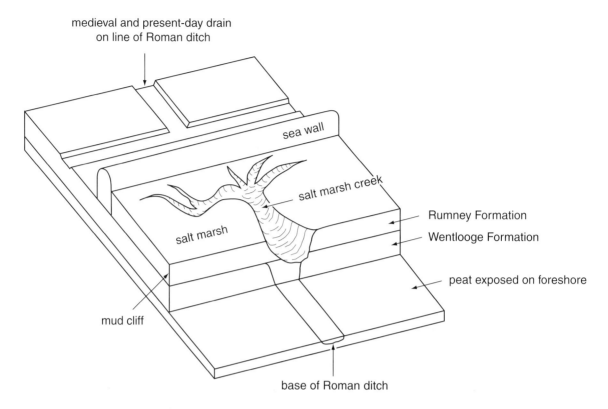

Fig. 7.11. Diagrammatic sketch of the relationship between Roman and later ditches, and saltmarsh creeks at Wentlooge Level (based on information in Allen and Fulford (1986)).

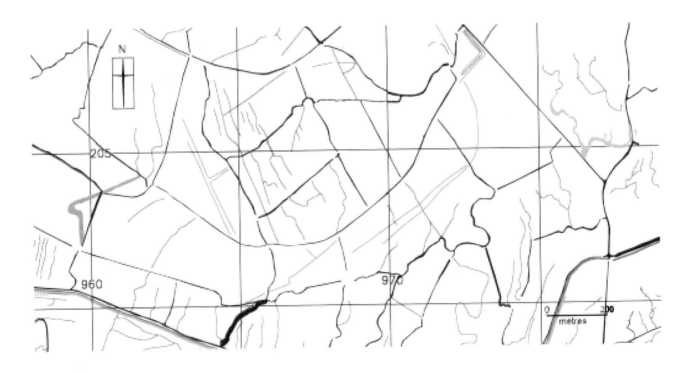

Fig. 7.12. Antediluvian features in Area VI (based on an initial plot by Air Photographic Services).

inside the later medieval sea-bank is notable, but another aspect of the survival of landscape at that site appears to have gone unremarked. The evidence for the line of Roman ditches has been traced in the silt-filled channels cut into the peat on the foreshore and in the section of the mud cliff on its inland side.[71] Between the sea-wall and the foreshore the ditches are buried beneath estuarine silt known as the Rumney Formation. Those silts were evidently deposited after the sea wall was constructed as they are found only on the seaward side (Fig. 7.11). The authors of the study do not comment that the saltmarsh creeks incised into the Rumney Formation bear in some places a definite relationship to the Roman ditches. Not every ditch is marked by a corresponding creek, and the creek system is more extensive than the Roman ditch system.[72] Nevertheless, it is notable that there is *any* relationship between the saltmarsh creeks cut into the Rumney Formation and the Roman pattern of drainage buried between 1 and 3 m beneath. The reason for this coincidence can only be speculated without further fieldwork. It is possible that the creek system first developed when the Roman ditches were still open and continued in more or less the same location as the estuarine silts were deposited. Alternatively, it may be that after the deposition of the Rumney Formation silts, the compaction of the ditch-fills was greater than in the surrounding Wentlooge Formation deposits, producing a slight depression on the surface of the saltmarsh in which the creeks subsequently developed.

The relationship between Roman and later marsh landscapes clearly deserves further investigation, both in the context of the Severn estuary and also on Romney Marsh. The study here has suggested that marshland should certainly not be treated as a *tabula rasa* upon which medieval reclaimers laid out a pattern of embankments and ditches. Not only did they utilize the natural creek system, but they were working in a landscape which may already have been modified by previous generations, and influenced by reclamation works of earlier date. Marshlands, no less than other English landscapes, have a 'time-depth', to use a term borrowed from ecology, a complexity of form resulting from a prolonged period of interaction between humans and nature.[73] Failure to acknowledge either the period of their development, or the role of the interaction, will mean that our understanding of the development of saltmarshes will continue to be incomplete.

Acknowledgements
I am grateful to Jill Eddison for discussing with me the dates of the innings by Sir Richard and Sir Edward Guldeford and for her comments on a draft of the text.

Notes

Abbreviations used:
BL   British Library
CCA   Canterbury Cathedral Archives
DCc   Canterbury Cathedral Archives, Dean and Chapter
ESRO   East Sussex Record Office
LPL   Lambeth Palace Library
PRO   Public Record Office

1. Lane and Hayes, 'Moving boundaries', 69; Hall and Coles, *Fenland*, 122.
2. Rippon, 'Medieval wetland reclamation in Somerset', 241–3; Rippon, *The Gwent Levels*; Silvester, *The Fenland Project, Number 3*.
3. Allen and Fulford, 'The Wentlooge Level', 91–117; Rippon, *The Gwent Levels*, 87–90.
4. Cook, 'Field-scale water management', 57.
5. Gardiner, 'Medieval settlement and society', 114–15.
6. Eddison, 'Catastrophic changes', 69.
7. Gardiner, 'Some lost Anglo-Saxon charters', 41.
8. LPL CM III/14, f. 3v.
9. *Idem.*
10. A number of tracks run eastwards from the upland in Playden and Iden towards the marsh, including those from Boonshill, Houghton Green and Saltcote Street. *Manuscripts Preserved Penshurst Place*, 57, 89–90. Although the site of the bridge has disappeared, its position can be inferred. Among the small number of tenants at *Morbrigge* in the early 14th century were Adam and Simon Bone,

suggesting that the bridge was to the east of Boonshill in Iden (ESRO AMS 4884).
11. On salt-making, see *Manuscripts Preserved Penshurst Place*, 55–6. For mention of Saltcot Street in 1345, ESRO ACC 6153. For *Eures*, see *Manuscripts Preserved Penshurst Place*, 57. Luke at Eure, a tenant of Playden manor, was otherwise called Luke at Revere (ESRO AMS 4883, 4884).
12. Salzmann, *Feet of Fines from 2 Richard I to 33 Henry III*, no.167.
13. Eddison, 'Catastrophic changes', 69–70.
14. For Winchelsea, see Royal College of Arms, Misc. Deeds 131; Archives Seine Maritime 7H57 (deed of resignation by Brother Hugh de Alneto of all tenements granted by Brother Manasses). For continuing enclosure until the 1240s, see *Manuscripts Preserved Penshurst Place*, 90, and Gardiner, 'Medieval settlement and society', 115.
15. Gardiner, 'Medieval farming and flooding', 130; PRO SC11/660, cf. PRO SC11/661; Gross and Butcher, 'Adaptation and investment', 112–3.
16. Eddison and Draper, 'Landscape of medieval reclamation', 78.
17. *Calendar of Patent Rolls 1330–34*, 202, 391; PRO E101/547/20, mm. 1, 2. For the location of the marshes, see Gardiner, 'Medieval farming and flooding', 131.
18. PRO E101/547/20, m. 3; *Calendar of Patent Rolls 1350–54*, 29, 82. For the suggested location of *Spadlond*, see Homan, 'The founding of New Winchelsea', map between 26 and 27.
19. Eddison, 'Catastrophic changes', 70.

20. *Calendar of Close Rolls 1310–13*, 190, 263; Sumption, *Trial by Battle*, 383
21. BL Add. Roll 16432; *State Papers and Manuscripts Relating to English Affairs in the Archives of Venice* **1**, frontispiece map, 36–7 (nos 120, 122 (1397–8)), 38 (no 126 (1398)), 42 (no. 148 (1406)) and 57 (no. 209 (1416)). The first reference identified to the Camber is a document of 1330 but, since it describes the limits of the liberty of New Winchelsea, the bounds may date to the foundation of that town in about 1290 (BL Add. Ch. 18623).
22. *Calendar of Patent Rolls 1334–38*, 259; *Calendar of Close Rolls 1354–60*, 315.
23. Gardiner, 'Medieval farming and flooding', 131–2
24. LPL CM VI/83.
25. CCA Register C, f. 255v.; LPL CM VI/96.
26. DCc Charta Antiqua F35; PRO E179/225/15.
27. *Calendar of Inquisitions Miscellaneous* **6**, no 319.
28. DCc Charta Antiqua A173.
29. DCc Charta Antiqua A165.
30. *Calendar of Patent Rolls 1476–85*, 138; *Manuscripts Preserved Penshurst Place*, 155
31. Draper, 'Farmers of Canterbury Cathedral Priory', 112–3.
32. LPL CM II/90; LPL CM III/3.
33. *Calendar of Patent Rolls 1476–85*, 51; LPL MS 951/1.
34. LPL CM III/3; DCc/DE 176.
35. *Victoria County History of Sussex* **9**, 151.
36. Pethick, 'Saltmarsh geomorphology', 53.
37. It is worth noting, however, that the saltmarsh creek pattern shown on the aerial photograph (Pethick, 'Saltmarsh geomorphology', fig. 3.7) has been influenced by a number of ditches and embankments which may be clearly identified.
38. Pethick, 'Saltmarsh geomorphology', 57–60.
39. Chapman, *Salt Marshes*, pls 20, 7.
40. Allen, 'Morphodynamics of Holocene salt marshes', 1172.
41. Crooks and Pye, 'Sedimentological controls', 210 and fig. 2.
42. Chapman, *Coastal Vegetation*, 112–17; Ranwell, *Ecology of Salt Marshes and Sand Dunes*, 92–5.
43. Chapman, *Salt Marshes*, 31–2.
44. Pethick, 'Drainage in tidal salt marshes', 725–30; French and Stoddart, 'Hydrodynamics of salt marsh creek systems', 244.
45. Knighton *et al.* 'Evolution of tidal creek networks', 171, 174.
46. Terminology for saltmarsh types is taken from Pye, 'Saltmarsh erosion', 360–2.
47. Shi *et al.* 'Geomorphic change', 73; Crooks and Pye. 'Sedimentological controls', 211.
48. Ranwell, *Ecology of Salt Marshes and Sand Dunes*, 86

gives a generalized figure of one hundred years for a marshland to reach maturity, ignoring the period of time for the formation of tidal flats.
49. Crooks and Pye, 'Sedimentological controls', 221; Cahoon *et al.* 'Vertical accretion', 235.
50. Crooks and Pye, 'Sedimentological controls', 210, 212.
51 Comments based on Crooks and Pye, 'Sedimentological controls', Fig. 7.4.
52. Note the presence in Fig. 7.4 of a creek in the embanked area to the north at (h).
53. Rippon, *Transformation of Coastal Wetlands*, 46–53.
54. Kestner, 'The loose-boundary regime of the Wash', 402–3.
55. Pethick, *Introduction to Coastal Geomorphology*, 161–2; Kestner, 'Loose boundary hydraulics and land reclamation', 31–40.
56. Allen, 'The sequence of early land-claims', 276–7; Allen, 'The geoarchaeology of land-claim', 5, 16–17.
57. For the Water of Chene, see Gardiner, 'Medieval society and settlement', 112–3.
58. All Souls College KeS/15; Mayhew, *Tudor Rye*, 14; LPL ED 204.
59. Green, *Soils of Romney Marsh*, 118 notes the presence of creek ridges on Romney and Agney soils in that area; All Souls College KeS/15.
60. Eddison and Draper,' Landscape of medieval reclamation', 81–2, 84.
61. LPL CM III/14, f. 5r.; CCA Register C, f. 270r.
62. LPL CM III/14, f. 1v.
63. Hallam, *Settlement and Society*, 162–9, 179–80; Lambert, 'Practical management', 333–9.
64. Barber, 'Medieval rural settlement', 92–3.
65. Green, *Soils of Romney Marsh*, 72, 74, 117–8.
66. LPL CM III/14, mm. 1v., 5r.
67. Dugdale, *History of Imbanking and Draining*, 101–2; Ordnance Survey first-edition six-inch map, Sussex sheets 32, 45, 46.
68. All Souls College KeS/17.
69. Thornham: Chapman, *Salt Marshes*, pl. 18 and see also the first-edition six-inch Ordnance Survey map, Norfolk sheet 6; Dengie Peninsula: Pethick, Saltmarsh geomorphology, Fig. 3.7.
70. Rippon, *The Gwent Levels*, 68, 87; Rippon, *The Severn Estuary*, 168–9.
71. Allen and Fulford, 'The Wentlooge Level'.
72. See particularly, Allen and Fulford, 'The Wentlooge Level', fig. 5 and Pl. II.
73. The term 'time-depth' is used in the context of historic landscapes by Fairclough *et al.*, *Yesterday's World, Tomorrow's Landscape*, 11–12.

References

Calendar of Close Rolls 1310–13.
Calendar of Inquisitions Miscellaneous **6**.
Calendar of Patent Rolls 1330–34, 1334–38, 1350–54, 1354–56, 1374–77, 1476–85.
Report on the Manuscripts of Lord De L'Isle and Dudley Preserved at Penhurst Place **1**.
State Papers and Manuscripts Relating to English Affairs, Existing in the Archives and Collections of Venice, and in other Libraries of Northern Italy **1**.
Victoria History of the County of Sussex **9**.

Allen, J.R.L. 1996. The sequence of early land-claims in the Walland and Romney Marshes, southern Britain: a preliminary hypothesis and some implications, *Proceedings of the Geologists' Association* **107**, 271–80.
Allen, J.R.L. 1997. The geoarchaeology of land-claim in coastal

wetlands: a sketch from Britain and the north-west European Atlantic-North Sea coast, *Archaeological Journal* **154**, 1–54.

Allen, J.R.L. 2000. Morphodynamics of Holocene salt marshes: a review sketch from the Atlantic and southern North Sea coasts of Europe, *Quaternary Science Reviews* **19**, 1155–1231.

Allen, J.R.L. and Fulford, M.G. 1986. The Wentlooge Level: a Romano-British saltmarsh reclamation in southeast Wales, *Britannia* **17**, 91–117.

Barber, L. 1998. Medieval rural settlement and economy at Lydd: preliminary results from the excavations at Lydd Quarry, in J. Eddison, M. Gardiner and A. Long (eds) *Romney Marsh: Environmental Change and Human Occupation in a Coastal Lowland* (Oxford University Committee for Archaeology **46**), 89–108. Oxford.

Cahoon, D.R., French, J.R., Spencer, T. Reed, D. and Möller, I. 2000. Vertical accretion versus elevational adjustment in UK saltmarshes: an evaluation of alternative methodologies, in K. Pye and J.R.L. Allen (eds) *Coastal and Estuarine Environments: Sedimentology, Geomorphology and Geoarchaeology* (Geological Society special publication **175**), 223–38. London.

Chapman, V.J. 1960. *Salt Marshes and Salt Deserts of the World*. London.

Chapman, V.J. 1964. *Coastal Vegetation*. Oxford.

Cook, H. 1994. Field-scale water management in southern England to A.D. 1900, *Landscape History* **16**, 53–66.

Crooks S. and Pye, K. 2000. Sedimentological controls on the erosion and morphology of saltmarshes: implications for flood defence and habitat recreation, in K. Pye and J.R.L. Allen (eds) *Coastal and Estuarine Environments: Sedimentology, Geomorphology and Geoarchaeology* (Geological Society special publication **175**), 207–22. London.

Draper, G. 1998. The farmers of Canterbury Cathedral Priory and All Souls College on Romney Marsh *c*.1443–1545, in J. Eddison, M. Gardiner and A. Long (eds) *Romney Marsh: Environmental Change and Human Occupation in a Coastal Lowland* (Oxford University Committee for Archaeology **46**), 109–28. Oxford.

Dugdale, W. 1882. *The History of Imbanking and Draining of Divers Fens and Marshes* (second edn). London.

Eddison, J. 1998. Catastrophic changes: a multidisciplinary study of the evolution of the barrier beaches of Rye Bay, in J. Eddison, M. Gardiner and A. Long (eds) *Romney Marsh: Environmental Change and Human Occupation in a Coastal Lowland* (Oxford University Committee for Archaeology **46**), 65–87. Oxford.

Eddison, J. and Draper, G. 1997. A landscape of medieval reclamation: Walland Marsh, Kent, *Landscape History* **19**, 75–88.

Fairclough, G., Lambrick, G. and McNab, A. 1999. *Yesterday's World, Tomorrow's Landscape: The English Heritage Landscape Project 1992–94*. London.

French, J.R. and Stoddart, D.R. 1992. Hydrodynamics of saltmarsh creek systems: implications for marsh morphologic development and material exchange, *Earth Surface Processes and Landforms* **17**, 235–52.

Gardiner, M.F. 1988. Medieval settlement and society in the Broomhill area, in J. Eddison and C. Green (eds) *Romney Marsh: Evolution, Occupation, Reclamation* (Oxford University Committee for Archaeology **24**), 112–27. Oxford.

Gardiner, M.F. 1989. Some lost Anglo-Saxon charters and the endowment of Hastings College, *Sussex Archaeological Collections* **127**, 39–48.

Gardiner, M.F. 1995. Medieval farming and flooding in the Brede valley, in J. Eddison (ed.), *Romney Marsh: the Debatable Ground* (Oxford University Committee for Archaeology **41**), 127–37. Oxford.

Green, R.D. 1968. *Soils of Romney Marsh* (Soil Survey of Great Britain, Bulletin **4**). Harpenden.

Gross, A and Butcher, A. 1995. 'Adapation and investment' in the age of the great storms: agricultural policy on the manors of the principal lords of Romney Marshes and the marshland fringe, in J. Eddison (ed.) *Romney Marsh: the Debatable Ground* (Oxford University Committee for Archaeology **41**), 107–17. Oxford.

Hall, D. and Coles J. 1994 *Fenland Survey: An Essay in Landscape and Persistence* (English Heritage Archaeological Report **1**). London.

Hallam, H.E. 1965. *Settlement and Society: A Study of the Early Agrarian History of South Lincolnshire*. Cambridge.

Homan, W.M. 1949. The founding of New Winchelsea, *Sussex Archaeological Collections* **88**, 22–41.

Kestner, F.J.T. 1975. The loose-boundary regime of the Wash, *Geographical Journal* **141**, 388–414.

Kestner, F.J.T. 1979. Loose boundary hydraulics and land reclamation, in B. Knights and A.J. Phillips (eds) *Estuarine and Coastal Land Reclamation and Water Storage*, 23–47. Farnborough.

Knighton, A.D. Woodroffe, C.D. and Mills, K. 1992. The evolution of tidal creek networks, Mary River, Northern Australia, *Earth Surfaces Processes and Landforms* **17**, 167–90.

Lambert, R. 2000. Practical management of grazed saltmarshes, in B.R. Sherwood, B.G. Gardiner and T. Harris (eds) *British Saltmarshes: Held as a Joint Symposium between the Linnean Society of London, the Royal Society for the Protection of Birds and English Nature*, 333–9. London

Lane, T. and Hayes, P. 1993. Moving boundaries in the fens of south Lincolnshire, in J.P. Gardiner (ed.) *Flatlands and Wetlands: Current Themes in East Anglian Archaeology* (East Anglian Archaeology **50**), 58–70. Norwich.

Mayhew, G. 1987. *Tudor Rye*. Falmer.

Pethick, J.S. 1969. Drainage in tidal salt marshes, in J.A. Steers, *The Coastline of England and Wales* (third edition), 725–30. Cambridge.

Pethick, J.S. 1984. *An Introduction to Coastal Geomorphology*, London.

Pethick, J.S. 1992. Saltmarsh geomorphology, in J.R.L. Allen and K. Pye (eds) *Saltmarshes: Morphodynamics, Conservation and Engineering Significance*, 41–62. Cambridge.

Pye, K. 2000. Saltmarsh erosion in southeast England: mechanisms, causes and implications, in B.R. Sherwood, B.G. Gardiner and T. Harris (eds) *British Saltmarshes: Held as a Joint Symposium between the Linnean Society of London, the Royal Society for the Protection of Birds and English Nature*, 359–96. London.

Ranwell, D.S. 1972. *Ecology of Salt Marshes and Sand Dunes*. London.

Rippon S. 1986. *The Gwent Levels: The Evolution of a Wetland Landscape* (Council for British Archaeology, research report **105**). York.

Rippon, S. 1994. Medieval wetland reclamation in Somerset,

120

Mark Gardiner

in M. Aston and C. Lewis (eds) *The Medieval Landscape of Wessex* (Oxbow Monograph **46**), 239–53. Oxford.

Rippon, S. 1997. *The Severn Estuary: Landscape Evolution and Wetland Reclamation*. London.

Rippon, S. 2000. *The Transformation of Coastal Wetlands: Exploitation and Management of Marshland Landscapes in North West Europe during the Roman and Medieval Periods.* Oxford.

Salzmann, L.F. 1902. *An Abstract of Feet of Fines Relating to the County of Sussex from 2 Richard I to 33 Henry III* (Sussex Record Society **2**). Lewes.

Shi, Z., Lamb, H.F. and Collin, R.L. 1995. Geomorphic change of saltmarsh tidal creek networks in the Dyfi Estuary, Wales, *Marine Geology* **128**, 73–83.

Silvester, R.J. 1988, *The Fenland Project Number 3: Marshland and the Nar Valley, Norfolk* (East Anglian Archaeology **45**). Gressenhall.

Sumption, J. 1990. *The Hundred Years War: Volume I. Trial By Battle.* London.

Romney Marsh: Coastal and Landscape Change through the Ages
(ed. A. Long, S. Hipkin and H. Clarke), OUSA Monograph 56, 2002, 121–126

8. The Rumenesea Wall, Romney and Walland Marshes: A Commentary

J.R.L. Allen

Recent synthetic accounts of the Walland and Romney Marshes accept to different degrees the definitive role advocated for the Rumenesea Wall in the critical early phases of the settlement of the area, but call for a further examination of several issues of fact and opinion, chiefly in the light of recent archaeological investigations. On the balance of evidence at present available, the Rumenesea Wall would seem to be a bridging seabank (Wealden scarp to New Romney barrier) of Saxon date which, with a contemporaneous coastal barrier and probably other engineered banks, allowed roughly one-half of the area to be transformed into a settled and farmed landscape. The context and role of the Wall call for further work, however, and a number of new and especially environmental research needs are suggested.

Introduction

Powerful natural forces and lengthy human interference have created, in the Walland Marsh and Romney Marsh proper on the English Channel, perhaps the most complex Holocene geological sequence and associated historic landscape to be found on the British coast. Despite research extending over many decades and recent monographic treatments (Eddison and Green 1988; Eddison 1995; Eddison *et al.* 1998), much remains either unknown or uncertain about the evolution of this considerable area (*c.* 250 km^2) of shifting gravel-sand barriers behind which sheltered sandy-muddy tidal inlets, including river outlets, and muddy-peaty marshes. Two attempts at a general synthesis (Eddison 2000; Rippon 2000) invite comment in the light of recent archaeological field work bearing on early reclamation or land-claim in the area and the role of the earthwork which has come to be known as the Rumenesea Wall. The analysis brings to light a number of future research needs.

The Rumenesea Wall

The numerous earthworks of especially Walland Marsh have long been recognised as important landscape features, but it is only recently that the significance of the structure variously called the Rumenesea Wall or Yoke Sewer Wall (see below) has been recognised. Hence it is appropriate briefly to summarise the evidence for, and character of, this structure.

The name Rumenesea Wall (Allen 1996) applies to a field monument which, although no longer a standing bank, can be traced continuously over the ground from New Romney to Snargate (Allen 1999) and which, between Snargate and the Wealden scarp at Appledore, arguably lies either beneath or very close to the impressive, later earthwork known as the Rhee Wall (Fig. 8.1). The Rumenesea Wall does not appear on Elliot's (in Lewin 1862) early maps of enclosing banks. In Green's (1968) important soil map, the Wall is shown as a definite bank only for a distance of about two kilometres northwest of

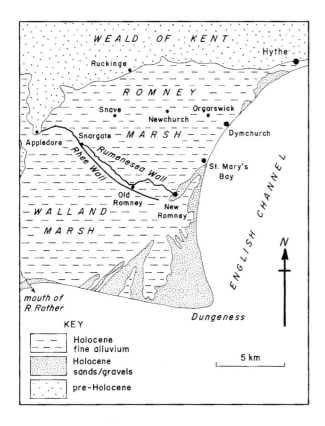

Fig. 8.1. The Walland and Romney Marshes showing the Rumenesea and Rhee Walls and places mentioned in the text. The Rumenesea lies between the Walls but is omitted for clarity.

Old Romney; elsewhere it appears merely as a 'probable sea wall'. Exactly how Green identified walls is nowhere explicit. However, as his survey occurred largely before highly mechanised arable farming became widespread in the area, many banks may have been visible at the time as upstanding features. Where these structures had already been removed or had become naturally degraded, he may have based his mapping on the survival of ramps (Allen 1997, 6, illus. 5), that is, consistent and fairly sharp changes in ground height across the line of the former bank. Green (1968, 17, fig. 18) had recognised that 'abrupt contrasts in levels and/or sedimentary patterns' could arise after the building of a sea wall. As is fully explained elsewhere (Allen 1997), this is because the erection of a bank, firstly, alters the hydraulics of a tidal marsh and, secondly, halts siltation on the enclosed area while allowing the continuing build-up of sediment on the portion that remains active.

The course of the Rumenesea Wall was recently confirmed instrumentally on the basis of a consistent southwestward increase in ground level across a continuous, narrow zone several metres wide that could be traced, with but one short break, from the coastal barrier at New Romney as far as Snargate (Allen 1999, fig. 1). Levelling was done at 44 randomly chosen sites roughly 200 m apart. The measured southwestward rise in elevation

averaged about 0.5 m, and in one place a rise of 1.61 m was noted; at only one of the selected sites did the ground prove to fall southwestward (by 0.15 m). This method failed only over an elevated, roughly one kilometre tract north-east of Old Romney, but where a bank had survived to be recorded in RAF (1946) air photographs. At Owen's Bridge, northwest of Old Romney, a modest rise of 0.18 m in level in the same direction was recorded over the line of a wall standing at right-angles to the Rumenesea Wall and apparently cut by the 13th-century Rhee Wall (Green 1968; Allen 1996).

The course of the Wall between Snargate and the Wealden scarp at Appledore is uncertain. It appears to emerge from beneath the Rhee Wall, a younger structure (Fig. 8.1), but may be represented in part by a lengthy bank Green (1968, soil map) recognised very close to the Rhee Wall on its northern side. As Green's map makes especially clear, the Rhee Wall between Appledore and Snargate pursues an irregular, almost meandering course, as if tracing a natural watercourse (? Rumenesea, see below), in contrast to the long, straight segments seen to the southeast of Snargate.

The Rumenesea Wall between Snargate and Old Romney (Fig. 8.1) pursues a sinuous course just to the northeast of, and in harmony with, an also sinuous watercourse, identified with the Rumenesea (Brooks 1988). Now called the Yoke or New Sewer, it has for some centuries been one of the larger, managed drains of the area.

A critical property of this watercourse is that its meanders rapidly and systematically roughly treble in wavelength southeastward to values near Old Romney in excess of 400 m (Allen 1999, fig. 3). In terms of empirical geomorphological evidence, as was explained, this means in the case of the natural channel that its width and the discharge of water through it increased rapidly toward the southeast. In form, the waterway very closely resembles the trunk channels of mature salt-marsh creek networks that expand into the heads of a small tidal inlets or estuaries, and hence is thought to be of tidal origin (Allen 1999). Indeed, the waterway has an almost axially central place within one of the larger occurrences of Green's (1968, fig. 10) 'land type with creek ridges'. The sinuosities of the Rumenesea Wall, however, although clearly in phase with those of the watercourse, are of a smaller amplitude and are locally impinged on by that channel in its present-day form. Consequently, it may be argued that the Rumenesea was (1) an active tidal system prior to the construction of the Wall, (2) already well-developed by the time the Wall was built, and (3), although constrained to the northeast by the Wall, continually or intermittently active up until the imposition of the man-made regime that finally changed it into a wholly freshwater drain. On the other hand, Eddison (2000, 84) suggests that 'the channel...was originally dug to provide soil for the bank' and that later 'the sea broke in, enlarged the eastern end of the channel and greatly magnified its curves'. As a dug channel among the unconsolidated sediments of Romney Marsh, however, the waterway may be expected to have been straight. Further evidence on the character and role of the Rumenesea comes from a recently completed, detailed analysis by Dr A.F. Pearson and Professor J.F. Potter of the distribution and geological provenance of building materials in the churches of the Marshes (Potter, personal communication, 2001). Mapping the occurrence of beach cobbles and boulders of Ashdown Sandstone and of flint, they found that these materials occurred in northwest-southeast belts roughly centred about the course of the Rumenesea. Their suggestion that boats brought stone at various times inland along this channel is not incompatible with the geomorphological evidence for the scale of the waterway (Allen 1999, 8), which in its natural state could at Old Romney have been about 30 m across, reducing to a width of about 10 m at Snargate. Rafts and boats of the order of 10 m in length could have been operated in such a channel, but there remain issues of dating before it can be said when the regime was either tidal or fresh.

Conditions Antecedent to the Wall

Beyond agreement that salt-making occurred on Romney Marsh proper during Roman times, at such widely dispersed sites (Fig. 8.1) as Dymchurch (Isaacson 1846), Ruckinge (Bradshaw 1970), and Snave (Reeves 1995), no final view can be given on the environmental character and evolution of the Marsh before the building of the Rumenesea Wall. There was some later Iron Age activity in the area, but of the now many known Roman sites, none post-date the early third century AD.

Most of the Marsh in the early Roman period is suggested by Eddison (2000, 52, fig. 14) to have been composed of a 'lagoon' filled with 'tidal sand and mudflats', on the basis of activity/occupation sites supposedly restricted to the northwestern margin below the Wealden scarp, and to the inner fringes of the coastal sand-gravel barrier in the southeast. Although so far restricted to modest areas, recent field investigations chiefly by Reeves (1995; personal communication, 1998) show that sites of this date occur much more widely and plentifully (Reeves 1995, fig. 5.3; Allen 1999, fig. 8A). For example, a loose cluster of thirteen sites occurs over a substantial area in Orgarswick parish (Fig. 8.1), in the middle of Eddison's supposed lagoon. Several sites near Newchurch lie within the outcrop of Green's (1968, soil map) calcareous soils, again coincident with much of the postulated lagoon.

On the other hand, Rippon (2000, 60, fig. 67A) states that at the time in question 'the whole of Romney Marsh was in fact a tidal saltmarsh'. One difficulty with this proposal, however, is that a proto-Rother is carried through the centre of the Marsh, to empty into the sea at Hythe in the far northeast (Fig. 8.1). This is groundless speculation, supported by neither the soil patterns and geomorphological features of the area (Green 1968, soil map) nor the long, high-resolution, stratigraphic profile completed by Long *et al.* (1998) on a north-south line across the middle of the Marsh (see also Spencer *et al.* 1998).

No late Roman occupation/activity sites are known from Romney Marsh proper. One among many possible explanations (Rippon 2000) is 'tidal flooding', so long as this is understood to mean the replacement of salt marsh, already subject to immersion by 100–200 tides annually, by environments (e.g. low marsh/mud flats/sand flats) lower still in the tidal frame, on account of a steeply increased rate of sea-level rise and/or a steep decline in the availability of suspended sediment (Allen 1990; French 1993). Eddison (2000, 46) favours such a drowning, writing that 'the Roman land-surface is generally buried beneath a metre or so of later sediments'. Rippon (2000, 138) also favours deep burial, for according to him 'palaeoenvironmental work has confirmed that around *c.* AD 300 there was a widespread episode of marine flooding (Long *et al.* 1998)'. No sudden, widespread marine transgression is claimed by Long *et al.* (1998, 45), who wrote that 'By *c.* 1700 cal. yrs BP intertidal conditions had returned to most of Romney and Walland Marshes', a reference to what they had shown to be the *gradual* retreat, westward and southward across Romney Marsh proper, of peat-forming conditions, begun in the north and east more than a millennium earlier.

In support of their conclusions, both Eddison (2000, 42) and Rippon (2000, 138) point to early Roman sites on Romney Marsh proper now buried many decimetres below present ground level. Although archaeological materials can achieve deep burial in coastal lowlands because they ended up in creeks or large drains (e.g. Hawkins 1973), some of the deeply buried finds noted from the Marsh appear to be genuinely related to subsequent episodes of sediment accretion outside of creeks, for extensive occupation *surfaces* were seen (e.g. Isaacson 1846). The known sites of deep burial are, however, few in number and, crucially, share the same, particular context. They all occur around the inner fringes of the narrow coastal barrier, in the Dymchurch-St. Mary's Bay area (Fig. 8.1), where storm overwashing and breaching may be expected to have spread raised plumes of sediment, and created short-lived creeks, that ranged inland for a little way. Sites further inland still – the great majority known from Romney Marsh (Reeves 1995, fig. 5.3; Allen 1999, fig. 8A) – have come to light through field-walking and other surface searches (Reeves 1995, personal communication, 1998). Consequently, they lie within normal plough depth. The totality of the evidence at present available does not suggest that deep burial is typical of early Roman occupation/activity sites in Romney Marsh proper.

Age and Function of the Wall

Charter evidence reviewed first by Brooks (1988) and later by Eddison (2000) and Rippon (2000) leaves little doubt that Romney Marsh proper was widely and probably quite densely populated by the 10th or 11th century AD, and that the process of settlement had begun by at least the seventh century. The wording of these charters implies that chiefly arable cultivation and little pasturing were being practised. On the coast lay fishing communities.

Recent archaeological discoveries vindicate these documentary sources. At least 23 Saxon activity/occupation sites are known from the Marsh (Allen 1999, fig. 8B), largely as the result of field-walking in a number of restricted but scattered areas (Reeves 1995; personal communication, 1998). Substantial sites existed on elevated tracts, such as Sandtun on a dune-covered spit near Hythe (Macpherson-Grant and Gardiner 1998; Eddison 2000, 58–60), at the former entrance to an east-west tidal system larger than, but resembling geomorphologically, the Rumenesea (Allen 1999, 8). Most sites lie, however, in Eddison's (2000) 'lagoon' or where Rippon (2000) envisages late Roman 'flooding'. Eddison (2000, 10, 64) expresses the belief that there is 'no relationship between the sites occupied in the Saxon period and those previously occupied by the Romans' and 'no known relationship between Roman and Saxon landscape'. Recently, however, it has been found that at least three substantial early Roman and Saxon find-spots coincide, in the widely dispersed Marsh parishes of Snave, Old Romney and Newchurch (Reeves, personal communication, 1998). Other occupation/activity sites of these periods lie only tens to a hundred metres or so apart, for example, in Orgarswick parish. That both early Roman and Saxon occupation debris should occur within plough depth, and in some instances lie mixed together in the soil at the same place, strongly points to the persistence of landscape features over a period of several centuries, and suggests how little, if at all, siltation modified the greater part of Romney Marsh during the earlier first millennium.

The question naturally arises as to how the change in land-use between early Roman and Saxon times was achieved. Given that the underlying trend of relative sea levels continued to be upward during the late Holocene, the transformation of a tidally-influenced coastal lowland into a permanently settled landscape would have demanded that any existing natural barriers be supplemented by engineered banks. To be effective these must in the first instance either form a continuous structure encircling the chosen area or be rooted at each end in natural high ground (Allen 1997, 16–17, illus. 12). There is little consensus on the prosecution of such reclamation or land-claim in the Walland and Romney Marshes

Like Elliott (in Lewin 1862) before them, Eddison and Draper (1997, fig. 2) appear to root marsh enclosures of later medieval date in the Rhee Wall (Fig. 8.1), but this earthwork, a 13th-century bivallate canal, is a comparatively late structure in the area, cutting parishes and estates, although it has come to serve as the administrative boundary of Walland Marsh (Teichman Derville 1936, 7). Eddison (2000, 67, figs 27, 29) subsequently repeated this mapping, briefly noting that the colonisers 'must have started in the north-east and moved progressively south-westwards'. Eddison and Draper's (1997, fig. 2) two 'cordons of connected embankments' in the Walland Marsh, similar to those of Green (1968, fig. 14), later become simply 'two embankments' (Eddison 2000, 67). Each cordon embraces a number of land-claims of various, chiefly later medieval dates, and probably records a major change in natural conditions which temporarily halted further reclamation and forced the repair and general upgrading of the outermost seabanks in a series of juxtaposed enclosures of different ages.

The Rumenesea Wall lies to the northeast of the Rhee Wall (Fig. 8.1) and is the most northeasterly bank of any substance in the Walland and Romney Marshes (Green 1968, soil map; Allen 1999). It was first proposed in 1996 that the Wall was of Saxon date, and that it was 'the earliest sea defence in the area', the 'defining monument of Romney Marsh', and the definitive boundary between the Walland and Romney Marshes as settled landscapes (Allen 1996, 275, 276). In support of this contention, reference was made to an eclectic range of partly published evidence: changes in land elevation, soil and stratigraphical patterns, archaeological finds, charters, churches, place names, and parish and field patterns. The later, detailed ground survey (Allen 1999, fig. 1) yielded no evidence against this view, and confirmed beyond reasonable doubt the persistence from New Romney to Snargate of Green's (1968) largely 'probable sea wall'. Together with the plausible segment between Appledore and Snargate, it appeared to form a 'bridging bank' (Allen 1997, illustration 12D) rooted in the high coastal barrier (New Romney) at one end and the Wealden scarp (Appledore) some 12 km away at the other (Allen 1996, 276; 1999, 13). Hence the Wall, supplemented by the coastal barrier and perhaps other seabanks in the north or east (see Green 1968, soil map), at a stroke made possible the transformation of the intertidal landscape of Romney Marsh proper, and provided high ground in which further land-claims spreading toward the southwest could be rooted (Allen 1996, fig. 1; 1999).

Although regarding it as a 'minor bank', and assigning to it no name, Eddison (2000, 83) later claimed the Rumenesea Wall as 'probably constructed in Saxon times as the defining boundary between the reclamations on Romney Marsh proper and the extensive salt marshes which then stretched away to the south-west'. It is thereby left unresolved as to whether the Wall was the single, definitive monument which allowed the start of permanent settlement or whether, like the cordons of later banks to the southwest, it merely consolidated the southwestward limit of a group of prior land-claims. The latter is perhaps unlikely, for the only enclosures so far identified to the northeast of the Wall lie remote from it, in the Newchurch area (Fig. 8.1). Here Reeves (1996, fig. 2) concluded that a sequence of modest 'innings' (see also Rippon 2000, fig. 56) had spread southeastward. The regional slope is from south down to north, however, and consideration should be given to the possibility of a staged northward advance of settlement from the vicinity of the coastal barrier toward a bank, which may itself have been settled, engineered along a diminished tidal waterway discharging near Hythe. Rippon (2000) also endorses views previously published on the crucial role played by the Rumenesea Wall, but prefers the name 'Yoke Sewer Wall' (surely a name for a freshwater drain) for the structure. Writing 'that this important landscape feature was in fact the original boundary between Romney Marsh proper and Walland Marsh', he too depicts the Wall as the root of further medieval land-claims to the southwest (Rippon 2000, 157, fig. 67B, C).

Concluding Discussion

The Rumenesea Wall merits serious consideration as the most significant earthwork on the Romney and Walland Marshes, but clarification of its status demands new research priorities and a shift of emphasis in the area.

A better understanding of the Rumenesea itself would result from a chronologically-constrained, stratigraphical and environmental study which aimed to establish the scale and character of this waterway over its known length. The northern tidal waterway merits a similar attack. Studies of foraminiferal assemblages in dated sediments from Romney Marsh proper would clarify the issue of the environments that existed there subsequent to the gradual westward retreat of the peat marshes identified by Long *et al.* (1998), that is, in the important interval from the late Bronze Age/Iron Age up to Saxon times.

At present, only circumstantial evidence dates the Rumenesea Wall to Saxon times. Although the bank is nowhere upstanding over its visible extent, enough may be preserved locally within the surviving ramp to allow excavations in search of organic material dateable by accelerator mass-spectrometry (AMS). Excavations and a detailed ground survey are also required in the area between Snargate and Appledore, where the Wall apparently was either subsumed into, or lay parallel with, the Rhee Wall. In conjunction with the environmental studies proposed, excavations are also needed on activity/occupation sites in Romney Marsh proper, at locations where only early Roman material is known and also where early Roman and Saxon remains coincide. The archaeological richness and potential of the area are clear from the work of Reeves (1995, 1996), and the results should provide critical evidence on what environmental and cultural changes took place in the Marsh in the centuries between early Roman abandonment, itself puzzling, and the inflow of Saxon peoples. Fieldwalking in the so-far unexplored, greater part of the Marsh should strengthen the evidence for the extent of both Roman and Saxon activities and settlement.

Acknowledgements

I am indebted to Andrew Pearson and John Potter for the opportunity to make reference to their study of the provenance and distribution of buildings materials in the marshland churches, in advance of its publication.

References

Allen, J.R.L. 1990. Salt-marsh growth and stratification: a numerical model with special reference to the Severn Estuary, south-west Britain, *Marine Geology* **95**, 77–96.

Allen, J.R.L. 1996. The sequence of early land-claims on the Walland and Romney Marshes, southern Britain; a preliminary hypothesis and some implications, *Proceedings of the Geologists' Association* **107**, 271–80.

Allen, J.R.L. 1997. The geoarchaeology of land-claim in coastal wetlands: a sketch from Britain and the north-west European Atlantic-North Sea coasts, *Archaeological Journal* **154**, 1–54.

Allen, J.R.L. 1999. The Rumenesea Wall and the early settled landscape of Romney Marsh (Kent), *Landscape History* **21**, 5–18.

Bradshaw, J. 1970. Ashford area, Ruckinge, *Archaeologia Cantiana* **85**, 1.

Brooks, N. 1988. Romney Marsh in the early Middle Ages, in J. Eddison and C. Green (eds) *Romney Marsh: Evolution, Occupation, Reclamation* (Oxford Committee for Archaeology **41**), 90–104. Oxford.

Eddison, J. (ed.) 1995. *Romney Marsh: the Debatable Ground* (Oxford University Committee for Archaeology **41**). Oxford.

Eddison, J. 2000. *Romney Marsh: Survival on a Frontier.* Tempus. Stroud.

Eddison, J. and Draper, G. 1997. A landscape of medieval reclamation: Walland Marsh, Kent, *Landscape History* **19**, 75–88.

Eddison, J. and Green, C. (eds) 1988. *Romney Marsh: Evolution, Occupation, Reclamation* (Oxford University Committee for Archaeology **20**). Oxford.

Eddison, J., Gardiner, M. and Long, A. (eds) 1998. *Romney Marsh: Environmental Change and Human Occupation in a Coastal Lowland* (Oxford University Committee for Archaeology **46**). Oxford.

French, J.R. 1993. Numerical simulation of vertical marsh growth and adjustment to accelerated sea-level rise, north Norfolk, U.K., *Earth Surface Processes and Landforms* **18**, 63–81.

Green, R.D. 1968. *Soils of Romney Marsh* (Soil Survey of Great Britain, Bulletin **4**). Harpenden.

Hawkins, A.B. 1973. Sea level changes around Southwest

England, in D.J. Blackman (ed.), *Marine Archaeology* (Colston Papers **23**), 67–87. Bristol.

Isaacson, S.I. 1846. The discovery of Roman urns and other ancient remains, at Dymchurch in Romney Marsh, *Archaeologia* **31**, 487–88.

Lewin, T. 1862. *The Invasion of Britain by Julius Caesar.* London.

Long, A., Waller, M., Hughes, P. and Spencer, C. 1998. The Holocene depositional history of Romney Marsh proper, in J. Eddison, M. Gardiner and A. Long (eds) *Romney Marsh: Environmental Change and Human Occupation in a Coastal Lowland* (Oxford University Committee for Archaeology **46**), 45–63. Oxford.

Macpherson-Grant, N. and Gardiner, M. 1998. Pottery from Sandtun, West Hythe, Kent, *Medieval Archaeology Newsletter* **18**, 7.

Reeves, A. 1995. Romney Marsh: the field-walking evidence, in J. Eddison (ed.) *Romney Marsh: the Debatable Ground* (Oxford University Committee for Archaeology **41**), 78–91. Oxford.

Reeves, A. 1996. Earthworks survey, Romney Marsh, *Archaeologia Cantiana* **126**, 61–92.

Rippon, S. 2000. *The Transformation of Coastal Wetlands.* Oxford.

Spencer, C., Plater, A. and Long, A. 1998. Holocene barrier estuary evolution: the sedimentary record of the Walland Marsh region, in J. Eddison, M. Gardiner and A. Long (eds) *Romney Marsh: Environmental Change and Human Occupation in a Coastal Lowland* (Oxford University Committee for Archaeology **46**), 13–29. Oxford.

Teichman Derville, M. 1936. *The Level and Liberty of Romney Marsh in the County of Kent*, Ashford and London.

Romney Marsh: Coastal and Landscape Change through the Ages
(ed. A. Long, S. Hipkin and H. Clarke), OUSA Monograph 56, 2002, 127–139

9. The Purpose, Construction and Operation of a 13th Century Watercourse: The Rhee, Romney Marsh, Kent

Jill Eddison

The Rhee, a prominent 12 km-long embanked waterway, crossed Romney Marsh from the upland to the sheltered marine inlet on which the medieval port of Romney was based. It crossed marshland which had previously been reclaimed. In contrast to early medieval channels used in other English coastal marshlands, whose purposes were to improve transport, land drainage or to by-pass the silted Wisbech estuary in the East Anglian Fenlands, the Rhee was constructed to supply water to flush away the sediment settling in the harbour of Romney. As such, it was unique in English marshlands.

This paper describes its progressive construction and operation as deduced from evidence of the Patent Roll of 1258 which describes the last stage of its construction, its operation and financing, and of the landscape and soils. This is discussed in the context of the terminal stages of a large tidal inlet where rapid silting was threatening disaster for New Romney, then still a port of international importance. Built in three stages, the Rhee became a large-scale human response to very rapid changes in the Romney Marsh coastline.

Introduction

The so-called Rhee Wall was an embanked watercourse which extended 12 km across the Romney Marsh coastal lowland from the upland near Appledore to Romney on the former coast (Fig. 9.1). Although it is the most prominent feature of the landscape of the Romney Marsh coastal lowland, its origin and purpose have long been an enigma, as is shown by numerous and varied theories about it. Dugdale hinted that it was a Roman sea wall, a hypothesis which was 'confirmed' by Elliott (Dugdale 1662; Elliott 1862; Furley 1880). Although that assertion was based on extremely flimsy evidence, it is a popular myth which continues in some quarters to this day. Scott Robertson (1880) realised that the very unusual boundary of the liberty of the medieval port of Romney implied that the Rhee had been a watercourse connected with that port, rather than a sea wall. On the basis of landscape and documentary evidence Ward (1940, 282) also discounted a Roman origin and any suggestion that it was a sea wall.

The Soil Survey map showed that, except for 2.2 km near Appledore, there is no difference between the sediments on one side and the other, confirming again that (with the exception near Appledore) the structure was never a sea wall (Green 1968). Brooks (1988, 92) showed that it was constructed directly across all the existing boundaries of parishes, manors and hundreds. Tatton-Brown (1988, 108) felt that it all dated from mid-13th century, and Vollans (1988, 128) was the first to state that it is clearly a composite feature, constructed in three different stages.

This article re-considers for what purpose, how and when the Rhee system developed and who was responsible for its construction and operation. It is based on evidence of documents, of the landscape and the detailed work of the Soil Survey (Green 1968). Evidence of walls and ditch patterns, a large proportion of which have disappeared or been degraded during the agricultural revolution of the last half century, is taken from tithe maps, the 1878 first edition six-inch and the 1960 1:25000 O.S. maps and from

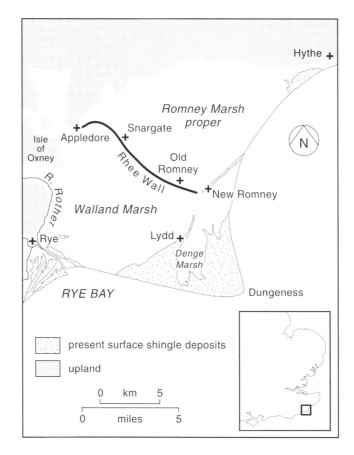

Fig. 9.1. Romney Marsh, with the so-called 'Rhee Wall' dividing Romney Marsh proper from Walland Marsh. This shows the present-day coastline which, owing to rapid and radical changes, is very different to that of the early medieval period.

Green's comprehensive map of the soils. The entry in the Calendar of the Patent Rolls of 21 June 1258 is fundamental to the discussion. It shows that the Rhee was constructed to supply water to scour away the silt being deposited by the tides in the harbour of New Romney, and that the last stage was built in or soon after 1258. The citizens of New Romney were responsible for constructing and operating it (*Cal. Pat. Rolls* 1247–58, 635). Although that entry has been frequently quoted it has never, remarkably, previously been explored in full, so it is printed here in the Appendix.

The Context of the Rhee

Romney Marsh developed naturally and was reclaimed behind a massive barrier beach of flint shingle. During the last two millennia major changes have taken place in that barrier and three very extensive tidal inlets have opened up successively through it, in the general areas of Hythe, New Romney and Rye (Fig. 9.1). Each of the inlets in turn provided an excellent sheltered haven for shipping and, on a coast facing the shortest crossing to the Continent, each in turn became the base for ports of local, national and international importance. But all of them were short-lived, succumbing to silting of their channels combined with narrowing of their entrances. It is necessary to

summarise this background evolution since, in one way or another, the Rhee is related to all three inlets (Fig. 9.2).

The tides flowed in through the inlets and deposited their loads of silt and other sediments, thus building up the surface of the marsh, and leaving behind a legacy of complex networks of marsh channels and creeks. The Rhee crosses headwater creeks of the first inlet, which had its opening in the north-east corner of the Marsh and was open in Roman times (Cunliffe 1988; Eddison 2000, 43–7). In the 1960s a radiocarbon date obtained from shells buried in the sands filling one of the major creeks gave a date of 1550 ± 120 years BP, which made it seem unlikely that the Rhee could have been a Roman structure (Callow *et al.* 1964; Green 1968). However, dating of shells is always problematical since they may have been reworked and redeposited. Suffice it to say that it seems likely that this creek was filled in after the Roman period (Gardiner and Long, personal communication, 2002).

The new land surface left by the silt deposited in this inlet had begun to be colonised by AD 700 and, judging by the widespread distribution of the documented estates, it is likely that most of the north-east (later to be known as Romney Marsh proper), as well as an estate at Misleham on Walland Marsh, had been colonised by 900 AD (Brooks 1988, 95–8). Domesday Book (1086) (Morgan

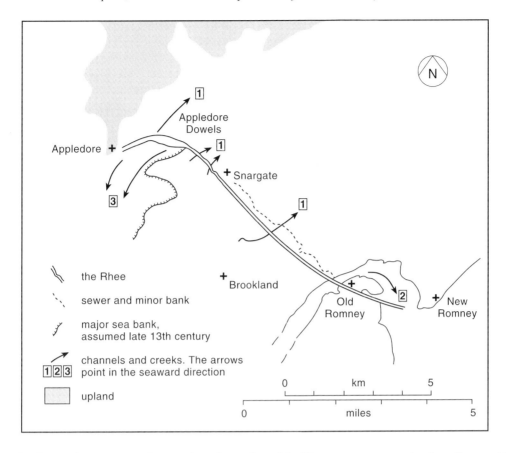

Fig. 9.2. A triple-phase schematic map showing the relationship of the Rhee watercourse to the three Romney Marsh inlets: It crossed some creeks of the Hythe inlet 1 *. It was constructed to bring a supply of water to the Romney inlet* 2 *. It served as a sea wall limiting the extent of the Rye inlet* 3 *.*

1983) and *Domesday Monachorum* (*c.* 1100) (Douglas 1944) together show that by *c.* 1100 most of the parish churches on Romney Marsh proper existed – with the exception of Snave and Snargate which notably were the furthest from the sea.

In contrast, none of the churches on Walland Marsh (south of the Rhee) is recorded until the 12th century, except for Midley, whose record is so anomalous as to suggest strongly that the Midley in Domesday refers to a parish not on the Marsh at all (Eddison and Draper 1997, 82). Brookland and Fairfield were established in the phase of colonisation which began in the 12th century and moved progressively south-westwards. The Rhee cuts across, and is therefore later than, the estates, the field boundaries and the associated parish boundaries established in this phase of colonisation. The remarkable sub-rectangular landscape of the estate of Misleham can be dated to *c.*1150 (Tatton-Brown 1988; Eddison and Draper 1997) and one which once belonged to Geoffrey Turcopule and subsequently to the hospital of St Stephen and St Thomas, New Romney, to *c.* 1190 (Butcher 1980, 19; Tatton-Brown 1988, 106–7).

In the meantime, while the land surface left by the first inlet was becoming occupied, a second tidal inlet, which

was to become the base for Romney, opened up. The sea must have broken through the shingle barrier and flowed into and 'captured' a major back-barrier channel lying behind the Dungeness mass (Spencer *et al.* 1998). The timing of this marine incursion is uncertain. It appears to have taken place after the Roman period because, apart from the occasional coin, no evidence of Roman activity has been found in that area, and it must have occurred before AD 741 because by then a settlement was based on it. Romney is not named specifically in the charter which describes that settlement. But the fishing and farming settlement described beside the inlet included an oratory dedicated to St Martin, the only such dedication on the Marsh, and that is assumed to be the predecessor of the large medieval church of St Martin which later stood in New Romney. A second charter, dated *c.* AD 920, refers to a channel known as the *Rumenesea* (Brooks 1988). There is no documentary evidence to indicate where this channel was, but the name seems much more likely to have referred to the wide inlet behind the barrier (shown on Green's map of 1968 and confirmed by Spencer *et al.* 1998) rather than the minor channel heading up towards Snargate suggested by Brooks (Brooks 1988; Allen 1996; 1999). Not long afterwards the name of that channel was adapted for the settlement, as *Rumenal* or *Romenal*. By mid-11th century ports on the Channel coast were growing fast as a direct response to a significant rise in maritime trade, and Romney became one of the most important, a member of the Cinque Ports (Gardiner 2000). Its strategic importance is illustrated by the raids by Godwin and his sons in 1052 and William of Normandy immediately after the Battle of Hastings in 1066, both of whom were anxious to suppress and secure the town and port (Whitelock 1962). Commercial, cultural, ecclesiastical and political links with the Continent became strong and the town probably reached its peak in the 12th century, as witnessed by the magnificent church of St Nicholas.

Inevitably, however, this inlet began to silt up. A radiocarbon date on a *Cardium edule* shell coupled with abrupt reduction in sediment grain size obtained from the higher reaches of the inlet near Little Cheyne Court (TQ 986216) suggests that between 789 and 659 cal. years BP (between AD 1161 and 1291) high energy conditions in the channel changed swiftly to much quieter conditions (Evans *et al.* 2001).

The last three quarters of the 13th century were marked by extraordinary storminess. The first documented storm occurred in 1236 (Holloway 1849, 67). Further great storms were recorded in 1250, 1252 and 1287/88 (Matthew Paris 175–6, 272–3; Gervase of Canterbury 293). The storms dealt a final blow to the long-established southern shingle barrier which had kept the sea out of Walland Marsh, and broke it down in mid-13th century (Eddison 1998, 68–70). This event affected both the operation of the Rhee and, apparently, the configuration of a small part of it. By 1258 the tides were running up to Appledore and sea water was taken in to amplify the flow down the Rhee (*Cal. Pat. Rolls* 1247–58, 635). Also, probably slightly later, the sea flooded out of the channels and over the marshland, and was arrested by the Rhee (Green 1968, map). In this way the 2.2 km of the Rhee nearest Appledore functioned for perhaps 100 years as a sea wall.

The Rhee

The Rhee itself is a narrow tract enclosed between a pair of earth banks with, locally, traces of a third bank. It stands proud above the level of the marshland on either side, and a road runs along the top of it from Appledore to Hammonds Corner, 1.4 km from St Nicholas' church, New Romney. As the Rhee was constructed across a landscape which had already been colonised, it must have interrupted existing drainage channels. It became the physical boundary between the drainage systems of Romney Marsh proper to the north and Walland Marsh to the south, and in 1308 was defined as the administrative boundary between those two levels (Teichman Derville 1936, 13). Only the Five Waterings Sewer crosses it, bringing the drainage of the western part of Romney Marsh south to reach the sea near Rye, which it has done since at least the early 16th century. Even where that sewer crossed Walland Marsh it remained under the jurisdiction of Romney Marsh proper (Eddison 1995, 159–60).

To describe the Rhee as a *wall*, the name by which it has been known since the 15th century, is very misleading. The place-name Rhee is derived from the Old English *ea* meaning a major watercourse, in contrast to many other terms used for minor courses (Wallenberg 1934, 479; Paul Cullen personal communication). This supports the conclusion of Scott Robertson who pointed out the extraordinary shape of the liberty of the port of New Romney, more than 16 km long but often no wider than 45 m up to Appledore, although widening out into a balloon shape in the valley west of that. He attributed this to Romney's need to control the Rhee watercourse (Scott Robertson 1880, 268–9, map). Importantly, the extraordinary boundary of the liberty also demonstrated the essential relationship of the Rhee to New Romney, which is further emphasised by the only surviving contemporary document.

The Patent Roll of 21 June 1258, the king's confirmation of a petition by the people of New Romney, explains both the purpose of the Rhee and describes its operation at that date (*Cal. Pat. Rolls* 1247–58, 635, see Appendix). Its purpose was to flush out silt settling in the inlet which served as the port of Romney. By 1258 that inlet had become blocked by 'obstacles' on the seaward side of Old Romney. Whatever else the 'obstacles' may have included, it certainly amounted to large quantities of silt and sand, and after attempts to clear it had proved useless, instructions were given for extending the Rhee eastwards, down to the remaining port. Compensation was to the paid by the 'barons and good men' of Romney to the tenants of the land to be taken up for this work, either with different land to the same value or with the equivalent in money.

The citizens of Romney were also to finance the operation of the whole system. Three new sluices were to be constructed. The first was to be made 'below Appledore' to take in at high tide the salt water which by then was flowing up from Winchelsea. That water was to be retained when the tide went down so that, together with the river water apparently already entering the system, it could be directed down the 'ancient course' (i.e. to Old Romney) and on down the new extension. A second sluice was to be made at Snargate, and a third had the dual purpose of releasing the Rhee water into the port of Romney and preventing the sea from entering the east end of the system. Since it lacks any documentation, the earlier, pre-1258, history of the system has to be considered in the light of this description of its purpose and operation.

Detailed Description

The Rhee and its immediate surroundings are described here in three sections, which are identical with the three stages in its construction. The first division is made at

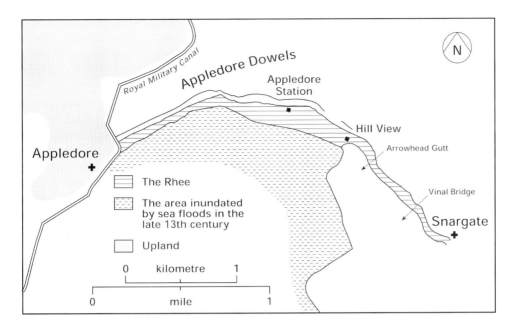

Fig. 9.3. Stage 1 of the Rhee. Irregularities in its width were apparently due to it acting as a sea wall sometime after initial construction. This also shows the third wall, running parallel to and north of the Rhee.

Snargate on the basis of a significant structural change, and the second near Old Romney at the point where the system ended before 1258 (*Cal. Pat. Rolls* 1247–58, 635).

Appledore to Snargate

The western end of the Rhee was, most unfortunately, obliterated when the Royal Military Canal was constructed in 1805. The site of the sluice 'below Appledore' may have been lost to those works. On the other hand the 'balloon' shape of the liberty in the valley between Appledore and the Isle of Oxney may be the administrative relic of a former holding basin for tidal water waiting to be released down the Rhee. If so, the sluice would probably now be obscured beneath sediments brought in by the tides at the end of the 13th century. At any rate, the Rhee now emerges from the disturbance of the Royal Military Canal beside the Appledore pumping station and then follows a broad curve in an east-north-easterly direction before heading south-east to Snargate (Fig. 9.3).

This length is markedly irregular. In the 2.2 km stretch from Appledore to Hill View (TQ 981295) great variations occur both in the width of the structure and in its relationship to the land on either side. The distance between the two walls varies from 90 m near Appledore to a maximum of twice that near Appledore Station. While the north wall follows a relatively regular gently curving line, it is the line of the south wall which provides the irregularities, which are to some extent at least related to other walls running down into the marsh to the south. To the north lies the Appledore Dowels where the main marsh peat is within 0.3 m of the surface and the land surface is

some 2.5 m below the top of the Rhee. To the south, in contrast, the land surface is only approximately 0.5 m below the Rhee.

These variations in the width of the Rhee and in its relation to the land on either side must have resulted from the influx of the sea from the south towards the end of the 13th century. The Rhee may have become exposed to the tides after the storms of the 1250s, and almost certainly was after those of 1287–8 succeeded in finally breaking asunder the Rye Bay shingle barrier (*Gervase of Canterbury*, 293; Eddison 1998). Subsequently, it probably remained accessible to high tides until around 1400, since in a dispute then between Christ Church Canterbury and Robertsbridge Abbey it was said that the boundaries of the 'towns' of Snargate and Appledore had been lost on account of the continual inundation of the sea (Holloway 1849, 126–7). The difference in height of the surface of the marsh on either side of the Rhee must be due in part to layers of additional sediments deposited on the south side, but also in part to wastage of peat on the north side where, without that covering of additional sediments, the peat can be expected to have been exposed to the atmosphere, at least seasonally.

In addition, the Soil Survey (Green 1968) mapped a third wall in the Dowels (still visible in low winter light), running closely parallel to the north wall and some 30 m to the north of it. It is continuous except, importantly, where it crosses a creek ridge at TQ 979296, indicating that when the wall was built the landscape had already been partially inverted and that the creek stood proud above its surroundings. The wall was therefore only necessary across the back-marsh surface, which was lower than the former creek. This third wall may have acted as a second line of defence, preventing any overflow from the Rhee from flowing further north across the Dowels.

Between Hill View and Snargate both the structure of the Rhee and its relationship to its surroundings become more regular. The two walls are a more uniform distance apart, though not yet parallel, the level of the marsh is the same on both sides of the Rhee and the patterns of soils and field boundaries are also the same on both sides. Significantly, the Rhee cuts across three field boundaries which were evidently established before it came into existence. Its course is, however, by no means straight. At Vinal Bridge, where the Five Waterings Sewer now passes under the road, there is a particularly tight S-bend. In addition, a significant dip in the road at Arrowhead (TQ 983292) marks the site of a culvert which collapsed some time after the Five Waterings Sewer ceased to cross under the road at that point in 1623 (Eddison 1995, 159–61).

Snargate to Old Romney

At Snargate the character of the Rhee changes abruptly. From there to Old Romney it is almost straight. Apart from slight bends for 400 m near Brenzett, long straight sections are connected by very minor changes in direction, giving an overall impression of a very gentle curve which is convex to the south-west. The width is a uniform 45 m, and the structure is consistently about one metre above the level of the marshes on both sides. The pattern of the soils it crosses is continuous from one side to the other. Until 1258 the Rhee ended near the later site of Sycamore House, Old Romney, where the water was released into the Romney inlet (*Cal. Pat. Rolls* 1247–58, 635; Green 1968, map) (Fig. 9.4).

This length of the Rhee cuts across the boundaries of five parishes whose churches stood on Romney Marsh proper and whose land was later extended in remarkable parallel slices in a south-westerly direction across Walland Marsh, in the phase of colonisation which began around 1150 (Brooks 1988, 92; Eddison and Draper 1997, 79–80). This length was therefore constructed later than that date. Nearer Old Romney, it sliced through an 80-acre estate which had been transferred from Geoffrey Turcopule to the hospital of St Stephen and St Thomas at New Romney sometime between 1186 and 1190 (Butcher 1980, 19; Tatton-Brown 1988, 106–7). In 1614, when that estate was mapped by William Web for the then owners, Magdalen College Oxford, it consisted of some 74 acres (six having been taken in by the Rhee). Significantly, the map also shows that while the Rhee sliced dramatically across the estate (taking in those six acres) the northern boundary of the property was the northern sewer which is described below (see Fig. 9.5). This indicates that the northern sewer existed but that the Rhee did not when this estate was laid out. This length of the Rhee must therefore be later than *c*. 1190.

It is also important to note a small meandering sewer running approximately parallel to the Rhee a short distance away to the north (see Fig. 9.4). This meandering sewer is bounded on the north side by a minor bank. Both sewer and bank decrease in importance as distance from the inlet at Romney increases. Elaborate meanders at the Romney end decrease in magnitude and the width of the sediments associated with the creek becomes narrower towards Brenzett, almost tapering away to extinction towards Snargate. The bank, almost all of which has now been disturbed by ploughing, changed from a 'major wall' to 'a minor or presumed wall' (Green 1968, map and fig. 20; see also Allen 1996; 1999). Significantly, this combined feature of sewer and bank approaches the Rhee closely at three points: at Snargate; at Sycamore House, Old Romney, where it comes within a few metres of the Rhee; and at Rheewall Farm, where it looks as though the Rhee may have been curved in order to keep clear of the sewer. East of Brenzett, the sewer and bank cross some field boundaries which are presumed to be part of the *c*. 1150 colonisation and therefore the sewer seems to have originated later than that.

Importantly, the landscape evidence of this sewer and bank may be complicated by its adoption for a secondary use. In 1592 it was part of the Yokes Sewer east of Brenzett, and the Abbatridge Sewer west of that church, both of which were part of the Five Waterings system which drained in a north-westerly direction to beyond Snargate and then south to reach the sea near Rye (Langdon 1592; Eddison 1995, 159–61). But subsequently, sometime in the later 18th century, the direction of drainage was reversed between Brenzett and TR 022261 when that length was adopted as the central portion of the New Sewer designed to take flood-water from the Appledore Dowels eastwards to enter the sea through Clobsden Gutt at the south end of the Dymchurch Wall, as it still does today. In order to maintain the flow of water down them, sewers have to be scoured frequently. Vegetation is often removed every three years, and accumulated sediment every five years. Particularly after its change of use in the 18th century, repeated scouring of this sewer may have increased its width, and dumping of sediment may have heightened the bank. It may be advisable to exercise caution when drawing conclusions about measurements of such features (see Allen 1999).

Old Romney to the Port of New Romney

Finally, in or very soon after 1258, the Rhee was extended for 2.9 km down to the much-reduced port (Fig. 9.6). It was the same width as before and consisted of three straight stretches with two slight but highly significant bends. Using the Soil Survey map, it is now possible to identify most of the places mentioned in the instructions to the surveyors involved in laying out the new course, including the two bends (*Cal. Pat. Rolls* 1247–58, 635). The extension started at the 'cross of the hospital of infirm persons of *Romenal*' which stands near *Aghenepend*'. The cross must

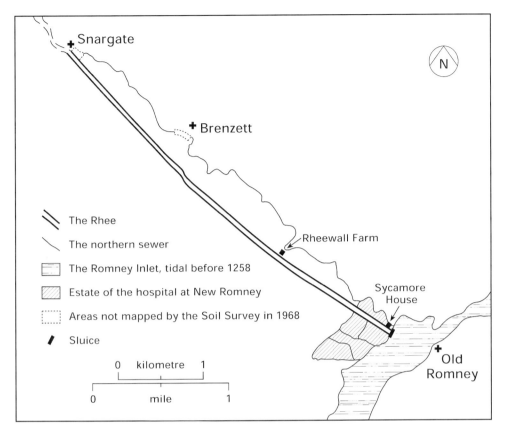

Fig. 9.4. Stage 2 of the Rhee, before 1258. The sewer running parallel to it on the north side forms the boundary of the estate of the hospital at New Romney.

have marked the north-east corner of the hospital (formerly Turcopule) estate, and up to 1258 also stood at the end of the Rhee, some 50 m east of Sycamore House (marked 1 on Fig. 9.6). The course then crossed the former tidal inlet to reach the next landmark, *Effeton*. That name has long been known, somewhat vaguely, to be associated with Old Romney: it is now shown to refer to the field in which St Clement's church stands (2 on Fig. 9.6). As soon as the Rhee was safely across the former inlet, it changed direction, turning east towards New Romney. At this point the Rhee cuts across some pre-existing field boundaries, as can be seen on Fig. 9.7. Also at this point, the glebe of Old Romney lies on both sides of the Rhee. Since it is reasonable to assume that the glebe of the 13th century was similar, if not identical, to that mapped in the 19th it is very probable that the 1258 extension of the Rhee bisected it (Gardiner 1995, 343, fig. 1). The third landmark, the house of William le Wyll, was ephemeral and eludes identification but presumably was mentioned because the surveyors needed an additional marker in the long, 2 km stretch between *Effeton* and the next bend. The fourth landmark was *melepend*, a millpond presumed to be connected with a tide mill, which very probably marked the final change in direction, at the present Hammonds Corner (marked 4? on Fig. 9.6). From there it headed

straight for a further 500 m to the new sluice where the water was to fall 'directly into the port' (5 on Fig. 9.6).

Discussion

The port of Romney, which rose to prominence in mid-11th century, was founded on one of the three major inlets of the sea which were such important features of the evolution of the Romney Marsh coastal lowland. As suggested by the reference to the *river of Newenden* (later known as the Rother) in the Patent Roll, this inlet may have been the conduit by which some river water reached the sea (*Cal. Pat. Rolls* 1247–58, 635). However, the quantity of fresh water flowing down the Rother, the principal river entering Romney Marsh, is very limited and it also varies seasonally. It has been shown elsewhere that in the 17th and early 18th centuries the flow into the Rye inlet was insufficient to lift the silt which settled outside the tidal sluices in the summer (Eddison 1988, 1995). Hence the sea retreated rapidly, and the inlet silted up. It is highly likely that this was also the pattern of events in the Romney inlet some four centuries earlier. One can infer that the effect of any fresh water entering the Romney inlet naturally would have been minimal in

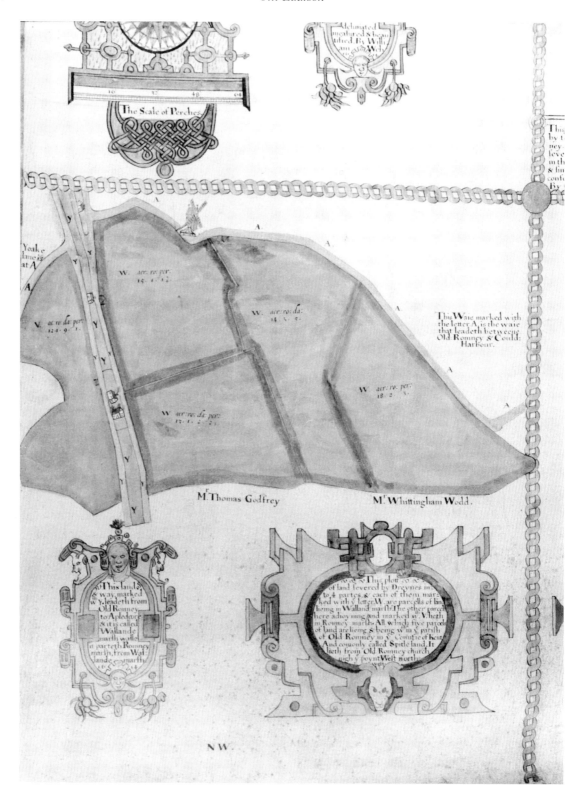

Fig. 9.5. The Spitleland *estate of the former hospital at New Romney, mapped by William Web in 1614 for Magdalen College Oxford, with north west at the bottom of the page. The sewer running south-east from Brenzett formed the northern boundary of the estate, and Yokes Lane from Ivychurch runs along the bank beside it. The Rhee (Y) is shown at left, cutting across the estate. (Part of Steer map 24. Magdalen College, Oxford).*

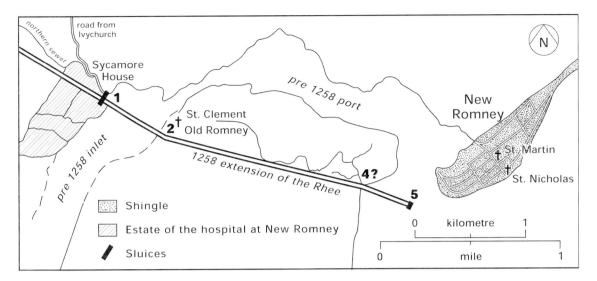

Fig. 9.6. Stage 3 of the Rhee, constructed in or soon after 1258. Numbers in bold refer to locations mentioned in the directions to the surveyors who laid it out.

comparison with the twice-daily influx of the silt-laden tides into an inlet of hundreds of hectares, particularly one which lay at the east end of the English Channel where the tidal range is high.

If, however, the outfall of water could be increased there was some hope of preventing, or at least delaying, the silting. In the 17th century the use of indraughts was common, whereby additional fresh and/or salt water was taken in and impounded behind the tidal sluices, and then released all at once at low tide. The combination of additional volume and the speed of the flow were sufficient to lift some of the silt. It must be assumed that the terminal sluices on the Rhee, first at Old Romney and after 1258 near New Romney were operated on similar principles. It was strategically placed on the side of the inlet, where silting would have been less than at the head.

Even before construction of the Rhee began, sewers would have drained the fresh water from the adjacent marshland and released it into the inlet through small tidal sluices. The long northern sewer from Brenzett to Sycamore House was no doubt one of these. But average annual rainfall on the Marsh is very low, less than 70 cm (Green 1968, 6), and therefore when the port was threatened by accumulating silt, the first stage of the embanked Rhee was built to bring additional water from more reliable, upland sources as far as Snargate, from whence it was channelled down that sewer to a sluice near the present site of Sycamore House. It is possible also that salt water may have been admitted through that sluice at high tide to increase the subsequent outflow. This system may have functioned satisfactorily for a short time but the multiple bends in the sewer must have seriously slowed down the passage of water. A wider, straighter watercourse would have been infinitely more efficient and beneficial. Therefore the embanked Rhee was extended 5 km from

Snargate to Sycamore House. This length was indeed almost straight, although it curved slightly to avoid the northern sewer. It entered the inlet very close to the outfall of that sewer. The dates of these first two phases remain uncertain, but the first appears to post-date the mid-12th century phase of colonisation and the second post-dates the establishment of Turcopule estate, which was 1190 at the latest. Looking laterally, in view of the rapid pace of silting in the 17th century in the Wainway, a major branch of the Rye inlet, it seems likely that the sequence of events at Romney was equally fast, and therefore that both of the first two stages of the Rhee were constructed within the 13th century (author's unpublished research).

Postscript

In the later 13th and in the 14th centuries a relatively small length of the original structure near Appledore was affected by incursion by the sea from the south, as described above. In 1337 an adjustment took place to 'an old trench leading from the arm of the sea called Appledore to the town of Romney', presumably part of the Rhee. This 'old trench' was said to have been so obstructed by shingle and sand for 30 years that ships could no longer pass by it to Romney 'as they used to do'. The sea had made another trench better adapted for the passage of ships, so the landowners were given a licence to fill in the old trench. The new trench was 2.5 km (500 perches) long and 100 m (20 perches) broad whereas the old trench had been 3.5 km long (700 perches) long and 50 m (10 perches) broad. The new trench crossed the manors of Aldington, Appledore, Kenardington and Woodruff, which belonged respectively to the archbishop, Christ Church Canterbury, a lay owner named Margaret de Basinges and Robertsbridge Abbey (*Cal. Pat. Rolls*, 1334–38, 457).

Fig. 9.7. An aerial photograph of the Rhee at Old Romney, looking east with the church at centre left. This shows the change in direction taken by the Rhee (at the place near the church described as Effeton *in the 1258 Patent Roll), after crossing the dried-up Romney inlet which lay across the foreground. It also shows clearly that the third, post 1258, phase of the Rhee crossed pre-existing field boundaries east of Old Romney. (Cambridge University Unit for Landscape Modelling, Aerial Photography Library DY 83, July 1949).*

Tatton Brown suggested that this adjustment took place in the part of the Rhee near Appledore (Tatton-Brown 1988, 108, fig. 9.1). Since that area was exposed to the sea at that time, that seems the likely location. Alternately, it may have been, as Scott Robertson believed, part of the system in the valley west of Appledore. Apart from that alteration, the topography of the original structure seems to have remained unchanged until about 1950. Since then most of it has suffered from ploughing and parts have also been disturbed by improvements to the A 259 which runs along the top of it, notably near Brenzett school and at Old Romney.

The question of whether and to what extent the Rhee was used for navigation must remain open. At present the evidence is very sparse, amounting to that in the 1337 Patent Roll cited above which mentions shipping, and possible further evidence in the cartulary and other records of New Romney (Scott Robertson 1880, 262). No doubt

an inland passage from Rye and Winchelsea to Romney, avoiding Dungeness, would have been welcome. But that would imply that either that cargoes had to be trans-shipped round each of the three sluices, or that each sluice had a navigation lock. The first would have been time-consuming, and the second expensive. So where is the evidence?

Other Coastal Marshlands

Early medieval river channels in other English coastal lowlands have not received a great deal of academic attention. However, the literature concerned with three major marshlands – the Fenlands, the Somerset Levels and the levels south of the Humber – gives a general impression that their waterways were probably used extensively at an early date, and that a number of river courses were straightened, embanked, diverted or even

---

newly constructed during or before the 13th century. But whereas those watercourses seem to have been used as transport arteries, or to improve land drainage or, in the southern Fenland, to divert river water *away* from the Wisbech estuary when that silted up in the 13th century, the Rhee was constructed to bring water *to* a silting inlet of the sea (Fowler 1934; Owen 1965; Darby 1970; Williams 1970; Gaunt 1975; Clarke and Carter 1977; Darby *et al.* 1979; Hall 1987; Silvester 1993; Rippon 1994; Dinnin 1997; Musgrove 1997; Taylor 2000).

Conclusion

The Rhee was an artificial waterway built in three stages, in a prolonged attempt to scour away the silt which was building up in one of the extensive marine inlets of Romney Marsh and threatening the livelihood of the port of New Romney. It was financed by that town, which serves to illustrate the dependence the town placed on the waterway. It began as a relatively short structure running from Appledore to Snargate and was later extended to Old Romney. Finally, in 1258 it was extended a second time, to within 1 km of New Romney. Thus, what began as a short 4 km waterway eventually became over 12 km long. By degrees, it became a very prominent feature, built in response to the rapid changes which characterise the Romney Marsh coastline. It is suggested, on the basis of better-documented silting in comparable terminal stages of a branch of the Rye inlet several centuries later, that all three stages of the Rhee were probably constructed during the 13th century.

Evidently the system must have worked well and the people of Romney must have had great confidence in it, otherwise they would not have considered undertaking not only the capital expenditure of twice extending it, but also the annual running costs of maintaining it. Because the 1258 extension crossed the former inlet, we can deduce that the tides had already retreated from Old Romney, and that by then New Romney had lost a large part of its former sheltered haven. Remarkably, the system remained in operation until *c.* 1400, or possibly as late as 1430 (Scott Robertson 1880, 273; Vollans 1988, 136–7). But by then it must have served a much-diminished harbour, the exact location and nature of which has yet to be explored.

Unlike channels in the other marshlands flowing across the peat fens, the Rhee was constructed across marshland which had already been reclaimed, some of which can be dated by referring to contemporary documentary sources. This is a great advantage for the landscape historian, since it provides the earliest dates at which part of the Rhee can have been constructed. Another advantage stems from the end of its operational life. When it was no longer economic to maintain the waterway, it was abandoned without any attempt to alter the 13th- and 14th-century topography. The land described as 'between the walls' was rented out

as pasture. Fortunately that happened at a time when, depopulated as a result of the sequence of the economic downturn in the early 14th century, the demographic disasters of the Black Death in 1348–9 and the recurring epidemics of bubonic plague, the marsh economy was turning over from arable to pastoral farming. The surface of the Marsh in general became turf and, including the Rhee, remained under grass until *c.* 1950.

Nothing comparable with the Rhee has emerged from a search of the literature of other marshlands, either in respect of its date, its age, its function, its size, or its relationship to the landscape it crossed. Indeed, the literature serves to emphasise the fundamental difference between Romney Marsh, whose evolution and occupation was dominated by extensive and rapidly-changing marine inlets and other marshlands which were dominated by equally extensive but much longer-lasting areas of fresh-water fen. It seems that the Rhee was indeed unique.

Acknowledgements

In 1996 Dr Mark Gardiner and I received a small grant from the Romney Marsh Research Trust to conduct a pilot investigation into the Rhee, which we acknowledge with gratitude. At that time we could reach few significant conclusions, but I benefited greatly from Mark's enthusiastic and stimulating input, and I have since been grateful to him for supplying references, for general discussions and for kindly commenting on a draft of this paper. The present article has arisen as a result of further reflection on my part.

I am grateful to Magdalen College Oxford for permission to reproduce part of Steer Map 24 which forms Fig. 9.5, and to Mike Scutt who photographed it. The aerial photograph appearing as Fig. 9.7 is from the collection of the Cambridge University Unit for Landscape Modelling, Aerial Photography Library. It is Crown Copyright 1949 and is reproduced with the permission of the Controller of Her Majesty's Stationery Office. Finally, I owe particular thanks to Ian Agnew who made fair copies of my drafts for Figs. 9.1, 9.2, 9.3, 9.4 and 9.6.

Appendix

The following is the complete text of the entry concerned with the Rhee in the *Calendar of the Patent Roll* dated 21 June 1258:

'As the king has understood that the port of *Rumenal* is perishing, to the detriment of the town of *Rumenal*, unless the course of the *river of Newenden*, upon which the said port was founded, and which has been diverted by an inundation of the sea, be brought back to the said port, and now hears by inquisition made by Nicholas de Haudlo whom he sent to those parts to provide measures for bringing the river back to the port by the old course or by another, that the river cannot be brought back or the port saved unless the obstructions in the old course be removed, and a new course made through the lands of certain men of those parts, near the old course, to wit, from a cross of the hospital of infirm persons of *Rumenal* which stands near *Aghenepend* as far as *Effeton*, and from *Effeton* to the house of William le Wyll, and so to *Melepend* and from *Melepend* down to the said port; so that a sluice be made below Appledore to receive the salt water entering the river by inundation of the sea from the parts of Winchelsea, and retain it in the ebb of the sea, that such water with the water of the river may come together by the ancient course to the new course, and so by that course fall directly into the said port; and so that a second sluice be made at *Sneregate* and a third by the port where the said water can fall into the sea, to retain merely the water of the sea's inundation on that side that it enter not into the said course;

reserving nevertheless the ancient and oblique course from the said cross to the port. The king therefore commands the said Nicholas to go to the said port and by jury of 24 knights and others of the vicinage make an estimate of how much of the land of other persons would have to be taken to make the new said course and sluices and the value of such land, and to assign to the tenants of such land of equal value or more out of land or money of the barons and good men of the said port, to remove the obstructions of the old course, and to cause the new course and sluices to be made in the lands of any persons whatsoever where it is expedient that they should be made for the common utility and improvement of the port and town; and the sheriff [of Kent] is to be aiding herein.'

References

Published works:

Calendar of Patent Rolls 1247–58, 1334–38.

Gervase of Canterbury *Opera* ii, ed. W. Stubbs 1880, Rolls Series **73**.

Matthew Paris *Chronica Majora v*. ed. H.R. Luard 1880, Rolls Series **87**.

Allen, J.R.L. 1996. The sequence of early land-claims on the Walland and Romney Marshes, southern Britain: a preliminary hypothesis and some implications, *Proceedings of the Geologists' Association* **107**, 271–80.

Allen, J.R.L. 1999. The *Rumenesea* wall and the early settled landscape of Romney Marsh (Kent), *Landscape History* **21**, 5–18.

Brooks, N. 1988. Romney Marsh in the early Middle Ages, in J. Eddison and C. Green (eds) *Romney Marsh: Evolution, Occupation, Reclamation* (Oxford University Committee for Archaeology **24**), 90–104. Oxford.

Butcher, A.F. 1980. The hospital of St Stephen and St Thomas, New Romney: the documentary evidence, *Archaeologia Cantiana* **96**, 17–26.

Callow, W.J., Baker, M.J. and Pritchard, D.H. 1964. National Physical Laboratory radiocarbon measurements II, *Radiocarbon* **6**, 25–30.

Clarke, H. and Carter, A. 1977. Excavations in King's Lynn 1963–70, *Society for Medieval Archaeology* monograph series **7**.

Cunliffe, B. 1988. Romney Marsh in the Roman period, in J. Eddison and C. Green (eds) *Romney Marsh: Evolution, Occupation, Reclamation* (Oxford University Committee for Archaeology **24**), 83–7. Oxford.

Darby, H.C. 1970. *The Medieval Fenland*, Cambridge.

Darby, H.C., Glasscock, R.E., Sheail, J. and Versey, G.R. 1979. The changing geographical distribution of wealth in England: 1086–1334–1525, *Journal of Historical Geography* **5.3**, 247–62.

Dinnin, M. 1997. The drainage history of the Humberhead Levels, in R. Van de Noort and S. Ellis, *Wetland Heritage of the Humberhead Levels, an Archaeological Survey*, (Humber Wetlands Project), 19–29. Hull.

Douglas, D.C. 1944. *The Domesday Monachorum of Christ Church Canterbury*. London.

Dugdale, W. 1662. *The History of Imbanking and Drayning of Divers Fenns and Marshes*. London.

Eddison, J. 1988. 'Drowned lands': changes in the course of the Rother and its estuary and associated drainage problems, 1635–1737, in J. Eddison and C. Green (eds) *Romney Marsh: Evolution, Occupation, Reclamation* (Oxford University Committee for Archaeology **24**), 142–61. Oxford.

Eddison, J. 1995. Attempts to clear the Rother channel, 1613–1624, in J. Eddison (ed.) *Romney Marsh: the Debatable Ground* (Oxford Committee for Archaeology **41**), 148–63. Oxford.

Eddison, J. 1998. Catastrophic changes: the evolution of the barrier beaches of Rye Bay, in J. Eddison, M. Gardiner and A. Long (eds) *Environmental Change and Human Occupation in a Coastal Lowland* (Oxford University Committee for Archaeology **46**), 65–88. Oxford.

Eddison, J. 2000. *Romney Marsh: Survival on a Frontier*. Tempus, Stroud.

Eddison, J. and Draper, G. 1997. A landscape of medieval reclamation: Walland Marsh, Kent, *Landscape History* **19**, 75–88.

Elliott, J. 1862. in Lewin, T. *The invasion of Britain by Julius Caesar*. London.

Evans, J.R., Kirby, J.R. and Long A.J. 2001. The litho- and biostratigraphy of a late Holocene tidal channel in Romney Marsh, southern England, *Proceedings of the Geologists' Association* **112**, 111–30.

Fowler, G. 1934. The extinct waterways of the Fens, *Geographical Journal* **83**, 32.

Furley, R. 1880. An outline of the history of Romney Marsh, *Archaeologia Cantiana* **13**, 178–200.

Gardiner, M.F. 1994. Old Romney: an examination of the evidence for a lost Saxon-Norman port, *Archaeologia Cantiana* **114**, 329–45.

Gardiner, M.F. 1998. Settlement change on Denge and Walland Marshes, 1400–1550, in J. Eddison, M. Gardiner and A. Long (eds) *Environmental Change and Human Occupation in a Coastal Lowland* (Oxford University Committee for Archaeology **46**), 129–45. Oxford.

Gardiner, M.F. 2000. Shipping and trade between England and the Continent during the eleventh century, *Anglo-Norman Studies* **22**, 71–93.

Gaunt, G.D. 1975. The artificial nature of the River Don north of Thorne, Yorkshire, *Yorkshire Archaeological Journal* **47**, 15–21.

Green, R.D. 1968. *Soils of Romney Marsh* (Soil Survey of Great Britain, Bulletin **4**). Harpenden.

Hall, D. 1987. The Fenland Project, Number 2: Fenland landscapes and settlement between Peterborough and March, *East Anglian Archaeology* **35**.

Holloway, W. 1849. *The History of Romney Marsh*. London.

Morgan, P. (ed.) 1983. *Domesday Book, 1, Kent*. Chichester.

Musgrove, D. 1997. The medieval exploitation and reclamation of the inland peat moors in the Somerset Levels, *Archaeology in the Severn Estuary* **8**, 89–97.

Owen, A.E.B. 1965. A thirteenth-century agreement on water for livestock in the Lindsey Marsh, *Agricultural History Review* **13**, 40–6.

Reeves, A. 1995. Romney Marsh: the fieldwalking evidence, in J. Eddison (ed.) *Romney Marsh: the Debatable Ground* (Oxford University Committee for Archaeology **41**), 78–91. Oxford.

Rippon, S. 1994. Medieval wetland reclamation in Somerset, in M. Aston and C. Lewis (eds) *The Medieval Landscape of Wessex*, Oxbow. 239–52. Oxford.

Scott Robertson, W.A. 1880. The Cinque Port Liberty of Romney, *Archaeologia Cantiana* **13**, 261–80.

Silvester, R.J. 1993. 'The addition of more-or less un-differentiated dots to a distribution map'? The Fenland project in retrospect, in J. Gardiner (ed.) *Flatlands and Wetlands*, East Anglian Archaeology **50**, 24–39.

Smith, G. 1998. White Kemp Gutt *c.* 1700: a time of change?, in J. Eddison, M. Gardiner and A. Long (eds) *Environmental Change and Human Occupation in a Coastal Lowland* (Oxford University Committee for Archaeology **46**), 183–90. Oxford.

Spencer, C., Plater, A.J. and Long, A.J. 1998. Holocene barrier estuary evolution; the sedimentary record of the Walland Marsh region, in J. Eddison, M. Gardiner and A. Long (eds) *Environmental Change and Human Occupation in a Coastal Lowland* (Oxford University Committee for Archaeology **46**), 13–29. Oxford.

Tatton-Brown, T. 1988. The topography of the Walland Marsh area between the eleventh and thirteenth centuries, in J.

Eddison and C. Green (eds) *Romney Marsh, Evolution, Occupation, Reclamation* (Oxford University Committee for Archaeology **24**), 105–11. Oxford.

Taylor, C. 2000. Fenlands, in Thirsk, J. (ed.) *English Rural Landscapes*. Oxford.

Teichman Derville, M. 1936. *The Level and the Liberty of Romney Marsh*, Ashford.

Vollans, E. 1988. New Romney and the 'river of Newenden', in J. Eddison and C. Green (eds) *Romney Marsh, Evolution, Occupation, Reclamation* (Oxford University Committee for Archaeology **24**), 128–41.

Wallenberg, J.K. 1934. *The Place-Names of Kent*. Uppsala.

Ward, G. 1940. In discussion of W.V. Lewis and W.G.V. Balchin, Past sea levels at Dungeness, *Geographical Journal* **96**, 258–85.

Ward, G. 1952. The Saxon history of the town and port of Romney, *Archaeologia Cantiana* **65**, 12–24.

Whitelock, D. (ed. and trans.) 1962. *The Anglo-Saxon Chronicle*. London.

Williams, M. 1970. *The Draining of the Somerset Levels*. Cambridge.

Maps

Langdon, T. 1592. *The plott of Romney Marsh, describing as well the common watercourses with their heads, arms and pinnocks, bridges and principal gutts...* All Souls College Oxford KeS/19.

Web, W. 1614. *Lands in Romney and Walland Marsh known as Spitleland ... held by Magdalen College and formerly held by the late chapel of St Stephen and St Thomas at New Romney*, Magdalen College, Oxford, Steer map 24.

Aerial photograph

The Rhee at Old Romney (19 July 1949). Cambridge University Unit for Landscape Modelling, Aerial Photography Library DY 83.

10. Land Holding and the Land Market in a 15th Century Peasant Community: Appledore, 1400–1470

Sheila Sweetinburgh

The late 15th and early 16th centuries were a time of significant change on Romney Marsh, where the landscape of large numbers of small farmsteads and mixed farming gave way to a landscape of few farmsteads and large blocks of grazing land. This paper examines peasant land holding and the land market for the period prior to these momentous changes using the court rolls series for the Christ Church Priory manor of Appledore for the period 1403–1471. These records are the best manorial records available for the Marsh, the manor of Appledore comprising the largest acreage of customary land of any of the priory's Marsh manors. However, the analysis of these records poses certain problems, and these are discussed in the first section. The second section suggests that generally there was an active customary land market in Appledore except during periods of economic difficulty, around 1430 and the 1450s. Those involved were local peasants, who bought and sold small parcels of land as the need arose or opportunity permitted, but there is nothing to indicate the accumulation of large holdings. Nor is there evidence of a move from mixed farming to specialised livestock production, instead farming families appear to have turned to by-employment to supplement their income. Although there is little to indicate a strong family-land bond, the records do suggest that these peasant farmers were keen to redistribute their lands among their offspring post-mortem.

Late medieval England was marked by continuing outbreaks of epidemic disease and this cumulative massive depopulation had a profound effect on agricultural practice nationwide, leading in many places to a slow shift from grain production or mixed farming systems, to one dominated by livestock production. Such fundamental changes might be expected to have implications for the rural peasantry, allowing some to exploit the new opportunities presented by the restructuring of English society.[1] In Kent, during the 15th century, the commercial opportunities presented by a rising demand for livestock – meat, wool and hides – for the east Kent and London markets, was further fuelled by the need to provision the garrison at Calais and the English forces in France.[2] Many of those involved in the livestock trade were butcher/graziers who frequently resided in Canterbury, the east Kent ports, or

the surrounding villages.[3] These townsmen were keen to build up their land holdings, seeking good grazing land in the hinterlands of the various ports. For the Romney Marsh region (Fig. 10.1), a significant effect of this development was the shift from a marshland landscape of relatively large numbers of small farmsteads, whose occupants employed a mixed farming regime on small plots of land, to a landscape dominated by large blocks of grazing land and a few farmsteads. This transformation appears to have begun during the last decades of the 15th century and continued throughout much of the 16th century, with men like Andrew Bate of Lydd and members of the Godfrey family of Romney increasing employing a policy of engrossment to form large holdings.[4]

One way of investigating these changes is to examine the local land market for the 15th century, since it has

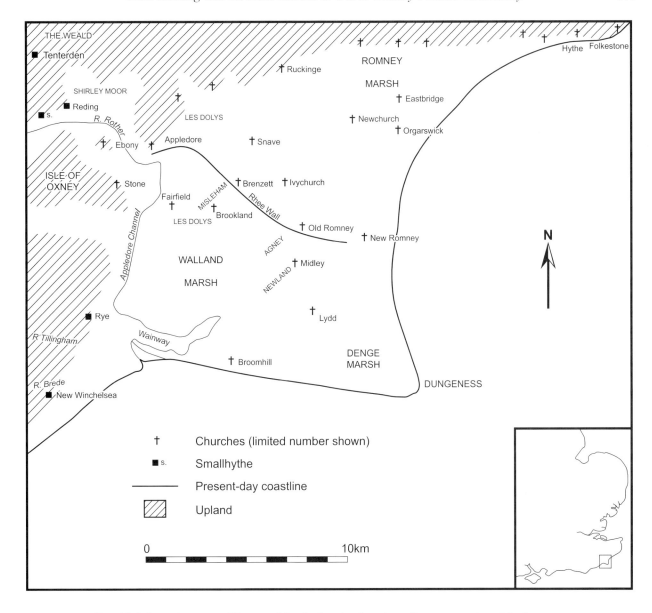

Fig. 10.1. Location map of Romney Marsh showing location of names mentioned in the text.

been argued that one of the determining factors in the growth of the market is the buoyancy of the local economy.[5] However, even though some work has been done on the late 15th and early 16th centuries, little detailed work on land holding and the land market in the Marsh has been done for the preceding period as a way of understanding the subsequent changes.[6] The intention of this paper is to try to provide an assessment of this earlier period with regard to the peasant farmers, but not those who leased the demesne lands of the various Marsh manors and whose land holdings were often considerable.[7]

Christ Church Priory's extensive holdings on Romney Marsh included the manor of Appledore as well as a number of other manors and lands located in Romney Marsh proper and Walland Marsh. Appledore was the priory's largest manor in the Marsh, comprising the demesne land and over 900 acres of tenant or customary land in the late 15th century.[8] Of this customary land the largest part was in Mistelham in the parish of Brookland, a further 369 acres were in Fairfield parish and the remaining 36 acres were in Appledore parish.[9] The scattered nature of the customary land and its total acreage in comparison with other Marsh manors means that a study of those who held it and the land market associated with it may provide useful evidence of peasant land holding in the Marsh more generally for the 15th century. Of particular importance with regard to this study is an assessment of land sales, the *inter vivos* transactions, though questions regarding the inheritance of land also need to be addressed. Like the rest of the county, partibility was the customary inheritance practice in the Appledore area, which might have been expected to have implications with regard to individual peasant holdings. It is fortunate, therefore, that the Appledore court rolls are probably the best surviving series of court rolls for any of the Marsh manors because such materials provide evidence of land transactions involving customary land. However, the Appledore records are far from complete and are considerably inferior to many court roll collections nationwide.[10] Consequently the first section of this paper will comprise a description of the evidence to illustrate its limitations and the problems of interpretation. This will be followed by an examination of the court rolls to see what they may tell us about peasant land holding and the market in customary land in the manor of Appledore.

The Nature of the Evidence

Although a few court rolls survive from the early 1380s and the late 1470s for the manor of Appledore, the main series covers the period 1403–1471.[11] In total for this period there are courts for 162 different dates, including four undated courts (see Table 10.1). These four, like a few of the other court records are incomplete, but it is possible to ascertain an approximate date from their position in the series and from the information in the entries. For 31 of the courts both draft and fair copies remain which means there are in total 193 court records surviving from the main series. Within this series there are no extant court records for four years, for a further 13 years only one court has survived, and for three years there are five courts. The court survival rate, therefore, varies considerably year on year, but in broad terms there are far fewer courts per year after 1445.

In addition to the uneven pattern of survival of these courts on an annual basis, there is the further problem that sequential courts very rarely appear to have survived. There were probably at least six courts per year (the seasonal distribution appears to imply there were more than five) during the first half of the century, though after *c.* 1450 this figure may have fallen. Under these circumstances the spread of surviving court rolls across the year may be important for an analysis of the sources. The seasonal pattern of survival does vary, but in most cases where at least two courts are extant there is often one from April or May, and one from October, or more occasionally November. Frequently these courts had been held on the day when the view of frankpledge for the borgs (tithings) of Appledore, Hothe and Redyng had also been held. The view was similarly under the jurisdiction of the priory and, like the courts, provided income for Christ Church, which may explain the greater survival of the combined records. Thus in terms of the seasonal distribution of the extant court records, in most cases there was one from the spring and one from the autumn. Though hardly an even spread throughout the year, this distribution pattern is especially important for the period after 1445 when generally it is these courts and views which have survived.

As well as looking at the differences in court record survival rates, it is necessary to examine the rolls themselves to ascertain how they varied with respect to the recording of land transactions (these primarily covered farm land, but might also include messuages, crofts, gardens, and occasionally designated types of land, like salt marsh). The land transactions may be divided into two main categories (see Table 10.2). Firstly, there were the *inter vivos* transfers or sales of land, though it is possible such transactions between family members may have been associated with pre-mortem inheritance. Other *inter vivos* land transactions may have involved leases or mortgages but the recording practices employed in these and other Kentish court rolls do not provide such details.[12] The other category of land transaction was post-mortem inheritance, the heir coming to the court to claim the land and to fulfil the necessary conditions.[13] However, there were other types of post-mortem transaction, like the employment of feoffees by the land holder, who passed his interest in the land to them before his death with instructions either to sell it or to enfeoffee the heir(s) he had chosen in the land concerned. Unfortunately the court records provide very few details about tenure, except on rare occasions when land under other types of tenure was listed in the rolls. For example, John Sedle and his wife appear to have wished to have their purchase of the inn called 'le George atte le Vyne' entered in the court roll in 1456, where it was stated that they held the inn in fee simple.[14]

Although the clerks also recorded other types of court business, like litigation covering cases of debt, trespass and the detention of chattels, it was the transfer of customary land which particularly concerned the court. The court officials were expected to ensure that 'relief' was paid and fealty sworn by the recipient in any transfer of land governed by the court, both *inter vivos* and post-mortem transactions. At times this task was extremely difficult to accomplish because some recipients were unwilling or unable to attend the court with the result that in certain cases the final recording of the transaction in the court rolls might be several years after the land transaction had actually occurred.[15] In such cases the clerk continued to list the recipient and whether he or she had yet to fulfil one or both criteria, the paying of relief and the swearing of fealty, alongside any fines which had been incurred as a result of the non-compliance. For the purposes of this study such entries are extremely useful. However, even for the years where the court survival rate is greatest, it is possible that the records of some transactions no longer exist. Thus, although the number of lost land transactions cannot be quantified, it should be considered in any analysis of the strength of the land market. Even where the survival rate of the courts is good, moreover, the first record of a particular land transfer may considerably post-date the actual transaction. Where the first record of the transaction occurs at a court for which there is at least one extant court from earlier in the year, it is unlikely to affect the analysis of land transfers per year, but may be problematic where the record is found in the first court of the year. Such difficulties become even greater where no court rolls survive for the previous year because it is unclear whether the transaction took place in that year or two years before the first entry. Furthermore, certain transactions have only survived in the records when the recipient had not paid relief before selling the land. In these cases both transactions were listed with a note of the double relief to be paid. On rare occasions a triplex relief was recorded in the Appledore court rolls, but unlike Sarah Campbell's study of the Christ Church manor of Adisham, there was no record of a quadruple or quintuple relief.[16]

Further problems included the condition of the rolls, some have sustained water and other damage, while others are fragmentary. In addition, on occasion the records in the draft and fair copies of the court rolls do not correspond entirely. Most of these differences are slight, like a difference in the recorded acreage, or in the degree of detail provided about the transaction, but sometimes they are more important. For example in the court dated 30 April 1465 the draft copy lists 20 land transfers but there are only 10 in the fair copy.[17] Yet the survival of both draft and fair copies is extremely useful for cross checking the progress of the land transactions through the courts, and also for locating transactions which are only recorded in one of the two courts. Unfortunately draft and fair copies are only available for 31 courts, four occur in 1421, and the rest are scattered across the whole period.

The pattern of survival where only the draft or fair copy is extant saw fair copies predominate for the period 1403–1426. Thereafter draft copies are more common in the late 1420s and early 1430s, though in the latter part of that decade there is an increase in the survival of draft and fair copies for particular courts. From 1440 to the mid 1460s draft copies predominate, and there are no fair copies at all surviving for the 1450s, though from 1465 to 1470 there are three years where at least one court survives in draft and fair form. This broad shift over time from the survival of fair to draft court rolls may also have important implications with regard to the analysis, but the effect is further complicated by an apparent change in scribal recording practice in the later court rolls. In the 1450s and 1460s the rolls are frequently less detailed than those for the first half of the century. This might reflect a decline in the amount of business transacted by the court, though, interestingly, the clerk recorded other matters, like the entry of young men to the borgs, which had not been included in the earlier rolls. Consequently, whereas the draft court records are often fuller than their fair counterparts for the earlier part of the century with regard to the land transactions, this apparent advantage may be offset for the period after 1450 by changes in recording practice and the smaller number of extant court rolls.

Thus the Appledore court rolls pose considerable problems, both with regard to total numbers and the pattern of survival over time when compared with other series

nationally. Furthermore, the quality and quantity of the land transaction entries vary considerably and generally provide far less information than can be found elsewhere. With respect to the land itself, few entries include location details, and even though the acreage involved was listed more often, 25% of the extant *inter vivos* land transfers are of unknown acreage. The clerk noted the relief when paid, but for a considerable proportion of the known transactions this entry has not survived, and only in a very few of the later court rolls did the clerk record the annual rent. The names of those involved in the transaction were almost invariably recorded, though this information was generally confined to the person's forename and surname, the clerk rarely adding details like occupation and family connections, which makes the identification of individuals extremely difficult. Such problems have been described in detail elsewhere, but it is worthwhile noting particular difficulties found in the Appledore court rolls.[18] These relate to the small pool of male forenames, the use of the same name for sons, fathers and brothers, and possibly other kin, the recording of certain individuals using occupational or other surnames, and, possibly most importantly, the difficulties of identifying individuals accurately in the court rolls and the views of frankpledge. Of these problems, the first three are fairly frequently encountered where the court record survival rate is not good and where the level of information provided in the various court entries is similarly poor. In such circumstances there are no solutions beyond the very careful use of all the available information and the realisation that some individuals may be wrongly identified and some family links, especially through marriage, will not be uncovered. The fourth problem, the identification of individuals in the courts and views, though not unique to Appledore, may be particularly significant here. Because the areas of jurisdiction covered by the Appledore court and view were different, the degree of overlap in terms of the personnel involved was limited, which means individuals and families are difficult to identify through record linkage.[19]

Whereas historians elsewhere have had other types of record, in particular rentals, to supplement their use of the court rolls, this is rarely possible for Appledore. Very few rentals survive for this manor – the best is dated 1503 – and other manorial documents, like demesne farmers' accounts, provide little information for the study of peasant land holding. Sources that do provide such information are deeds and wills. Unfortunately, however, almost no deeds and only a small number of wills survive from 15th-century Appledore and the surrounding parishes. Consequently, although it may be possible to cross reference a few individuals or families using the court records, views and wills, there are some instances where the fragmentary nature of the evidence appears to produce considerable problems of identification. When looking at land holding, moreover, there are major difficulties regarding apparent under-recording in the will of the testator's land and

Table 10.1. The number of surviving courts per year and a comparison between the land transfers (first record) per year and the land transfers (first record) per court per year for the manor of Appledore, 1403–1471.

Date	Extant courts	Land transfers	Land transfers (rolling 9 year average)	Land transfers per court	Land transfers per court (rolling 9 year average)
1403	2	12		6	
1404	3	13		4.33	
1405	2	7		3.5	
1406	2	16		8	
1407	1	4	14.9	4	5.33
1408	0	0	14	0	4.88
1409	3	33	13.2	11	4.74
1410	5	39	13.1	7.8	4.57
1411	3	10	12.9	3.33	4.46
1412	2	4	14.2	2	4.9
1413	2	6	16	3	5.26
1414	3	6	14.3	2	4.54
1415	2	14	11.55	7	4.45
1416	2	16	12.7	8	4.01
1417	5	16	14.4	3.2	4.97
1418	4	18	16.3	4.5	5.14
1419	2	14	17.4	7	5.51
1420	4	20	18.55	5	5.4
1421	4	20	18.1	5	5.18
1422	5	23	16.4	4.6	4.94
1423	3	16	15	5.33	4.71
1424	4	24	13.4	6	3.94
1425	2	12	13.5	6	3.96
1426	1	1	12.4	1	3.96
1427	2	5	9.9	2.5	3.45
1428	0	0	8.7	0	3.05
1429	4	21	6.3	5.25	2.49
1430	2	10	6.6	5	2.24
1431	2	0	8.7	0	2.66
1432	3	5	8.8	1.66	2.71
1433	3	3	9.55	1	3.49
1434	4	15	9.1	3.75	3.65
1435	3 + 1 undated	19	9	4.75	3.23
1436	2	6	11.7	3	3.9
1437	1	7	14.1	7	4.46
1438	3	17	16.2	5.66	5.17
1439	4	9	15.3	2.25	5.01
1440	4	24	17.3	6	5.51
1441	4	27	17.55	6.75	5.62
1442	3	22	19.9	7.33	5.87
1443	3	7	20	2.33	5.92
1444	4	37	19.1	9.25	5.78
1445	2	8	17.1	4	5.33
1446	2 + 1 undated	28	15.1	9.33	5.58
1447	3	18	13.8	6	5.32
1448	1	1	14.9	1	6.01
1449	3	6	12.8	2	5.98
1450	1	9	12.9	9	6.04
1451	1 + 1 undated	10	9.9	5	5.11
1452	2	17	8	8.5	4.55
1453	2	18	8.5	9	4.77
1454	2	9	9.1	4.5	5.77
1455	1	1	8.3	1	5
1456	1	1	7.7	1	4.88
1457	2	6	6.2	3	4.17
1458	1	11	5	11	3.55
1459	1	2	4.4	2	3.28
1460	1	4	4.55	4	3.39
1461	2	4	7.4	2	4.27
1462	2	7	8.2	3.5	4.67

Table 10.1. continued.

1463	1 + 1 undated	4	8.3	2	4.11
1464	1	2	8.4	2	4.22
1465	3	27	8	9	3.78
1466	2	13	7.5	6.5	3.56
1467	2	12	6.9	6	3.27
1468	1	3		3	
1469	0	0		0	
1470	0	0		0	
1471	1	1		1	

Table 10.2. An assessment of the different types of land transactions (first record) for the manor of Appledore, 1403–1470.

Date	Extant courts	Total transactions	Post-mortem including feoffees	Inter vivos same surname	Inter vivos others
1403–1405	7	32	8	4	20
1406–1410	11	92	19	3	70
1411–1415	12	40	10	1	29
1416–1420	17	84	22	4	58
1421–1425	18	95	30	3	62
1426–1430	9	37	5	5	27
1431–1435	16	42	5	1	36
1436–1440	14	63	22	3	38
1441–1445	16	101	18	2	81
1446–1450	11	62	13	1	48
1451–1455	9	55	13	2	40
1456–1460	6	24	8	3	13
1461–1465	10	44	12	1	31
1466–1470	5	28	9	1	18
Total	161	799	194	34	571

property, and, with regard to what is recorded, a lack of detail concerning acreage, location, and tenure. Also, the will was often the product of a particular stage in the testator's life cycle, near the point of death, which meant the level of land holding recorded failed to take account of changes over the lifetime and issues relating to pre-mortem inheritance.[20] However wills may, on occasion, reveal something of the complexity of an individual's land holding – the holding of customary land under a number of manors, the holding of free land, the leasing of demesne land, and other lands – which is extremely valuable.[21] But this does highlight the problem of having to rely pre-dominantly on the court rolls of a single manor when analysing land holding and the land market in the Appledore area.

The Manor of Appledore – Land Holding and the Land Market

Having demonstrated the difficulties associated with using the court rolls, and other evidence, to investigate land holding and the land market, it is necessary to indicate how they may be used while allowing for these limitations. Firstly, there seems little option except to record the land transactions by first known date on the understanding that even though a small proportion might be allocated the year after the transaction actually took place, this degree of inaccuracy would not adversely effect the pattern of land transactions seen over time. In addition, although court survival rate was not good for the whole period, so leading to an underestimate of the number of land transactions, the length of time taken for such transactions to pass through the court, especially during the first half of the century, might again suggest the degree of inaccuracy would not affect the trends seen in the land market. For the period 1450–1470 the small number of surviving courts may be a problem. Yet, by comparing the rolling averages of land transfers per year and land transfers per court per year (Fig. 10.2) for this later period, it appears that initially the land transfers per court only declined slightly at a time when transfers per year were falling considerably. There-after, as transfers per court declined more sharply, the level of land transfers per year continued to fall, though indicating a slight recovery c. 1465. This seems to show an interesting and changing correlation between the two rolling averages, and suggests that the apparent fall in land transactions per court over the last two decades of the study, the most important part of the court's business, was a real trend. Under these circumstances the priory may have felt it was unnecessary to hold as many courts per year, especially as it seems to have been less necessary to distrain the recipients to fulfil their obligations. Consequently it should be possible to investigate the land market and land holding.

Analysis of the land market and holding was achieved by counting the number of land transactions, using the first known date, on an annual basis and on a five-year basis. The transactions were categorised by type of transaction (*inter vivos* and post-mortem) and then sorted into groups based on the acreage of the land transfer. In order to provide an indication of the scale of the turnover of land involved it was decided to look at the amount of land sold on a five-year basis using the figures in Tables 10.4 and 10.5. The acreage was calculated using the maximum and minimum figures for each of the different groups. Thus, for group two the minimum was one acre and the maximum five acres, whilst for those transactions over 30 acres the actual acreage was used. No additional acreage was added with regard to the transactions of unknown acreage. These figures are provided in Table 10.3 and are intended to show the broad trends with regard to the acreage transferred through the courts. Having examined the land transactions in terms of numbers and acreage and, to a lesser extent, location (location details were generally limited), the investigation focused on the types of transaction involved. For example, an assessment was made of the frequency of group involvement, the incidence of transfers of land between known kin and, where possible, a profile of various individuals and their involvement in the land market. From the results it was possible to draw some tentative conclusions.

During the period 1400–1470 the evidence suggests that the customary land market in the manor of Appledore was fairly active. There were some fluctuations over time (Fig. 10.2): a short-term peak 1409–10, and more sustained peaks around 1420 and during the first half of the 1440s; and the troughs around 1430 and the 1450s. In part the peaks were fuelled by years of high mortality, 1410, 1421

and 1444, though there were also higher than average numbers of *inter vivos* transactions or sales during these periods (see below).[22] The drop in the number of land transfers per year and per court (see the rolling nine year average figures in Figure 10.2) around the year 1430 is interesting, possibly reflecting a degree of difficulty within the community. The decline in the number of land transactions from the early 1450s to 1470, the end of the main series of records, may be more problematic because it broadly coincides with the fall in the number of extant court rolls. However, for the reasons outlined above, this finding appears to reflect a decline in the land market, especially with regard to *inter vivos* transactions. Such a downturn might reflect a period of hardship for the local peasantry, probably in part associated with the problems of the mid-century slump.[23]

Although it is impossible to produce precise figures for the acreage of customary land transferred through the Appledore courts, the figures in Table 10.3 do show some interesting trends. They seem to suggest that in terms of total acreage as much as two thirds of the 900 acres of customary land in the manor was transferred at times of peak activity in the land market.[24] This high turnover of land seems to have been greatest in the decade 1416–1425 and the decade 1436–1445, with a slightly lower peak 1406–1410. The minor peak of 1406–1410 coincides with a time when there were a high number of land transfers, which may indicate that compared to the other two peaks the size of the average land transfer was slightly smaller. A decade later the turnover of land was apparently even higher, and again this was due to a high annual number of land transactions, and a slight increase in the average acreage transferred (in part a reflection of a small number of 50 acre or more pieces of land). The third peak of 1436–1445 was a product of a peak in the number of land transactions per year and, like the previous peak, an increase in the average size transacted (again in part a few larger pieces of land). Interestingly, even though the acreage figure transacted fell for the period 1450–1470, the relative fall seems to have been slightly less than the decline in the number of transactions. This may indicate that there was a slight rise in the average acreage transacted for this period (possibly a reflection of a greater proportion of the larger pieces of land). Because the majority of these were *inter vivos* land transfers this may suggest (see also Table 10.4 below) that there was a slight decline in the frequency of the very small sized transfers, though the actual numbers involved are small and there remains the problem of the 'unknown acreage' transactions.

Two further characteristics of the Appledore land market were the high proportion of land transactions involving small, but not tiny pieces of land, and the predominance of local interest; very few 'outsiders' appear to have taken an active interest in acquiring Appledore land.[25] With regard to both types of land transaction, the most common size was between one and five acres and, even these, as well as the large transactions of over 30

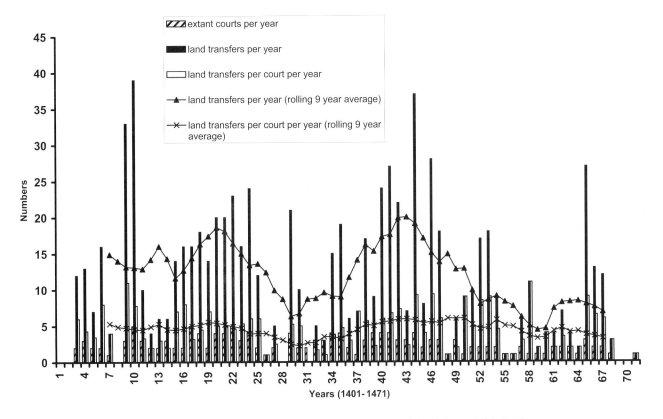

Fig. 10.2. The customary land market in the manor of Appledore, 1403–1471.

acres, might comprise a number of parcels of land, often in different locations.

Sales accounted for the majority of land transactions and out of a total of 799 known transactions for the period, 605 were *inter vivos* transfers. In broad terms the number of land sales was greatest during the first half of the century and, thereafter, there appears to have been a marked decline in the land sales per year. During the first half of the century there were a number of peaks and troughs.[26] There were two major periods of activity, *c.* 1410 and the period 1441–1445, though during the intervening period the market was also relatively active from 1416 to 1425. These peaks were presumably due to a range of factors, and, as noted above, land sales were apparently sensitive to periods of high mortality (*c.* 1410, 1421, 1444). The other factors are difficult to ascertain, but the apparent presence of both buyers and sellers might suggest the market was demand led, or at least in a state of equilibrium (there were sufficient buyers for those wishing to sell).[27] One way of trying to establish the buoyancy of the land market might be to analyse the levels of relief and rent paid over time to see if they were sensitive to market conditions. The data from the Appledore court rolls rarely includes rents, and, even though relief payments are relatively frequently recorded, the amount per acre was generally extremely low.[28] Furthermore, although there was some variation in the relief payment per acre, this

appears to be linked to the type and location of the land rather than to the level of activity in the land market.[29] However, even if it is difficult to ascertain the strength of interest in buying land, the low costs involved throughout the period presumably allowed many within the local peasantry to purchase land readily compared to their counterparts on manors where seignorial demands were heavy. This suggests that a fall in the level of *inter vivos* transactions may reveal the presence of local difficulties. Thus the apparent downturn in land sales during the late 1420s and early 1430s may in part reflect certain problems in the local agrarian economy, a situation that may have been even more acute during the 1450s and 1460s, a time of severe hardship in the national, and local, economy.[30]

With regard to the acreage sold, such transactions rarely involved more than 30 acres, and all were under 100 acres. One of the largest concerned the sale of 73 acres in Ovenham to Laurence and John Kynet by John Watte and Walter Ledenne in 1421.[31] Instead, vendors were far more likely to sell small pieces of land, a situation that seems to have remained fairly constant, though the proportion of the larger pieces (15–30 acres) sold did increase slightly towards the end of the period. About a third of the total sales involved areas of between one and five acres, and a further 20% were of pieces of land under an acre. Although the location details of such small pieces of land are frequently unknown, except in terms of the area, like

Table 10.3. An indication of the scale of the acerage transferred through the courts of the manor of Appledore, 1403–1470.

Date	'Minimum' acreage (acres)	'Maximum' acreage (acres)	Total land transactions	Transactions of unknown acreage
1403–1405	71	143	32	5
1406–1410	223	428	92	28
1411–1415	128	229	40	9
1416–1420	268	486	84	17
1421–1425	418	724	95	15
1426–1430	113	208	37	8
1431–1435	91	206	42	12
1436–1440	406	615	63	15
1441–1445	236	473	101	43
1446–1450	195	413	62	11
1451–1455	109	277	55	18
1456–1460	102	202	24	7
1461–1565	101	245	44	14
1465–1470	47	111	30	15

Table 10.4. The pattern of inter vivos land transactions (first record) for the manor of Appledore, 1403–1470.

Number of transactions – by acreage

Date	under 1 acre	1 to 5 acres	Over 5 to 10 acres	Over 10 to 15 acres	Over 15 to 30 acres	Over 30 acres	Acreage not known	Total transactions
1403–05	11	8	1	2	0	0	2	24
1406–10	16	26	5	1	1	1	23	73
1411–15	8	10	3	2	0	0	7	30
1416–20	18	18	7	2	1	1	15	62
1421–25	14	28	8	0	4	2	9	65
1426–30	5	15	3	3	0	0	6	32
1431–35	6	15	4	2	1	0	9	37
1436–40	4	13	6	5	3	1	9	41
1441–45	13	17	13	4	3	1	32	83
1446–50	11	23	3	2	3	0	7	49
1451–55	6	15	4	0	3	0	14	42
1456–60	2	5	2	1	3	0	3	16
1461–65	5	10	4	2	1	0	10	32
1466–70	1	5	2	0	0	0	11	19
Total	120	208	65	26	23	6	157	605

Mistelham in Brookland parish, or in a named *tenementum*, it seems likely that some comprised whole fields, and others were sections of larger fields. For example, at least some of the relatively recently reclaimed fields of *les Dolys* or *les Doolez* (each 25 acres), were not sold as complete fields but were subdivided in some way.[32] This subdivision allowed John Ian in 1443 to sell to Richard Marchall five rods of land in *les Dolys* in Mistelham, and in the same year Richard bought a further acre of land there.[33]

Almost 60% of the sales were between two individuals but there was some group buying and selling, and at least one group comprised seven men. The surname evidence would seem to suggest that of these groups only a very small number (6%) comprised brothers, a father and son,

or others with the same surname acting together as buyers or sellers.[34] Instead, over 85% of these groups contained men who were apparently unrelated, though it seems likely a considerable proportion were linked through marriage, but the paucity of the sources means these kin groups cannot be recovered. Other group buying may indicate the presence of feoffees or other financial arrangements, and in some cases these men may have intended to manage the land jointly. Very few married couples entered the land market (6% of the group buyers and sellers), and of these few two-thirds sought joint tenancies, like John Kynet and Godelena his wife who bought 12.5 acres from Robert Clement and William Thomas atte Layne in 1404.[35] Women, however, rarely entered the land market on their

Table 10.5. The pattern of post-mortem land transactions (first record) for the manor of Appledore, 1403–1470.

Date	Under 1 acre	1 to 5 acres	Over 5 to 10 acres	Over 10 to 15 acres	Over 15 to 30 acres	Over 30 acres	Acreage not known	Total transactions
1403–05	2	0	2	0	1	0	3	8
1406–10	3	4	5	0	1	1	5	19
1411–15	1	4	1	0	1	1	2	10
1416–20	4	9	3	1	2	1	2	22
1421–25	4	11	6	1	1	1	6	30
1426–30	1	0	1	0	0	1	2	5
1431–35	0	0	1	1	0	0	3	5
1436–40	0	8	4	1	0	3	6	22
1441–45	0	6	0	0	1	0	11	18
1446–50	0	4	2	0	2	1	4	13
1451–55	1	7	0	0	1	0	4	13
1456–60	0	0	2	2	0	0	4	8
1461–65	0	6	0	0	2	0	4	12
1466–70	0	1	3	0	1	0	4	9
Total	16	60	30	6	13	9	60	194

own account and where they were involved they were most frequently selling land. Unfortunately the records rarely indicate the woman's marital status, but for a few individuals it was possible to ascertain this through record linkage. Presumably a large majority of these women were widows, like Agnes the widow of John Suttone who bought a messuage from Thomas Blakbourne and William Chaloner in 1409.[36]

Although record linkage is quite difficult, for the reasons outlined above, it is possible to gain an idea of the relative interest of 'outsiders' in the Appledore land market. Of those involved in buying and selling land, the majority appear to have resided in Appledore, or the two neighbouring settlements of Hothe and Redyng, or on their own farmsteads locally. A relatively large number of family names were found across the whole period, and though there were occasional new surnames among the buyers which may indicate the presence of migrants, this is extremely difficult to quantify from the available evidence. However, on 19 occasions the clerk did note the presence of those buying land or selling land who were not from Appledore or the surrounding villages. Of these the majority were from the small towns of the southern Weald or the coastal ports and only a very few were from other parts of the Marsh (Bilsington and Ivechurch).[37] Four men were said to be from Tenterden and of these two had the same surname as families in Appledore.[38] It is difficult to ascertain whether many of the others had family connections with Appledore because even though very few had surname links with those recorded in the court rolls, they may have been connected through marriage. For example, it is possible that the acre of land William Launder and Johanna his wife sold in 1411 had been inherited by her and it was she who provided the connection between her husband and Appledore.[39] From the surviving evidence there is little to suggest that these men were

seeking to buy large areas of customary land in the manor. One possible exception was Thomas Thundour of Winchelsea who purchased over 35 acres in the 1450s, including land in Mistelham and fresh and salt marshland in *les Dolys* in Benequike.[40] As a townsman from Winchelsea he may have held lands from other lords in the region, including land in Sussex, but without further investigation this remains speculation. Interestingly, there is little to suggest the major lay land holders in the region were involved in the Appledore land market, the only reference to such an individual relates to Sir John Cheyne who was recorded selling a messuage, garden and three rods of land in 1450.[41]

There is little evidence, moreover, to suggest the local peasantry from Appledore and the local Marsh parishes were accumulating large land holdings through the Appledore land market. Although it is extremely difficult to map the activities of particular individuals over time, even the most active individuals, like John Hornbroke the butcher, rarely amassed more than 50 acres. John inherited a messuage and three rods of land from his father in 1416.[42] Two years later he sold three rods of land and then purchased a small acreage with Henry Passour in 1420.[43] The next known record concerns 1438 and between that date and 1449 he bought various pieces of land, providing in total over 50 acres.[44] Yet there is nothing to indicate these acquisitions should be seen as a deliberate strategy of accumulation or consolidation, nor that John's activities were geared towards specialisation, especially with regard to pastoralism, either in his case or more generally. The Appledore area had supported a mixed farming regime even during the pre-Black Death period because certain areas, like the salt marshland, were only suitable for livestock, and this remained the dominant peasant farming strategy for most of the later Middle Ages.[45] Moreover, John was following his father's profession and it seems likely the presence of butchers at Appledore was not a new phenomenon in the 15th century, rather the local livestock market had been in operation in the town from at least the 14th century.[46] Some of John's contemporaries seem to have entered the land market to sell as frequently as they bought, and, in most cases, it is difficult to establish patterns of activity among the participants. For example, except in a few cases, there is little to show individuals bought more than one piece of land in a particular area. In part this is a reflection of the recording practices in the court rolls but also reflects the personal circumstances of those involved and their own individual needs and responses.[47]

However the evidence does show that very few (6%) *inter vivos* transactions were between men with the same surname. Of the few known instances, a minority appear to have involved brothers, rather then fathers and sons, and in some cases this strategy appears to have been used to maintain the family holding intact. For example, in 1405 Andrew, Thomas and John Dendemere each inherited a third of the family messuage following the death of their father, whereupon Thomas and John sold their shares to Andrew.[48] One reason for this apparent absence of transfers of land between fathers and sons may be the unwillingness or the perceived lack of necessity by fathers to provide their sons with customary land pre-mortem, though some may have given other types of land to their sons which were not governed by the Appledore court.[49] These findings are not dissimilar to those recorded by Jones for 15th-century Bedfordshire (the manor of Arlesey Bury), where 13% of the *inter vivos* transactions were between family members; and the figure of nine percent calculated by Lomas from various ecclesiastical manors in late medieval south-east Durham.[50] Neither discusses his findings in detail, but both consider the absence of specific family ties to the land was significant. Dyer, in his study of west midland villages in the 15th century, considered that, in addition to the decline in family size, migration was an important factor. He believed surviving adult sons either sought land elsewhere or migrated to areas where there were alternative sources of employment. As well as affecting the likelihood that sons would inherit their father's land (pre- and/or post-mortem), this also resulted, at times, in a significant proportion of the land being transferred to the lord, a situation that was not found at Appledore.[51] Instead the apparent presence of sons to inherit post-mortem (see below) might suggest migration was less significant there. Though a minority may have moved to the towns, especially to Tenterden, but also to the other Wealden towns and the coastal ports, others considered opportunities elsewhere in the region were not particularly attractive, preferring to follow their fathers as farmers in the Marsh.[52] The situation with regard to land transfers within the family, however, may be more complex, and it seems likely some of the *inter vivos* transactions involved those related by marriage, land

representing a commodity to be traded as necessary for the benefit of the individual and his family.

Post-mortem inheritance was an important method of land transference among the Appledore peasantry. Of the 194 known post-mortem transactions, 50% were between fathers and sons and, as noted earlier, the customary system was partible inheritance. The land involved was predominantly less than 10 acres, and about a third of these transactions included a messuage. Interestingly, such transactions were between the father and one son in two thirds of the known cases, and for the much smaller number of mother-son transactions, the majority were again with one son. Although the missing court rolls may have contained entries relating to post-mortem transactions with other sons, this seems unlikely and may indicate that for a considerable number of families only one son outlived his father or parents. These findings are not dissimilar to those discovered by Smith for a number of Suffolk manors for the late 13th and early 14th centuries, another area where partible inheritance was customary. As at Appledore at least one son inherited land on his father's death, but the earlier, more buoyant demographic times saw more than one son inheriting on almost half of these occasions, rather than the one third at Appledore. Yet even for the earlier period in Suffolk, as Smith points out, where partibility was customary the likelihood that more than one son would inherit was still relatively infrequent, and the 15th century Appledore figures are even more striking.[53] Thus it appears that with regard to the frequency of father-one son inheritance the local system of customary inheritance was not a significant factor.

The slightly larger size of the holdings involved in the post-mortem transactions compared to the sales presumably mirrors the type of transaction, and in some cases may represent the donor's entire holding. Yet less than 15% of the post-mortem transactions involved holdings of over 15 acres and of these only five percent exceeded 30 acres. Furthermore, all the holdings were less than 100 acres, the largest being a messuage and 81 acres John Wolbald inherited from his father in 1440.[54] John Wolbald, however, was exceptional and, even where fathers were succeeded by one son, the land holding that son inherited was often small (under 10 acres), which meant some sons sought further parcels of land to supplement their inheritance.[55] Consequently, even though fragmentation of holdings was not an important issue with respect to post-mortem inheritance at Appledore, the small size of the inherited land holding may have fuelled the level of activity in the local land market, and increased the likelihood that some households would, in addition to farming, have undertaken small-scale craft or trading activities.[56] Furthermore, if some of these transactions are representative of the total acreage held at death, this suggests that even the largest peasant holdings on the Marsh in Appledore were relatively small. Yet it is possible a few of those who began to enter the Appledore land market from the 1460s did acquire and retain slightly larger, though still scattered, holdings compared to their predecessors, so that at death in the early decades of the 16th century their son(s) inherited a greater acreage.

Although the evidence from the post-mortem transactions indicates the importance of inheritance through the male line (brothers were also occasionally post-mortem donors and recipients), women were involved in over 15% of these transactions. Mothers and daughters were most frequently concerned, though on a few occasions sisters were similarly involved in these post-mortem transfers. At death, therefore, in most cases customary land and property were successfully retained within the nuclear family (only 11% of the post-mortem transfers were to non-designated heirs, or to people with a different surname from the deceased, who were not listed as kin), families using a range of strategies to pass on such assets between generations. Occasionally this might include inherited land, but often most of the land had been acquired by the deceased over his lifetime, and there is nothing to suggest the family-land bond was important to these families in the Appledore area.[57]

As well as providing land for their offspring, mothers might act as guardians on behalf of their under-age children. Even though there are only three known instances in the Appledore court rolls, it is possible such actions were more common, and may indicate that mothers might play a significant role in the transfer of land between generations.[58] For example, when John Page died in 1406 his wife Agnes paid relief on behalf of their two young sons, John and Laurence, for four acres of land with the agreement that they would swear fealty when they came of age.[59] The record of this part of the post-mortem land transfer has not survived but it seems both sons reached their majority, and presumably inherited the land as agreed. When John died in 1417 Laurence inherited three acres and one rod of land from his brother.[60]

One practice that may have become more widespread by the third quarter of the 15th century, or at least was more likely to be recorded by the clerk at Appledore (the first known record is from 1446, thereafter there are 13 other instances), was the use of feoffees.[61] Like the making of wills, the employment of feoffees provided individuals with the opportunity to make choices with regard to their inheritance strategy, including the ability to modify the customary practice of partible inheritance. As a result individuals were able to devise a complex post-mortem devolution of their property which might, for example, include instructing their feoffees to sell part of their customary holdings to those outside the kin group to provide money for post-mortem bequests; or to sell to particular family members. William Newland appears to have used such a strategy, but it is difficult to establish the details from the surviving evidence. Between 1417 and 1441 he purchased over 30 acres, the majority in Mistelham. At some stage in the year of his death (1446)

he sold 25 acres to a group of men, while his unnamed feoffees sold two acres to Thomas Batberd and an acre to Richard Tylden, and Simon Dod received an acre and three rods of land from William post-mortem.[62] At this point it is not clear how much land William's feoffees still held, nor what had happened to the 25 acres in Mistelham. In 1452 William's feoffees sold two acres to Thomas Newland (his relationship to William is not known) and another small plot to two men and a woman.[63] These transactions may have been intended to keep part of the holding in the family and to raise a small sum of money. In the following year the group of men who had bought 25 acres from William in 1446, sold the same acreage to John Newland (possibly his son but no details were recorded apart from John's name).[64] Although the location of the land was not recorded, it seems likely that it was the piece of land in Mistelham. The final transaction appears to have taken place in 1458 when William's feoffees sold a piece of land in Mistelham to John Newland.[65] This case, though highlighting the problems of trying to construct the processes involved, may indicate William's intention to pass on the majority of his holding to John Newland, and to produce a small sum from his estate, possibly for pious purposes.

Having looked at the characteristics of the market in customary land in the manor of Appledore in terms of sales and inheritance, it is necessary to look at the implications for peasant land holding. It would appear that most of those holding customary land were local peasant farmers whose livelihood was primarily dependant on agriculture, but who might be involved in some form of by-employment (brewing, baking, the butchery trade, tanning, spinning and weaving, or as a craftsman or labourer for the priory).[66] Many of the farmers seem to have lived on farmsteads, presumably as close as possible to their scattered land holdings, whereas others lived in Appledore, or in the vicinity, and so were under the Appledore tithing.[67]

It is difficult to gauge the size of these land holdings, and for some their holdings varied considerably over their adult life. Yet, if the post-mortem transactions are a useful guide, it would appear that few individuals built up a large holding (or if they did they subsequently sold much of it pre-mortem) and instead most held no more than 10 acres at death. Some of these land holdings appear to have been in the same area, though this may not mean the land was in a single block, or even in adjacent parcels, and others seem to have held different sized plots in a variety of places. Unfortunately there is nothing in the court rolls or testamentary evidence to suggest how these holdings were farmed, nor whether some peasants rented out part of their holding.[68] However the testamentary materials do suggest that some of the more prosperous local peasants held land from a number of landlords, though even these men appear to have held less than 100 acres, assuming that all or most of their land was recorded in the will. Stephen Adam of Brookland was one of these more prosperous peasants, and in his will made in 1472 he left 87 acres scattered across five parishes.[69]

Although there is no evidence of large-scale accumulation of land by individual peasants during the last two decades of this study, there does seem to have been a slight increase in acreage of the average sale. This slight increase and the drop in the number of land sales might indicate that the structure of the Appledore land market was beginning to change. The loss of the post 1470 court rolls means this cannot be ascertained, but it is possible testamentary materials from the mid 16th century might provide more information on this matter. If these showed the acquisition of larger land holdings by testators compared to those making wills in the last decades of the 15th century, it might be argued that these later testators had been active in the local land market after 1470, and so provide circumstantial evidence of changing practices.

Conclusion

Even though the sources pose certain problems with regard to analysing the workings of the land market and the nature of peasant land holdings in the Marsh, they do provide useful indicators concerning the state of the rural economy and the place of the peasantry in Romney Marsh. The small peasant farmers of Appledore and the surrounding parishes appear to have used the local land market for a number of different purposes. For some individuals and families epidemic disease and other difficulties may have necessitated the selling of land, and such people appear to have found buyers from among their neighbours. Local, as well as national, conditions may explain the fall in the level of activity in the land market around 1430 and during the 1450s, in particular. This latter period presumably reflects the mid-century slump, though whether this marked a prolonged period of hardship for the Appledore peasantry is difficult to gauge from the surviving evidence.

In contrast, others may have been able to use the land market, especially during the first half of the century, to establish themselves as small farmers where they employed a mixed farming regime, though possibly with an increasing emphasis on livestock. These householders may have been involved in various by-employment, like the production and distribution of bread and ale, as cloth producers or wage earners, such craft and trade activities providing, at times, valuable extra cash for the farmer and his household. Yet demand for such commodities and services was presumably limited, and may have fallen still further over the third quarter of the 15th century, and, as before, the land remained the main source of the family's income.[70] Consequently these peasant farmers were keen to re-distribute their lands among their offspring post-mortem, possibly through their wives as an intermediary as they

sought to perpetuate the family's involvement in the Appledore area. By so doing they sought to overcome the problems caused by massive depopulation, the continuing outbreaks of epidemic disease, and the consequent reduction in the local and regional economy, which severely affected peasant society on Romney Marsh in the 15th century. However, there is little to suggest that these peasant farmers were breaking with tradition, and it seems likely that their forebears had also sought to sustain themselves through a combination of mixed farming and by-employment. Lordship on Romney Marsh had never been strong in terms of the restrictions placed on the customary land market or the provision of labour services. This had provided the local peasantry with the opportunity to buy and sell irregularly sized, small parcels of land that had been part of the *tenementa* or other areas of reclaimed land, the priory apparently allowing this freedom of peasant action merely claiming small relief payments from the new tenant.[71] In addition, during the 15th century this relaxed policy was extended to the manor's demesne land, which was leased as a single block to one or two local men.[72]

Consequently, customary land continued to be a valuable capital asset, useful in the raising of liquidity through mortgaging, leasing or selling where the cash raised might be employed for other purposes. For the peasant farmer in Appledore, his scattered small parcels of land offered him considerable flexibility, thereby providing him with the chance to buy and sell on a short-term basis as the need arose or as he saw the opportunity. This flexibility within the land market favoured buyers who were able to adopt a pragmatic approach, so possibly providing opportunities for a few of the small farmers to become increasingly involved in the growing livestock trade after the mid-century crisis. Yet, these men do not appear to have sought to become large-scale accumulators of land, and instead it was their sons and, more particularly, their grandsons, who had the chance to become large-scale livestock farmers on Romney Marsh.

Acknowledgements

I should like to thank Andrew Butcher for appointing me as his research assistant on the 'Medieval Structures of Land-holding in Romney Marsh' project, and to the Romney Marsh Research Trust for funding this project. Moreover, I should like to thank Andrew for his guidance and assistance while working on the project and for his comments and suggestions during the writing of this paper. Gill Draper very generously shared her ideas about the history of land holding in the Appledore area with me, and allowed me to use her map of Appledore and its hinterland. John Hills kindly produced the fair copy. Finally, I should like to thank the two anonymous referees for their comments and suggestions.

Notes

1. Britnell indicates the changes which took place *c.* 1300–1520 in terms of urban demand, for example rising standards of living and the growth of the meat trade; Britnell, 'Urban demand in the English economy', 9–19.
2. The renewal of hostilities in the Hundred Years War seems to have stimulated a demand for all kinds of livestock for export during the early 15th century; Mate, 'Pastoral farming', 524–5, 534. Harvey, *Jack Cade's Rebellion*, 13.
3. Butcher, 'The families of Hythe'.
4. Dimmock, 'Accumulation and poverty in Lydd'.
5. However, as Harvey noted, the relationship between local prosperity and the presence of a land market was not simple, and in places like Kent light seignorial demands were a contributory factor; Harvey, 'Conclusion', 349–50.
6. Carlin, 'Christ Church and its lands'.
7. For an assessment of the demesne farmers of Christ Church Priory and All Souls College during the later Middle Ages; Draper, 'The farmers on Romney Marsh', 109–28. As Draper notes, it was these lessees who were closest in outlook to the 'capitalists' Dyer found in the 15th century in the west midlands; Dyer, 'Capitalists in fifteenth-century England', 10–16.
8. Butcher, personal communication.
9. For an assessment of the development of Mistelham; Eddison and Draper, 'A landscape of medieval reclamation', 76–84.
10. To provide some idea of comparison, Halesowen (Worcestershire) has a superb series of court rolls running from 1270–1500 and has been used by Razi to construct a detailed study of the area; Razi, *Life, Marriage and Death*; 'Family, land and the village community', 3–36; 'Myth of the immutable family', 3–44. For Kent one of the best series is for the manor of Adisham, covering the period 1271–1480; Campbell, 'History of Adisham', 254–302.
11. CCA U15 10/12 1378–1379, U15 10/13 1382–1383, U15 10/14–42 1403–1471, U15 10/43 1467–68, 1477–1482.
12. However, even though the numbers are very small, the recording of cases in the court rolls concerning non-payment of rent and trespass might imply that sub-renting between tenants of customary land did take place at Appledore; CCA U15 10/16, 18, 19, 21.
13. The payment of a 'relief', not an entry fine, was due on land associated with freehold tenure, and this system also applied to customary land in Kent. The relief seems to have been about half the annual rent in Appledore, though this is based on a small number of entries where the rent was also listed. Moreover, tenants on neither category of land owed 'heriot' in Kent; Campbell, 'History of Adisham', 258.
14. CCA U15 10/34.
15. A land transaction which took a particularly long time concerned Richard and John Knyght who took more than six years to fulfil the court's requirements; CCA U15 10/14–16.
16. Campbell, 'History of Adisham', 259.
17. CCA U15 10/35, 10/36.
18. There is a considerable literature on the value, use and limitations of court rolls, including; Razi, 'The Toronto School's reconstruction', 141–57; Razi, 'The erosion of the family-land bond', 295–304; Razi, 'The use of manor court rolls', 191–200; Razi, 'The transparency of court rolls', 523–35; Poos and Smith, 'Legal windows onto historical populations?', 128–52; Poos and Smith, 'Shades still on the window', 409–29; Campbell, 'History of Adisham', 26–32; Jones, 'Bedfordshire: fifteenth century', 237; Dyer, 'Changes in the link between families and their land', 305–11; Dyer, 'Documentary evidence', 12–35; Campbell, B. 'Land market in a fourteenth century peasant community', 92–4.
19. Dyer noted similar problems of identification; Dyer, 'Changes in peasant holdings', 279.
20. Butcher, 'Introduction'.
21. For example, in his will dated 1471 John Curteys of Brookland held two plots of land (half an acre and a quarter of an acre) from Christ Church, a three acre plot from St Augustine's Abbey, and a messuage and other unspecified pieces of land on the Marsh; CKS PRC17/1, f.378r.
22. The highest yearly figures of post-mortem transfers for the period occurred in 1410 (9 transfers), 1421 (11 transfers) and 1444 (12 transfers). Mortality in these years at Christ Church Priory was not the highest experienced there, but as Hatcher has noted it might be said that the priory experienced mortality crises during the 15th century of more than once every four years, a situation which may also have occurred on the Marsh; Hatcher, 'Mortality in the fifteenth century', 30–1.
23. Hatcher, 'The great slump', 245–8.
24. Using the 'maximum' figure for Appledore, but without adding any extra for the 'unknown acreage', the acreage of the manor was transferred once every 13 years during the period 1403–1470; for the decade 1416–1425 it was once every seven and a half years and for the decade 1436–1445 it was once every eight and a quarter years. This is comparable to Whittle's figure of once every 11 years for the manor of Hevingham Bishops, 1444–1558, a manor she characterised as having an active land market in small parcels of land; Whittle and Yates, '*Pays réel* or *pays légal*?', 16–7.
25. Schofield found that *extranei* were interested in customary land for the Essex manor of Birdbrook from the mid 15th century, though he too noted this became more prevalent from the 1470s; Schofield, 'Market for customary land', 6–7.
26. Campbell found that at Coltishall, Norfolk, the land market was not harvest-sensitive after the Black Death; Campbell, 'Land market in a fourteenth century peasant community', 110. Comparing harvest yields (Winchester manors), grain prices (national), and land transfers for Appledore, there was no indication of a strong correlation between harvest quality and the number of land transfers; Farmer, 'Prices and wages', 503–5, 507–8. However, in a mixed farming region the situation is more complex and livestock production is also important. As Mate has indicated, there were considerable problems in Kent during the 1430s, 1440s and 1450s, with severe storms on Romney Marsh in the 1460s; Mate, 'Pastoral farming', 525–8, 534.
27. This is in contrast to other parts of the country, for example some west midland villages, where customary land passed into the lord's hands because buyers were not eager to acquire land immediately it became available; Dyer, 'Changes in peasant holdings', 283–4.
28. The low level is similar to the level of entry fine found by

Whittle on certain Norfolk manors; Whittle and Yates, '*Pays réel* or *pays légal*?', 8–9.

29. In 1425 the relief for half an acre of land in *les Dolys* was 4*d.*, whereas for four acres in Ovenham it was only 3*d.*; CCA U15 10/20. In 1447 the priory sought a relief of 40*d.* for five acres in *les Dolys* and 3*d. ob.* for five acres in Ovenham; CCA U15 10/21. In 1458 the relief for 13 acres of land in Ovenham was 9*d.ob.q.*; CCA U15 10/34.

30. Hatcher, 'The great slump', 248, 250, 253; Mate, 'Kent and Sussex', 121–3.

31. CCA U15 10/19.

32. This land was also known as *Les Doolez* and had been reclaimed before 1416; Eddison and Draper, 'A landscape of medieval reclamation', 87, 88.

33. CCA U15 10/29.

34. These findings are very different from those presented by Smith for the manor of Redgrave for the period 1260–1319; Smith, 'Families and their land', 186–7.

35. CCA U15 10/14.

36. CCA U15 10/16.

37. Those from the Weald came from Tenterden, Newenden, Woodchurch, Bethersden and Hawkhurst; and those from the coastal towns came from Rye, Winchelsea, Romney and Lydd.

38. It seems likely John Roulf and Stephen Adam of Tenterden had familial connections with Appledore; CCA U15 10/18.

39. CCA U15 10/18.

40. CCA U15 10/33, 10/34.

41. CCA U15 10/31.

42. CCA U15 10/18.

43. CCA U15 10/19.

44. CCA U15 10/21, 10/26.

45. Though impressionistic, the small number of debt and other cases recorded in the court rolls would suggest the continuing importance of mixed farming. For example a case in 1405 concerned a bullock and a pig; of two cases in 1422 one concerned the pasturing of 13 gimmers and the other oats; in 1435 there was a dispute over a cow in milk with her calf; a case in 1459 concerned two bushels of wheat, and in 1465 Robert Hornbroke was said to have sold 10 quarters of wheat and a quarter of peas to John Spicer; CCA U15 10/14, 19, 21, 34, 36.

46. Although Edward III granted a licence to the priory to hold a weekly market, and annual fair at Appledore in 1358, it seems likely the town had been a trading centre for produce from the Marsh from a much earlier date; Hasted, *History of Kent*, 254; CCA DCc Ch. Ant. A164.

47. Using the continuous series of court rolls for Kempsey for the 15th century, Dyer was able to draw up 109 biographies of tenants involved in the local land market. Even though he found some whose holding size over their life time related to life cycle changes, in other cases the pattern of land transfers appeared to 'defy rational explanation', a situation which was not dissimilar, at times, for the manor of Appledore; Dyer, 'Changes in peasant holdings, 286–7.

48. CCA U15 10/14.

49. The absence of maintenance agreements in the Appledore court rolls was mirrored by Dyer's findings for a number of west midland villages for the 15th century. However, he did find that land transfers within the family represented a higher proportion of the total *inter vivos* transactions compared to the findings for Appledore; Dyer, 'Changes in peasant holdings', 284–9.

50. Jones, 'Bedfordshire: fifteenth century', 217–9; Lomas, 'Durham: land and its transfer', 297–8.

51. Dyer, 'Changes in peasant holdings', 284–6. In the Appledore court rolls there was only one transaction involving the lord. In 1412 Johanna, the daughter and heir of John Haldeune died without heirs, her messuage, 20 acres of arable and 10 acres of woodland was transferred to the priory; CCA U15 10/18.

52. Although impossible to quantify, from the biographies of those known to have inherited land and been involved in the Appledore land market, it would appear few bought land in the manor before inheriting (but they may have leased land or purchased land outside the manor), which may imply they were involved with the family holding, or were working locally. With regard to migration, employment opportunities in the region were probably limited before the last decades of the century when the Wealden cloth and iron industries began to develop rapidly; Zell, 'Industry in the countryside', 56, 153–4, 233–4. The New Romney freemen's lists do suggest migration between the countryside and the town was important during the 15th century, though almost 60% of Romney's freemen were enrolled between 1450–1470; Butcher, 'Origins of Romney Freemen', 20–2, 24–7.

53. Smith, 'Families and their property', 50.

54. CCA U15 10/21.

55. For example John Edolf inherited an unknown acreage (probably small) from his father in 1406. Thereafter he made two further purchases of land, four acres with other men in 1430 and four acres, three rods in 1443. His two sons, Thomas and William, inherited seven acres of land on the death of their father in 1447; CCA U15 10/14, 21, 29.

56. Thomas Brykenden inherited a messuage and just over 20 acres (in seven parcels of land) from his parents in 1422. He presumably farmed his scattered holdings, his wife providing additional income through her brewing activities during the 1420s and 1430s; CCA U15 10/19, 20, 21.

57. In 1383–4 the customary land of the manor included 36 *tenementa*; Butcher, personal communication. These were frequently named after tenant families and most of the names survived into the 15th century, but a few seem to have been replaced. The *tenementa* varied in size between one and a 100 acres, and all were apparently capable of being sub-divided, and it was these parcels of land which were transferred in the court rolls. As a consequence individuals might hold small parcels of land in a number of *tenementa* and these might be sold within one transaction. In the 15th century, the Feldiswell family was one of only two known to have held land within a *tenementum* bearing its name, and in this case the name was not in the 1383–4 list; CCA U15 10/18, 21, 29, 34. For differing views on the strength over time of the family-land bond; Razi, 'The erosion of the family-land bond, 295–304; Dyer, 'Changes in the link between families and their land', 305–11.

58. Interestingly in the courts they studied, Poos and Bonfield found that mothers were not always appointed as guardians, and that other family members or strangers might be appointed; Poos and Bonfield, *Select cases in manorial courts*, cxxxii–cxxxiii. At Appledore the only known

guardian who was not the heir's mother was William Gerard (there is nothing to suggest the mother was living at the time). In 1439 he paid relief and had custody of young William Kenet's inheritance from his father until the boy came of age. There is nothing in the court rolls to indicate the relationship between them but William Gerard may have been young William's godfather, and they may have been related through marriage; CCA U15 10/21.

59. CCA U15 10/14.

60. CCA U15 10/18.

61. The use of feoffees with regard to the disposal of customary land post-mortem was a fairly common practice in 15th century Kent; Butcher, personal communication. Interestingly Poos and Bonfield do not appear to have found this practice, though they did find a few cases where the sick or dying sought to transfer their customary land outside the court. Such transfers were made before witnesses to a manorial official, who subsequently registered the transfer in the court rolls at the next court, a simpler and less flexible system; Poos and Bonfield, *Select cases in manorial courts*, cxxxvi–cxxxvii.

62. CCA U15 10/21.

63. CCA U15 10/33.

64. *Ibid*.

65. CCA U15 10/34.

66. Using record linkage for those listed in the views of frankpledge and in the land transactions, it would appear that some households might bake and/or brew commercially, like the Benet, Lang, Knight, and Sedelyde families. Others, like the Adams, Chesemans and Hornbrokes, were butchers, while three members of the Coteler family and two members of the Henxden family were listed as tanners, and each had been involved in the land market. Evidence for local cloth making in these peasant farmer households is more limited but John Webbe owned a wool loom in 1438, John Scraybard, fuller, was fined for washing woollen cloth illegally in 1432, and Robert Ford and his wife were involved in a case in 1479 concerning wool and spinning equipment; CCA U15 10/ 21, 43. The lessees of the priory's demesne were charged

with the upkeep of the property which might necessitate work on the farm buildings, embankments and ditches, such work was done for wages. For example in 1468–9 a carpenter repaired the cowstalls and did further work at the grange; CCA DCc Bedels' Rolls, Appledore 75.

67. The field walking evidence from Romney Marsh proper indicates that during the Middle Ages scattered or dispersed settlement was the dominant picture across the marsh; Reeves, 'The field walking evidence', 89–90.

68. As noted earlier, the evidence from the debt and other cases seems to imply some sub-renting took place, but the ease with which land could be bought might suggest sub-renting was not common. All the cases appear to be concerned with grazing land, which might indicate that, like some of the small-scale land transfers, individuals were seeking to take advantage of short-term market opportunities; CCA U15 10/16, 18, 19, 21.

69. CKS PRC17/1, f. 160r.

70. Though difficult to quantify, with regard to the food trades, there appears to have been a noticeable decline in the number of regular brewers and bakers fined in the views of frankpledge from *c.* 1450, and with respect to the brewers especially, a marked increase in the number of women presented only once or twice; CCA U15 10/ 33–43.

71. As Mate noted, the tenant services on Christ Church Priory's marsh manors were negligible during the 14th century; Mate, 'Labour and labour services', 55. In their article on the contrast in peasant land holding between Norfolk and Berkshire, Whittle and Yates discuss the significance of landlord policy on the development of the customary land market in the 15th century. Whittle indicates that the less restrictive landlord policy in Norfolk provided the local peasantry with greater opportunities, a situation which had many similarities with the position in Kent; Whittle and Yates, '*Pays réel* or *pays légal?*', 3–18.

72. For example, in the late 1420s and early 1430s the priory leased the demesne land to John Lang and Richard Philipp, their successor was John Lambsyn, who held the lease during the 1430s and 1440s; CCA DCc MA137, 139, 140, 144; Bedels' Rolls, Appledore 60, 64.

References

Britnell, R. 2000. Urban demand in the English Economy, 1300-1600, in J.A. Galloway (ed.) *Trade, Urban Hinterlands and Market Integration c. 1300-1600* (Centre for Metropolitan History Working Papers Series **3**), 1–22. London.

Butcher, A.F. 1974. The origins of Romney freemen, 1433-1523, *Economic History Review* 2nd series **27**, 16–27.

Butcher, A.F. 1997. The marshland economy of the families of Hythe in the later Middle Ages, lecture given at the tenth anniversary of the Romney Marsh Research Trust.

Butcher, A.F. Forthcoming. Introduction: inheritance and cultural transmission in late medieval English society, in A.F. Butcher (ed.) *Strategies of Inheritance in Late Medieval Kent*.

Campbell, B. 1984. Population pressure, inheritance and the land market in a fourteenth century peasant community, in R.M. Smith (ed.) *Land, Kinship and Life-Cycle*, 87–134. Cambridge.

Campbell, S. 1981. Some Aspects of the Social and Economic

History of the Manor of Adisham, *c.* 1200 to the Dissolution (unpublished M.Phil. thesis, University of Kent at Canterbury).

Carlin, M.N. 1970. Christ Church, Canterbury, and its lands from the beginning of the Priorate of Thomas Chillenden to the Dissolution (1391–1540) (unpublished B. Litt. thesis, University of Oxford).

Dimmock, S. 1996. Accumulation and poverty in Lydd, *c.* 1450–1550, paper given at the Kent University conference on 'Poverty'.

Draper, G. 1998. The farmers of Canterbury Cathedral Priory and All Souls College on Romney Marsh *c.* 1443–1545, in J. Eddison, M. Gardiner and A. Long (eds) *Romney Marsh: Environmental Change and Human Occupation in a Coastal Lowland* (Oxford University for Archaeology **46**), 109–28. Oxford.

Dyer, C. 1984. Changes in the size of peasant holdings in some west midland villages, 1440–1540, in R.M. Smith (ed.) *Land, Kinship and Life-Cycle*, 277–94. Cambridge.

Dyer, C. 1984. Changes in the link between families and their land in the west midlands in the fourteenth and fifteenth centuries, in R.M. Smith (ed.) *Land, Kinship and Life-Cycle*, 305–11. Cambridge.

Dyer, C. 1988. Documentary evidence: problems and enquires, in G. Astill and A. Grant (eds) *The Countryside in Medieval England*, 12–35. Oxford.

Dyer, C. 1991. Were there any capitalists in fifteenth-century England?, in J. Kermode (ed.) *Enterprise and Individuals in Fifteenth-Century England*, 1–24. Stroud.

Eddison, J. and Draper, G. 1997. A landscape of medieval reclamation: Walland Marsh, Kent, *Landscape History* **19**, 75–88.

Farmer, D. 1991. Prices and wages, 1350–1500, in E. Miller (ed.) *Agrarian History of England and Wales, III: 1348–1500*, 431–525. Cambridge.

Harvey, I. 1991. *Jack Cade's Rebellion of 1450*. Oxford.

Harvey, P.D.A. 1984. Conclusion, in P.D.A. Harvey, (ed.) *The Peasant Land Market in Medieval England*. 328–56. Oxford.

Hasted, E. 1972 (reprint). *The History and Topographical Survey of the County of Kent, vii.* Canterbury.

Hatcher, J. 1986. Mortality in the fifteenth century: some new evidence, *Economic History Review* 2nd series **39**, 19–38.

Hatcher, J. 1996. The great slump of the mid-fifteenth century, in R. Britnell and J. Hatcher (eds) *Progress and Problems in Medieval England*, 237–72. Cambridge.

Jones, A. 1984. Bedfordshire: fifteenth century, in P.D.A. Harvey (ed.) *The Peasant Land Market in Medieval England*, 179–252. Oxford.

Lomas, T. 1984. South-east Durham: late fourteenth and fifteenth centuries, in P.D.A. Harvey (ed.) *The Peasant Land Market in Medieval England*, 253–327. Oxford.

Mate, M. 1985. Labour and labour services on the estates of Canterbury Cathedral priory in the fourteenth century, *Southern History* **7**, 55–67.

Mate, M. 1987. Pastoral farming in south-east England in the fifteenth century, *Economic History Review* 2nd series **40**, 523–36.

Mate, M. 1991. Kent and Sussex, in E. Miller (ed.) *Agrarian History of England and Wales, III: 1348–1500*, 119-36, 680–703. Cambridge.

Poos, L. and Bonfield, L. (eds) 1998. Select Cases in manorial Courts 1250–1550. Property and Family Law (Seldon Society **114**). London.

Poos, L. and Smith, R.M. 1984. 'Legal windows onto historical populations?' Recent research on demography and the manor court in England, *Law and History Review* **2**, 128–52.

Poos, L. and Smith, R.M. 1986. 'Shades still on the window': a reply to Zvi Razi, *Law and History Review* **4**, 409–29.

Razi, Z. 1979. The Toronto School's reconstruction of medieval peasant society: a critical view, *Past and Present* **85**, 141–57.

Razi, Z. 1980. *Life, Marriage and Death in a Medieval Parish: Economy, Society and Demography in Halesowen, 1270–1400*. Cambridge.

Razi, Z. 1981. Family, land and the village community in later medieval England, *Past and Present* **93**, 3–36.

Razi, Z. 1984. The erosion of the family-land bond in the late fourteenth and fifteenth centuries: a methodological note, in R.M. Smith (ed.) *Land, Kinship and Life-Cycle*, 295–304. Cambridge.

Razi, Z. 1985. The use of manor court rolls in demographic analysis: a reconsideration, *Law and History Review* **3**, 191–200.

Razi, Z. 1987. The demographic transparency of manorial court rolls, *Law and History Review* **5**, 523–35.

Razi, Z. 1993. The myth of the immutable English family, *Past and Present* **140**, 3–44.

Reeves, A. 1995. The field walking evidence, in J. Eddison (ed.) *Romney Marsh: the Debatable Ground* (Oxford University for Archaeology **41**), 78–91. Oxford.

Schofield, P.R. 2001. *Extranei* and the market for customary land on a Westminster Abbey manor in the fifteenth century, *Agricultural History Review* **49**, 1–16.

Smith, R.M. 1984. Some issues concerning families and their property in rural England 1250–1800, in R.M. Smith (ed.) *Land, Kinship and Life-Cycle*, 1–86. Cambridge.

Smith, R.M. 1984. Families and their land in an area of partible inheritance: Redgrave, Suffolk 1260–1320, in R.M. Smith (ed.) *Land, Kinship and Life-Cycle*, 135–95. Cambridge.

Whittle, J. and Yates, M. 2000. '*Pays réel* or *pays légal?*' Contrasting patterns of land tenure and social structure in eastern Norfolk and western Berkshire, 1450–1600, *Agricultural History Review* **48**, 1–26.

Zell, M. 1994. *Industry in the Countryside. Wealden society in the sixteenth century*. Cambridge.

*Romney Marsh: Coastal and Landscape Change through the Ages
(ed. A. Long, S. Hipkin and H. Clarke), OUSA Monograph 56, 2002, 157–172*

11. "To fasten itt upon his successors, heirs and owners of that howse...so longe as the world standeth": Family Identity and Romney Marshlands in Early Modern Kent

Mark Merry and Catherine Richardson

This paper investigates the dynamic between land and family identity, and is concerned to connect the symbolic and ideological constructions of both to landholding practices. The paper shows that, for some families at least, holding and using parcels of land in the Level was a tangible and explicitly exploited means of constructing familial identity, for the purpose of maintaining and promoting their social status, and cementing the local and regional networks which located them among their peers. These parcels were passed on between generations using a form of 'testamentary metonymy' which facilitated the transmission of a family identity consisting of the moral norms and social practices commensurate with social status. The value of marshland on the Level may have meant this land in particular was seen as more closely synonymous with status than other holdings.

Introduction

This paper investigates the dynamic between land and family identity, and is concerned to connect the symbolic and ideological constructions of both to landholding practices. In 1977 Peter Clark identified the 16th century as a period in which a nexus of issues including the "growing prosperity" of the gentry and their "increasing administrative experience" led to an "enhanced political awareness, social self-confidence, articulateness and class consciousness to match their rising political and economic aspirations".[2] This paper offers an example of the nature and significance of such issues within and between the generations of the Scotts of Scotts Hall and the Hales' of Tenterden. Examination of these branches of two prominent Kentish families, who were significantly active in the possession and use of land in the Level of the Romney Marsh in the late 16th and 17th centuries, makes it possible to situate the generation of family identity within their connections to local and regional society. The subject is approached through an examination of both the economic activities of those families, and the language in which they discuss issues of lineage and land in their wills.[3] The paper will show that, for some families at least, holding and using parcels of land in the Level was a tangible and explicitly exploited means of constructing familial identity, for the purpose of maintaining and promoting their social status, and cementing the local and regional networks which located them among their peers.

The Level of the Romney Marsh has been seen as a distinctive place: its peculiarities of geography, administration and self interests distinguished it from the rest of Kent.[4] Part of the reason for this lies in the sheer value of the marshland in the Level: pasture was at a premium throughout the period, making marshland holdings valuable assets and the land market extremely fluid. Frequent changes of ownership and occupation with the resulting focus on land use required close management, and the Level consequently developed a virtually urban administration.[5]

The Scott and Hales families have been chosen for a number of reasons. Firstly, they are significant land owning families of Kentish elite, about which much is known throughout the period. Both fall into the category of 'substantial marshland owner' identified by Stephen Hipkin as being resident on the fringes of the Level.[6] Secondly, although not resident on the Level, they were particularly involved in its politics and economies. The minute books of the corporation make it clear that both families were at the heart of the politicised offices of its peculiar administration. In the 1640s, for instance, sir Robert Scott is succeeded in the office of deputy surveyor by Edward Hales first knight and baronet, while the office of surveyor was held by sir Edward Scott (Robert's brother) until his death in 1645, then occupied by his eldest son Edward esquire.[7]

Thirdly, at the county level, the records show members of the two families acting as justices or on various commissions throughout the period.[8] Thomas Scott esquire attained the position of Sheriff, while Edward Hales knight and first baronet served in numerous capacities (see below). Members of these families were involved at every level of the administration of justice in Kent.[9]

Finally, the marriages of both families were crucial to their immersion into the economics and politics of the Level.[10] Their family trees (see Figs. 11.1 and 11.2) show marriages into well established Kentish families, who were prominent not only in gentry society but also in the land market in the Level. A series of marriages in the second decade of the 17th century between the Scotts and the Honywoods linked the senior Scott heir with a family heavily involved in direct farming in the Level throughout the century.[11] The Hales family was also married into the Honywood family early in the period (see Fig.11.2),[12] and into other families involved in the owning and farming of the marshland in the Level.[13]

Part of the purpose of this paper is to complement recent work done on the structures of land ownership, occupation and use in the Level.[14] The broad trends depicted by this work are extremely illuminating, particularly with regard to the obscure question of land use, while the material that it draws upon lends itself to various statistical analyses. This paper takes the findings of these quantitative studies, and elucidates them with deeds, probate materials, and court materials. The activities of the Scott and Hales families can be considered as a response to the developing economic conditions on the Marsh, while at the same time indicating how these broad economic contexts could shape the strategies adopted for social promotion by particular families.

The Extent of the Marshland Holdings of the Scott and Hales Families

Local Taxation Materials

The wall scots levied for the upkeep of the Dymchurch wall provide (with varying comprehensiveness) details of owners and tenants of marshland holdings totalling some 23,500 acres in the Level of the Romney Marsh from the 1580s.[15] They indicate that two trends were developing across the Level. Firstly, they show that owner occupation of holdings had steadily diminished by the end of the century.[16] Owning and occupying marshland holdings increasingly became entirely separate pastimes, as a response to the rapidly changing national economic conditions that prevailed in the early part of the 17th century.[17]

The second trend is associated with the crisis in the wool industry in the early 17th century. The depression seems to have had the dual effects of coalescing owners and occupiers in the Level into distinct groups and altering the structure of occupation across the Level in the 17th century.[18] The larger tenant farmers rose to dominance during the course of this century, accumulating growing numbers of separate holdings into increasingly large concerns.[19] Analysis of the scot book material indicates that this rise of the larger tenant farmer was principally at the expense of the middle ranked farmers, although the humblest of farmers also lost holdings.[20] There was a clear trend whereby those who could afford to do so increasingly turned to exploiting their marshland for their rent yield rather than employing them as pasture for their own herds. These two broad trends, both of which can be seen to have been well underway by the early 1650s, resulted in a fluid land market, which was characterised by high levels of extremely short term leasing of often very small parcels of marshland, often (although this is notoriously difficult to elucidate) with a degree of very small scale sub-tenancies.[21] Indeed the activity in the land market seems most energetic in relation to the smaller holdings in the Level, and it appears that, from the early 17th century, the more substantial owners strove to accumulate large piecemeal farms in order to exploit their rent value.[22]

Scot Book Evidence for the Scott and Hales Families

As mentioned, the scot books cannot be used to examine systematically land ownership in the Level until the 1650s, but in our period they do indicate the Scott and Hales families holding substantial marshland. In 1587 the Scott family owned (or had recently owned) over 500 acres mostly in Orlestone, while the Hales family were listed as owning 176 acres in Ivychurch.[23] Clearly this does not reflect anywhere near the complete holdings of either family, particularly as we know from the common expenditors accounts that both families were holding ancient manors of the Level in the 1580s.[24] In the early years of the 17th century both families were still substantial owners: the Scotts owning 582 acres and the Hales family owning 429 acres.[25] However, in terms of their *occupation* of holdings in the Level, both families were clearly heavily involved in the market.[26] In both families, individual owners also occupied the lands that were owned, which is quite typical of the general pattern at the end of the 16th

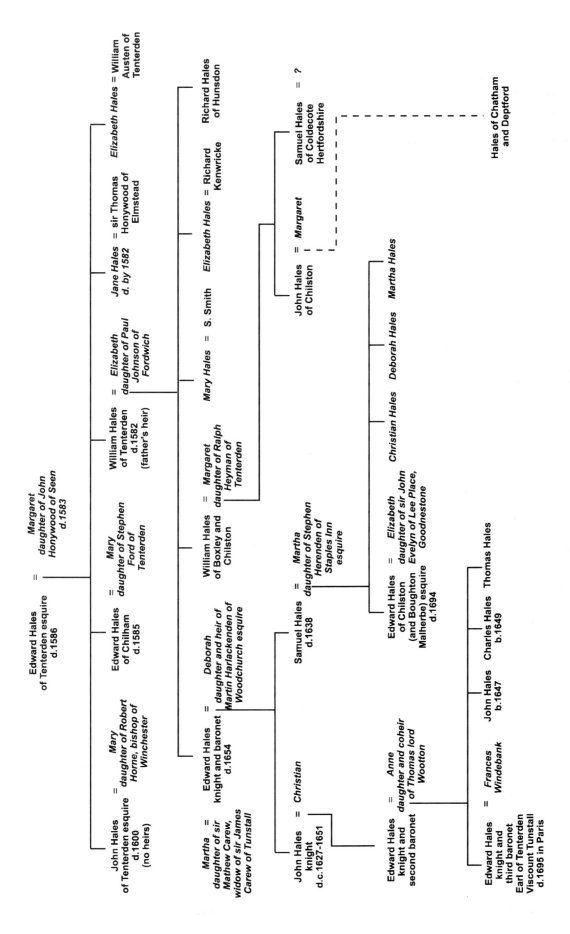

Fig. 11.1. Simplified family tree of the Hales' of Tenterden.

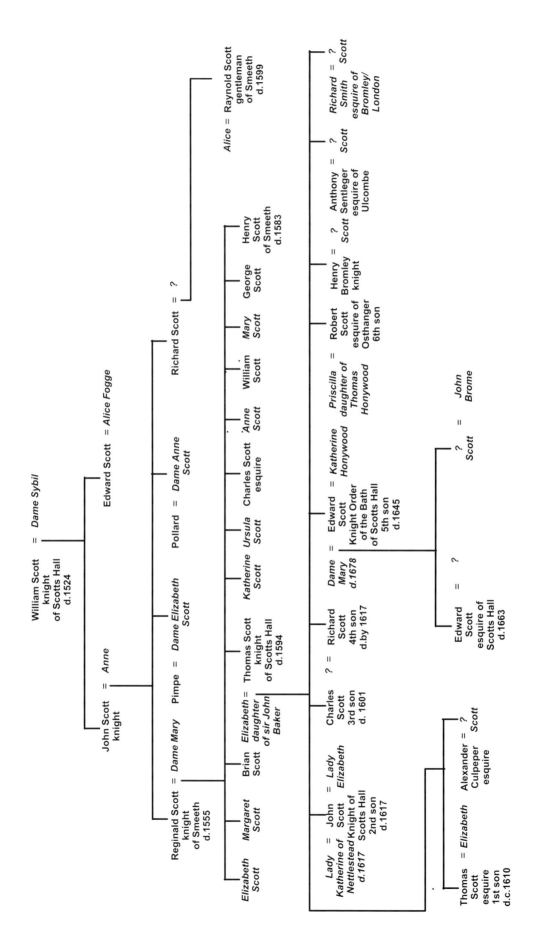

Fig. 11.2. Simplified family tree of the Scotts of Scotts Hall.

century.[27] At the level of the individual, both families again boast members that fit into the highest category of tenant.[28]

Crucially, however, the picture had changed by the middle of the 17th century, when both families sought to buy more marshland,[29] again in line with the trends affecting the Level as a whole. The Scott family withdrew from direct farming, and had largely stopped occupying any holdings in the Level by the mid 17th century; whereas the Hales family, bucking the trend somewhat, seems to have maintained its direct farming interests until at least the end of the 17th century whilst increasing its possessions. While the amount of land occupied by the Hales family remains reasonably constant throughout the century, it becomes coalesced into the hands of one or two individual farmers in the latter half of the century:[30] this suggests that within the Hales family there might have been differing perceptions as to just what their role as prominent investors in the Level ought to be.

The scot books also indicate that multiple members of both families were engaged in buying, selling and leasing holdings; that the holdings themselves varied greatly in size and location across the Level's waterings; and that those that they did business with came from diverse social and geographical backgrounds.[31] This was true of the market as a whole, and it paints a vivid picture of the fluidity of business on the marsh.

The Scott and Hales families thus appear fully engaged in the business of the Level. Both were committed to their positions in the Level financially; and business transactions, marriage settlements and the administration of Level 'rules' all served to visibly associate the families with the Level, and they thus accrued a particular kind of status. In the period 1550 to 1650 two things are evident from the scot books: both families adapted in some measure to changing economic conditions and the different policies these entailed; and both families maintained a substantial presence in the Level. The longevity of this presence, as we shall see, was an important factor in the generation of familial identity.

Testamentary strategies

Marshland Holdings and Family Strategy

Will evidence is important here because it enables the analysis of discourses of identity over time. Such an analysis demonstrates testators' attitudes towards the land they held, and situates such thoughts within a discourse of family identity. For that reason it is important to consider land bequests in relation to the broader strategies being employed in the testaments.

There is evidence that testators are not only aware of the practices of their relatives whilst writing their own testaments, but also attempt to emulate them. The Scott family offer an example of this with their tradition of leaving their best coach and best coach horses to their

wives.[32] The repetition of such a detail is richly suggestive of the extent to which they regard their wills as related to one another, and their testamentary strategies as a matter of family convention. This suggests that, as a group, the documents do offer concepts of family identity, and the following sections therefore identify patterns which are apparent across the wills: patterns suggestive of the rhetoric of identity.

The wills of these two elite families exhibit particular characteristics, which, although not unusual for testators of comparable social status, are vital to an understanding of the value of the evidence contained within them. There is no space here for a detailed discussion of gentry testamentary practices, but three interrelated issues are particularly relevant: self-consciousness, literacy, and intertextuality.

An example will explicate these issues: sir Edward Hales of Tunstall, baronet, makes his will in 1651, in the "threescore and fifteenth yeare" of his life.[33] At the end of the document he describes the text he has just written:

> this my last will and testament, consisting of six sheets of paper written with my owne hand, being filed and ioned together at the Topp with a faire sheete of paper to Cover them and sealed therewith twoe seales.[34]

Hales demonstrates an awareness of his own actions which arises from his consciousness of their importance and the significance of the manuscript itself. In doing so he posits a putative reader of the text, and confronts the modern reader with his pre-engagement with their reading. This striking self-awareness is facilitated by Hales' literacy, his ability to explain his actions in writing. Clark notes the importance of literacy in constructing and reflecting the identity of the Kentish gentry,[35] and the period examined here was one in which Kentish gentry were producing a number of literary texts, most significantly in this context, Reginald Scott's *Discovery of Witchcraft*.[36] The involvement of the will-writers in local and national government must also have developed their awareness of the authority of the written word and the coercive power of rhetorical construction. In addition, mention is made of other documents which the testators have produced,[37] and such intertextual references are an important part of the functionality of their testaments: the latter do not make operative sense without the range of supporting documentation which together makes up these individuals' methods of organising and managing their affairs.

Attending to the particular place which the will occupies within these different kinds of texts identifies the nature of the information about land and identity it offers. It is read and rehearsed in numerous different contexts in front of a variety of audiences, and can therefore be seen as a public document, intended on some level to relay the conception of family and status held by the testator.[38] The continuum which exists between the different types of writing these individuals produced facilitates and shapes the self-consciousness of their testamentary writing. It also indicates the degree of consciousness with which discourses are employed within these documents, and suggests the level on which the concepts of land ownership and reputation they contain are being worked out.

The Scott Family

This paper takes for its material the branch of the Scott family based at Scotts Hall. The quality of the evidence for the landholding behaviour of this branch of the family is particularly strong, and their sense of identity is interestingly centred within the house itself.

The Scotts were involved in two types of land holding in the Romney Marsh: they owned often quite small parcels of marshland in the Level which were coalesced into substantial farms; and they held manors, which included parcels of marshland in the Level. The attitude of the Scott family to the two differed in important ways: while the former could be traded freely as essentially economic assets, the latter were jealously protected.

From the middle of the 16th century the Scott family's presence as landowners in the Level was substantial. The inquisition post mortem of Reginald Scott knight (1555) attests to this: the manors of Orlestone, Sevington, Brenzett, Ham, Warehorne, Snave and Ruckinge are listed among his considerable possessions in the region. Also listed is the manor of Thevegate in Smeeth, one of the most central of the Scotts' capital properties.[39] These are the manors which the Scotts kept within the family throughout the period.[40] Reginald, as Zell puts it, occupied a position among the 'top rank of office-holding gentry' who were taxed on large landed incomes; and this was a position that he cultivated during his lifetime through the marriages of his children.[41]

Even in simple numerical terms the will and the inquisition make it clear that the holdings in the Level comprised the bulk of Reginald Scott's patrimony, and any attempt he made to establish himself and his family based upon his landed wealth therefore needed to focus around these possessions. This centrality is clear, even from the fact that the profits for 15 years from his named marshlands in Snave and Ivychurch are to provide his executors with the income needed to fulfil the will.[42] The testamentary strategy of sir Reginald Scott with regard to his Romney Marsh holdings should be seen in terms of the careful manipulation of something fundamental to the status of his family.

In the will, key family holdings were referred to in concrete detail: manors like Thevegate, Ham and Orlestone, which stayed in the family for at least another century; as well as specific, named pieces of marshland in the Level with information about their size and value. These 'detailed' holdings were by no means all of Reginald's patrimony, and his naming of them in this manner is indicative of special concern or knowledge about them. The key holdings are bequeathed intact to individuals: his smaller marshland holdings go as a unit to his

son Charles, while Henry receives the Scotts' smaller manors in Bilsington and elsewhere. Reginald's chief heir, Thomas, is to have the most important and central of the Scott holdings: the manors of Scotts Hall and Thevegate in Smeeth, Orlestone, Bircholt, Combe, Ham, Capell and Hernden. A complicated series of reversionary and conditional bequests led to Reginald's widow enjoying virtually all her husband's landed possessions for life, and she was to be responsible for maintaining them and making sure his heirs came into them.

The core Scott holdings which descended to Reginald's heir Thomas were important units in the region,[43] and the fact that they are maintained in their entirety and placed in the hands of a single heir is significant. The will is explicit in its conditions that these holdings are to remain intact with all their lands and appurtenances, and already it is possible to see a different mode of treatment between different kinds of holdings. The grouping and protecting of these manors became a pattern common to the testamentary strategies of the later senior Scotts. Reginald's will refers explicitly to a series of pre mortem deeds and settlements which were designed to safeguard the transmission of key holdings. An indenture dated 16th February 1540 places the manor of Thevegate in the hands of some eminent gentry notables to ensure its safe retention by the Scotts. Similarly, the marriage settlement of Reginald's son Thomas made it very difficult for Reginald's heirs to lose the equally key manor of Orlestone.[44] Reginald's trustees and executors were to be his heir Thomas and sir John Baker, the father of his heir's wife to be.[45]

The treatment of these core holdings, many with appurtenances in or on the fringes of the Level, should be seen in contrast to Reginald's other holdings, including prime pasture holdings in the Level. Small parcels of marshland, which, although highly lucrative and important economically, are not bundled together with these core holdings.[46] Other properties, like the manor of Shrimpenden on the fringes of Bilsington (which do not appear in the later Scott material), and lands and messuages in Newington, Aldington, Bonnington and Brabourne, are not protected in the same way either.

This then was the situation for the Scott family leading up to the end of the 16th century, and in many ways the will of Reginald Scott knight established (or reflected an existing) pattern. He is substantially more forthcoming about marshland holdings in his will than his successors, and that is principally because across the period the latter share the obvious concern to transmit them prior to the testamentary process.

Thomas' will makes clear how significant his Romney Marsh interests were to his family.[47] Among his bequests he lists the manors of Capell, Hernden, Combe, Orlestone, Ham and Thevegate. To this he has added the manors of Brenzett and Brabourne. Indeed Thomas seems to have added substantially to his inheritance, with named lands, woods, properties and parks in Smeeth, Aldington, and Brabourne, and sizeable parcels of marshland in Eastbridge; and although these were only partially connected with the Level, they would have had a considerable effect upon his association with the region. Many of these additions to the Scott patrimony may have resulted from his marriage to Elizabeth Baker, daughter of sir John Baker.

The scot book of 1587 attests to the activities of Thomas in the Level, as both owner and occupier; and one might identify the 1590s as the high point of Scott establishment in the physical landscape of the Level. Between the scot books and the will we have a pretty vivid picture of Thomas Scott as landlord, tenant and farmer in large pockets of land across the Level, firmly rooted in holdings that had been his father's. His testamentary strategy is reminiscent of his father's: for example references to pre mortem agreements; detailed descriptions of the most important holdings; conditions imposed upon the bequests of Romney Marsh holdings. Also like his father, Thomas chose to aggregate the family's principle Romney Marsh possessions into a single heir, his eldest son Thomas esquire. Thomas senior served to consolidate the identity of the family by extending the presence of the family in the region of their influence, and to coalesce the respective holdings into single entities placed into the possession of single heirs.

Thomas Scott esquire rose to the political heights of Sheriff of Kent, justice of the peace, and royal commissioner.[48] He survived his father by little over a decade, and there is no extant will, but a survey of his widow's possessions in 1627 is suggestive.[49] He died heirless, and so the careful reversionary instructions of his father sir Thomas (and indeed his grandfather sir Reginald) came into force. What is left in the inquisition post mortem of his widow Elizabeth is therefore what she had acquired in her own right, and presumably the holdings that her husband was in a position to leave to her. Among them are considerable marsh and pasture in Newington, Hythe, Saltwood, Bonnington, Bilsington, Aldington, Eastbridge and Lympne.[50] An indenture dated 1619 records the transfer in trust of these holdings to Thomas Bedingfield senior of Smeeth and Thomas Tournaye of Saltwood:[51] after the death of Elizabeth, they are to be conveyed to the heirs of her uncle sir John Honywood. The Scotts were closely connected by marriage with the Honywoods throughout the period, but even so what Elizabeth and the Honywoods receive does not originate from the core Scott holdings (and indeed may have been brought by Elizabeth into the marriage).

Thomas clearly followed the pattern established by his father by placing the core Scott possessions at the centre of his testamentary strategy. He did introduce an innovation, however, by establishing the house and lands at Nettlestead (possibly acquired as part of his marriage settlement) as a jointure piece for the wife of the senior Scott, who took up residence there after the death of her husband. This develops the situation whereby land becomes firmly embedded in family practice.

The significance of this is clear: the core possessions of Thomas Scott were protected, and by the default of heirs, were transferred horizontally (in this case to his brother sir John). Everything else, including substantial accretions to these critically important Romney Marsh holdings, left the control of the Scotts. The dispersal of these possessions not only led to a weakening of the family's economic condition, it also led to a dilution of the Scott presence in the region. This in turn may have led to familial anxiety about how their identity as a long standing and substantial influence in the Level was viewed by their peers.

That the brother, John Scott knight, was possessed of the core Scott Romney Marsh possessions is manifest in his will of 1616.[52] Following this will, however, detailed information about the Scott possessions virtually disappears from the probate material, and this is especially true of those core possessions in the Marsh. We know from the scot book material that the family was still in possession of these in the 1650s, and so their absence from the wills can only indicate pre mortem transfer. This would suggest a degree of care taken over the transference of assets crucial to the family's status, a feature of gentry inheritance patterns in the period.[53]

Although John does not specify parcels of land, he does make an explicit statement of their critical role in his strategies for preserving the Scott position in the region. His executors are to levy cash from his estate to buy lands worth £50 *per annum*, which is to be conveyed to Katherine, the first wife of his younger brother Edward esquire. This money is to be used for "the redemption and bringing back into the family of 43 acres 3 perches of marsh lately conveyed" to Edward, which is part of the "ancient inheritance of the Scotts". The marshland, once retrieved, is to be given back to Edward.

At a time when a response in the Level to economic depression comprised buying up parcels of prime pasture to exploit diminishing margins by sheer scale, contemporaries may have viewed losing any parcel as unsound business sense.[54] However, there seems to be more to this incident than prosaic financial considerations. The stressing of the land's long association with the family hints at issues bound up with the family's identity as regional leaders: a self-conscious part of their role in the social and political (and economic) networks of the Level was based upon the reality of their *presence* there.[55] From their principle 'bases' at Scotts Hall in Smeeth and Brabourne manor (along with the other core holdings of the family, which are *never* disposed of in Scott wills), these parcels of marshland and other possessions brought the family into widespread and repeated contact with neighbours, peers, and partners. Possession of land in the Level was at the heart of familial identity, and longevity was of as much importance as scale of possession.

As sir John Scott produced no male heirs, the core Scott holdings passed to the same younger brother Edward, eventually knight and Order of the Bath, who had sold off the 43 acre parcel previously. By the time of his own death in 1645 he seems to have learned his lesson: like his elder brother John he lists among his bequests a series of limited cash annuities funded from marshland holdings, but the holdings themselves have been disposed of by pre-testamentary agreement.[56] He also seems to have been engaged in a process of adding to the Romney Marsh holdings, as evidenced in the 1663 will of his son and heir, Edward esquire.[57] Like his predecessors, sir Edward maintained the policy of guarding the core holdings and concentrating them into the hands of single heirs, although other valuable parcels of land in the Level were bequeathable.[58]

By the end of the 17th century the Scotts seem to disappear from the scot books. Although it is clear that the family did not actually disappear from the Level, the extent of their holdings definitely diminish, and it is perhaps no coincidence that this happens at a time when senior Scotts are appearing at Chancery to answer cases of debt and broken agreement.[59] By the end of the 17th century George Scott of Scotts Hall esquire was answering to the heirs and executors of sir Francis Pemberton over the jointure of Pemberton's daughter Anne. The jointure settled upon Scott's wife Anne Pemberton (in return for the marriage portion of £4000) was to include a number of manors, which after the death of Anne were to pass to the heirs of sir Francis for 500 years. Significantly, one of the manors included was that of Brabourne, which had been jealously guarded by Scott's predecessors.[60] A decade later, in 1712, Pemberton's son is pursuing Scott at Chancery for a debt of £5300, and acquiring parts of the Scott patrimony to defray the money owed.[61] The gradual dissipation of their holdings in the Level, which had always been central to their income, led to a reduction in wealth, and perhaps also to the family's relationships with its peers.

The Hales Family

The Tenterden, rather than the more prestigious Canterbury, branch of the Hales family provides a useful counterpoint to the Scotts of Scotts Hall. There are a number of important similarities between the two with regards to patterns of landholding, for example. The Hales family also possessed two distinct kinds of holding in the Level: the core possessions that were protected in the strategies of the Hales testators, and the economically significant marshlands that were more commoditized. The nature of the testamentary evidence differs slightly from that of the Scotts, however, in that the broad family practices established in the period tended to skip generations, leaving us with less material. As marshland owners the Hales' belonged to the group who were based outside the Level,[62] like the Scotts, with their seats at Tenterden, and later at Tunstall.

Edward Hales of Tenterden esquire[63] bequeathed his holdings in the Level to his grandson Edward (later first

baronet).[64] The latter's father William, who is explicitly confirmed as *his* father's heir, receives all other lands and properties, but not those in the Romney Marsh which are singled out and described in detail. The skipping of a generation in this fashion, even though the grandson Edward is a minor, identifies a keen interest regarding the inheritance of the Romney Marsh possessions. There may have been a particular concern about William Hales (although this is doubtful as he is deemed fit to receive the prodigious non-Romney Marsh possessions);[65] or a concern more generally about the continuity of ownership of these parcels of marshland.[66]

The testamentary strategy of Edward Hales of Tenterden esquire also affected his other sons.[67] The complex will of John Hales esquire of Tenterden indicates the wrangling that may have gone on to ensure that the marshland holdings found their way to Edward Hales knight and baronet.[68] Among John's possession were lands and properties in Stone, and a parcel of marshland called Mores Court; as well as marshland in Appledore, Burmarsh and Fairfield which he had received from his father in trust until his nephew's coming of age.[69] The Stone properties were to go to Edward Hales baronet (the intended heir of the Hales patrimony), while John bequeathed the marshland to his other nephew Edward (son of Edward Hales of Chilham), contrary to the instructions of his father. Codicils later appended to John's will reverse these bequests through a series of detailed and restrictive clauses, so that all the marshland holdings are concentrated into the hands of the intended heir, who was still a minor at this stage, just as John's father intended. If nothing else, this indicates that not all of the Hales family approved of the principle Hales holdings skipping a generation to the grandson of Edward esquire of Tenterden: his uncle for one, seems to have required compensation for losing out on the estates that the family's position in society was based on.

Edward Hales knight and first baronet of Tunstall, the heir of his grandfather, was one of the most notable and wealthiest Kentish figures of his time.[70] His office holding included that of MP and deputy lieutenant of Kent, and through a series of far-sighted marriages was integrated with the inheritance and influence of the Dering, Cromer and Wootton families.[71] His role in national politics was influential and pragmatic, siding with one party while covertly supporting the other, although his interests in these matters were often more concerned with old relations among the families of his regional peers.[72] Indeed his influence in the region was prodigious, and not least through his business practices: as Clark puts it, "... his ruthless depopulation of Romney Marsh and engrossing of property made him feared and hated through much of South Kent".[73]

Edward first baronet's will of 1651 follows closely the pattern of his grandfather's. Firstly, there is essentially no detail about any of the lands and properties held by this leading light of Kentish gentry society; and secondly he leaves what is mentioned to grandchildren.[74] As with the Scotts, the Hales wills are indicative of pre mortem transfers of critical assets, and Edward first baronet follows this model. The lack of detail about his possessions is complemented by the explicit statement that he does not have lands "convenient and fitting in his power" to dispose of freely, except those he has formerly settled. These must have included the Romney Marsh holdings that warranted the special testamentary treatment of his grandfather.[75]

The land and property dealings of this Edward Hales in the first half of the 17th century are accessible through the collection of documents known as the Hales Place deeds.[76] These deeds serve to complement the absence of detail about the family's landholding behaviour during this period, and provide an excellent opportunity for witnessing the *actual*, rather than intended, strategies of the Hales family. They also provide excellent information about the details of holdings, and who the Hales' were doing business with. The immediate and inescapable impression provided by these deeds is that the family were holding land and property all over Kent and further afield by this period. They had a particular interest in marshland pasture, indicating sound business acumen, and not just in the Level; but it was those possessions in the Level which were perceived to be at the heart of their family identity. The deeds suggest that the role of the Hales family in the Level became more prominent as the 17th century went on, in contrast to the Scotts.

Edward (and his family as a whole) pursued a mixed policy with regard to the acquisition and use of his holdings.[77] He bought, sold, leased to and from in many different places; and the details of these individual deeds show that his business was conducted with many different individuals, some of which he had manifest business and familial associations with, others that he did not. But there are trends discernible in the deed material. It is evident, for example, that Edward Hales was busy accruing marshland holdings, and that he exploited them for their rent value in a series of short term high rent leases. It is also clear that he was a tenant who commanded favourable terms, with very long and cheap leases.[78] What the deed material also suggests is that in the half century or so after Edward Hales' death, his policies were still in operation within the family, with the pursuit of a balance of acquisitions and leases which reflect the continuing importance of marshland holdings to the economic survival of the family.[79] The ruthlessness of Edward Hales' business practices during his life may well have informed the subsequent patterns of patrimony management amongst his successors.

By the end of the 17th century, the Hales family's concern with their Romney Marsh holdings was still palpable and explicit. One of Edward first baronet's grandsons, Edward Hales of Chilston and Boughton Malherbe esquire, makes this evident in his will of 1694.[80] The executors of this will are instructed that none of the lands in the Romney Marsh or belonging to Bellaview are

to be sold to fulfil the testator's just debts and legacies, unless all of his personal estate and the manors of Chilstone, Bowley and Borden "withall the lands and hereditaments unto them belonging" are not enough to pay them.[81]

In other words, the Hales family was still protecting its Romney Marsh holdings. That they still appear as leading owners in the Level in the mid 18th century stands testimony to the importance attached to these components of their enormous landed wealth. But the tenacity with which both families held onto their holdings in the Level suggests that the value of the marshland lay not just in its income generating value, but also in their cohesive effects. That is to say, the role of the marshland holdings was to anchor the families firmly within the regional society in which they operated as land owners, social and cultural leaders and officers.[82] The networks that were created by ownership in the marsh were extensive: they brought individuals and families into repeated contact with whole groups of others, in relationships founded on economic interaction and administrative effort. This was perhaps more so in the Level than in other regions, due to the extremely fluid, short-term nature of land holding and leasing. The marshland parcels and manors thus cemented the critical interrelationships that drove gentry society to a degree greater than land held outside the Level.

Family and Individual Identity

This analysis has seen marshland to be productive of situations in which individual identity is shaped and expressed because of its complex administration and frequent trading. In testamentary practice, however, it is the manor which is the important unit, and it has been shown to be central to the definition and dissemination of family identity. It is important therefore to investigate the evidence which the wills offer about the relationship between individual and family identity if we are fully to understand the role of marshland within their construction. Particular items are obviously selected to be bequeathed in wills rather than passed on by other means, and attending to other types of object which are described in this context is instructive. Bequests of specific objects are much rarer in Scott and Hales wills than in those of their lower status neighbours, and by far the most prominent type of item given is individual items of silverware. In 1600, for example, John Hales of Tenterden gives to Edward, son of his brother William, "my bason and we[a]re of silver percell guilte".[83] The function of these objects is vital to an understanding of their position within the will. They are used in a domestic setting, but at ritual occasions on which both family and non-family members are likely to have been present.

Such objects define the status of the household in terms of the amount and quality of silverware which the family can afford, and they are at the heart of a complex level of domestic routine which is increasingly indicative of elite status from the late-sixteenth into the seventeenth centuries. Whilst the newness of their design may have been suggestive of aesthetic and artistic precocity, the more or less traditional form which they took harked back to a medieval past of feudal hospitality and the moral codes which reinforced it.[84] Such objects are, in other words, vital in the construction of elite identity, and passing them on is an important part of the transferral of social status from one generation to the next. Identity is encoded within the metonymic qualities of the individual bequest: the patriarchal responsibilities of governance and lordship within the household and the community are embodied in the ceremonial actions associated with the object and symbolised in the moral codes which inform those actions.[85]

These bequests are often limited by age: the child is to receive them when he or she reaches maturity. When they come into the new adult's possession they are already associated with a series of patterns of behaviour, seen throughout childhood to be appropriate to their use. In this way, the bequest of a piece of silverware is also the bestowal of a responsibility to use it appropriately, and to be explicitly aware of the nature of the family whose status it represents.

Inheriting such objects, then, is not about possessing something new, but rather about being the owner of something very familiar. The shift from use to control is one of the central paradigms of maturity in such a family. There is a clear sense here of an identity on a scale larger than that of the individual, one to which the personal is intimately related, but which is partly independent of it. This switch from use to control can be seen to operate even more crucially with respect to land. Edward Hales first baronet receives his grandfather's marshlands. His uncle John is to have the profit of the lands until Edward is of age, "to bestowe yearely in or upon the bringing upp of the saide Edward".[86] Before he reaches his majority, the land will be converted into money for his benefit, with the use of which he will be moulded into a suitable adult to undertake the responsibilities of its ownership. Once he achieves maturity, personal and familial identity become much more closely related as he is the head of the family. The use/control dynamic defines the individual in relation to the family in a hierarchy with the leading male heir at its head: numerous bequests to daughters and other female kin "out of the profittes of my landes",[87] draw attention to their subservient position and the underlying importance of land to family status simultaneously. It provides the financial basis for the establishment and maintenance of status, and the physical basis for the local impact of social standing, its negotiation within a local community. It is given expression in these wills as an asset which is productive of many different kinds of material and social credit, permitting all to participate in a domesticity which defines and expresses status, whether as users or controllers of the assets on which it depends.

Family Identity and the Importance of Location

Wills display a range of testators' attitudes towards location and locality which offer a context for an understanding of the importance of land in broader terms. These attitudes are generated by the social practices of gentry families within their local communities.

Members of both families are clearly at pains to stress their commitment to a charitable rhetoric of Christian and communal responsibility. They leave money to the poor of various parishes; invariably those in communities in which they own land, in the case of Edward Scot knight and Order of the Bath, in Smeeth, Brabourne, Nettlestead, Aldington, Orlestone, Postling, Yalding, Mereworth and Lympne, amongst others.[88] This stress upon a range of parishes indicates the testators' appreciation of the connections between the receipt of profit and a responsibility to the sustenance of parish life. Land ownership is seen as productive of obligation.

Edward Hales first baronet specifically requests that his money be given to "the honest poore persons there and not to such as inhabit or dwell in Cottages illegallie erected on warfs or in the high waies or live idlely by freeboothing, begging, filching or stealing or otherwise dissorderlie in theire lives".[89] The distinction used here is one at the heart of the heavily moralised attempts to distinguish between the worthy and the unworthy poor.[90] It is one of a range of aspects of testamentary provision which as a whole underline the self-consciously constructed moral and religious identity which these individuals display in their wills.

As a counterpart to their pious concern for their souls, the Scotts and Hales pay careful attention to the manner of disposal of their bodies.[91] Edward Hales of Tunstall wishes to be buried in the parish church of Tunstall, "without any pompe or ceremonies at all no funerall sermon no vaine Commemoracon no Invitacon [to] Strangers or friends farr of but such friends onlie as are neare at hand, my honest neighbours of the parish of Tunstall aforesaid and servants".[92] Acknowledging the protestant aversion to the superstitions of ritual funerary display, these instructions offer another example of Hales' godly piety, and they stress the sensitivity of the issue of public gentry behaviour within the local community.[93]

The wills also illustrate the increasing interest in ancestry which Clark sees as central to Kentish gentry identity in this period.[94] Edward Hales bequeaths his granddaughter his "best jewell at her Choyce my Cheine of pearles and all other the pearles which are in her or the said Edward Hales her husband his Custodye". In doing so, he describes her as,

...wife of Edward Hales my Grandsonne and only Sonne of Sir John Hales knight my sonne, deceased, by Dame Christian his wife one of the foure Daughters and Coheires of Sir James Cromer late of Tunstall aforesaid knight, deceased, being one of the foure Daughters and Coheires of Thomas Lord Wotton Baron of Marley, deceased, by Dame Mary his wife one of the foure Daughters and Coheires of Sir Arthur Throckmorton late of paulesperry in the Countie of Northampton knight, deceased...[95]

His intricate noting of the connections between his family and those to which they are linked in marriage stresses the importance of lineage and, indeed, of memory in the construction and maintenance of status. The need to display these links stresses the ability of rank to overcome location: Hales is connected through marriage with individuals all over the country, presumably the same kin whom he suggests should not be invited to his funeral. He depicts rank and locality in tension as a result of the importance of the regulation of display. In Hales' rhetoric, the moral impetus to limit ostentation reads as a prioritisation of his local community over his connections to the 'community of the elite'.

Despite the strength of this 'localising principle', it is land which provides the resources that make horizontal, inter-locational connections possible, and which define the family's vertical position above others in the village, town and county within which their principle holdings are located. The family's rootedness in particular areas is the prerequisite for their connections to other similarly located kin-groups across the country as a whole, and it gives them a distinctiveness through their association with a specific place.

Many of the Scott family wills address similar issues of situation in their repeated reference to Scotts Hall, where being 'of' the house identifies the particular branch of the family to which the individual belongs, and their relative status within a wider kin network. The symbolic power of the house, along with many of the other issues raised in this paper, is epitomised by a bequest of Katherine Scott, widow of sir John Scott, whilst he lived of Scotts Hall. Since she is the widow of the Scott heir she is, in line with family convention, living in Nettlestead at the time of her death. She leaves her

> best silver saltseller to the owner of Scottshall, and pray him in the Lord to take good care to fasten itt uppon his successors heires and owners of that howse with as such Care of mee, as I shew kindnesse to him, that itt maye be theire abiding as testimony of my infinite affection thereunto (if it may bee) so longe as the world standeth.[96]

The house becomes the repository for a sense of connection and belonging, and the perpetuation of patrimony is linked to the endurance of domesticity. Her husband was concerned in his will to leave money to retrieve marshland which was part of the "ancient inheritance of the Scotts". Taken in conjunction the two testaments demonstrate an overt awareness of the almost visceral relationships between house, household, family and land.

Conclusions

The preceding analysis has suggested that longevity of family identity was dependent upon a sense of the distinction between the personal and the familial, where the latter is underpinned by the former but ideologically separate from it. The Scotts and Hales' in part expressed their idea of family by focusing the meanings of dynasty and patriarchy into material culture and the ritualised transfer of land. This practice of 'testamentary metonymy' facilitated the transmission of a family identity which consisted of the moral norms and social practices commensurate with their status. It was passed on through a bequest with its own family history: one which marked out the relationships connecting the generations by its passage between them.

Particular manors appear to have functioned in this way, figuring the longevity and continuity of physical presence on specific pieces of land as a vital aspect of social status. It seems likely that the morality of land-holding which both families expound in their wills, issues like the intimate knowledge and sense of responsibility towards the communities whose surrounding land generated their wealth, were discourses they held in common with others of similar rank.

However, the nature of the land market on the marsh may well have made the Scotts and the Hales' situation slightly different. The value of marshland on the Level may have meant that such land was seen as more closely synonymous with their status than their other holdings, facilitating the levels of display and provision which defined them against their peers. In addition, the intensive administration of the marshland was productive of increased interaction with neighbours and associates. As members of both families were officers within this administration, it clearly provided a key local arena within which they exercised their status in relation to other owners and occupiers of the marsh. In other words marshland may have made these individuals particularly conscious of their identity in the first place. Administration also necessitates concentration on its object, time spent in understanding the operation of the marsh, and therefore a heightened awareness of the position of marshland within the operation of family finances and of county economics. This particular land seems to have affected the prominent families who owned it in fairly precise ways, perhaps facilitating an especially close set of perceived connections between the Romney Marsh and family identity.

Two issues are related to this particularity. Firstly, the distinct nature of Kentish inheritance patterns in the time of these individuals' ancestors produced specific types of family structure. Gavelkind resulted in a series of large and prominent families, amongst them the Scotts and Hales', which were divided into several clearly defined branches within the county.[97] Within the extended kinship networks generated by gavelkind, individual groups defined themselves partly by locality.[98] Location on the edge of the marsh was therefore significant for both of the branches studied here as a further level of distinction within families.

The grouping of 'types' of holding, especially those in the Romney Marsh, and their transmission to single heirs noted above represents neither the practice of gavelkind nor primogeniture:[99] it is related to the former, but is a distinct inheritance practice. The division of estates by the Scotts and the Hales' suggests a more directed and at the same time less pragmatic approach to inheritance, with the central goal being the safeguarding of those possessions mostly closely associated with their respective family identities. This paper has demonstrated that the division of lands was not entirely, perhaps not even primarily, economically motivated.

Secondly, it is also instructive to consider these issues in relation to Peter Clark's characterisation of the role of the Kentish gentry in this period. He sees their "primary function in county society" as "an intermediary between different concepts of the community", where members of the ruling elite who were most active locally where also most effective at a national level.[100] Their power was *derived from* their close supervision of their locality, and their status outside the county was additionally located within a notion of a coherent Kentish community.[101] Landownership, for Clark, makes control possible through supervision and interaction, and the closeness of this supervision both inspires a notion of community and gives these men their key role in relating the local to the national.[102]

The tensions identified in the wills above (the dual focus of a gentry identity concentrated inwards towards the administration of local estates with its moral responsibilities, and outwards towards wider kinship networks based on social parity) appear in a different light in relation to this 'connectivity' dynamic. It becomes possible to see the level of self-consciousness with which these tensions are exhibited in the Scott and Hales testaments as a way of explicitly and publicly foregrounding the dynamic set of connections which empowered these men to govern their county.[103]

This dynamic between the local and the national should also be seen in relation to a nationwide interest in quantifying land. Saxton's maps and Leland's travels charted the country, exploring metaphorically whilst recording systematically the relative character of distinct locations within a whole.[104] In Kent, while Lambarde was compiling his *Perambulations*, the ruling gentry groups were developing an interest in the history of their county and their own families, commissioning pedigrees and family trees.[105] Inspired by a growing awareness of their relation to Kent's historical and geographical distinctness, they began to investigate its potential as a discrete community through the metaphor of land management: the symbolic correlations between their cultivation of the land as gentry farmers and the proper husbandry of a protestant county. Reginald Scot, for example, produced his *Perfite Platforme of a Hoppe Garden* in 1574 as an exploration of 'spiritual husbandry'.[106] The men discussed in this paper must have appreciated the temporality of the marshland they owned and farmed: a terrain filled with potential for the future; simultaneously suggestive of their ancestral past and overflowing with promise for their personal, familial and county future.

Notes

1. With thanks to the Romney Marsh Research Trust for the funding to undertake this research. Quote is from will of Dame Katherine Scott; PRO PCC 11/129/188, 1616.
2. Clark, *English Provincial Society*, 147, 216 and *passim*.
3. Family identity as a term is used here to describe the practices and possessions which individuals who are related to one another consider important in the expression of their connections with one another. The high levels of self consciousness with which kinship is regarded amongst people of social standing in early modern society makes it essential to attend to the *expression* of family identity in contemporary terms. Influenced by these issues, we have tried to develop a methodology which attends to both the qualitative evidence of the display of identity (in testamentary material), and the quantitative evidence of the events and exchanges in which such attitudes were expressed, intensified and modified (in land transactions). For an example of such a methodology being used upon a 15th century urban community, see Merry, *Public and Private Lives*.

4. For a brief summary of the agricultural development of the Romney Marsh see Zell, *Early Modern Kent*, 94–100.
5. Rents rose from 8s per acre in the 1570s to 20s in the 1610s, and apart from a dip in the middle of the century, stayed at this level throughout the 17th century. The purchase price of land rose from £12 per acre at the start of the 17th century to £20–22 by the 1660s; Hipkin 'Tenant farming', 646–61.
6. Hipkin, 'Tenant farming', 649–53.
7. CKS S/Rm/sm1 ff.21v, 26v, 37, 53v.
8. See for example the role of Thomas Scott in 1569; CPR Eliz. **5**, 1569–72, 225.
9. For a snapshot of the role of the families in the administration of county justice at the start of the 17th century, see Knafla *Kent at Law, passim*. For the structures of county administration see Zell, *Early Modern Kent*, chapter 1; Clark, *English Provincial Society*, chapter 4.
10. For more on the marriage strategies of the Scott and Hales families *a propos* their economic polices, see below. For the wider context of Kentish marriage practice see Everitt, *The Local Community*; Bonfield, *Marriage Settlements*.

11. The scot book material indicates that the Honywood family were occupying 243 acres in the Level in *c.* 1612, while by 1650 they were still farming over 100 acres; CKS S/Rm/fs5, S/Rm/FSz10. Sir Edward Scott of Scotts Hall made his first marriage to Katherine Honywood *c.* 1616, while his younger brother Robert had married Priscilla (daughter of Thomas) Honywood in *c.* 1610.

12. Edward Hales esquire took a Honywood heiress for a wife, while his sister Mildred also married into the family. The connection with the Honywoods was 'renewed' by the Hales' throughout the period.

13. Other families connected to the Hales' and mentioned in the scot book material include the Fords, the Johnsons, the Austens, the Harlackendens; S/Rm/fs5, S/Rm/fs3, S/Rm/fs6, S/Rm/FSz10.

14. Hipkin, 'Tenant farming', 646–76; and 'The structure of land occupation', 147–63.

15. Unlike the majority of land taxes, they were imposed upon those who occupied land rather than those who owned it. Indeed is should be noted that the scot books only provide patchy information about ownership in the Level. Surviving wall scot records date from 1587, *c.* 1612, a number of records from 1650 to 1654, 1699 and later.

16. Hipkin, 'Tenant farming', 659–66.

17. Bowden, 'Agricultural prices', 631–41.

18. Hipkin, 'Tenant farming', 658–60.

19. In the early part of the century the largest farmers (those occupying 200 acres or more), some 3% of tenants, accounted for a little over 20% of the Level; by the middle of the century they comprised some 5% of tenants and were occupying a little over a third of the Level; while by the end of the century, they comprised 7% of tenants and held over 40% of the Level; Hipkin, 'Tenant farming', 653–56.

20. Bowden, 'Agricultural prices', 602–5, 642–8, 662–72.

21. The scot book and watering map material for the first half of the 1650s provides the greatest amount of serial information, and it appears that holdings as small as 16.5 acres could change hands four times in as many years: during the period 1650 to 1654, at least two fifths of the Level saw a change in occupier; Hipkin, 'Tenant farming', 649–52.

22. Hipkin, 'Tenant farming', 652.

23. CKS S/Rm/fs3.

24. CKS S/Rm/FAe3.

25. CKS S/Rm/fs5. With thanks to Stephen Hipkin for extracting these figures.

26. The Scotts were in occupation of 476 acres (in Newchurch and Orlestone), while the Hales family occupied at least 317.5 acres (in Bonnington, Ivychurch and elsewhere). CKS S/Rm/fs3.

27. Hipkin, 'Tenant farming', *passim*.

28. Charles Scott occupied 92 acres; Thomas Scott 204 acres; Edmund Scott 106 acres; Roger Scott gent 51 acres; Henry Scott 23 acres. From the Hales family: sir James occupied 99.5 acres; Charles 77 acres; William 20 acres; John Hales gent 102 acres; Edward Hales gent 19 acres. CKS S/Rm/fs3.

29. The figures for 1612 are somewhat sketchy as CKS S/Rm/fs5 provides only patchy information about ownership of the holdings.

30. In the 1650s Mrs Elizabeth Hales was recorded as being in occupation of 310.5 acres owned by Colonel Kendrick, while by the end of the century she had added a further 9.5 acres to this. Also by 1699, Richard Hales was occupying 55 acres across two waterings; CKS S/Rm/fs6.

31. This is evident from the scot book material; Hipkin, 'Tenant farming', 658.

32. See for instance PRO PCC 11/131/57, 1616; PCC 11/195/49, 1645.

33. PRO PCC 11/237/150v, probate 1654.

34. PRO PCC 11/237/153.

35. Clark, *English Provincial Society*, 202–220. For comparative material on non-Kentish gentry see Larminie, 6, and chapter 8.

36. For the relationship between Reginald Scott and the Scotts of Scotts Hall, see Fig. 11.1.

37. For example, Edward Hales leaves jewels "the number whereof are specified in a paper under my hand writeing kept with them"; Edward Scott provides for his son to buy back his goods "by vertue of the said recyted deed given by me"; PRO PCC 11/237/150v, PCC 11/312/232v.

38. In addition, several wills mention the dealings these men had in local and national courts, underlining their familiarity with public exchanges and public image; see for example PRO PCC 11/96/320, 1600.

39. PRO C142/102/85. Also listed are 60 acres of marsh called Ermynerdes in Eastbridge, the manor of Shrympesden in Bilsington, and substantial holdings in Aldington, Bircholt, Newington, Wye, Smeeth, Bilsington, Bonnington and Saltwood.

40. In addition Reginald Scott's will refers to 85 acres of named marshlands in Snave, Ivychurch and Aldington; PRO PCC 11/37, 1555.

41. Zell, *Early Modern Kent*, 49, 63. Reginald's children were married to a son and daughter of sir John Baker, one of the largest scale landowners in Elizabethan Kent, who held very significant estates in the Romney Marsh.

42. Along with unspecified lands in Aldington.

43. Interestingly both Orlestone and Scotts Hall are to be administered by Reginald's executor: the former until Thomas marries Elizabeth Baker, the latter until Thomas reaches 21 years of age. In both cases the executor receives the profits in order to maintain the testator's daughters.

44. These include: sir Brian Tuke, George Tychit esquire, sir Edward Boughton, sir John Williams, Anthony Cooke esquire, and Charles and George Tuke gentlemen. Quoted in the inquisition post mortem of Reginald Scott; PRO C142/102/85.

45. PRO PCC 11/37, 1555.

46. Thus the nine acres in Snave and Ivychurch, which are to provide the executor with an income to maintain Reginald's daughters for 15 years, are bequeathed to a younger son who gets little else.

47. PRO PCC 11/ 85/1. His brother Henry, who received manors in Bilsington from his father, may well have withdrawn his interests from the Romney Marsh, as by the end of his life he indicates little in the way of a foothold in the Kentish land market. All his lands and properties are located in some detail in London; PRO PCC 11/66, 1583.

48. For the political career of Thomas Scott, Scott, *Memorials*, 213; PRO C142/322/178; SP 12/Case F; SP 12/208/25; BL Add. MS. 33924, f.23.
49. Inquisition post mortem, PRO C142/738/15.
50. The parcels amount to just short of 400 acres. There is also the manor of Oaseborne and other holdings in Cheriton, as well as several messuages and mills.
51. Both men appear as occupiers in the Level in the scot books of 1587 and *c.* 1612; S/Rm/Fs3, S/Rm/Fs5. The indenture, quoted in the inquisition post mortem, provides considerable detail about the provenance of these holdings. For example, the manor of Blackoose was bought from Edward Hales knight and baronet: see also CCA U85 box 3 for the indenture (the price was £1000; the sale took place in 1612). Elizabeth is said to have bought lands from William Finch esquire and wife, and John Cooper esquire and wife.
52. PRO PCC 11/131/57.
53. For an extended discussion of pre mortem inheritance strategies see Larminie, *Wealth, Kinship and Culture*, especially 21–5.
54. It should not be forgotten that recouping a plot of top quality Romney Marsh pasture (the value of which would have been somewhere in the vicinity of £20 per acre in the 1610s) would not have been an insignificant proposition, even for a family as wealthy as the Scotts.
55. That is, the presence of their financial interests there: the traditional seats of both the Scott and Hales families were just beyond the boundaries of the Level.
56. PRO PCC 11/195/49. An annuity of £20 goes to his grandson Richard Brome, and one of £5 goes to his servant Timothy Rooke, from a well documented parcel of 30 acres in Burmarsh bought from Edward Berry of Canterbury.
57. It refers to all the lands bought by his father in Brookland, also bought from Captain Berry of Canterbury; PRO PCC 11/312/232v. Edward esquire's mother, Mary, removed to Stanstead in Hertfordshire after her husband's death, and her will refers only to substantial properties in Mersham which she leaves to her daughter Elizabeth Westrowe; PRO PCC 11/356/321.
58. He leaves what marshland he mentions to his servants Peter Bedingfield and William Hartridge: again the parcels involved do not come from the core group of the family's Romney Marsh possessions.
59. See for example PRO C5/417/52, C5/301/39 and C5/261/13.
60. PRO C5/301/39. A passing reference also indicates financial difficulties for George Scott. At the time of his marriage he had mortgaged the manor of Nettlestead for £7,000 plus interest to Samuel Grimston baronet: for almost a century Nettlestead had been preserved for the wife of the senior Scott heir.
61. PRO C5/261/13.
62. Hipkin, 'Tenant farming', 659–64. Although a branch of the Hales family were established at Woodchurch.
63. Who died in 1586; PRO PCC 11/69/423.
64. PRO PCC 11/69/423. We know that some of his marshland holdings were in the parish of Warehorne, and that he had recently bought marshland from William Marden the elder of Tenterden, Thomas Asshenden and Humphrey Clerk gentleman of Romney Marsh. Clerk was a substantial occupier in 1587 and 1612, and Marden was an owner-occupier in 1587.
65. The extent of the estates he inherited away from the Level is evident from the Hales deeds; CCA U85 boxes 1–8.
66. The will of William Hales confirms the transfer of the marshlands from his father to his son Edward, which also contain holdings in Appledore and Fairfield. To this he adds his own inheritance in Tenterden, Ebony and Stone; CCA PRC 17.44.58.
67. Edward Hales of Chilham seems to have been in possession of nothing in the Romney Marsh. He died before his father, and so was not involved in the transmission of Edward senior's Romney Marsh holdings CCA PRC 17.46.335.
68. PRO PCC 11/96/320.
69. Mores Court comprised 100 acres in the parish of Burmarsh, and was occupied by Thomas Honywood of Elmstead, gentleman, who was the brother-in-law of John Hales.
70. Everitt, *Continuity and Colonization*, 74.
71. Zell, *Early Modern Kent*, 309-311; Everitt, *Continuity and Colonization*, 79
72. Everitt, *Continuity and Colonization*, 116, 145, 191–199, 219, 246; Clark, *English Provincial Society*, 369, 476.
73. Clark, *English Provincial Society*, 344.
74. PRO PCC 11/237/150v.
75. His late servant William Barham of Tunstall is made 'keeper', overseer and rent collector of a number of the Hales' core holdings, including the testator's lands in the Romney Marsh; PRO PCC 11/237/150v. These also will have included recently reclaimed marshland that he had acquired in 1636; Zell, *Early Modern Kent*, 99.
76. Hundreds of deeds are bundled into CCA U85 boxes 1–8.
77. For example, in one area of Sellindge parish, probably that adjacent to Blackmanstone manor that he bought in 1630, the deeds show him buying land he already occupies, buying other land in order to lease out, and leasing land (presumably in order to sublet); CCA U85 box 4.
78. Frequently, where Edward Hales acquires a lease, it is part of a complicated family settlement, which is why the rent figures are often negligible.
79. Although like the Scotts, Edward Hales seems to have run into financial difficulty at the end of his life, as suggested by the sale of 578 acres of marsh in the Level to William Sedly of Diggesworth in Hertfordshire esquire, particularly as the price he obtained (£5,000) is well below the average per acre in the period (approximately £20); CCA U85 box 3. This may have been connected with the financial penalties he incurred (a 'voluntary donation' of £6,000) to obtain his release from the Tower in 1648 after Parliament's suspicion at his involvement in the Kentish insurrection earlier in the decade.
80. CCA PRC 17.79.141.
81. Bellaview had passed to his father Samuel in a pre mortem transfer of his grandfather Edward first baronet. In the latter's will, Samuel's widow Martha is said to owe rent

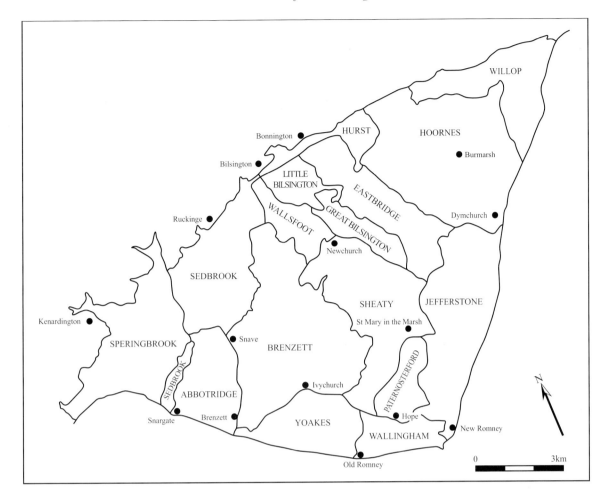

Fig. 12.1. The Waterings of the Level of Romney Marsh.

Table 12.1. Turnover of land occupiers in Denge Marsh 1677–1723 (Sources: EKAC S/D/FS 2,3).

	Nov 1677	May 1683	Aug 1688	June 1693	June 1698	May 1703	May 1708	May 1713	June 1718	June 1723
Nov 1677	**49**	26	11	7	4	2	2	1	1	1
May 1683	–	**52**	17	12	7	4	3	2	2	1
Aug 1688	–	–	**48**	30	20	14	12	9	7	4
June 1693	–	–	–	**50**	30	22	18	12	10	6
June 1698	–	–	–	–	**48**	30	25	16	11	7
May 1703	–	–	–	–	–	**47**	33	21	15	8
May 1708	–	–	–	–	–	–	**49**	24	18	10
May 1713	–	–	–	–	–	–	–	**46**	33	20
June 1718	–	–	–	–	–	–	–	–	**47**	29
June 1723	–	–	–	–	–	–	–	–	–	**42**

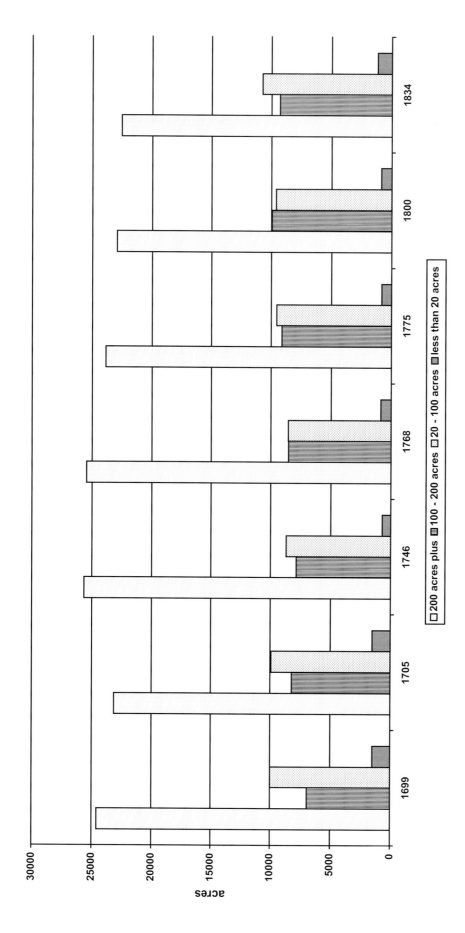

Fig. 12.2. The distribution of land among occupiers in Romney Marsh region 1699–1834 (Sources: EKAC S/Rm/FS 6, 10, 13, 56, 173, FSz 10; S/W/FS 1A, 2, 4, 5A, 6, 6A, 6B, 7, 7A, 8, 9, 39; S/D/FS 3, 5, 6, 7).

Table 12.2. The New and Old Romney Hearth Tax, 1663* (Source: EKAC NR/RTh 2).

Number of hearths	New Romney	Old Romney	Half-year arrears (New and Old Romney)	Exempt households	Household total
1	5	4	5	5	19
2	5	4	6	4	19
3	6	4	10	3	23
4	5	1	4	–	10
5	3	2	3	1	9
6	2	1	3	–	6
7	3	–	2	–	5
8	4	–	–	–	4
9+	2	1	1	–	4
Household total	35	17	34	13	99
Empty houses	–	–	4	–	4
1–2	10	8	11	9	38
3–6	16	8	20	4	48
7+	9	1	3	–	13

* The hearth tax was levied on households according to the number of hearths each household possessed.

more populous post-Restoration parish of perhaps 450 souls,[8] but even this figure is barely able to carry late-Stuart New Romney across the threshold of the least demanding demographic qualification for urban status posited by any historian of early modern England. There were Kentish villages with no such pretensions that could boast significantly larger populations.[9] Nonetheless, as Fig. 12.3 shows, simply to sustain its modest population, New Romney relied on net immigration, for periodic bouts of exceptionally high or crisis mortality (1666, 1668, 1677, 1679 and 1682) helped contribute to a burial total 116 in excess of that for baptisms between April 1662 and December 1701.[10] Most immigrants – like Daniel Langdon himself – probably hailed from within the marsh region, but some travelled further, and a few much further, including Thomas Gyles and Margaret his wife, who, having made the arduous trip back from New England, had their children baptised in the church of St Nicholas in March 1675.[11]

Despite the relatively small number of households exempt from the 1663 hearth tax, many of New and Old Romney's inhabitants were ordinarily considered too poor to contribute to national taxation. Thirty-eight households, or approximately two in every five, were granted certificates of exemption from the 1666 hearth tax, while a poll tax schedule compiled in the immediate wake of the Restoration lists just 124 adults in New Romney, and a mere 38 in Old Romney.[12] More were assessed for the 1667 poll tax (168 adults and 63 children at New Romney,

and 41 adults and 17 children at Old Romney), and very similar numbers – 292 and 285 respectively – were included in poll taxes levied a generation later in 1692 and 1694.[13] But if the overall population of the two settlements did approach 500, two-fifths of their inhabitants were either evading poll taxation or otherwise exempt on grounds of poverty. On the other hand, as will be shown, post-Restoration New Romney could boast a core of remarkably wealthy inhabitants. How then did they make their money?

The answer, emphatically, is not via New Romney's port. During the 15th and early-16th centuries the town's maritime economy had succumbed to a combination of political, military and competitive economic pressures, and, not least, to the retreat of the sea. Similar fates later befell the maritime economies of Rye to the west and of Hythe to the east.[14] By the Restoration New Romney was, and had long been, a port in name only, and its inhabitants had turned their gaze westward to the marsh landscape. The extent of the reorientation of New Romney's economy is apparent from a reconstruction of the primary occupational distribution of poll taxpayers in 1692 and 1694. Altogether, as Table 12.3 shows, it is possible to recover the primary occupation of 59 of the 75 male heads of household in New Romney paying poll tax in 1692, and 49 of the 65 paying in 1694.[15] No merchants, mariners or seamen appear in either schedule. Indeed, in 1692 only two men derived their living from the sea – one fisherman and one rippier (a carrier of fish), and by 1694 only the

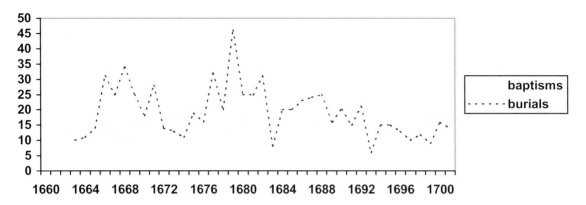

Fig. 12.3. New Romney baptisms and burials 1663–1700 (Source: CKS P309/1/1).

rippier remained. By contrast, the marsh was vital to New Romney's economy. One-third of poll taxpayers with known occupations were graziers, and the remainder of the town's population lived by servicing the needs of the regional agrarian economy. The signal importance of wealth generated in the countryside to the material comfort of the town's leading citizens is even more readily apparent from Table 12.4, which analyses the occupational structure of the governing freeman class.

As was common in the small towns of 17th-century England, New Romney was ruled by a narrow self-perpetuating oligarchy. Often, in such towns, oligarchic control was promoted and sustained by the institution of a common council exercising legislative powers transferred from the commonalty of freemen, and comprising typically 24 of the 'wiser and discreeter sort' of freemen, who were carefully selected – usually by the magisterial bench – from among a commonalty that normally embraced between one-third and one-half of the adult male population. At New Romney, however, as at neighbouring Rye, admission to the franchise marked a man's entry into the ruling elite, for the commonalty remained the legislative forum of town government, and oligarchic rule was promoted and sustained by restricting freeman admissions, which took place under the watchful and largely controlling eyes of the incumbent mayor and his jurats (typically four per annum) – who together comprised the executive arm of the governing class and the town's magisterial bench.[16] The mantle of citizenship was conferred on just 129 men between 1623 and 1700, and these included a number of the county's elite who scarcely set foot in the town, but whose honorific admission was dictated by broader external agenda, particularly the necessary corporate politics of ingratiation.[17] The internal agenda governing the pattern of admissions was to sustain political control in the hands of a resident plutocracy.

Throughout the later-17th century, admissions to the franchise were successfully manipulated to maintain a commonalty comprising an elite score. There were 20 freemen among those paying the demobilisation tax in 1660, 22 among New Romney hearth tax payers in 1663,

20 among the town's poll tax payers in 1692, and 20 again in 1694. And, as Table 4 shows, graziers comprised more than half of New Romney's governing class. Among them, tax assessors in 1694 reckoned Edmund Marten and Stephen Brett each 'worth £600', and John Norman 'worth £300', but such judgements characteristically and substantially underestimated the real wealth of New Romney's leading citizen-graziers.[18] Of those dying during the 1660s, Jeremy Standford and Stephen Brett senior each left flocks of over 900 sheep, Robert Wilcocke possessed 2,046 sheep and 76 cattle, and Thomas Chalker left 3,526 sheep and 31 cattle. Standford and Brett both bequeathed goods valued at more than £1,000, Wilcocke's inventory was assessed at £1,829, and Chalker's at £2,989. As I have observed elsewhere, decayed and depopulated port it may have been, but post-Restoration New Romney contained residents whose inventorial wealth dwarfed that of most of contemporary Canterbury's leading citizens.[19]

Nor, it must be emphasised, was an interest in marshland confined to those citizens whose primary occupation is described in contemporary documentation as grazier. Thirty-one male poll taxpayers returned as residents of New Romney in 1694 – including Daniel Langdon – can be found among tenants of the 42,945.75 acres scotted in Walland Marsh, Denge Marsh and the Level of Romney Marsh in 1699; altogether they occupied 4,166 acres, 9.7 per cent of the land in the Romney Marsh region. Their holdings at the turn of the century ranged from the 2 acres in the hands of William Tayler, to the 570 acres occupied by Richard Baker, gentleman-grazier. Among the 31 were Thomas Fagge (butcher, 69 acres), Richard King (tailor, 36 acres), John Pope (innholder, 23 acres), Thomas Shorte (carpenter, 4.5 acres) and William King and Edward Reynolds, 'day labourers', who occupied 14 and 3 acres respectively.[20] Of course, for men like William Tayler and Edward Reynolds, a 2- or 3-acre holding merely represented the opportunity to keep a dairy cow or a few pigs for domestic consumption, but a 69-acre tenancy such as Thomas Fagge's represented a commercial enterprise, as indeed did the 36-acre tenancy of Richard King, tailor-grazier! Nevertheless it is the big commercial tenant farms

Table 12.3. Primary occupations among male New Romney poll taxpayers in 1692 and 1694 (Sources: EKAC NR/RTp 12, 15, /Rta 2–32; S/Rm/FS 6, /W/FSz 2, /W/FS 1A, 2, 6, /D/ FS 2; CKS, P 309/1/1; CKS PRC 27, 11).

	1692	1694
Attorney	2	2
Blacksmith	1	1
Butcher	2	2
Carpenter	3	3
Clergy	4	4
Drover	1	–
Fisherman	1	–
Glover	1	1
Grazier	20	18
Innholder	2	3
Labourer	10	6
Looker	1	1
Miller	1	1
Rippier	1	1
Sadler	1	1
Shoemaker	1	2
Tailor	6	3
Wheelwright	1	–
Unknown	16	16
Total	75	65

Table 12.4. Primary occupations among New Romney Freeman poll taxpayers in 1692 and 1694 (Sources: as Table 12.3, plus EKAC NR/AC 2 (unfoliated)).

	1692	1694
Attorney	2	2
Blacksmith	–	1
Butcher	1	1
Carpenter	–	1
Clergy	1	1
Fisherman	1	–
Grazier	12	11
Sadler	1	1
Shoemaker	–	1
Tailor	1	1
Unknown	1	–
Total	20	20

that catch the eye. In 1699, across the marsh region, there were a dozen tenant farmers holding more than 500 acres, and a further 54 occupying between 200 and 500 acres. Among New Romney's inhabitants, such farms were largely the preserve of freemen. Ten of the 11 freeman graziers poll taxed in 1694 were still farming in 1699. All held more than 100 acres, six occupied in excess of 200

acres, and, overall, these ten leading 'townsmen' were farming 2,678 acres at the turn of the century.

By contrast with that which survives for land occupation, evidence for landownership in the Romney Marsh region during the late-17th and early-18th centuries is frustratingly patchy. Nonetheless, it is clear that New Romney men owned as well as leased marshland, though on nothing approaching the same scale. For example, the 50 private landowners assessed on 572 acres in the immediate vicinity of the town in 1662 included 16 inhabitants of New Romney, who owned a total of 188 acres, but among tenants there were 33 New Romney men occupying 397 acres of the privately owned land, and a further 106 of the 289 acres of corporately owned land that was also assessed for taxation. Similarly, of the 843 acres of 'lands in New Romney ... sessed to the King's tax' in October 1667, 795 acres were privately owned by 34 landlords, nine of whom (owning 160 acres in total) were New Romney residents, whereas 18 of the 32 tenants were townsmen, and they occupied 348 acres, or 41 per cent of the land. Nine of the 16 New Romney landowners assessed in 1662, and four of the nine assessed in 1667, were owner-occupiers; the proportion of owner-occupied land among this group amounting to 63 per cent in 1662, and 59 per cent in 1667. However, one might expect owner-occupation rates among landowning townsmen with respect to a modest area in the immediate vicinity of New Romney to be unrepresentative of the wider picture, and this is indeed the case. Overall, just 16 per cent of the 861 acres assessed in 1662, and only 21 per cent of the 843 acres taxed in 1667, were owner-occupied, and, as we have seen, on Walland Marsh and Denge Marsh less than one acre in ten was being farmed by its owner at the turn of the 17th century.[21]

The Commercial Farming World of Daniel Langdon

Two years after the young and single Daniel Langdon, 'grazier', contributed to the 1694 poll tax in New Romney, he moved out of the town, first to St Mary-in-the-Marsh, where he was still living in 1699, and then, in 1701, with his recently acquired wife Esther, to the well-appointed Honeychild House in the parish of Hope-All-Saints, latterly the home of Mr Thomas Noble, a Romney Marsh justice of the peace, whose widow's death in 1693 doubtless occasioned the sale. Shortly after their arrival, in July 1701 Esther gave birth to Robert. Two more sons, Daniel and Martin, followed in 1704 and 1707.[22] Already a wealthy man, the 270 acres Langdon was farming in 1699 made him the 35th largest occupier (of 513) in the entire Romney Marsh region. By 1705, when he held 362 acres, he had risen to 20th in the list of 507 farmers.[23] Thereafter, as entries in the calendar scot books for the Level of Romney Marsh detail, the size and distribution of his holdings oscillated as existing tenancies came to an end and new leases were taken out, but right up to his death, in January 1751, the total acreage of his leaseholdings at any one time remained well above 200 acres.[24] Daniel's first wife, Esther, did not survive long into the 18th century, and at some point – probably in the early 1710s – he married Elizabeth, daughter of Thomas Handfield senior, a minor gentleman of Ulcombe, and an ex-bailiff and common expenditor of the Level and Liberty of Romney Marsh.[25] As we shall see, the acquisition of a family tie with Thomas Handfield was to prove a convenience to Daniel's private commercial enterprise. Indeed it was probably as a direct result of his second marriage that Langdon also became a landowner on the marsh – albeit a modest one – acquiring 10.5 acres in Hoornes watering from his father-in-law by 1715. As for the eldest child of his first marriage, it did not prove necessary for Robert to endure the long wait for a deathbed inheritance before following in his father's footsteps, for in 1722, at the age of 21, Robert Langdon began his own career as a commercial tenant farmer, leasing 79 acres in Jefferstone and Sheaty. By 1732 Robert had built up his tenant farm to 167 acres, comprising seven parcels dotted across Jefferstone, Paternosterford and Sheaty waterings, which he leased from three different owners. By 1739, 'Mr Robert Langdon' had retraced his father's steps and joined the ranks of the gentleman-grazier inhabitants of the town of New Romney.[26]

For the later-18th century, historians interested in farming practice on Romney Marsh are able to turn, amongst other sources, to the invaluable account bequeathed by the Reverend Daniel Jones of New Romney in a letter, composed in 1786 though apparently never sent, to his Welsh brother, Thomas Jones, of Llanio Tregaron, near Lampeter.[27] For the early-18th century, on the other hand, thus far, evidence has proved more elusive. So the chance survival of two small volumes of Daniel Langdon's 'almanacs', covering the years 1723–5, provides what may prove a rare opportunity to examine the nature and diversity of the commercial farming activities of a tenant farmer on the marsh in the early-Hanoverian period.[28] That said, Langdon's almanacs, and the clutch of loose letters, notes, bills of sale or purchase, and other ephemera that has survived with them,[29] are sometimes more frustrating than they are enlightening. Alas, for instance, there is nothing to throw light on the circumstances that led one Thomas Kennard to compose the following anguished letter (original spelling retained),

'For Mr Langdon at St Mary's near New Romney, Kent April 28th, London.
Sir, I wonder that you can sarve any porman so as you have don me and my credetors, for the want of that money which you and Mr Toul kep back keps me so long from hom and from my family.
I wold have you consider of it and some way make an end to it, for it is very hard upon me, for I have lost on I with the smal poks, so tis very hard to get min own living abroad and til you have ben my frend I must suffer.
So pray sor I beg of you to be my frend and to doo what you can for me, and I hope if you be my frend that God will reward you of it, so wishing you and your family all health, so all from your desalat chap'.

The content of the pages between which this and other items of correspondence were unceremoniously stuffed reveal Langdon's almanacs as general purpose notebooks, in which he recorded – albeit sporadically, often haphazardly, and frequently in incomplete or cryptic fashion – a wide range of activities (concerning both private business and public office) provided they involved money. Langdon's almanacs have none of the completeness or coherence that might merit their description as accounts, but they comprise entirely financial jottings. If entries throw any light on Langdon's private family life, they do so purely as a by-product. Daniel certainly cared enough for his wife to purchase 'two pounds of chocolate ... the best to be bought' in November 1724, but it was not the occasion of the purchase that prompted a note in the almanac, it was the cost – 8 shillings.[30]

Langdon did produce a small commercial surplus of wheat, which was either sold at the farm gate or sent to Dymchurch, and he also occasionally had one or two pigs to sell,[31] but he was, of course, primarily a sheep farmer, and entries in the almanacs include payments for the annual cycle of tasks attendant on maintaining flocks, very much as described in detail by Daniel Jones in 1786. To carry out the day-to-day work of overseeing his flocks, Langdon found it necessary to hire just one farm servant on annual contract. Thus, at Michaelmas 1723 William Catt was retained for a wage of £4, plus the right to keep three sheep at Langdon's cost, while the following year George Mount was contracted as a living-in servant with a correspondingly reduced wage of £3 5s., plus the keeping of just two sheep at Langdon's charge, for which, in order for Mount to purchase, Langdon advanced £1 2s. of his wage. The many marshland graziers who, unlike Langdon, were not domiciled on the marsh, employed 'lookers', who often worked for a number of tenant farmers simultaneously, to carry out the duties performed for Langdon by Catt and Mount. To meet the rest of his labour requirements, Langdon relied on buying in men to carry out specific tasks during the year.[32]

Labour costs for the marshland grazier were, however, a minor element in the profit and loss equation. Far more significant were the overheads associated with the purchase and maintenance of stock and, particularly, the tenancy of land, to which we shall shortly turn. With regard to the former, Daniel Langdon was in the fortunate position of being an established grazier with an existing breeding flock, and, beyond taking the wise precaution of hiring rams at riding time (for a mere £1 in 1723),[33] his main concern was to safeguard the resulting and vulnerable lambs in the face of the harsh winter climate on the marsh. The general solution, widely – though not universally – adopted by graziers, was to winter lambs on uplands away from the marsh:[34] Langdon's particular solution made use of his father-in-law. Thus, on 21 August 1723, Langdon noted that he had 'sent to my father at Ulcombe 140 lambs to keep, at a penny a lamb by the week to Ladyday', and on 17 September he 'sent more of lamb to my father Handfield a keeping, 31 in all'. In 1724 a similar entry records 'sent to my father Handfield 126 lambs a keeping at 1d. per lamb by the week from the 26 August to Ladyday, being 30 weeks every live lamb comes to keeping of it just 2s. 6d. a lamb'. Family ties notwithstanding, both Handfield and his son-in-law seem to have regarded the arrangement as strictly commercial – albeit conveniently simple to devise. On the one hand, evidence from elsewhere suggests that Handfield was charging the going rate, and, on the other, Langdon carefully recorded winter losses on the uplands (13 lambs in 1723–4 and 12 in 1724–5), and made deductions accordingly from the money he paid his father-in-law.[35]

If it was common practice for marsh lambs to be wintered on the uplands, Daniel Jones's late-18th century observations and Davison's ongoing research suggest that in summer much livestock belonging to upland farmers was brought down to feed on the pastures of marsh graziers 'at a certain price per head'.[36] But, as Davison also shows, agistment was a multi-dimensional phenomenon, occurring *within* marsh and upland regions as well as between them. Agistment is exceptionally difficult to quantify, but the indications are that it was a frequent money-raising resort for tenants with spare capacity, and its scale and significance in shaping the character of agrarian and tenurial regimes in both the marsh and contiguous upland regions in the early modern period are perhaps only now beginning to be appreciated. Practised on any scale, agistment should properly be regarded as a particularly flexible species of sublease, and as an alternative to the formal subletting of land. That there was comparatively little subletting of land on the marsh was certainly due in part to the availability of short-term leases, but probably also to a widespread reliance on agistment; indeed what for some farmers amounted to a *strategic* reliance upon agistment.

There are no clear indications in the almanacs that Langdon was receiving payment for the summer pasturing of livestock belonging to upland farmers, but animals were agisted on his land. In September 1723, for instance, 'Mr Fowl put into my land at Dymchurch two cows at three shillings per week'.[37] More significant were his dealings with the neighbouring but absentee French farmer Mr Justinian Champney, the owner-occupier of 57 acres in Sheaty, for whom Langdon was evidently acting as managing agent on commission, and in which capacity he organized the local and metropolitan sale of Champney's sheep and cattle, and paid his land taxes and poor rates.[38] In the winter of 1724–5, moreover, 223 of Champney's 'ewes, wether tegs and old barrens' were agisted on Langdon's farm. Just as he noted the casualties among his own lambs wintered at Ulcombe, so Daniel listed the winter casualties among Champney's sheep. Only 15 died, but the list makes macabre reading: three were simply noted

as dead, six had drowned, one was found 'in the snow', four had been 'torn to pieces' and, finally, 'one old barren' was described as 'mislaid and killed by the beast'.[39]

During the 1780s, Jones observed, rents for marsh pasture 'are in general from 20s. to 35s. per acre, but some prime fatting pieces so high as 40s. and even 50s. per acre', adding that 'the few acres that are ploughed let from 40s. to £3 per acre'. Our attentive cleric also registered the recent impact of stiffening competition for tenancies:

> '...it is exceedingly difficult to get land for it requires almost as much interest to get at, as it would to procure a place at court, and besides, of late years it is become so excessively dear as to be hardly worth the hazard of using'.[40]

The conditions of 'late years' in fact stretched back until at least the early 1770s. In November 1773, in a letter to his kinsman William Pattenson, Josias Pattenson reported on the efforts of potential tenants to outbid each other for marsh holdings. On getting wind of the availability of one estate, he wrote, 'no less than four graziers ... substantial men, went to London ... on purpose either to buy or hire the same ... and you know how the graziers ride after every parcel of land that is to be let in the marsh'.[41] But circumstances half a century earlier were very different.

For the early-18th century, payments authorized by the Lathe of Romney Marsh to compensate owners of land excavated to provide earth to repair Dymchurch Wall offer reasonable indications of what were probably regarded as average commercial rents, and these may be supplemented by information contained in leases, account books and, in Daniel Langdon's case, the almanacs. Without exception, between 1700 and 1720, the Lathe offered compensation at rates of between 20 shillings and 24 shillings per acre.[42] Among the packages approved were two (in 1704 and 1705) on land belonging to Peter Godfrey and occupied by Daniel Langdon. On both occasions 23 shillings per acre was granted.[43] Among rent payments recorded by Langdon at Michaelmas 1723, that for £40 to John Sawbridge, his landlord on 34 acres in Jefferstone, suggests a very similar rent of *c.* 23s. 6d. per acre. Other entries in the almanacs would appear to indicate somewhat lower rents of between 16 shillings and 22 shillings on his holdings elsewhere, but such variations may reflect not only differences in the quality of land but also in the precise terms of leasehold agreements. Langdon paid the land tax and manorial quit rents (liability for both of which technically fell to owners) on land leased from 'landlord Godfrey', but not – it would appear – on other lands he occupied. It is therefore likely that some, but not all, of his rent payments reflected reductions to compensate for additional liabilities that had been agreed at the original negotiation of leases. More research is needed on the topic, but it is clear that marsh rents in the first half of the 18th century remained depressed at levels first achieved a century earlier, and well below those to which Daniel Jones's contemporaries in the 1780s had 'of late years' become accustomed.[44] Indeed, during the late 1730s, Henry and Jeremy Read, both substantial tenants on the marsh, were negotiating rent abatements from the leading rentier in the Romney Marsh region, Sir Wyndam Knatchbull of Mersham, and in June 1739, another of Knatchbull's tenants, Mr Stace, offered to renew his lease on one parcel of marsh for a further five years, but only if there was some abatement of the rent. Stace 'complained chiefly of the low price of wool, of which', Knatchbull wrote, 'he told me he usually sheared 25 packs, but could not get more than £4 or £4 10s. at most'.[45]

Rent apart, Langdon paid poor and church rates for land occupied in the parishes of Hope, Dymchurch and St Mary-in-the-Marsh, and water and wall scots to the Level of Romney Marsh.[46] Among these, the burden of wall-scot payments in some years during the first quarter of the 18th century was particularly onerous. Typically 2 shillings per acre per annum before the late 1720s (and hence for Langdon an annual bill in excess of £20), the sum demanded by the Lathe could rise to more than 4 shillings per acre in years when exceptionally heavy expenditure on repairs was authorized, as was the case between 1704 and 1708. In 1705, when he was occupying 362 acres on the Level, Langdon's bill for wall scots amounted to £74 13s. 3d. It is scarcely surprising that the ensuing outcry from occupiers was sufficient to force the Lathe to agree, in February 1706, that it was 'reasonable' henceforth to expect owners to make some contribution in years when 'excessive' scots were levied.[47]

Rent, scots, local rates, the costs of labour, and of maintaining or augmenting buildings, fences, flocks and herds – all these had to be met. 'It must be observed', commented Reverend Jones,

> 'that it is not every one who is capable of being a good grazier ... it requires a man of sense and judgement to do that to the most advantage, whether we consider it with respect to the grazing of their land, or to bring their stock to market with the quickest return and greatest profit'.[48]

Marshland graziers sold a proportion of their stock locally, and at the 'lower markets' of Tonbridge, Maidstone and Rochester, but metropolitan demand meant that, for the bigger graziers particularly, the London market figured prominently in the drive to achieve 'greatest profit'.[49] For this trade, of course, drovers were vital to oversee the sheep and cattle that made the 70-mile trip to Smithfield on the hoof. But what was their precise role, and how was the livestock of the marsh traded in the capital?

In his exhaustive study of middlemen, Westerfield (1915) points out that 16th and 17th century statutes assume that drovers performed 'the double function of dealing in cattle and of driving them to the market', and argues that it was during the 18th century that the two functions were differentiated, with jobbers assuming the buying and selling part of the process and, before 1750, gaining 'a monopoly of the livestock market'. Nowhere was the impact of this monopoly more in evidence than at

Smithfield. Jobbers bought at farms, at fairs and markets, at towns along the roads by which animals were being driven to market, and at Smithfield itself, and they bought from graziers, drovers, farmers, and from one another. Early-18th century commentators reckoned that of all the cattle and sheep that came to Smithfield, as many as three-quarters (one estimate suggested as much as 90 per cent) had been jobbed. Sales at Smithfield were conducted by factors working on small commissions (during the 1770s reported rates were 1s. 6d. per bullock or 3d. per sheep). When factors sold for jobbers, they were set minimum prices for consignments. When graziers who had resisted the blandishments of jobbers consigned stock to the commission factor they usually put no price on them, relying instead on the factor's discretion. The buyers from commission factors (apart from speculating jobbers) were the wholesale - or carcass - butchers, who in turn sold to the retail – or cutting – butchers.[50]

Whoever the purchasers of sheep and cattle sold in the local and lower markets of Kent were – about which he ventures no opinion – so far as the direct traffic into Smithfield is concerned, if the Reverend Jones's general commentary is to be believed, the late-18th-century graziers of Romney Marsh were among the minority who had resisted the overtures of speculative drovers and jobbers. Drovers are portrayed as mere employees, contracted by graziers to drive livestock to the outskirts of London, 'a few at a time. i.e. from half a score and upwards according to the extent of their business', where they were received by the commission factor,

> 'who has them to the next market at Smithfield, two of which are held weekly, i.e. Mondays and Fridays; he sells them to the carcass butchers and writes by that day's post to the owners informing them to whom he has sold them and at what price, and deducting the expense of droving and selling which comes on the whole to about 1s. a head'.[51]

Jones may not have been particularly well-informed, but his portrayal matches evidence for the early 1720s in the almanacs and surviving correspondence of Daniel Langdon.

As his dealings on behalf of Mr Champney show, Langdon was not averse to playing the middleman, but in his trade with Smithfield he was not keen to surrender margins. So, as they were driven to London, the sheep and cattle in the care of Thomas Weldon (Langdon's regular drover) remained in Daniel's ownership. Weldon had to be content with a wage that appears to have varied according to the time of year as well as to the number of animals despatched to the capital, but which averaged approximately 3d. for every sheep in his charge.[52] On reaching the outskirts of London, Langdon's livestock were consigned to his commission factor, Mrs Mary Moone, who, either in person or by proxy, conducted the sales at Smithfield, informing Langdon of the outcome in letters, some of which – sent in 1723 and 1724 – have survived.

Moone's letters, though always brief and to the point, suggest a firmly established and perhaps even warm working relationship. It is evident from a number of comments that Langdon occasionally visited London to assess the state of the market for himself, but for the most part he relied on intelligence from Mary Moone, and then conveyed his instructions in letters 'to put in the Hythe bag to be carried to' her.[53] Thus, on 4 July 1723, she wrote informing him that 'at present we sell fat wethers and mutton for near 3¼d. the lb forequarters', and on 5 October that 'our markets at present are something better than when you was last up'. Sometimes, when the market was good, a note of urgency was injected. On 22 November 1723 Moone advised that 'yesterday we sold fat wethers' mutton for full 3¼d. the lb forequarters, and in our opinion, the sooner you send it the better in all', and, on 2 July 1724, she reported that 'at present, fat beef is worth 4s. 6d. if fat and fine, and do believe the sooner you send it the better. Fat mutton 2s. 2d. per stone'. At other times, the tone is apologetic. In a brief note appended to an account, dated 7 September 1724, of '19 sheep sold for Mr Dan Langdon', Moone sought to reassure her client. 'Sir, you may depend that my cousin Crew took all possible care for your advantage to the utmost of a full and bad market, the worst we have had this year'.[54] Clients, of course, might turn to others, not least to those jobbers who 'endeavoured to tempt the grazier by offering a price higher than he intended to give or than prevailed at Smithfield'.[55]

But if she may occasionally have feared for future commissions, one factor cementing the relationship between Langdon and his London agent was Mary Moone's willingness to arrange for supplies of life's little luxuries to be delivered to the Langdon household on the often bleak Romney Marsh. Among these, 'bath water' (bath oil) figured prominently. Six bottles were despatched in July 1723, 12 'by John Hale, master of the Elizabeth for Folkestone' in September, and a further dozen by the same route in November. A veritable flood of bath water was shipped in 1725. Spa water was also sent, as were mace, nutmegs and 'imperial queen tea', some of which subsequently found its way to 'my father Handfield' at Ulcombe. And, as previously noted, there was the *very* expensive chocolate that Mary Moone 'sent by the bearer' from London on 6 November 1724; 'which', she ventured delicately, 'therefore hope your spouse will like'.[56]

Langdon's almanacs are less informative about his other main source of farming income, though it is clear that sales to wool buyers occurred on a considerable scale. A loose account for 'my fleece wool, locks and lambs wool sold' in November 1723 reveals an income of £190 2s. 6d., a series of cryptic notes in the almanac for 1724 culminates with '790 fleeces in all entries this year', and further jottings show that fleece wool worth £108 6s. 1d. was sold in February 1725.[57] But if it is impossible to glean much detail about Langdon as a wool producer from the pages of the almanacs, they do provide frequent

reminders that he did not have to rely entirely on farming for an income. Indeed, for the great majority of his adult life, Daniel Langdon was devoting a significant amount of time to public offices and, in fine 18th-century fashion, to harvesting the fruits of a number of them.

The Public World of Daniel Langdon

Had he chosen to remain in New Romney there seems little doubt that the suitably qualified – not least, wealthy – young Langdon would have been looked on favourably by the magistracy and granted his citizenship before the end of the 17th century. But to move out of New Romney was to step into the peculiar jurisdiction of the Level and Liberty of Romney Marsh, and it was to the executive and administrative bureaucracy spawned by this jurisdiction that Langdon turned for a public career.

As an administrative and governmental entity, the Level of Romney Marsh had originally developed in response to the need for a body capable of funding, organizing and carrying out sea-defence measures and the maintenance of sewers. After 1462 the area covered by the drainage authority also acquired a political and legal identity as the Liberty of Romney Marsh. The Liberty of Romney Marsh enjoyed chartered corporate status, with legislative, tax-raising and, notably, judicial powers equivalent to those exercised in the Cinque Ports.[58] At the beginning of the 17th century, doubtless influenced by recent trends in the Cinque Ports, the doors at meetings of the drainage authority of the Level (General and Petty Lathes) were closed to ordinary owners and occupiers on the marsh. Likewise, in 1604, the general legislative and judicial arm of local government, the Liberty of Romney Marsh, excluded the commonalty of male residents on the marsh from any further say in its business by the simple expedient of importing the concept of 'freemen' and instantly confining their number to 24 of the 'chiefest, substantialist, most sufficient, discreetest and richest inhabitants of the commonalty'. The Level and Liberty thus effected a sweeping transference of power into the hands of a two-branched self-perpetuating oligarchy consisting of a drainage authority comprising the lords of the 23 manors (or their designated representatives), the bailiff and jurats, and a Liberty comprising the same bailiff and jurats, and up to 24 freemen. The bailiff of the Level and Liberty was appointed annually by the 23 lords of the Level, and the jurats of the Level and Liberty were selected from among the freemen of the Liberty. New freemen of the Liberty were selected by the existing bailiff, jurats and freemen. Among their roles, bailiffs served as justices of the peace and coroners, and the practice of annually electing four other justices of the peace (and, like the bailiff, coroners *ex officio*) from among the jurats, first enshrined in the 1462 charter, was continued.[59]

In 1697, Daniel Langdon was selected as a freeman of the Liberty of Romney Marsh and began his ascent through the ranks of both the Liberty and the Level. In May 1705 he was appointed one of the jurats of the Level, and, at its annual assembly the following Michaelmas, the Liberty not only confirmed the appointment but also elected Langdon as one of the four justices of the peace for Romney Marsh to serve for 1705–6.[60] Between 1708 and 1720 he combined these roles with that of churchwarden for his home parish of Hope-All-Saints, but although he relinquished parish office during the 1720s, he went on to be elected as a JP for Romney Marsh on 32 occasions between 1705 and his death in January 1751, and sat on the magisterial bench in an unbroken stint between 1736 and 1750. By 1714, Daniel was the second ranking jurat of the Level and Liberty, and he graduated to senior jurat in 1726, thereafter delivering the vote of thanks for the sermon that accompanied the annual deliberations of the 'discreetest and richest' inhabitants of the marsh. There can have been few if any more widely recognized figures in the Romney Marsh region during the 1730s and 1740s than its senior jurat and most experienced justice and coroner.[61]

If the offices of the Liberty conferred power and authority, it was the bureaucracy of the Level that promised financial remuneration, for the business of maintaining the sea defences and drainage of the Level of Romney Marsh had generated a number of offices and duties commanding salaries, fees and perquisites. The land drainage bureaucracy can be broadly divided between those officials primarily concerned with tax collection, and those overseeing expenditure on walls or sewers. There were distinct bodies of revenue raising and spending officials for the Dymchurch Wall, and for each of the main sewers of the Level, but it was Dymchurch Wall that required most money and attention, and the principal revenue raising and spending officials for the wall, respectively the common clerk and the common expenditor of the Level, were also the principal bureaucrats of the drainage authority.

Apart from major structural alterations (which required the authority of a General Lathe), decisions over repairs to the wall were taken by the bailiff, jurats and two proprietorial lords – or their deputies – appointed annually as surveyors, the latter rotating according to the alphabetical order of the 23 manors. Wall scots were then authorised by the bailiff, jurats, a surveyor and the common expenditor, and the money was collected under the auspices of the common clerk. During the early-18th century, repairs were carried out under the general supervision of a salaried director of works, William Markwicke, and of the common expenditor, who also hired and paid workmen, contracted for materials and accounted to the General Lathe. The bailiff and jurats of the Level also exercised supervisory functions at Dymchurch Wall, and in the woodlands rented or owned by the Level from which timber to 'arm the walls' was supplied.[62]

Daniel Langdon entered the Level's bureaucracy in May 1703 when he was elected common expenditor for Clobsden watering. His rapid promotion to common expenditor for the Level followed in May 1706, Langdon succeeding his future father-in-law to the office. Thereafter, Langdon was annually re-elected to the position by the lords, bailiff and jurats of the Level until he died.[63] That he was roundly approved of by the narrow clique of proprietors in possession of the keys to the office does not, however, indicate that he, or his fellow senior officials, or for that matter those who sustained him in power, were popular among the ordinary run of owners and occupiers on the marsh. For most of his period in office there were popular rumblings of discontent that occasionally flared into overt accusations of greed and malpractice on the part of drainage authority officials.

Popular resentment of the perceived excesses of corporate hospitality at the Lathe had a long history, but it was honed in the difficult economic conditions facing the majority of tenant farmers during the late-17th and early-18th centuries. Deprived of any formal voice, occupiers could only petition, and petition they did, 'complaining', in 1677 for example, 'of the great charge as well of the General Lathe as the Petty Lathe and other meetings of the officers of the marsh'.[64] The petitions prompted gestures, but the complaints went on, and were reaching one of their periodic crescendos when Daniel Langdon came on the scene. As we have seen, the unprecedented sums of money expended on Dymchurch Wall did call forth a declaration from the Lathe in 1706 that owners ought reasonably to contribute to 'excessive and extraordinary scots', and in May 1708, in an effort to defuse another high tide of resentment, a schedule of attendance fees for Lathes was issued. It nonetheless authorized payments to each of the lords, the bailiff, the jurats, the common expenditor, common clerk and sergeants of the Level, and the collectors and expenditors for the waterings.

Another source of popular resentment was the myriad of fees claimed by jurats for their attendance at land surveys and on accounting days, for days spent 'attending the walls' and, increasingly as the 18th century wore on, 'for journeys to the country's woods and other services'. It was not necessary, complained Robert Austen in 1713, for 'too many' jurats – in addition to the bailiff and the expenditor or collector for the watering – to turn up for surveys, claim fees, and thus 'greatly increase the charge' on occupiers. The Lathe apparently concurred, and ordered that henceforth just one jurat 'that lives near the place' should take a fee. But orders were one thing, enforcement quite another. In May 1708 it had been agreed that only the bailiff and 2 jurats should attend to supervise repairs to Dymchurch Wall on any given day, but in 1723 the Lathe admitted that the order had been widely disregarded by jurats charging 'promiscuously' for their attendance. In the capacity of jurat, Daniel Langdon claimed £6 9s. for 86 days attending the walls between June 1718 and March 1719, enough to prompt the Lathe to pause for thought and freeze payment. But Langdon got his fees in

June 1720, and entries in the almanacs, and in his accounts as common expenditor over the following 30 years, suggest no diminution in the jurats' promiscuous regard for the indispensability of their presence at the walls. In the accounting year 1722-3 Daniel Langdon claimed £12 13s. for attendance at the walls, and the total fees paid to the bailiff and six jurats for this duty amounted to £64 2s., while in 1748–9 – by which time he may have been into his late seventies – Langdon claimed £5 8s. for 72 days spent supervising repairs at the walls. Nor did the enthusiastic presence of jurats always prevent less guileful appropriations of corporate resources. In 1721, several workmen were reported to have taken wood intended for use on the walls 'on pretence that the same is only rotten and broken'. This brand of opportunism the Lathe intended not to regard lightly. Future culprits would be 'prosecuted and punished with the utmost severity the law will allow'.[65]

Between 1705 and 1750 the fees Daniel Langdon took as a jurat for attending at the walls and woods, at the taking of surveys and accounts, and for being present at General and Petty Lathes, amounted to between £10 and £20 per annum. On top of this was his annual salary as common expenditor, which stood at £20 when he came into office. However, it had become routine practice in the era of Robinson Beane – the common expenditor throughout the later-17th century – for the 'extraordinary pains' of the office to be recognized with an annual gratuity, usually equivalent to the basic salary of the office, and Langdon enjoyed just such a gratuity from 1706 until 1716, when a Lathe under pressure from disgruntled taxpayers discontinued it 'until further order'. Langdon suffered this inconvenience until 1732, when, 'in consideration of his good and faithful service for several years past', his basic salary was doubled to £40 per annum, at which level it remained until his death. Furthermore, often in the years before 1744, and regularly thereafter, Langdon also received £5 per annum for 'extraordinary journeys to buy wood and timber' for the use of the Level. Of course he did incur some expenses, but as jurat and common expenditor Langdon's average net income from salaries, fees and perquisites between 1706 and 1716, and from 1732 until his death, may be roundly estimated at £55 per annum.[66]

It is probably more than a coincidence that the decision to double Langdon's basic salary took place just in advance of the interim report of a committee of enquiry into officers' 'salaries, fees and perquisites' that the General Lathe had finally set up in response to a recrudescence of popular complaint in the early 1730s. As a memorandum written on 7 June 1734 by Sir Wyndam Knatchbull makes clear, such complaints were by no means confined to Romney Marsh proper.

'At the commission of sewers for Walland Marsh at the Saracen's head this day, it was very reasonably objected by Mr Faussett that the expenditors and other officers were in a manner paid twice over, because they were not only paid their salaries, but were likewise paid for their attendance in seeing the works performed which had been ordered, and for which attendance he did suppose the salaries were their only proper payment. ... I likewise mentioned the unreasonableness of paying 4 shillings into the commissioners pockets after they had been treated at the expense of the Level. And the gentlemen there whom I spoke to were of the same opinion, but nothing was offered publicly for the reforming of it'[67]

The interim report of the committee for the Level of Romney Marsh, received in July 1733, offered some encouragement to critics. Having perused the abstract of salaries, fees, and perquisites that had been provided, the committee announced them 'very uncertain' and deserving 'further consideration'. It was particularly unhappy about the profits of the common clerk 'chiefly arising from his perquisites', and recommended that these be abolished henceforth, in favour of a 'certain salary'. It is some indication of the level of fees extracted by the common clerk in the early-18th century that the recommendation was to quadruple his salary to £80 per annum. To this the Lathe assented, as it did to the recommendation that ways should to be sought to make payments to other officers 'more certain for the ease of the country, and ... by salaries only, without any fees or perquisites whatsover'. The halving of fees paid to all those attending Lathes, and reductions of fees for those attending at surveys were also proposed. But it seems that plans to trim their income met with stubborn and effective resistance from the Level's officers, for the committee subsequently reported that, on further investigation, it had found 'no considerable excess in such salaries, fees and perquisites'. The Lathe was thus able to order that they 'remain and be received by the officers in such manner as heretofore hath been, excepting only the fees concerning the measurement of sewers'. No further reforms of the fee structure for officials seem to have been contemplated during the lifetime of Daniel Langdon.[68]

This does not mean, however, that the complaints of hard-pressed tenants on the marsh had no impact on the drainage authority. It was not difficult to appreciate the link between the burden of taxation authorized by the Level and the volume of complaint amongst taxpayers, even if it did tend to rise in the form of protests over officers' fees. As noted above, heavy taxation was authorized between 1704 and 1708, and in excess of £4,000 was spent in 1714 and again in 1717, but thereafter, and particularly during the later 1730s and 1740s, sustained efforts were made to appease taxpayers by, where possible, cutting expenditure on Dymchurch Wall.

During the early-17th century all repairs to Dymchurch Wall were carried out, as one contemporary account has it, by workmen whom the common 'expenditor with the assistance of the bailiff of Romney Marsh and the jurats doth daily appoint', and who were paid 'every night with ready money' for 'such days as they work'.[69] Although the common expenditor continued to hire workmen on a day-to-day basis during the early-18th century, it was

William Markwicke's practice, as director of works, to contract out portions of the work to consortia in order to reduce costs. Throughout the 1720s, Markwicke placed successive contracts for 'arming and keeping in repair the several walls and sea groins' with consortia led by Henry Cane. Cane and his partners' willingness to take on the bulk of the work for less than £400 per annum helped peg the total burden of wall scots on the Level's farmers to below £2,500 in all but one year of the decade, and to below £2,000 in 1729 and 1730. But in 1732–3 the contract agreed with Cane's consortium was extended to include the 'finding of piles and overlatts' for the walls and sea groins, and, at £679 (and similar amounts in 1733–4 and 1734–5) may not have represented such good value. It did not help that storm damage sometimes necessitated expensive emergency repairs to sections of Dymchurch Wall, and an additional £507 was spent in the summer of 1732, and £492 the following summer, on remedial work at Kingsland. Wall-scot demands rose from £1,980 in 1731-2 to over £2,500 in both 1732–3 and 1733–4.[70] Taxpayers complained loudly about officers' fees. But if, as we have seen, the resulting committee of enquiry finally rejected thorough reform of fees, the Lathe did agree, in July 1734, that the contract for the repair and maintenance of walls and groins had been 'put out to the several workmen at too great a price or yearly salary', and that sealed bids would be invited for future contracts. The following year it was also decreed that the Level's surveyors would have power to treat with 'any person for the recarrying of wallstuff upon the cheapest and best terms they can get'.[71]

Cane's consortium still had the contract for 'arming the wall' in 1735–6, but in the summer of 1736 the successful bidder for a three-year contract to 'arm, sustain and keep in repair' the wall and groins, and to transport 'wallstuff and other materials', was none other than John Fowle of Dymchurch, the long-standing common clerk of the Level. Over the next three years, Fowle received £500 per annum as main contractor, and his £80 salary as common clerk, principally for collecting the scots that would pay him for carrying out the work. On completing the contract, apparently to its satisfaction, in June 1739 the Lathe ordered Fowle (as common clerk) to organize the next round of bids. Public notice was to be given, an advertisement was to be placed 'in the Canterbury newspaper' and, since this was all being done rather late in the day, the common expenditor – Daniel Langdon – was ordered to 'have charge and care of the walls and sea groins' until a new contract could be finalized at a meeting scheduled for 19 July. This temporary arrangement finds its reflection in the details of the common expenditor's account for 1739–40, with payments to labourers he directly employed by the day in June, July and August 1739 amounting to £44 18s. 6d., compared with just £12 3s. 8½d. for the whole of the accounting year ending May 1739, and £14 7s. 8d. for the period September 1739 to May 1740.[72]

There is no record of what went on at the meeting on 19 July 1739 'to receive proposals from any person or persons in what manner and upon what terms and conditions they will undertake all on any part' of the work on offer. What *is* known is that the contract to maintain the wall and groins (for £270 per annum) went to John Smith, Nicholas Rolfe and Richard Coleman, three jurats of the Level, that this contract was renewed annually, on the same terms, in 1740, 1741, and 1742, and then renewed for a four-year term in 1743 at the slightly reduced cost of £255 per annum. In 1747 Smith, Coleman, and another jurat, Stephen Pilcher, secured the contract for the next year. Their contract was, in turn, renewed for a further two years at Midsummer 1748, and for a further three years at Midsummer 1750.[73]

Thus, from the summer of 1736 until Daniel Langdon's death and beyond, contracts for the repair and maintenance of Dymchurch Wall were placed with the Level's own officers, and it is difficult not to view such in-house deals with at least a modicum of suspicion. Perhaps there was little response to the public advertisements, perhaps the successful bidders beat off stiff competition, but if they did, the common clerk and jurats may well have had the opportunity to weigh in advance the contents of other 'sealed' bids, and to adjust their own accordingly, offering just the right amount to preserve a margin whilst undercutting the opposition and being able to satisfy scrutineers (themselves, among a handful of others) of the sufficiency of work they would carry out.

But whatever its demerits, the contracting-out of maintenance work to its own officers did contribute to keeping a lid on the Level's expenditure, and, thus, on the tax demanded of tenant farmers struggling through the difficult years of the 1730s and 1740s. John Fowle's contract of 1736 represented a saving of more than £150 per annum compared with that which it replaced, and the contract agreed with Smith, Rolfe and Coleman in 1739 for the same work, in turn, cost the Level just over half as much as had that with Fowle. As a result, during the early 1740s, occupiers on the Level were being asked to pay less than £1,500 per annum in wall scots, a lighter burden than at any point earlier in the 18th century. It was not until the beginning of the 1750s that occupiers were again asked to raise in excess of £2,000 in an accounting year.

Conclusion

In the minutes of the meeting of the General Lathe convened on 30 May 1751 there is an entry that reads, simply, 'Daniel Langdon, dead'. His eldest son and executor, Robert Langdon, grazier of New Romney, received the outstanding fees and salary due to his father from his successor as common expenditor, and remained a farmer on the marsh until 1763. But with Robert's passing, the surname 'Langdon' disappears from the tax registers of occupiers on 18th-century Romney Marsh and joins the long list of tenant farming families that eventually vanished from the region. However, in the evidence of his private commercial dealings, Daniel Langdon bequeaths us glimpses of many aspects of the world of a larger early-18th-century tenant farmer on the marsh. In some respects we can be sure Langdon was a typical farmer, for instance in his hiring of scattered parcels of land from different owners on a wide variety of terms and conditions. Equally, the young Daniel Langdon, and later Robert, were typical of New Romney's wealthy inhabitants in their reliance on income generated on the marsh. Less certainly, we may suppose Langdon typical in his reliance on agistment, and hypothesize that it was a crucial and complex component in the calculations of many commercial farmers. But just how vital was the metropolitan market to the commercial viability of marshland graziers, and how typical were Langdon's methods of trading with Smithfield? These questions await further investigation.

In other respects, as his public career amply demonstrates, Daniel Langdon was a privileged insider, annually 'elected' by a small and thoroughly unrepresentative clique, not formally accountable to any wider constituency. Detailed scrutiny of the 44 years of his common expenditors' accounts suggests that his behaviour in office, no better and no worse than any of his contemporaries among the 'chiefest, substantialist, most sufficient, discreetest and richest' sort, was that of a man who felt no unease about harvesting private profits from public office. These he doubtless rationalized as merely just reward for his 'great pains', but if the pursuit of fees by jurats fell short of outright peculation, it was, and remained, as the Lathe was on one occasion forced to admit, 'promiscuous'.

Acknowledgements

My ongoing research on the Romney Marsh region has been facilitated by the generous support of the Romney Marsh Research Trust. Jill and David Eddison carefully read a draft and – as ever – saved me from a number of errors, some hilarious. I am also grateful to Anne Davison for kindly supplying a number of references unearthed in the course of her current doctoral research, and for much stimulating discussion.

Notes

Abbreviations:

CCA	(Canterbury Cathedral Archives)
CKS	(Centre for Kentish Studies)
EKAC	(East Kent Archives Centre)

1. CKS P317/1/1, P309/1/1.
2. Hipkin, 'Tenant farming', 656, Table 2; EKAC S/D/FS 1, 2, /W/FSz 2.
3. EKAC S/W/FS 5A, 6B, 7A, 8, /D/FS 6, /Rm/FSz 10. These findings are explored in depth in Hipkin, 'Land ownership and land occupation', forthcoming.
4. EKAC S/Rm/FS 6, /FSc 4 p.221, /FSc 5 p. 182.
5. The following three paragraphs summarize arguments fully developed in Hipkin 'Tenant farming', and *idem*, 'Land ownership and land occupation'.
6. Bowden, *Wool Trade*, 185–217; CCA DCc/CH ANT C1222/a; EKAC S/Rm/SO 3, 21 (1697).
7. EKAC NR/AC 1, 2.
8. EKAC NR/RTh 2; The population estimate of 420–450 based on hearth tax data assumes mean household size to have been between 4.25 and 4.5; Chalklin, 'The Towns', Appendix III A. 280. Adoption of a multiplier of 1.67 instead of 1.5 would raise the population estimate based on the 1676 Compton census from 345 to 385. Between 1670 and 1699 recorded baptisms at New Romney ran at decennial averages of 16.3, 16.6 and 16.3. The suggested parish population of 450 assumes a mean birth rate of 36 per thousand. CKS P309/1/1.
9. Chalklin, *Seventeenth-Century Kent*, 24; Clark and Slack, *English Towns in Transition*, 5; Hipkin, 'Penny rent', 4–9.
10. Totals (exclusive of figures for 1676 and 1677, for which evidence is incomplete) are 708 burials and 592 baptisms.
11. CKS P309/1/1 f. 12r.
12. See Table 12.2; EKAC NR/RTh 6, /RTp 3.
13. EKAC NR/RTp 4, 12, 15.
14. For detailed analysis of developments at Rye see Hipkin, 'Maritime economy', and *idem*, 'Marshland drainage', *passim*.
15. Information contained in Table 12.3 is based on occupational data derived from the following five sources: (1) the poll tax assessments themselves, EKAC NR/RTp 12, 15; (2) the St Nicholas parish burial register for the 1690s, CKS P309/1/1; (3) probate material, CKS PRC 11, 27; (4) surviving local assessments for direct taxes authorized by post-Restoration parliaments on land, fees, offices, goods, stock and merchandize, EKAC NR/RTa 2–32. For general discussion of these taxes see Jurkowski *et al.*, *Lay Taxes*, 255-75, and Chandaman, *English Public Revenue*, 138–95 esp. 157; (5) the superb Romney, Walland and Denge Marsh scot book material that survives for the turn of the century. EKAC S/Rm/FS 6, /W/FSz 2, /FS 1A, 2, 6, /D/FS 3. For general discussion of scot book material see Hipkin, 'Tenant farming', 650–2 and *idem*, 'Land occupation', 148–54.
16. Hipkin, 'Closing ranks', 319–32.
17. These included: Norton Knatchbull, 1640; Sir Robert Honeywood, 1658; Sir Charles Beckley, 1660; Sir Charles Sedley, 1668; Sir Benjamin Bathurst and Sir William Goulston, 1685; Henry, earl of Romney, 1694; Sir William Twisden, 1695.
18. EKAC NR/RTp 15.
19. Hipkin, 'Tenant farming', 671 and n.
20. EKAC NR/RTp 15; S/Rm/FS 6, /W/FS 1A, 2, 6, /D/FS 3.
21. EKAC NR/RTa 4, 13.
22. CKS P317/1/1, P191/1/1; CCAL DCb/BT1/200, /122.
23. EKAC S/Rm/FS 6; S/W/FS 1A, 2, 6; S/D/FS 3.

24. EKAC S/Rm/FSc 4 p. 221; /FSc 5 pp. 182, 187; /FSc 6 p. 348; /FS 10; CCA DCb/BT1/200 p. 116. For most of the 1720s, 1730s and 1740s Daniel Langdon was occupying in the region of 225 acres, all of it within the Level of Romney Marsh.
25. CKS PRC 17/91/3. I owe this reference to Ann Davison; EKAC S/Rm/SO 3 pp. 21, 30–37.
26. EKAC S/Rm/FSc 5 p. 186; /FSc 6 p. 349.
27. Jones, 'Sheep on Romney Marsh'.
28. EKAC S/Rm/ Z 2, 3.
29. EKAC S/Rm/ Z 4.
30. EKAC S/Rm/Z3 f. 21r.
31. EKAC S/Rm/Z 2 ff. 41v, 62v, /Z 3 ff. 3v, 5–6, 42v.
32. EKAC S/Rm/Z 2 ff. 1v-2, 20v, 22v-23r, /Z3, f.0-1r, 30v; Jones, 'Sheep on Romney Marsh', 5.
33. EKAC S/Rm/Z 2 f. 21v.
34. Jones, 'Sheep on Romney Marsh', 13.
35. EKAC S/Rm/Z 2 ff. 17v-19r, /Z 3 ff. 18v-19. For evidence of similar rates for winter pasturing of marsh sheep on the uplands see Davison 'Symbiotic relationship'.
36. Jones, 'Sheep on Romney Marsh', 13; Davison, 'Symbiotic relationship'.
37. EKAC S/Rm/Z 2 f. 64v.
38. EKAC S/Rm/FSc 5 p. 60, /Z 2, ff. 19v-23r, /Z 3 20v, 29v-31r.
39. EKAC S/Rm/Z 3 ff. 28v-29r.
40. Jones, 'Sheep on Romney Marsh', 4–5, 7.
41. CKS U2140, E25. I owe this reference to Anne Davison.
42. EKAC S/Rm/SO 3 pp. 25, 32, 36, 38, 39, 42, 45, 47, 66, 70.
43. EKAC S/Rm/SO 3, pp. 32, 36.
44. EKAC S/Rm/Z 2, ff. 24, 27v, 30r, 32r, /Z 3, ff. 23v, 24, 40v-41r; Hipkin, 'Tenant farming', 667.
45. In 1768, Sir Edward Knatchbull, the inheritor of Sir Wyndam's estate, owned 1,920 acres in the Romney Marsh region, making him the largest private owner on the marsh. EKAC S/Rm/FSz 10; CKS U951/E12 (Hatch Memoranda). I owe this reference to Anne Davison.
46. EKAC S/Rm/Z 2, ff. 3v-5r, /Z3 f. 2r.
47. EKAC S/Rm/FAe 32-3, /FS 6, /SO 3, p. 38.
48. Jones, 'Sheep on Romney Marsh', 7.
49. Among local markets, that at Dymchurch appears to have been particularly active. Stock sold locally, or in the 'lower' markets at Tonbridge, Maidstone and Rochester was not, of course, necessarily consumed within Kent. Jobbers' purchases of livestock in these markets may well have resulted in much of it eventually serving the metropolitan consumer.
50. Westerfield, *Middlemen*, 187–202; Chartres, 'Marketing', 231–7.
51. Jones, 'Sheep on Romney Marsh', 11–12.
52. EKAC S/Rm/Z 19v, 21v, /Z 3, 29v-30r.
53. EKAC S/Rm/Z 2, f. 65r.
54. EKAC S/Rm/Z 4. Langdon correspondence bundle (unsorted), Z/2, ff. 24, 29v, 31v, /Z 3, ff. 20v, 31r, 40v.
55. Westerfield, *Middlemen*, 191.
56. EKAC S/Rm/Z 2, ff. 18v, 30-32, Z/3, ff. 20–21, /Z 4.
57. EKAC S/Rm/Z 2 ff. 42v-43, /Z3, ff. 40v-41r, /Z 4.
58. Teichman Derville, *Level and Liberty*, is the standard work on the subject, though now rather dated and not in all respects convincing.
59. EKAC Rm/AC 1 pp. 1–7. esp. p. 2; S/Rm/SO 2.
60. EKAC S/Rm/SO 3, p. 34; Rm/AC 1, pp. 157, 165–6.
61. CCA DCb BT1/122; EKAC Rm/AC 1, pp. 166–224.
62. EKAC S/Rm/ SO 1–4; /FAe 1–35; For an early 17th-century account see Beck 'Drainage of Romney Marsh', 165-7.
63. EKAC S/Rm/ SO 3, esp. pp. 30, 36-7, /SO 4, pp. 1–74, /FAe 33–35.
64. EKAC S/Rm/ SO3, p. 8.
65. EKAC S/Rm/ SO3, pp. 38, 43, 54, 70, 72, 76; /Z 2, ff. 10v-11r, /Z3 f. 12v, /FAe 33–35.
66. EKAC S/Rm/SO 3, esp. p. 62, /SO4 p. 5. Estimates based on analysis of common expenditors' accounts, 1708–1751, EKAC S/Rm/Fae 33–35.
67. CKS U951/E12 (Hatch Memoranda, 1734–5). I owe this reference to Anne Davison.
68. EKAC S/Rm/SO 4, pp. 5, 12–13, 15, 19.
69. Beck 'Drainage of Romney Marsh', 165.
70. EKAC S/Rm/FAe 34, 35.
71. EKAC S/Rm/FAe 35, /SO 4 pp. 19, 22.
72. EKAC S/Rm/FAe 35, /SO 4 pp. 26–27, 36, 38.
73. EKAC S/RM/SO 4, pp. 36, 40, 42, 46, 48, 61, 64, 72, /FAe 35.

References

Beck, D. 1995. The drainage of Romney Marsh and maintenance of Dymchurch Wall in the early 17th century, in J. Eddison (ed.) *Romney Marsh: The Debatable Ground* (Oxford University Committee for Archaeology 41), 164–8. Oxford.

Bowden, P. 1962. *The Wool Trade in Tudor and Stuart England.* London.

Chalklin, C.W. 1978. *Seventeenth-Century Kent: A Social and Economic History.* Rochester.

Chalklin, C.W. 1995. The Towns, in A. Armstrong (ed.) *The Economy of Kent, 1640–1914*, 205–34. Woodbridge.

Chandaman, C.D. 1975. *The English Public Revenue 1660–1688.* Oxford.

Chartres, J.A. 1990. The marketing of agricultural produce, 1640–1750, in J.A. Chartres (ed.), *Agricultural Markets and Trade 1500–1750*, 157–255. Cambridge.

Clark, P. and Slack, P. 1976. *English Towns in Transition, 1500–1700.* Oxford.

Davison, A. A "particularly convenient and useful" arrangement: the symbiotic agrarian economy of Romney Marsh and the surrounding region in the 18th century, in A. Long, S. Hipkin and H. Clarke (eds), *Romney Marsh: Coastal and Landscape Change Through the Ages* (Oxford University School for Archaeology 56), 190–204. Oxford.

Hipkin, S. 1995. The impact of marshland drainage on Rye Harbour, 1551–1650, in J. Eddison (ed.), *Romney Marsh: The Debatable Ground* (Oxford University Committee for Archaeology 41), 138–47. Oxford.

Hipkin, S. 1995. Closing ranks: oligarchy and government at Rye 1560–1640, *Urban History* **22**, 319–40.

Hipkin, S. 1998. The structure of land occupation in the level of Romney Marsh in the late 16th and early 17th centuries, in J. Eddison, M Gardiner and A. Long (eds) *Romney Marsh: Environmental Change and Human Occupation in a Coastal Lowland* (Oxford University Committee for Archaeology **46**), 147–63. Oxford.

Hipkin, S. 1999. The maritime economy of Rye 1560–1640, *Southern History* **20/21**, 108–42.

Hipkin, S. 2000. Sitting on his penny rent: conflict and right of common in Faversham Blean, 1595–1610, *Rural History* **11**, 1–35.

Hipkin, S. 2000. Tenant farming and short-term leasing on Romney Marsh 1587–1705, *Economic History Review* **LIII**, **4**, 646–76.

Hipkin, S. forthcoming. The structure of land ownership and land occupation in the Romney Marsh region, 1646–1834.

Jones, D. 1956. Sheep on Romney Marsh in the eighteenth century, a letter sent in 1786 and transcribed by D. Skilbeck. *Wye College, Occasional Publications* **7**.

Jurkowski, M., Smith, C.L. and Crook, D. 1998. *Lay Taxes in England and Wales 1188–1688*. London.

Teichman Derville, M. 1936. *The Level and Liberty of Romney Marsh*. Ashford.

Westerfield, R.B. 1915. *Middlemen in English Business: Particularly Between 1660–1760*. New Haven, Conn.

13. A 'Particularly Convenient and Useful' Arrangement: The Symbiotic Relationship between the Agrarian Economy of Romney Marsh and the Surrounding Region in the 18th Century[1]

Anne Davison

This paper examines the relationship between Romney Marsh and the surrounding region in the 18th century, placing the agrarian economy of the Marsh in a wider context. The substantial minority of 'absentee' Marshland occupiers and the 'lookers' they employed are considered, together with a re-evaluation of the contemporary typecasting of the 'looker'. Special consideration is given to the seasonal migration and agistment of livestock practiced in both regions. Upland farmers could own and rent land in both areas, taking in livestock for other Marshland graziers while at same time putting out their own livestock with other Upland farmers. Not all graziers over-wintered livestock on the Uplands, although many did, and while amicable, long-term arrangements were made between many farmers, marshland graziers were often exploited and their livestock suffered. The sometimes complex mechanics of this symbiosis are exemplified in the mixed farming economy of Upland farmer Samuel Flint of Biddenden, who was also a Marshland grazier. His livestock operations are considered, together with the reciprocal arrangements made between Flint and Marshland graziers for the agistment of sheep and cattle on each other's lands. The evidence suggests that agistment was a complex affair, and practiced on a wider scale than perhaps previously realised.

Introduction

The extremely fertile[2] region of Romney Marsh has long been famous for its rich pastures. Equally renowned has been its liability to flooding that necessitated 'auncient and wholesome ordinances ... for the preservation and maintenance of the bankes and walls, against the rage of the Sea.[3] Even today, the Marsh still relies on the protection afforded by Dymchurch Wall, which in the 18th century alone could require as much as £7,000 per annum to maintain,[4] funded from taxes levied on the occupiers of the land. From 1587 onwards, many of these taxation records (scot books) have survived, and early listings of occupiers, acreages held and payments due have yielded evidence of unprecedented quality for the early modern period as to the structure of land occupation over a consolidated chunk of land covering over two per cent of the county of Kent.[5] The inhabitants too were vulnerable,

not so much from the incursion of the sea but from the exceptionally high rates of death and disease brought on largely by the prevalence of 'marsh ague' that made the Level a 'sickly and contagious country'.[6] Actually living on the Marsh itself was indeed a precarious business, so that despite the immense value of the land, relatively few people lived there.[7]

For the purposes of this particular research, recent work on the scot book evidence has served to provide a skeletal framework for the 18th century in the form of lists of names of those who occupied land in the region.[8] This in turn has acted as a spring-board for further work, enabling the names listed to be linked with probate material,[9] and memoranda and account books, which, taken together, have put flesh onto the bones of those individuals who had a stake (whether large or small) in the Marsh. What follows in this paper is an insight into the often extremely

Table 13.1. Domicile of occupiers of the land in the level of Romney Marsh (source: for 1699, 1705, Hipkin (2000); for 1768, 1834, information supplied by Dr. S. Hipkin (personal communication).

complicated working lives and relationships of some of these people as revealed by the records they have left behind. These documents also shed further light onto the often close yet complex relationship of the Marsh with the surrounding region. In what follows, specific reference is made to transhumance and the agistment of livestock practiced to a greater or lesser degree by farmers and graziers in both areas. But, as will be shown, this practice also occurred *within* the Uplands as exemplified in the cases of Samuel Pattenson and Samuel Flint, who, while at the same time being Marshland graziers, also appeared to over-winter at least a proportion of their lambs, not on their home farms in the Weald, but instead with fellow Upland farmers. The overall picture is one of a kaleidoscope of activity, with frequent movement of livestock from one place to another, whether between the two regions, or simply within the Uplands. This rather complicated state of affairs is perhaps more understandable when the practicalities of the often scattered nature of landholdings are considered. According to Daniel Jones writing in 1786, many Marshland graziers would ' ... hire their land of different owners in any parcels, and at any distance, neither the compactness of their business, nor the distance being any object with them.'[10]

The mutually beneficial working partnerships that frequently arose between farmers and graziers in both regions also serves to place the agrarian economy of Romney Marsh into its proper and wider context. Moreover, this symbiotic process embraced a wide range of farmers, rich and poor alike, who either occupied land or agisted their livestock on the Marsh while living some distance away.[11] Daniel Jones wrote that Marshland graziers were 'generally in easy circumstances, though not very rich and live chiefly in villages or towns in the style of private gentlemen... If they live near they ride over their ground attended by their looker perhaps once or twice a week or perhaps not so often ... In general they have not much to do and what is done they always do before dinner.'[12]

It was usually 'absentee' graziers such as these who employed 'lookers', who lived in the immediate vicinity of the Marsh, to take care of their land and livestock, and their role will also be considered, particularly as their social status and range of occupation could often be greater than has previously been appreciated. Kinship networks contributing to financial or other arrangements also played their part within the farming fraternity, influencing the plans of those who lived, worked or drove their sheep and cattle to and from the Marsh and surrounding area. The scheme of things as a whole is brought sharply into focus in the farming account book of Samuel Flint of Biddenden,[13] a man who was at the same time an Upland farmer and Marshland grazier. His account book illustrates both how Wealden cattle rearing could be a complex affair in terms of the agistment, movement and foddering of livestock, and also – part-and-parcel of that process – how the mechanics of the partnership between Marsh and

Upland actually worked in the lives of individual farmers in the second half of the 18th century. It also reveals the extent to which the working out of this relationship influenced Flint's sphere of operations. This is of particular interest as Flint lived a full 10 miles away from Romney Marsh while remaining to some extent economically dependent on it.

Romney Marsh – an 'Absentee Society'

Table 13.1 and Figure 13.1[14] demonstrate that a substantial minority[15] of occupiers of the land on Romney Marsh at four different points in time from 1699 to 1834 lived away from the area. Approaching matters from a different angle – the study of land occupation in Kent (and the Romney Marsh region in particular) – Kain has identified two groups of farmers taken from the tithe surveys of 1840.[16] One group held land solely in the Marsh region itself, irrespective of whether they themselves lived there. However, a second group comprised farmers, who, while holding land elsewhere in the county, also occupied more than half of the land on the Marsh. Certainly, in the 18th century, the Marsh was virtually devoid of resident gentry[17] although it was not only those with money who could afford to live in the somewhat healthier upland areas of the Weald or sandstone ridge. Thus, typical of the 'middling sort' was Robert Brissenden of Woodchurch,[18] whose estate was valued at £250 14s. in May 1741 and who rented 11 acres in Kenardington from a substantial landowner John Austen of Canterbury.[19] Brissenden's widow also continued the lease after his death, for she is recorded as the tenant in 1745.[20] The humble farmer, William Raynor of Sellinge[21] kept two heifers in the Marsh, the value of which comprised nearly one third of his entire estate of £38 6s. 10¾d. devised in January 1771.

The people of Tenterden had certainly prospered as a direct result of sheep farming on the Marsh. Writing in the 18th century, Hasted found it a ' ...well-built town, having many genteel houses, or rather seats, interspersed throughout it.'[22] These belonged to well-to-do families such as Curteis, Haffenden, Blackmore and Stace, ' ... and several others, most of whose wealth, as well as that of the inhabitants of this town in general, has arisen from its near neighbourhood to Romney-Marsh, where most of them have some occupation in the grazing business.'[23] Hasted cited one Tenterden grazier, Mr John Mantel, as an earlier example 'of one of the instances of the quick accumulation of the riches from Romney Marsh ...'[24] because it had taken him just 14 years (to 1687) to make enough money to buy not only a substantial residence, but also other land and property, which in terms of rental income alone was worth £800 per annum. Equally representative of those who had profited from their association with Romney Marsh half a century later was Humphrey Wightwicke,[25] who on his death in 1721, left an estate worth £2,434 9s. 8d., half of which consisted of

19: (margin top left)

wright John Martin[35] gained an income from a variety of sources. Apart from his trade, he was paid 14s. 8d. in 1763 for keeping six bullocks for yeoman-farmer Thomas Merrells of Tenterden, and in addition to being the owner-occupier of one acre of marshland close to his home in Hamstreet, gained rental income from properties both there and in Smeeth, and also owned a shop in Brabourne occupied by his daughter.[36]

The examples of Reynolds and Carpenter warn us to not necessarily take too readily Hasted's contemporary descriptions of the 'looker', who was typecast as a rather wretched individual 'of mean condition', who, along with other Marsh dwellers, were 'of the lower sort ... mostly men as are employed in the occupations and management of the level, or a kind of seafaring men, who follow an illicit trade, as well by land as water'.[37] Defoe erred in equal measure in lumping them together with others of the 'lesser sort', who, perhaps throwing caution to the wind, formed part of the steady stream of migrants to the bleak landscapes of the marshlands of south-east England in the hope, at the very least, of earning higher wages in this unhealthy area, perhaps 'for the advantage of good farms'– or even of making a living out of the lucrative profits to be gained from smuggling.[38] The living conditions of these diseased, worn down and threadbare people added to the already grim picture. Marshmen were graphically described as huddling together in dark, damp and cramped conditions in their ill-ventilated huts, such as the dilapidated dwellings in Appledore described by Hasted as 'meanly built, and mostly inhabited by graziers, lookers and smugglers'.[39] This depiction may well have been true to an extent, and, what is more, if animals were kept inside as well, such places would have made ideal 'incubating chambers'[40] for the mosquitoes responsible for 'marsh fever' and the debilitating bouts of shaking and shivering that went with it. However, *all* inhabitants of the marshlands were susceptible to the scourge of endemic malaria[41] – and neither Reynolds, Carpenter nor Martin were exempt. Equally, the sight of people who were quite obviously extremely unwell, their teeth chattering uncontrollably in the summer heat and in no fit state for anything, must certainly have contributed to the stereotype.

Yet it was people such as these who played a crucial role in the symbiosis between Marsh and Upland. Indeed, Daniel Jones was at pains to describe the 'looker' as one who had more of a full-time, even desirable occupation, enjoying,

> '... a house at an easy rent; ... the keep of a cow at a moderate charge, ... all the fat of the dead sheep and the lamb skins if he lambs them and has the privilege of keeping a horse upon his master's ground *gratis* and is paid besides for whatever work he does upon the land; all which enables him to live in a comfortable manner and with a few other privilege if prudent, he can even save money.

> 'His business is to ride about ground, which he generally

does once a day ... to see whether there be any sheep fallen into the ditches, and whether the fence is anywhere broken down; he also counts the sheep and sees whether any of them is ailing or has been struck by the fly. He has always a dog with him ... He also attends and assists his master in everything with regard to the stock, that is done upon the land. One man can look after from three to five hundred acres of land or more, and very frequently looks after land for several different masters at the same time and if any of them live at a considerable distance he perhaps has a bed in his house to accommodate them ...'.[42]

Transhumance: Romney Marsh and the Seasonal Migration of Livestock

Romney Marsh has always been an area of 'detached' pasture in the sense of being used for distant communities for transhumance. Evidence of this ancient practice of seasonal migration can be seen in the many sunken lanes running south and west across Kent that were originally droveways for those who took their flocks and herds to the Weald and Marshlands for the summer.[43] It is also reflected in place-names. Burmash, for example, means 'borough marsh' – in this case, one belonging to the people of Canterbury.[44] The interdependence of Marsh-Upland has arguably long been fundamental to the agrarian economy, with migration of livestock between the two regions every spring and autumn so that ' ... all the narrow little lanes leading up from the Levels were alive with the plaintive bleating of the droves.'[45] John Boys reported in 1796 that during the summer, while their own pastures were reserved for hay, Upland farmers would need to place some of their cattle out to keep with Marsh graziers, for a period lasting for about 20 weeks commencing in mid-May. This arrangement was reciprocated, with Upland farmers keeping Marsh lambs for the graziers for around 30 weeks over the winter.[46] Indeed, for the Marsh grazier, this seasonal migration was important, firstly because of climate conditions and also due to the problems of maintaining the same stock levels all-year-round.

Firstly, the Marsh climate, 'evill in winter, grievous in summer and never good'[47] has low rainfall, hot dry summers, cold, windy, rather bleak winters, and often bad weather in late spring.[48] The strong constitution of the Romney Marsh breed of sheep has persisted in the region to the virtual exclusion of other breeds as it can withstand the severe weather better than most. Nevertheless, lambs are still by nature vulnerable and hence, have preferably been kept on the Uplands in the winter, then taken down to the Marsh in the spring.[49]

Secondly, although the Marsh could arguably carry more sheep per acre than anywhere else in the country, this was only true for the summer months. Even today, although the land can support the equivalent of seven mature sheep per acre in the summer, this is cut to just over two sheep per acre in the winter months.[50] Likewise

Fig.
pari:
Snar
Lym
Selli
Broo
Pluc

a 12:
on th
Wigl
by m
part
Mars
was t
they
sheep

Farr

Typic
Mars
Wille
5s. 2:
home
at Ne
both
and £
simil

in the 18th century, whereas typically, five sheep per acre could be kept 'according as the summer may turn out for grass',[51] this might be greatly reduced in the winter. Some farmers had sufficient pasture at their disposal elsewhere to over-winter stock. Upland farmers would put lambs on their own stubble, meadows, pasture or turnip fields, and in addition feed them on beans, peas, straw or hay in order to prevent scouring. In the 1760s, Wealden gentleman-farmer Jeremiah Smith[52] ran just such a mixed farm, with 130 acres at home and a further 121 acres leased on Romney Marsh Level. With 52 cattle plus 290 sheep he would have needed land in both regions to support their needs throughout the year. No doubt at least some of his cattle would have spent the summer fattening on the Marsh, with a good proportion of lambs on the home farm for the winter.

However, not every farmer was in such a fortunate position. For the late 1730s, Sir Wyndham Knatchbull's 'Hatch Memoranda'[53] demonstrate that even a substantial grazier like Henry Read (the largest tenant farmer on the Marsh at the time) could have problems in finding enough winter pasture for his sheep. From time to time Knatchbull would meet informally with Read as well as some of his other tenants and Knatchbull's notes provide a unique insight into some of their conversations. In July 1735, he noted that Read was to have some of his tegs, but at the same time Read had asked Knatchbull whether he would be prepared to take in some of his lambs to keep on part of his Upland estate. Knatchbull had promised to send him word when he had made up his mind. At some point he had clearly agreed to do so, and by July 1739 he noted that Read was to send him 80 lambs to keep from August until Ladyday 1740. In the meantime Knatchbull had been advised that the going rate for taking in 80 to 100 lambs for that period would be 1d per week per lamb. Interestingly, as Hipkin's research on Daniel Langdon shows, a similar rate for agistment was being charged as far back as the early 1720s, for on August 21st 1723, Langdon recorded that he had 'Sent to my father at Ulcombe 140 lambs at 1d. per week to Ladyday …'.[54] Knatchbull had calculated that the 20 acres he had in mind for the keeping of Read's lambs would then be laid in for hay after they had been taken off again in the Spring. In this case, the ratio of stock to winter pasture on the Uplands was between four and five lambs per acre.

Knatchbull, the largest landowner on the Marsh, was himself not immune from the problem of over-wintering livestock. He too used land on his home farm (the 'Mersham Hatch' estate) to over-winter sheep. In October 1742, 67 sheep kept on the Marsh at the 'Schoolland' besides a further 92 ewes and ewe tegs were 'brought home for want of grass'.[55] While some farmers would keep their lambs until the following year and then sell them off as tegs, it was common practice at Michaelmas for those who had insufficient winter pasture to sell off

their old sheep, all their weather lambs and the refuse of their ewe lambs. These were then bought up by the upland farmers who bred few if any sheep themselves. Instead, they would simply go down to the Marsh and buy up as many as they could accommodate in the winter.[56] Knatchbull did likewise later that October when he 'Sold to Mr Andrews all the ewes, barrens and weather lambs belonging to the Schoolland; so remain only the 28 ewlambs, which I did not sell'.[55]

Although Knatchbull's documents paint a positive picture of generally good working relationships between landlord and tenant, and of amicable deals struck between them for the keeping of livestock, this state of affairs was not necessarily the norm. Insufficient pasture to over-winter stock could be the scourge of many a grazier, who might find himself in the unhappy position of being dependent on, or even exploited by, Upland farmers. In a letter dated March 25th 1797 to Sir Joseph Banks, William Deedes junior commented that Marshland graziers needed to shear their lambs, who were 'very subject to the Fly, and that our Graziers are obliged to put out their Lambs where the Keep is often very indifferent.'[57] Daniel Price, writing somewhat later during the Napoleonic Wars, noted that many complained that the Upland farmers who took in their marsh lambs would

' … take every unfair advantage of them if they can: they advance the price of keep every year, or every other year; they keep more lambs than they usually did, or ought to keep; and they continue to maintain them worse. These are serious things, that ought to occupy the attention of the graziers more than they do; and were they to hold together, an effectual remedy might be provided against this imposition.'[58]

Winter keep of lambs was not without its risks for the animals themselves. Writing in 1796, Boys reported that lambs returning from the Uplands after a bad winter 'frequently go home nearly starved; from which they sometimes die in great numbers when they get into good keep'[59], and this situation had apparently not improved half a century later when Buckland reported that

'The greatest disadvantage which the flock masters of Romney Marsh experience is the necessity of sending their lambs long distances up the country to keep during winter. The period extends from September to the beginning of April (30 weeks) and the price commonly paid is £5 or £6 per score. The young sheep are thus placed beyond the control and care of the graziers during a large portion of that most important period in the life of an animal – the first year – a period on which will depend, according to the treatment it has received, its entire future condition. Vast numbers of 'tegs' (as the young sheep are termed) return to the marsh in the spring in a half-starved condition and so debilitated are they that many die soon after they are put upon richer pasture…'[60]

Agistment: 'A Particularly Convenient and Useful' Arrangement

Transhumance and the agistment of livestock was not only for graziers wishing to over-winter their stock on the Uplands, for they were also obliged to keep a strict watch on their marshland pastures in the summer. To ensure that the grass would not grow too long, they took in cattle to keep at very low prices.[61] According to Daniel Jones, many Wealden farmers, whose emphasis lay traditionally in cattle rearing and fattening for the meat market, found the Marshland pastures essential during the summer months, for at this time, ' ... when the grass is sufficiently grown the graziers take in the barren and fatting cattle of the [Upland] farmers while their meadows are laid in at a certain price per head, *so that the one party is particularly convenient and useful to the other*' [my italics].[62] Such arrangements ran right through the spectrum of the farming community and could be even more flexible than those suggested by Jones. Hence, the evidence suggests that Sir Wyndham Knatchbull agisted his sheep on Henry Read's marshland over the summer months: for in July 1735, when Read had asked Knatchbull if he would take in his 80 to 100 lambs to keep for the winter, Knatchbull had already noted that Reed would have his tegs.[63] A successor, the rentier Sir Edward Knatchbull (who by 1763 had inherited Mersham Hatch) also kept cattle there in the summer. Knatchbull also made various arrangements with some of his other tenants. For instance, he kept lambs over the winter on his Mersham estate for John Dunk, a substantial tenant farmer who leased 439.5 out of his 591.5 acres on Romney Marsh from Knatchbull. At the same time Knatchbull put his own lambs out to keep with tenant farmer Joseph Frind of Postling. Moreover, Frind grazed his own cattle on the Mersham estate – and all of these arrangements appeared to have been on an ongoing, regular basis.[64] The Knatchbull-Read relationship was certainly still going strong some 30 years later – and on October 12th 1770 Knatchbull paid Read £3 18s. for keeping his bullocks on the Marsh for 13 weeks.[65] Indeed, Sir Wyndham had earlier made a similar arrangement, and in working out what he might sell his cattle for in 1737, had calculated that 'My 3 cows which are come out of the Marsh will probably weigh out 20 score a piece, and will be worth by Michaelmas £12; but I must not refuse £11.'[66]

So widespread were these arrangements that farmers and graziers had their own recognised set of unwritten rules for the over-wintering of lambs and summer keep for cattle. A Cranbrook farmer reported to Daniel Price that as a rule of thumb, 'The proportion of lambs to bullocks, is five lambs to be kept by the farmer in winter, for one head of cattle by the grazier in summer; but if more sheep or cattle are admitted, the price varies in consequence'.[67] As soon as they first came to the Uplands, our Cranbrook farmer would divide up the sheep into lots of about 10 each, and put them on his stubble, then onto the seeds, and a month prior to their return to the Marsh in the Spring they were fed on old pastures. By changing lamb pasture regularly – perhaps as often as once a week - losses were minimised, and although winter was by its very nature the worst time for casualties Price noted that, ' ... the grazier that has the least refuse in his flock, discovers the greatest share of merit ...'.[68]

Upland Farmers, Marshland Graziers: 1. Samuel Pattenson

The reciprocal relationships in the later 18th century and early 19th century as described by contemporary writers (like Boys, Jones and Price) might seem relatively simple at first glance. In reality however, often complex arrangements were entered into, as the examination of the gentleman-grazier Samuel Pattenson of Biddenden amply demonstrates. Pattenson was an Upland farmer, who owned 12 acres of pasture on the home farm, and a few jottings on a small scrap of paper that have survived from the 1730s give some vital clues as to the complex nature of Pattenson's farming economy.[69]

In terms of income, besides recent sales of wool, cattle and oats, Pattenson noted rent received from Messrs Carpenter and Rolf respectively for land on the Marsh.[70] On the debit side, he owed £11 to other farmers in the Biddenden area for winter 'lamb keeping'. £10 was set aside to buy some more bullocks. Rental was also due for lands in Biddenden and also for 20 acres of fresh marshland in Ivychurch in Walland Marsh that Pattenson occupied from the early 1730s to 1763.[71] A further £14 rent was due to Stace (probably Robert) – for land in Ebony, lying on the Marsh-edge, a few miles south-east of Biddenden.[72]

Thus, Pattenson owned land in Biddenden and on the Marsh, some of which he rented out. He was also a tenant himself – again, not only in his locality, but also in the Marsh. He had a sheep flock, from which he gained an income from wool – but despite having landholdings in both Marsh and Upland, he apparently put a proportion of his lambs out to keep with other Upland farmers, most probably over the winter period. He was also a commercial arable farmer – and in addition, as per the traditional emphasis of Wealden farming – he concentrated on cattle rearing.

Furthermore, executorship accounts in 1770 also reveal that Pattenson – who put his own lambs out to keep with other farmers – actually *kept* lambs for Marshland grazier Henry Read – son of the late Henry Read – whose mutually beneficial relationship with the Knatchbull family has already been mentioned. On May 6th 1770, Read paid £5-17s for the keeping of 39 lambs for 30 weeks through the winter. Indeed, this arrangement was to continue without interruption as Pattenson's successor, Samuel Flint, was to continue keeping Read's 39 lambs for a further five weeks, and for which Flint received 19s-6d. Indeed, they did similar business until the following year. Thus, Read's working relationship with Messrs. Pattenson and Flint, and the previously discussed long-term business link with the Knatchbull family, show the continuity of relationships within the farming community that existed at this time.

Upland Farmers, Marshland Graziers: 2. Samuel Flint

Samuel Flint had strong family connections with the Marsh. By 1714, his grandfather Samuel Pattenson had already married Hannah, daughter of William Blackmore, part of the same Tenterden family whose wealth had come directly from marshland livestock farming.[73] There were also early connections between the Pattenson and Flint families, as Samuel Flint's maternal great-aunt had married Abraham Flint, a wealthy brazier and minor landowner (of some 54 acres) on the Marsh.[74] In the early 1730s Abraham had set up his youngest son James in business by going halves with him on a lease of land in Bonnington owned by Nicholas Toke. In 1737, James also inherited a further 34 acres in Bilsington from his father (some of which he later rented out).[75] Styled 'Grazier' in 1772, James had graduated to 'Gentleman' some 14 years later,[76] which status was doubtless augmented by the purchase of some 96 acres of land in Walland Marsh, an area reputedly the most rich and fertile in the whole region.[77]

By 1766 the now elderly Samuel Pattenson had decided to give up active involvement in at least a proportion of his farming business and this provided the opportunity for his grandson (who lived with him at the time)[78] to take it on. (Flint was probably also already farming some 60 acres in Biddenden belonging to his mother.)[79] Goods and stock in Biddenden were appraised that November, and Flint also borrowed £160 from his grandfather Pattenson to complete the purchase of 129 sheep, two oxen, a black mare, 21 loads of hay, farm equipment, eight acres of seeds plus all the wood growing on land that Pattenson rented in Biddenden. There follows a full account (at least for the first three years or so) on almost a day-to-day basis, of expenditure, both large and small, ranging from a bill for 2d. to mend the lock on a stable door, purchase of personal items, mole-catcher's bills and wages paid out, to records of produce sold, sales, purchases and movement of livestock. In later years entries regarding the minutiae of expenditure tail off somewhat, but nevertheless Flint still recorded wages paid to local farm labourers involved in the arable side of the business, and kept careful records of the movement, feeding and keeping of livestock – especially cattle – both locally and on the Marsh. The shift in emphasis in Flint's account keeping may be due, at least in part, to the fact that in the early days he apparently had to borrow quite heavily to get established, and probably needed to keep track of every penny. Certainly during the earlier years, even small purchases like three new mole traps for 3d. or the occasional sale of a lamb skin at 1s. did not go unrecorded. In addition to the initial £160 borrowed from his grand-father in November 1766, he also borrowed extensively from his brother Richard and sister Hannah, and by August 1769 his mother had lent him a total of £100. In January 1768 he repaid £38 4s. 10½d. (loan plus interest) due to his sister Ann Love – but had to borrow a further £28 from Samuel Pattenson in order to do this.[80] In January 1768 he also took out a further loan of £25 from a Mr Pullen, which he repaid in June. Being in debt to ones relatives did not excuse Flint from paying the going rate of interest[81] and he made various payments until the last recorded entry relating to loans, made in August, 1771. Once Flint came into his share of Pattenson's estate sometime after July 1770, his cash-flow would have eased somewhat[82] and therefore noting down every expense was perhaps less necessary.

Variations in incompleteness notwithstanding, Flint's account vividly portrays a labour-intensive mixed farm – a hive of activity with everything put to good use. The summer of 1769 saw his only personal spending spree which included five new shirts (made by his sister) and two pairs of new shoes. His shorts, watch and shoes were also repaired – and he bought a spaniel puppy for 1s. 6d. There was little room for luxuries, and even after Pattenson's death Flint still economised, and rather than buy a new coat, he paid out 1s. 6d. to have his grandfather's coat altered to fit. His was an operation in a different league to that of Sir Wyndham Knatchbull, who (some 20 years earlier) was often preoccupied with making a careful note of the contents of his wine cellar, sometimes especially replenished from London. Flint's forays in this direction were frugal by comparison. He bought one gallon of brandy in 1767 (and more two years later) and wine was home brewed.[83] Nevertheless, there were limits to Flint's frugality, for he did manage to go to the theatre on at least one occasion, for inside the account book is a playbill for a production in Cranbrook by the Canterbury Company of Comedians. (He completely covered the back of the sheet with notes of wood sold to various customers.) He also subscribed to a newspaper – probably 'The Kentish Post' – which he shared with someone else by going halves, paying an annual contribution of 9s-3¼d. His desire to keep up-to-date also extended to matters agricultural: Flint was prepared to try out new things, for in April 1770 he paid 10s. for two bushels of 'this new sort of barley'.

Flint's recorded 'overheads' were quite high, and as can be seen from Table 13.2, in 1767–68, he incurred a deficit of just over £34. The introduction of capital in the form of loans must have provided a much-needed boost to help offset the loss. However, Flint was in good company: Sir Edward Knatchbull made no profit at all in 1770–71 and a loss of £56 in 1775.[84]

Flint's arable operations were highly labour-intensive. In the early years his chief farm hand, John Day, (who rented a house from Flint) did the lion's share of the work, and they had an informal arrangement whereby every so often they would tally up bills for work done or monies owed and settle up accordingly.[85] 1767–1768 was a fairly

Table 13.2. Samuel Flint of Biddenden – Recorded income and expenditure, October 1767 – October 1768 (source: CKS U301 E6).

		£ s. d.
Income:	Sales of sheep, wool, cattle, etc.	152–04.–00.
	Sales of crops, etc.	27–04.–10¼.
	Keeping sheep/cattle for others	01–17.–00.
Sales total		180–05.–10¼.
Expenditure:	Rental, taxes, on land/property	81–12.–04½.
	Livestock purchase, materials + wages	99–06.–05¾.
	Agisting cattle/sheep	15–05.–05.
	Interest paid on loans /part repayments	
	Of Principal monies (see note)*	18–01.–04.
Expenditure total		214–05.–07¼.
Leaves total deficit for year		£34–09s.–07d.

* Note : Samuel Flint paid interest during the year on the loans he had already taken out and in January 1768 he borrowed a further £28 from his grandfather to repay principal money borrowed + interest to his sister Ann Love. He therefore used £10 4s. 10½d. from his own funds to repay the interest and some of the principal money, and the same day paid interest of £1 8s. 5½d. on the existing loan from his mother. (The £28 loan from Samuel Pattenson was repaid in April 1769, along with board and lodging allowance from Michaelmas 1767-68, at £10 8s.) On May 6th 1768 he took out another loan from his mother, for £40. In June, he paid £6 8s. interest on the original loan of £160 from Samuel Pattenson, which paid for his purchase of Pattenson's stock and effects, etc.

	£ s. d.
Own funds used	10–04.–10½.
Interest to Mary Flint	01–08.–05½.
Interest to Samuel Pattenson	06–08.–00.
Total	**£18–01s.–04d.**

typical year. In the autumn, apart from ploughing, lime and marle were spread on the fields. Barley and oats were threshed, the clover stack thatched and wheat seeds purchased. In January and February 1768 much hedging and ditching was done and 150 loads of dung spread on the fields. Lime was brought in from Brenchley, Day spent 10 days ploughing, and Flint purchased barley seeds. There was more hedging and ditching work in April, while five acres of tares and nearly four acres of barley were sown. In June, attention was paid to weeding and control of thistles, more ditching, stacking straw and making faggots. In addition to John Day's labour, Flint employed extra help at 'peak' times, especially for autumn and spring ploughing, and also during the busy summer months – for the crucial harvesting period. Day's family joined in with several others in this on-going task that began in July and continued well into September, during which time nearly four acres of clover and six acres of grass were cut, wheat and barley gathered in and a haystack prepared. Corn then had to be cleaned, threshed and stored in the granary. More than £26 was paid out in wages for that year. However, this would have been largely offset by the steady stream of income amounting to just under £25, from

recorded sales of barley, oats, wheat and wood products over the same period.[86] Flint also grew apples and pears commercially, and purchased plum, peach and apricot trees. There are also recorded sales of willow, ash, hoppoles, turnips and flax – and a small quantity of pork.

While crop sales generated enough income to cover most of the wages bill, much was produced to cater for Flint's own specialised livestock operation, the importance of which is reflected in the £152 4s. income generated in 1767–68 from recorded sales of sheep, wool, cattle and associated products.[87] While cattle manure improved soil fertility, tears, hay and clover provided essential winter fodder for cattle and sheep. As for the Marshland dimension of Flint's enterprise, Daniel Jones presumed that Marshland graziers kept a register of all their stock, noting down numbers and in which fields they were kept, how many died, sales, purchases and expenses incurred, in order to keep precise accounts for each year.[88] Flint's account book is not quite so exact, but nevertheless gives some insight into livestock movement, sales and purchases.[89]

For 1767–68, recorded sheep and cattle sales took place in six months of the year. In October-November 1767, 10

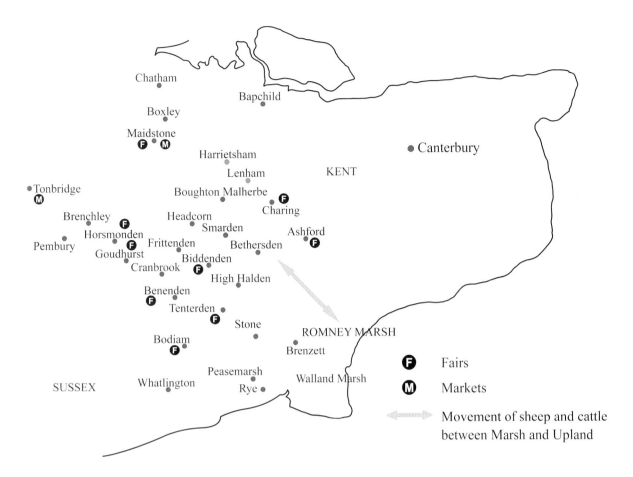

Fig. 13.2. Samuel Flint of Biddenden – sphere of operations, 1766–82.

fatt sheep were sold locally[90] and a further seven to a regular customer, butcher Thomas Avery of Bapchild. In March 1768 Flint sold four sheep locally and also drove another 26 to Maidstone Market where he sold half to Avery and the rest to a man from Chatham.[91] In April 1768 Avery bought two fatt oxen for £29, and in July one fatt calf was sold, probably to a local. In August 1768, William Wildish of Harrietsham (another regular customer) bought eight sheep, but this was part of a £47 deal that also included seven cattle. In this and the following years, apart from local customers who bought mainly sheep skins, mutton or the odd calf or sheep, Flint continued to sell further afield. His brother-in-law from Headcorn bought a steer, and two old rams were sold to James Blackmore of Tenterden. (Blackmore also hired a ram in 'the riding season'[92] each November, as did 'Cousin' Austen). Other customers came from Halden and Frittenden – and Flint also took his stock to sell at some of the 'lower markets'[93] such as Tonbridge or Maidstone. He regularly attended local fairs where, in the main, he purchased cattle, and Fig. 13.2 shows their location and the geographical extent of Flint's sphere of operations. Fairs and markets provided a good opportunity for farmers and graziers to meet and arrange deals. Thus, on 6th May

1770, at Tenterden Fair, Flint not only purchased two steers from Richard Woodman of Peasemarsh in Sussex, but also met up with Henry Read – for it was on that date that Read paid him for lamb-keep on Pattenson's Upland pastures for the previous winter, and they also made arrangements together for future business. From 1779 to 1781 Flint recorded sales of livestock (mainly cattle) to just two customers, Robert Colebrook of Tenterden and Robert Cobb, both of whom occupied land on Romney Marsh.[94] As for wool sales, these averaged just over £13 each year from 1767 to 1770.[95]

Much of Flint's record-keeping concerned the rearing of livestock within the vicinity of Biddenden, which discloses the traditional emphasis of the Upland farmer on cattle rearing and fattening. Careful notes were made as to exact winter foddering requirements (with clover or straw) not only for cattle, but also for the working oxen and horses that were kept in the Pound and Close on the late Pattenson's home farm, or taken down to the Marsh-edge Stace Land. Examination of the account book shows that in both the keeping and movement of cattle and sheep, nothing remained static for long. Not only was there a nearly constant stream of livestock traffic from one place to another, but the evidence suggests that a significant proportion of cattle agisted on Flint's land was for locals. Thus, on 9th October 1771, Flint took in to keep a bullock for a local, Mr Witherden, for an unspecified period, for which he charged £2 2s. Five days later, he drove six of his own lambs 'To Freeman's' (an Upland farmer) where they stayed for the next 23 weeks over the winter. On November 11th 1771, two of Flint's steers were taken up to the Pound in Biddenden,[96] to be foddered three times a day. A week later, Flint took in to keep one cow for John Day. On November 20th 1771, a further 15 of Flint's lambs were driven to Thomas Brittenden's (another Upland farmer) where they were kept until April 4th 1772. On December 20th 1771, Flint took two of his own cows to 'The Old House' in Biddenden – again, to be foddered three times a day. One week later, he took in to keep 12 sheep belonging to his brother-in-law. As for cow agistment, although John Day initially paid £3 a year, Flint's charges gradually increased, so that in June 1772, he made a special note that he had agreed to keep Day's cow at £3 10s. per annum, excluding foddering. By 1775 Flint was charging £4 per annum to keep a milch cow for another local. Flint's charges may have been on the high side, for in 1772 it was Knatchbull's belief that 40s. per dairy cow per annum was the going rate.[97]

As we have already seen, 'lookers' on Romney Marsh were more diverse in their social status and range of occupation than the contemporary typecasting would lead us to believe. Moreover, the terminology was not confined to the Marsh, for just as there were 'lookers' who kept an eye on the land and livestock of farmers who lived a distance away, so too there could be similar arrangements made for livestock on the Uplands. Thus, in November 1769, the respectable Flint received 10s. 6d. 'for half a year's looking' for Jonathan Austen, an Upland farmer.

Moreover, even as Flint was taking in sheep for Marshland graziers, in terms of his own flock (standing at 125 sheep and 36 lambs in May 1767) although it is uncertain where they were kept in the summer, it appears that he moved a good proportion of his lambs to the fields of other Upland farmers for the winter months every year up to 1775. This included 12 weather tegs driven to 'granpapas ground' in September 1767. In August 1768, Flint 'drove to my granpapa Ground 11 weather taggs for him to keep the winter at 2s. 6d. per score' followed by a further 10 weathers that October (1768). Five of these were taken away in February 1769, the rest in April. There were apparently few casualties, part from one lamb recorded as lost over the summer of 1769. Like his grandfather Samuel Pattenson before him, Flint kept lambs over the winter for Marshland grazier Henry Read (and additionally James Blackmore) while wintering his own lambs elsewhere.

Commercial connections were also facilitated by the convenience of kinship networks. This is illustrated in an entry for September 7th 1769, when Flint 'Then took in to keep of my Cousin James Blackmore of Tenterden 20 Marsh Lambs at two shillings per score'. These were kept for 30 weeks until April 1770, with only one lamb lost. Flint was paid £2 17s., but at the same time bought seven teggs from Blackmore for £5. The following month Flint 'Then put out to keep to my Cousin James Blackmore three steers to fatt ... ' on Walland Marsh,[98] where they were kept until 4th September, at a cost of £2 5s. In the meantime, on June 7th 1770, Flint drove a further two runts down to Blackmore's to fatten, where they remained until 30th July[99] – and similar arrangements continued between them until Blackmore's death. On the same day (4th September) that Flint collected his steers, he also took in 50 lambs to keep for 'Mr Reeds' – and Flint's steers and Read's lambs were probably driven together up to the farm in Biddenden, where the lambs remained until May 8th 1771. Flint kept several fatting steers over the winter at the Pound in Biddenden, foddered three times a day. On 2nd February, 1771, two of these were taken on Flint's behalf by Thomas Paine to Tunbridge Market where they were sold for £18. Flint noted, 'Bought the same in and gave £10 10s.'– a differential of £7 10s.

Flint also had dealings with Henry Earle of Brenzett – ranked among the top five per cent of tenant farmers on Romney Marsh in 1775.[100] Unusually, but indicative of the flexibility that marked so many of the complex Marsh-Upland arrangements, it was Flint – the Upland farmer – who in September 1773 looked after Earle's bullocks. In June 1775 he was also paid 3s. 1d. 'For washing of young Mr Earle's sheep, also for tarr [and] also for shearing of the said 20 sheep and winding wool .' Flint then carried Earle's wool to Tenterden for which he charged 1s. Conversely, Flint also put bullocks into Earle's keep to fatten on the Marsh over the summer of 1774, and in June 1779 kept a bay colt on Earle's ground at Brenzett. In 1775, curiously, and for reasons that remain unclear, Flint kept 20 lambs for 13 weeks for Earle through the summer (from May to August) – presumably on the Uplands, although precisely where they were kept is unknown.[101] By May 1779 Philip Ovenden of Tenterden had taken over occupation of the 78 acres in Walland Marsh[102] previously occupied by his late brother-in-law Blackmore, and thereafter Flint and Ovenden agisted sheep and cattle on each other's lands.

Conclusion

This paper has examined some aspects of the symbiotic relationship of the agrarian economy that existed in the 18th century between the Romney Marsh and surrounding Upland region, and has tried to hint at some of the complexities involved therein. The Marsh has been considered, not in isolation, but in its proper, wider context for the period. For an 'absentee society', an area of low population density, the Romney Marsh region has shown itself to be a remarkably complex arena in terms of the business arrangements made by those absentee occupiers of the land, in relation to others who lived, worked and farmed in the area. The evidence has demonstrated that there was much more to the 'looker' in terms of social status and diversity of occupation than the contemporary stereotyping would have us believe – and also that the terminology associated with 'looking' was not confined solely to the Marsh, but could also apply to the Weald.

The common aim of the farming fraternity – the well-being of their respective agrarian economies, whether on the Marsh or Uplands, or a combination of the two – resulted in the forging of a myriad of business relationships – and this paper has attempted to catch a glimpse of some of these. Many of the arrangements made between individual farmers were amicable, continuing through succeeding generations of landlords and tenants, and appeared to work well, as shown in the examples of the reciprocal relationships made between Knatchbull and Read and also between Pattenson, Read and Flint. However, as has been illustrated from the reports of contemporaries, many Marshland graziers found themselves at the mercy of the less diligent – or possibly even unscrupulous – Upland farmers who provided winter pasture for Marsh lambs.

The Marsh-Upland farming economy of the 18th century worked in a variety of dimensions. The scot book listings of apparently unconnected occupiers of the land in the region belie the reality – a huge network of inter-dependent people, both substantial and modest landowners and tenants, rich and poor alike – rubbing shoulders with one another on the roads, in the fields, or at the various local markets and fairs that provided a natural rendezvous for members of the farming community, where deals were struck and reciprocal arrangements made.

It has been claimed that the seasonal migration of livestock dominated the agrarian economy of the region in the 17th century, and in modified form until the 20th century.[103] However, in the light of the evidence presented in this paper, this argument, at least in one respect, is somewhat exaggerated, and needs some qualification. Firstly, much of the movement of sheep specifically affected vulnerable Marsh lambs removed to the Uplands for the winter, whilst the burden of transhumance with respect to cattle had to do with summer fattening on the Marsh. Moreover, not all farmers moved all of their sheep and cattle. On the other hand, however, for those farmers who did agist a proportion of their livestock on each other's

lands, especially within their local neighbourhood, the mechanics of this process would appear to be a much more commonplace – and complex – affair than has previously been realised. There is no doubt, then, that taken as a whole, the scale of the importance of livestock movements both within and between regions should not be under-estimated. Indeed, the scale and complexity may indeed have been greater than previously appreciated. The multi-faceted nature of agistment is exemplified in the farming operations of Samuel Flint, and the study of his account book has shown the degree to which agistment occurred: Flint agisted his own lambs with other Upland farmers while taking in cattle to keep on the home farm for his neighbours – which usually involved perhaps just one or two beasts per individual local farmer at any one time. However, he also took in lambs over the winter for some of the highest-ranking graziers on the Marsh – for those such as Read, Blackmore and Earle. Yet this particular practice worked both ways: for Flint, the Wealden cattle farmer, the Marsh was at the very least a valuable asset, and quite possibly essential to his farming economy, for it enabled him to fatten some of his beasts on the lands of these selfsame substantial graziers, while a proportion of his acreage at home was laid in for hay. Such arrangements appeared to work well and to the mutual benefit of all concerned – and the fact that in the main, these partnerships were long-standing, would indicate that all parties were satisfied with the level of care provided for their livestock, and the virtual absence of recorded losses or casualties would lend weight to this. For them at least, the symbiosis certainly was, as Daniel Jones suggested, a 'particularly convenient and useful' arrangement.

Acknowledgements

This paper forms part of ongoing postgraduate research at Canterbury Christ Church University College, examining the agrarian economy of the Romney Marsh region during the 18th century. Special thanks are due to my supervisor, Dr Stephen Hipkin, for his enthusiasm, encouragement, advice and constructive criticism, all of which have been very much appreciated. Thanks are due to the staff of the Centre for Kentish Studies in Maidstone and the East Kent Archives Centre at Whitfield. I am also grateful to Paul Davison for drawing up the maps.

Notes

Abbreviations used:
CKS   Centre for Kentish Studies
EKAC   East Kent Archives Centre

1. Jones, 'Sheep on Romney Marsh', 13. Taken from ' ... in the summer when the grass is sufficiently grown the graziers take in the barren and fatting cattle of the farmers while their meadows are laid in at a certain price per head, *so that the one party is particularly convenient and useful to the other.*' [My italics.]
2. A mixture of alluvial soil combined with marine deposits and Wealden clay – Roper, 'Romney Marsh – the Fifth Quarter' in *Cantium 4, Summer 1972*, 28.
3. Lambarde, cited in Roper, 'Romney Marsh – the Fifth Quarter' in *Cantium 4*, Summer 1972, 31.
4. Bendall, 'Mapping and displaying', passim.
5. Hipkin, 'The structure of land occupation' and 'Tenant', passim.

6. Hasted, *History and Topographical Survey* **8**, 258.
7. Dobson, 'Death and disease' passim. There was just one person to every 44 acres on the Marsh, compared to one person to every seven to eight acres in the Weald, as indicated by the Compton Census of 1676 – cited in Everitt, *Continuity and Colonisation*, 61.
8. In particular, EKAC S/W/Fs4 and S/Rm/FsZ10, covering 1745 and 1768. Special thanks are due to Dr Stephen Hipkin for supplying me with databases he compiled as a result of his research into the scot book evidence. See also Hipkin, 'The structure of land occupation' and 'Tenant farming', passim.
9. Wills, probate inventories and probate accounts.
10. Jones, 'Sheep on Romney Marsh', 6.
11. This could be anything up to 20 miles away. See Jones, 'Sheep on Romney Marsh', 5.
12. Jones, 'Sheep on Romney Marsh', 6.
13. CKS U301 E6.
14. For 1699 and 1705, information taken (with permission) from Hipkin, 'Tenant farming'. For 1768 and 1834, taken from information supplied by Hipkin (forthcoming).
15. Between 37.5% and 46.2%.
16. Kain, 'Tithe surveys', 89–90.
17. Everitt, *Continuity and Colonisation*, 36.
18. CKS PRC11/82/124.
19. CKS PRC32/65//372.
20. EKAC S/Rm/Fs10. Widow Brissenden probably continued to rent the land until the end of the term of the lease, which was likely to be seven years. EKAC S/Rm/FSz10 shows that William White was the tenant of Austen's 10.5 acres in 1768.
21. CKS PRC11/85/57.
22. Hasted, *History and Topographical Survey* **7**, 203.
23. Hasted, *History and Topographical Survey* **7**, 204.
24. Hasted, *History and Topographical Survey* **7**, 212.
25. CKS PRC27/41/104. The sheep and cattle were valued at £1,202 12s. 6d. and fleece wool at £137 10s. He also had enough resources to lend out considerable sums of money. Not only was he owed £50 for debts due upon Bond, but a further £716 19s. 'for debts due upon several Notes'.
26. Dobson, 'Death and disease', 25.
27. Buckland, 'On the farming' passim, cited in Whyman, 'The unchanging face', 48–52.
28. CKS PRC11/84/185.
29. Probably Boxley, near Maidstone.
30. CKS PRC32/65/157 – will of Richard Reynolds, Newchurch, grazier. CKS PRC32/66/271 – will of Edward Carpenter, New Romney, grazier (which mentions 'All my Freehold Lands in the parish of Hope all Saints' which he left to his wife Amy).
31. This was rather more than the going rate of 8d. per acre as suggested for the 1780s. See Jones, 'Sheep on Romney Marsh', 5.
32. Note that in the probate account of Thomas Merrells of Tenterden (CKS PRC11/85/66), £1 1s. was paid to Samuel Farmer and Thomas Paine in 1762, for making an inventory and appraising the intestate's goods and chattels.
33. EKAC S/Rm/FSz10. Reynolds widow leased 71.5 acres from the heirs of Rev. Clare.
34. EKAC S/Rm/FSz10.

35. CKS PRC17/98/459.
36. EKAC S/Rm/FSz10 – one acre in Springbrook CKS PRC17/98/459 – Martin's will, made in 1770. CKS PRC11/85/66 (probate account of Merrells).
37. Hasted, *History and Topographical Survey* **8**, 469. Also Hasted, cited in Dobson, 'Death and disease', 170.
38. Defoe, cited in Dobson, 'Death and disease', 170.
39. Hasted, cited in Dobson, 'Death and disease', 170.
40. Dobson, 'Contours of Death and Disease', 326.
41. Dobson, 'Contours of Death and Disease', passim.
42. Jones, 'Sheep on Romney Marsh', 5.
43. Everitt, *Continuity and Colonisation*, 36.
44. Everitt, *Continuity and Colonisation*, 58.
45. Everitt, *Continuity and Colonisation*, 34.
46. Boys, *General View*, 171–72.
47. Quoted from Lambarde's *Perambulation of Kent*, c. 1540, cited in Hasted, *History and Topographical Survey* **8**, 469.
48. Allanson, *Kent or Romney Marsh Sheep*, 3.
49. Jones, 'Sheep on Romney Marsh', 2. Allanson, *Kent or Romney Marsh Sheep*, 11.
50. Allanson, *Kent or Romney Marsh Sheep*, 11.
51. Jones, *Sheep on Romney Marsh in the 18th Century* **9**, 13.
52. Parish of Bethersden. CKS PRC11/85/59.
53. CKS U951 F18/2.
54. EKAC, S/Rm/Z2, Folio 17v. Hipkin, 'The Worlds of Daniel Langdon', this volume, passim.
55. CKS U951 F18/2.
56. Jones, 'Sheep on Romney Marsh', 9.
57. Carter, *The Sheep and Wool Correspondence*, 290.
58. Price, *A System of Sheep-Grazing*, 59–60.
59. Boys, *General View of the Agriculture*, 126.
60. Buckland, 'On the farming of Kent', passim.
61. Boys, *General View of the Agriculture*, 121.
62. Jones, 'Sheep on Romney Marsh', 13.
63. CKS U951 E12.
64. EKAC S/Rm/FSz10, CKS U951 A42, CKS U951 A21.
65. CKS U951 A21. By this time, Henry Read's son (Henry) had taken over from his late father.
66. CKS U951 E12. It is unclear, however, whether these were kept on Read's land, or somewhere else on the Marsh.
67. Price, *A System of Sheep-Grazing*, 68.
68. Price, *A System of Sheep-Grazing*, 70.
69. CKS U301 E12. See also CKS PRC17/98/353 (Pattenson's will).
70. CKS U301 E12. A rental receipt dated October 27th 1735 for rent paid by Mr Edward Rolf refers to 'one publick water scot payable the 20th September 1734 and two other scots, one payable in August 1734 and the other in March 1734 Rolf allowing ten shillings toward it …'.
71. CKS U301 T24. Dated 28th August 1740 – a renewal of 7 year lease at £16 per annum. This is the same parcel of land referred to in EKAC S/W/Fs7a – North Walland scot book for 1760–79, showing that scot payments amounting to £1 10s. were due each time a tax was levied. This, plus the £16 rental for the land, makes up the figure of £17 10s. that was applicable for the rental due to Wyvil, Pattenson's landlord, as referred to in CKS U301 E12 (the jottings on the scrap of paper).

72. CKS PRC17/99/266 – will of Robert Stace of Tenterden. He would have come from the same Tenterden family referred to by Hasted earlier in this paper. See also CKS U301 E12 where Samuel Pattenson refers to various disputes with his cousin William Pattenson, who had allegedly taken advantage of Samuel's good nature, and without asking had driven 'all those lambs through my Stace Land to go down in the Marsh ... '. This reinforces the idea that Pattenson's 'Stace Land' lay between Biddenden and Walland Marsh. William Pattenson's interest lay in the 241 acres of prime marshland in Walland Marsh rented from the wife of the late Sir George Rooke, sometime Vice-Admiral of the Fleet – see CKS U2140 T12, U2140 E24, and also Hasted, *History and Topographical Survey* **8**, 403.

73. Hasted, *History and Topgraphical Survey* **7**, 204. See also CKS U301 E10 – 1713-27 (Executorship papers of Samuel Pattenson senior, related to Blackmore and Flint families). See also EKAC S/Rm/Fs10 1745 (Romney Marsh Level), S/Rm/FSz10 – 1768 (Romney Marsh Level), S/W/FS7a – 1760–779 (North Walland Scot Book) for land held on Romney Marsh. CKS U1575 E6 – on Blackmore family (waterscotts receipts for 16 acres of 'summerlands' in Ebony), and Land Tax receipts. CKS PRC17/97/453 = will of James Blackmore senior, 1767 – refers to Dean Cort Land and various other parcels of land on Romney Marsh. Also CKS PRC17/100/99 – will of James Blackmore the elder, 1778.

74. CKS PRC17/90/23. See also CKS U301 E10.

75. CKS PRC17/90/23 – will of Abraham Flint. CKS U301 T30 – renewal of lease for 68 acres (15 acres in Ruckinge and 53 acres in Orlestone and Snave) from Isaac Rutton of Ashford. EKAC S/Rm/FSz10 – 1768 – shows Flint as landlord of 15 acres. EKAC S/Rm Fs13 (Calendar Scot Book for Level of Romney Marsh, Ladyday 1775) – lists James Flint as tenant/occupier of 51.5 acres. Earlier, EKAC S/W SO5a (Decree and Order Book for Walland Marsh, 1744–55 – shows that in June 1748 James Flint was returned as Juror at a General Sessions Meeting in Brookland. (Samuel Turner was also a juror, and he appraised Samuel Pattenson's goods' livestock as shown in Flint's diary – CKS U301 E6.)

76. CKS PRC17/102/106.

77. Price, *A System of Sheep-Grazing*, 24.

78. CKS U301 E6. An entry dated April 7th 1769 shows he paid Pattenson £10 8s. for 'One year's Board due at Michaelmas last in 1768 ... '.

79. CKS PRC17/101/30 – will of Mary Flint.

80. CKS PRC17/98/353 – shows that Ann Love was married to Stephen Love of Headcorn (Gentleman). Flint did not repay the further £28 loan from Pattenson until April 1769.

81. Currently 4% per annum.

82. CKS PRC17/98/353 – Pattenson's will was proved in July 1770. Flint inherited all the land and property in Biddenden plus his one-quarter share of £1,111 4s. 4½d. – the sum total of the estate.

83. He outlaid 3s. for '1 dozen of corks and 2 pound of Shigar Candy for to put in my wine'. There are also other entries for beer money allowed for his men working in the heat of summer – and this ale was also doubtless of the home-brewed variety.

84. CKS U951 C84/16 and CKS U951 A21 – Estate Accounts, 1763–79.

85. The rental for Day's house was £3 per annum. Flint also charged £3 per annum for the keep of Day's cow.

86. The total recorded wages bill for October 1767–October 1768 was £26 4s. 10¼d. Totals for crop sales for the same period amounted to £12 11s. 9d. (barley), £6 10s. 2¼d. (oats), £2 10s. 1d. (wood), £2 16s. (Wheat) and £2 16s. 10d. (income gained as a result of Flint's labourers doing odd jobs on other farms, for example, helping with ploughing). Total for sales of barley, oats, wood, wheat and labour = £27 4s. 10¼d.

87. This figure includes ram hire (£1 4s.), sales of mutton (18s. 5d.), skins (13s. 5d.) and carcases (£1 9s. 8d.).

88. Jones, 'Sheep on Romney Marsh', 14. These accounts ran from Michaelmas to Michaelmas each year.

89. Flint noted down casualties, although there are only a very few recorded. In August 1769 one lamb (out of a total of 29) was lost while in his grandfather Pattenson's keep, and two heifers drowned and one weaning colt was lost in 1771.

90. To a Mr Merrals of Milkhouse Street.

91. Flint allowed £1 15s. in expenses for driving them to market.

92. Jones, 'Sheep on Romney Marsh', 7.

93. Jones, 'Sheep on Romney Marsh', 12.

94. EKAC S/Rm/FSz10 – (Scot Book for Romney Marsh Level, 1768) shows that Robert Cobb = a tenant of 415.5 acres, and Colebrook a rentier of 68 acres. EKAC S/Rm Fs13 (Romney Marsh Calendar Scot Book for Ladyday 1775) shows a Robert Cobb of Orlestone as occupier of 12.5 acres.

95. Two year's worth of wool was sold for £25 5s. 7d. to John Winsor of Tenterden in July 1768 (rate = £5 10s. per pack). In July 1769 it was sold to Edward Elsted of Charing for £13 8s. 9d. (£6 per pack). In October 1770 Edward Summers (local to Biddenden) bought 110 fleeces for £13 9s. 3½d. (£6 per pack) and the total included lambs wool (£5 per pack) and locks (£3 per pack).

96. CKS PRC17/98/353.

97. CKS U951 A21, Estate Accounts, 1763–79.

98. EKAC S/Rm/FSz10 and S/W/FS7a (North Walland Scot Book). In 1769 Blackmore was the owner-occupier of 78 acres in Walland Marsh, and tenant of a further 345.5 acres elsewhere on the Marsh.

99. This was for a period of seven weeks and four days – for which Flint paid 15s. – i.e. 1s. per week per runt.

100. EKAC S/Rm/Fs13, S/W/Fs 5a, 6b, S/D Fs6. Information supplied by Dr Stephen Hipkin. Earle was ranked 20th out of 423 tenants for the entire Romney Marsh region in 1775.

101. One of Flint's farm workers also did some 'gapping' for Earle, for which Flint was paid 2s. 8d.

102. EKAC S/W/Fs7a, 1760–79. North Walland Scot Book. In 1779 Thomas Blackmore is entered as the owner of the 78 acres (New Watering).

103. Everitt, *Continuity and Colonisation*, 61.

References

Allanson, G. 1961. *Kent or Romney Marsh Sheep: A Study of a Famous Breed in its Local and National Settings.* Ashford.

Bendall, S. 2000. Mapping and displaying an English marshland landscape in the mid-eighteenth century, in L. Daston and P. Reill (eds) *The Display of Nature in Eighteenth-Century Europe.*

Boys, J. 1805. *General View of the Agriculture of the County of Kent.* London. (2nd edition).

Carter, H. (ed.) 1970. *The Sheep and Wool Correspondence of Sir Joseph Banks, 1781–1820.* The Library Council of New South Wales.

Dobson, M.J. 1997. *Contours of Death and Disease in Early Modern England.* Cambridge.

Dobson, M.J. 1998. Death and disease in the Romney Marsh area in the 17th to 19th centuries, in J. Eddison, M. Gardiner and A. Long (eds), *Romney Marsh: Environmental Change and Human Occupation in a Coastal Lowland* (Oxford University Committee for Archaeology **46**), 166–81. Oxford.

Everitt, A.M. 1986. *Continuity and Colonization: The Evolution of Kentish Settlement.* Leicester.

Hasted, E. 1797–1801. *The History and Topographical Survey of the County of Kent.* Canterbury.

Hipkin, S. 1998. The structure of land occupation in the Level of Romney Marsh during the late sixteenth and early seventeenth centuries, in J. Eddison, M. Gardiner, and A. Long (eds) *Romney Marsh: Environmental Change and Human Occupation in a Coastal Lowland* (Oxford University Committee for Archaeology **46**), 147–63. Oxford.

Hipkin, S. 2000. Tenant farming and short-term leasing on Romney Marsh, 1587–1705, *The Economic History Review* **LIII**, 646–76.

Hipkin, S. 2002. The worlds of Daniel Langdon: public office and private enterprise in the Romney Marsh region in the early eighteenth century, in A. Long, S. Hipkin and H. Clark (eds) *Romney Marsh: Coastal and Landscape Change Through The Ages* (Oxford University School for Archaeology 56) 173–189. Oxford.

Jones, D. 'Sheep on Romney Marsh in the 18th Century' A letter sent in 1786 and transcribed as *Occasional Paper of Wye College No. 7,* 1956.

Kain, R.J.P. 1976. Tithe surveys and the study of land occupation, *The Local Historian* **12**, No. 2.

Price, D. 1809. *A System of Sheep-Grazing and Management as Practiced in Romney Marsh.* London.

Reeves, A. and Eve, D. 1998. Sheep-keeping and lookers' huts on Romney Marsh, in J. Eddison M. Gardiner and A. Long (eds) *Romney Marsh: Environmental Change and Human Occupation in a Coastal Lowland* (Oxford Committee for Archaeology **46**), 191–207. Oxford.

Roper, A. 1972. Romney Marsh – the Fifth Quarter, *Cantium* **4**, 28.

Whyman, J. 1972. The unchanging face of Romney Marsh: selected references, *Cantium* **4**, 48–52.

Romney Marsh Publications

Papers published by members of the Romney Marsh Research Trust which concern the Marsh, including those in the first three Romney Marsh monographs. Short papers included in The Romney Marsh Irregular *are not listed.*

Allen, J.R.L. 1996. The sequence of early land-claims on the Walland and Romney Marshes, southern Britain: a preliminary hypothesis and its implications, *Proceedings of the Geologists' Association* **107**, 271–80.

Allen, J.R.L. 1999. The Rumenesea Wall and the early settled landscape of Romney Marsh (Kent), *Landscape History* **21**, 5–18.

Baillie Reynolds, D.H. 1986. Dungeness, its shingle ridges and what lies under them, *Geographical Journal* **152**, 81–87.

Barber, L. 1998. Medieval rural settlement and economy at Lydd, in J. Eddison, M. Gardiner and A. Long (eds) *Romney Marsh: Environmental Change and Human Occupation in a Coastal Lowland* (Oxford University Committee for Archaeology **46**), 89–108. Oxford.

Barber, L. 1998. An early Romano-British salt-working site at Scotney Court, *Archaeologia Cantiana* **118**, 327–53.

Barber, L. 2000. Lydd: how the marsh was colonised, *Current Archaeology* **168**, 482–3.

Beck, D. 1995. Drainage of Romney Marsh and maintenance of the Dymchurch Wall in the early 17th century, in J. Eddison (ed.) *Romney Marsh: The Debatable Ground* (Oxford University Committee for Archaeology **41**), 164–8. Oxford.

Beck, R. 1997. Earth resistivity meter, *Everyday Practical Electronics*, 12–21, 102–4.

Bendall, S. 1995. Enquire 'When the same platte was made and by whome and to what Intent': sixteenth-century maps of Romney Marsh, *Imago Mundi* **47**, 34–48.

Bennell, M. 1995. Hope all Saints: a survey and discussion of the ruins and earthworks, in J. Eddison (ed.) *Romney Marsh: The Debatable Ground* (Oxford University Committee for Archaeology **41**), 99–106. Oxford.

Brooks, N.P. 1988. Romney Marsh in the Early Middle Ages, in J. Eddison and C. Green (eds) *Romney Marsh: Evolution, Occupation, Reclamation* (Oxford University Committee for Archaeology **24**), 90–104. Oxford.

Burrin, P. 1988. The Holocene floodplain and alluvial deposits of the Rother valley and their bearing on the evolution of Romney Marsh, in J. Eddison and C. Green (eds) *Romney Marsh: Evolution, Occupation, Reclamation* (Oxford University Committee for Archaeology **24**), 31–52. Oxford.

Cunliffe, B.W. 1988. Romney Marsh in the Roman Period, in J. Eddison and C. Green (eds) *Romney Marsh: Evolution, Occupation, Reclamation* (Oxford University Committee for Archaeology **24**), 83–7. Oxford.

Dimmock, S. 1998. Class and the Social Transformation of a Late Medieval Small Town: Lydd *c.* 1450–1550 (unpublished Ph.D. thesis, University of Kent at Canterbury).

Dimmock, S. 2001. English small towns and the emergence of capitalist relations, *c.* 1450–1550, *Urban History* **28**, 5–24.

Dix, J., Long, A.J. and Cooke, R. 1998. The evolution of Rye Bay and Dungeness Foreland: the offshore seismic record, in J. Eddison, M. Gardiner and A. Long (eds) *Romney Marsh: Environmental Change and Human Occupation in a Coastal Lowland* (Oxford University Committee for Archaeology **46**), 1–12. Oxford.

Dobson, M.J. 1997. *Contours of Death and Disease in Early Modern England.* Cambridge.

Dobson, M.J. 1998. Death and disease on Romney Marsh in the 17th to 19th centuries, in J. Eddison, M. Gardiner and A. Long (eds) *Romney Marsh: Environmental Change and Human Occupation in a Coastal Lowland* (Oxford University Committee for Archaeology **46**), 165–81. Oxford.

Draper, G. 1998. The farmers of Canterbury Cathedral Priory and All Souls College Oxford on Romney Marsh *c.*1443–1545, in J. Eddison, M. Gardiner and A. Long (eds) *Romney Marsh: Environmental Change and Human Occupation in a Coastal Lowland* (Oxford University Committee for Archaeology **46**), 109–28. Oxford.

Draper, G. Forthcoming. Inheritance practices and the transmission of real property in the Romney Marshes, *c.*1150–1390, in A.F. Butcher (ed.) *Strategies of Inheritance in Late Medieval Kent.*

Eddison, J. 1983. The evolution of barrier beaches between Fairlight and Hythe, *Geographical Journal* **149**, 39–53.

Eddison, J. 1983. The reclamation of Romney Marsh: some aspects reconsidered, *Archaeologia Cantiana* **99**, 95–110.

Eddison, J. 1983. An intensive ditching system in the Wicks, south-west of Lydd, *Archaeologia Cantiana* **99**, 273–6.

Eddison, J. 1983. Flandrian barrier beaches off the coast of Sussex and south-east Kent, *Quaternary Newsletter* **39**, 25–9.

Eddison, J. 1985. Developments in the lower Rother valleys up to 1600, *Archaeologia Cantiana* **102**, 95–110.

Eddison, J. 1988. 'Drowned Lands': changes in the course of the Rother and its estuary and associated drainage problems 1635–1737, in J. Eddison and C. Green (eds) *Romney Marsh: Evolution, Occupation, Reclamation* (Oxford University Committee for Archaeology **24**), 142–63. Oxford.

Eddison, J. 1998. Catostrophic changes: the evolution of the barrier beaches of Rye Bay, in J. Eddison, M. Gardiner and A. Long (eds) *Romney Marsh: Environmental Change and Human Occupation in a Coastal Lowland* (Oxford University Committee for Archaeology **46**), 65–87. Oxford.

Eddison, J. 2000. *Romney Marsh: Survival on a Frontier.* Stroud: Tempus.

Eddison, J. and Draper, G. 1997. A landscape of medieval reclamation: Walland Marsh, Kent, *Landscape History* **19**, 75–88.

Evans, J.R., Kirby, J.R. and Long, A.J. 2001. The litho- and biostratigraphy of the late Holocene tidal channel in Romney Marsh, southern England, *Proceedings of the Geologists' Association* **112**, 111–130.

Gardiner, M. 1988. Medieval settlement and society in the Broomhill area, and excavations at Broomhill church, in J. Eddison and C. Green (eds) *Romney Marsh: Evolution, Occupation, Reclamation* (Oxford University Committee for Archaeology **24**), 112–27. Oxford.

Gardiner, M. 1994. Old Romney: an examination of the evidence for a lost Saxo-Norman port, *Archaeologia Cantiana* **114**, 329–45.

Gardiner, M. 1995. Medieval farming and flooding in the Brede Valley, in J. Eddison (ed.) *Romney Marsh: The Debatable Ground* (Oxford University Committee for Archaeology **41**), 127–37. Oxford.

Gardiner, M. 1996. A seasonal fishermen's settlement at Dungeness, Kent, *Medieval Settlement Research Group Annual Report* **11**, 18–20.

Gardiner, M. 1998. Settlement change on Walland and Denge Marshes, 1400–1550, in J. Eddison, M. Gardiner and A. Long (eds) *Romney Marsh: Environmental Change and Human Occupation in a Coastal Lowland* (Oxford University Committee for Archaeology **46**), 129–45. Oxford.

Gardiner, M. 1998. The exploitation of sea-mammals in medieval England: bones and their social context, *Archaeological Journal* **154**, 173–95.

Gardiner, M. 2000. Shipping and trade between England and the continent during the eleventh century, *Anglo-Norman Studies* **22**, 71–93.

Gardiner, M. and Macpherson-Grant, N. 1998. Pottery from *Sandtun*, West Hythe, Kent, *Medieval Archaeology Newsletter* **18**, 7.

Gardiner, M., Stewart, J. and Priestley-Bell, G. 1998. Anglo-Saxon whale exploitation: some evidence from Dengemarsh, Lydd, Kent, *Medieval Archaeology* **42**, 96–101.

Gardiner, M., Cross, R., Macpherson-Grant, N. and Riddler, I. 2001. Continental trade and non-urban ports in Mid-Anglo-Saxon England: Excavations at *Sandtun*, West Hythe, Kent, *Archaeological Journal* **158**, 161–290.

Gibbard, P.L. and Preece, R.C. (with contributions from M.R. Bates, D.H. Keen, M. Waller and A.J. Long) 1999. South and Southeast England, in D.Q. Bowen (ed.) *A Revised Correlation of Quaternary Deposits in the British Isles*, The Geological Society special report **23**.

Green, C.P. 1988. Palaeogeography of marine inlets in the Romney Marsh area, in J. Eddison and C. Green (eds) *Romney Marsh: Evolution, Occupation, Reclamation* (Oxford University Committee for Archaeology **24**), 167–74. Oxford.

Gross A. and Butcher, A. 1995. Adaptation and investment in the age of the great storms: agricultural policy on the manors of the principal lords of the Romney Marshes and the marshland fringe, in J. Eddison (ed.) *Romney Marsh: the Debatable Ground* (Oxford University Committee for Archaeology **41**), 107–17. Oxford.

Hipkin, S. 1995. The impact of marshland drainage on Rye Harbour, 1550–1650, in J.Eddison (ed.) *Romney Marsh: The Debatable Ground* (Oxford University Committee for Archaeology **41**), 138–47. Oxford.

Hipkin, S. 1995. Closing ranks: oligarchy and government at Rye, 1570–1640, *Urban History* **22**, 319–40.

Hipkin, S. 1995. Buying time: fiscal policy at Rye, 1600–1640, *Sussex Archaeological Collections* **133**, 241–54.

Hipkin, S. 1998. Land occupation in the Level of Romney Marsh during the late 16th and early 17th centuries, in J. Eddison, M. Gardiner and A. Long (eds) *Romney Marsh: Environmental Change and Human Occupation in a Coastal Lowland* (Oxford University Committee for Archaeology **46**), 147–63. Oxford.

Hipkin, S. 1998/9. The maritime economy of Rye, 1560–1640, *Southern History* **20/1**, 108–42.

Hipkin, S. 2000. Tenant farming and short-term leasing on Romney Marsh, 1587–1705, *Economic History Review*, 2nd series, 646–76.

Holgate, R. and Woodcock, A. 1988. Archaeological and palaeoenvironmnetal investigations at Pannel Bridge, near Pett Level, East Sussex, in J. Eddison and C. Green (eds) *Romney Marsh: Evolution, Occupation, Reclamation* (Oxford University Committee for Archaeology **24**), 72–6. Oxford.

Hutchinson, J. 1988. Recent geotechnical, geomorphological and archaeological investigations of the abandoned cliff backing Romney Marsh at Lympne, Kent, in J. Eddison and C. Green (eds) *Romney Marsh: Evolution, Occupation, Reclamation* (Oxford University Committee for Archaeology **24**), 88–9. Oxford.

Hutchinson, J. and Bromhead, E.N. 1997. Back-analysis of the collapse of a Roman wall built on a landslip. *Proceedings of Seventh International Symposium on Landslides, Trondheim.*

Innes, J.B. and Long, A.J. 1992. A preliminary investigation of the 'Midley Sand' deposit, Romney Marsh, Kent, UK, *Quaternary Newsletter* **67**, 32–9.

Long, A.J. 1998. Dungeness Foreland, in J.B. Murton, C.A. Whiteman, M.R. Bates, D.R. Bridgland, A.J. Long, M.B. Roberts and M. Waller (eds) *The Quaternary of Kent and Sussex: Field Guide*. Quaternary Research Association, 88–94. London.

Long, A.J. 2000. The mid and late Holocene evolution of Romney Marsh and the Thames Estuary, *Archaeology of the Severn Estuary* **11**, 55–68.

Long, A.J. and Hughes, P.D.M. 1995. Mid- and late-Holocene evolution of the Dungeness Foreland, United Kingdom, *Marine Geology* **124**, 253–71.

Long, A.J. and Innes, J.B. 1993. Holocene sea-level changes and coastal sedimentation in Romney Marsh, southeast England, UK, *Proceedings of the Geologists' Association* **104**, 223–37.

Long, A.J. and Innes, J.B. 1995. The back-barrier and barrier depositional history of Romney Marsh and Dungeness, Kent, *Journal of Quaternary Science* **10**, 267–83.

Long, A.J. and Innes, J.B. 1995. A palaeoenvironmental investigation of the 'Midley Sand' and associated deposits at the Midley Church Bank, Romney Marsh, in J. Eddison (ed.) *Romney Marsh: The Debatable Ground* (Oxford University Committee for Archaeology **41**), 37–50. Oxford.

Long, A.J. and Innes, J.B. 1998. Midley Church bank, in J.B. Murton, C.A. Whiteman, M.R. Bates, D.R. Bridgland, A.J. Long, M.B. Roberts and M. Waller (eds) *The Quaternary of Kent and Sussex: Field Guide*. Quaternary Research Association, 87. London.

Long, A.J., Plater, A.J., Waller, M.P. and Innes, J.B. 1996. Holocene coastal sedimentation in the Eastern English Channel: new data from the Romney Marsh region, United Kingdom, *Marine Geology* **136**, 97–120.

Long, A.J., Waller, M., Hughes, P. and Spencer, C. 1998. The Holocene depositional history of Romney Marsh proper, in J. Eddison, M. Gardiner and A. Long (eds) *Romney Marsh: Environmental Change and Human Occupation in a Coastal Lowland* (Oxford University Committee for Archaeology **46**), 45–63. Oxford.

Long, A.J. and Waller, M. 1998. Introduction: The Romney Marsh depositional complex, in J.B. Murton, C.A. Whiteman, M.R. Bates, D.R. Bridgland, A.J. Long, M.B. Roberts and M. Waller (eds) *The Quaternary of Kent and Sussex: Field Guide*. Quaternary Research Association, 61–64. London.

Long, D., Waller, M. and McCarthy, P. 1998. The vegetation history, stratigraphy and pollen data for the Shirley Moor region, in J. Eddison, M. Gardiner and A. Long (eds) *Romney Marsh: Environmental Change and Human Occupation in a Coastal Lowland* (Oxford University Committee for Archaeology **46**), 31–44. Oxford.

Needham, S. 1998. A group of Early Bronze Age axes from Lydd, in J. Eddison and C. Green (eds) *Romney Marsh: Evolution, Occupation, Reclamation* (Oxford University Committee for Archaeology **24**), 77–82. Oxford.

Pearson, S. 1995. The medieval houses of the Marsh: the missing evidence, in J. Eddison (ed.) *Romney Marsh: The Debatable Ground* (Oxford University Committee for Archaeology **41**), 92–8. Oxford.

Plater, A.J. 1992. The late Holocene evolution of Denge Marsh, southeast England: a stratigraphic, sedimentological and micropalaeontological approach, *The Holocene* **2**, 63–70.

Plater, A.J. and Long, A.J. 1995. The morphology and evolution of Denge Beach and Denge Marsh, in J. Eddison (ed.) *Romney Marsh: The Debatable Ground* (Oxford University Committee for Archaeology **41**), 8–36. Oxford.

Plater, A.J., Long, A.J., Spencer, C.D. and Delacour, R.A.P. 1999. The stratigraphic record of sea-level change and storms during the last 2000 years: Romney Marsh, south-east England, *Quaternary International* **55**, 17–27.

Plater, A.J., Spencer, C.D., Delacour, R.A.P. and Long, A.J. 1995. The stratigraphic record of sea-level change and storms during the last 2000 years: Romney Marsh, south-east England, *Terra Nostra, Schriften der Alfred-Wegener-Stiftung* **2/95**, 248.

Reeves, A. 1995. Romney Marsh: the field-walking evidence, in J. Eddison (ed.) *Romney Marsh: The Debatable Ground* (Oxford University Committee for Archaeology **41**), 78–91. Oxford.

Reeves, A. 1996. Earthworks survey, Romney Marsh, *Archaeologia Cantiana* **116**, 61–92.

Reeves, A. and Eve, D. 1998. Sheep-keeping and lookers' huts on Romney Marsh, in J. Eddison, M. Gardiner and A. Long (eds) *Romney Marsh: Environmental Change and Human Occupation in a Coastal Lowland* (Oxford University Committee for Archaeology **46**), 191–207. Oxford.

Reeves, A. and Williamson T. 2000. Marshes, in J. Thirsk (ed.) *The English Medieval Landscape*, 150–66. Oxford.

Robinson, G. 1988. Sea defence and land drainage of Romney Marsh, in J. Eddison and C. Green (eds) *Romney Marsh: Evolution, Occupation, Reclamation* (Oxford University Committee for Archaeology **24**), 163–6. Oxford.

Smith, G. 1998. White Kemp Gutt *c*.1700: a time of change?, in J. Eddison, M. Gardiner and A. Long (eds) *Romney Marsh: Environmental Change and Human Occupation in a Coastal Lowland* (Oxford University Committee for Archaeology **46**), 183–90. Oxford.

Spencer, C.D. 1997. The Holocene evolution of Romney Marsh: a record of sea-level change in a back-barrier environment (unpublished Ph.D. thesis, University of Liverpool).

Spencer, C.D., Plater, A.J. and Long, A.J. 1998. Holocene barrier estuary evolution: the sedimentary record of the Romney Marsh region, in J. Eddison, M. Gardiner and A. Long (eds) *Romney Marsh: Environmental Change and Human Occupation in a Coastal Lowland* (Oxford University Committee for Archaeology **46**), 13–29. Oxford.

Spencer, C.D., Plater, A.J. and Long, A.J. 1998. Rapid coastal change during the mid- to late-Holocene: the record of barrier estuary sedimentation in the Romney Marsh region, southeast England, *The Holocene* **8**, 143–63.

Stupples, P. 2002. Tidal cycles preserved in late Holocene tidal rhythmites, the Wainway Channel, Romney Marsh, Southeast England, *Marine Geology* **182**, 231–46.

Sweetinburgh, S. Forthcoming. Hooks, nets and boats: sharing the catch in Kentish fishing communities, in A.F. Butcher (ed.), *Strategies of Inheritance in Late Medieval Kent*.

Tatton-Brown, T. 1988. The topography of the Walland Marsh area between the eleventh and thirteenth centuries, in J. Eddison and C. Green (eds) *Romney Marsh: Evolution, Occupation, Reclamation* (Oxford University Committee for Archaeology **24**), 105–11. Oxford.

Tatton-Brown, T. 1989. Church Building on Romney Marsh in the later Middle Ages, *Archaeologia Cantiana* **107**, 253–265.

Tooley, M.J. 1990. Sea level and coastline changes during the last 5000 years, in S. McGrail (ed.), *Maritime Celts, Frisians and Saxons* (Council for British Archaeology Research Report **71**), 1–16. London.

Tooley, M.J. 1990. Broomhill Level, East Sussex, in S. Jennings (ed.) *Field Excursion Guide – IGCP 274* (IGCP Project 274 UK Working Group: Coastal Evolution in the Quaternary).

Tooley, M.J. 1995. Romney Marsh: the debatable ground, in J. Eddison (ed.) *Romney Marsh: The Debatable Ground* (Oxford University Committee for Archaeology **41**), 1–7. Oxford.

Tooley, M.J. and Switsur, R. 1988. Water level changes and sedimentation during the Flandrian Age in the Romney Marsh area, in J. Eddison and C. Green (eds) *Romney Marsh: Evolution, Occupation, Reclamation* (Oxford University Committee for Archaeology **24**), 53–71. Oxford.

Vollans, E. 1988. New Romney and the 'river of Newenden' in the later Middle Ages, in J. Eddison and C. Green (eds) *Romney Marsh: Evolution, Occupation, Reclamation* (Oxford University Committee for Archaeology **24**), 128–41. Oxford.

Vollans, E. 1995. Medieval salt-making and the inning of tidal marshes at Belgar, Lydd, in J. Eddison (ed.) *Romney Marsh: The Debatable Ground* (Oxford University Committee for Archaeology **41**), 118–26. Oxford.

Waller, M. 1993. Flandrian vegetation history of south-eastern England. Pollen data from Pannel Bridge, East Sussex, *New Phytologist* **124**, 345–69.

Waller, M. 1994. Flandrian vegetation history of south-eastern England. Stratigraphy of the Brede valley and pollen data from Brede Bridge, *New Phytologist* **126**, 369–92.

Waller, M.P. 1998. An investigation into the palynological properties of fen peat through multiple pollen profiles from south-eastern England, *Journal of Archaeological Science* **25**, 631–42.

Waller, M.P., Burrin, P.J. and Marlow, A. 1988. Flandrian sedimentation and palaeoenvironments in Pett Level, the Brede and lower Rother valleys and Walland Marsh, in J. Eddison and C. Green (eds) *Romney Marsh: Evolution, Occupation, Reclamation—* (Oxford University Committee for Archaeology **24**), 3–30. Oxford.

Waller, M., Entwistle, J.A. and Duller, G.A.T. 1995. TSPPlus – a menu driven program for the display of stratigraphic data, *Quaternary Newsletter* **99**, 32–9.

Waller, M., Long, A.J., Long, D.J. and Innes, J.B. 1998. Walland Marsh: wetland vegetation, sea-level change and coastal evolution, in J.B. Murton, C.A. Whiteman, M.R. Bates, D.R. Bridgland, A.J. Long, M.B. Roberts and M. Waller (eds) *The Quaternary of Kent and Sussex: Field Guide*. Quaternary Research Association, 70–81. London.

Waller, M., Long, A.J., Long, D. and Innes, J.B. 1999. Holocene vegetation history of Romney and Walland marshes, southern England, *Quaternary Science Reviews* **18**, 1419–44.

Wass, M. 1995. The proposed northern course of the Rother: a sedimentological and microfaunal investigation, in J. Eddison (ed.) *Romney Marsh, The Debatable Ground* (Oxford University Committee for Archaeology **41**), 51–77. Oxford.

Contributors

JOHN ALLEN
Postgraduate Research Institute for Sedimentology
University of Reading
PO Box 227
Whiteknights
Reading RG6 6AB

HELEN CLARKE
Kynance, Clarence Road
Tunbridge Wells TN1 1HE

ANNE DAVISON
50 Park Avenue
Maidstone
Kent ME14 5HL

JILL EDDISON
Langley Farm
Bethersden
Ashford
Kent TN26 3HF

JOHN EVANS
Department of Earth Science
Cardiff University
PO Box 914
Park Place
Cardiff CF10 3YE

MARK GARDINER
Department of Archaeology
The Queen's University of Belfast
Belfast BT7 1NN
Northern Ireland

STEPHEN HIPKIN
Centre for Early Modern Kentish Studies
Department of History
Canterbury Christ Church College
Canterbury
Kent CT1 1QU

JASON KIRBY
Department of Geographical Sciences
University of Plymouth
Drake Circus
Plymouth PL4 8AA

ANTONY LONG
Department of Geography
University of Durham
Science Site
South Road
Durham DH1 3LE

MARK MERRY
History Data Service
UK Data Archive
University of Essex
Colchester CO4 3SQ

CAROLINE OWEN
Department of Geography
University of Liverpool
PO Box 147
Liverpool L69 3BX

ANDREW PLATER
Department of Geography
University of Liverpool
PO Box 147
Liverpool L69 3BX

CATHERINE RICHARDSON
The Shakespeare Institute
Mason Croft
Church Street
Stratford-upon-Avon CV37 6HP

STEPHEN RIPPON
Department of Archaeology
University of Exeter
Laver Building
North Park Road
Exeter EX4 4QE

HELEN ROBERTS
Institute of Geography and Earth Sciences
University of Wales
Aberystwyth SY23 3DB

Paul Stupples,
Department of Environmental and
Geographical Sciences
Manchester Metropolitan University
John Dalton Building
Chester Street
Manchester M1 5GD

Christopher Spencer
School of Geography and
Environmental Management
Faculty of the Built Environment
University of the West of England
Coldharbour Lane
Bristol BS16 1QY

Sheila Sweetinburgh
11 Caledon Terrace
Canterbury
Kent CT1 3JS

Martyn Waller
Centre for Earth and
Environmental Science Research
School of Earth Science and Geography
Kingston University
Penrhyn Road
Kingston
Surrey KT1 2EE

Wendy Woodland
School of Geography and
Environmental Management
Faculty of the Built Environment
University of the West of England
Coldharbour Lane
Bristol BS16 1QY

Index

This index includes the names of places on, and related to, Romney Marsh and also the names of landowners, tenants and other individuals connected with the history of the marsh. Names are listed as they appear in the text of this monograph.